The

UYGHURS

The

UYGHURS
Strangers in Their Own Land

GARDNER BOVINGDON

COLUMBIA UNIVERSITY PRESS   NEW YORK

Columbia University Press

Publishers Since 1893

New York   Chichester, West Sussex

Library of Congress Cataloging-in-Publication Data

Bovingdon, Gardner.

The Uyghurs : strangers in their own land / Gardner Bovingdon.

p. cm.

Includes bibliographical references and index.

ISBN 978-0-231-14758-3 (cloth)—ISBN 978-0-231-14759-0 (pbk.)—

ISBN 978-0-231-51941-0 (e-book)

1. Uighur (Turkic people)—China—Xinjiang Uygur Zizhiqu—History—20th century.

2. Xinjiang Uygur Zizhiqu (China)—History—Autonomy and independence movements.

3. Nationalism—China—Xinjiang Uygur Zizhiqu. 4. China—Ethnic relations.

I. Title.

DS731.U4B68   2010

305.89'4323—dc22   2009052787

DESIGN BY MARTIN N HINZE

CONTENTS

CONTENTS

ACKNOWLEDGMENTS

This book began as a dissertation, and I owe a great debt to the members of my committee. My chair, Vivienne Shue, deserves gratitude beyond measure. She guided me patiently in the study of Chinese politics, volleyed ideas with me over an unusually protracted research and writing process, and pushed me to think more deeply and clearly from the moment of my arrival at Cornell. Ben Anderson challenged me to get beneath the facade of the "unitary" Chinese nation and to interrogate sources with care and humor. Valerie Bunce labored for years to make me into a comparativist; I began to see the light during a marathon series of meetings one spring. To Jonathan Lipman I owe thanks for advice not only here at home but also in an impromptu meeting over a steaming bowl of cöcürä in Ürümci on a frigid winter night. Other Cornell faculty gave generously of their time, counsel, and expertise. Peter Katzenstein supervised me in the world's longest-running seminar, conducted regularly after matches in a nearly ten-year squash rivalry; he and Mary helped me hone my ideas in the later stages of writing. Isaac Kramnick passed on to me information about time zone irregularities in New Mexico and also helped me secure support from Cornell's government department for a conference I organized with Barry Sautman in Boston, where I was able to exchange ideas with many experts on Xinjiang and Uyghurs. Other Cornell faculty who provided valuable advice on my writing include Tom Christensen, Sherm Cochran, Brett de Bary, Ed Gunn, and Keith Taylor. The late Knight Biggerstaff made a generous gift of books from his library. Members of the Cornell staff without whom I could not have completed my program include the government department's amazingly competent trio of Laurie Coon, Kim Shults, and Michael Busch; Laurie Damiani of the East Asia program; and librarian Charles D'Orban, who gleefully helped me with numerous bibliographic questions.

I have great debts to fellow graduate students and friends at Cornell, including Ken Forsberg, Rob Culp, Rich Calichman, Mao-Mao Zhong Yumei, Lee Haiyan, Jee-Sun Lee, Paul Festa, John Gibson, Smita Lahiri, Thamora Fishel, Erick White, John Norvell, and Leda Martins. Rawi Abdelal and Adam Segal I thank for advice, critical comments, and squash. Lee Haiyan and Eric Karchmer helped me locate key texts in China.

My research was supported by generous fellowships or grants from the National Science Foundation, Cornell's peace studies and Asian studies programs, Cornell's government department, and the Mellon Foundation.

The staff and faculty of Xinjiang University provided me a home, a community of scholars, and excellent resources. I am especially grateful to Fu Chunlei of the Foreign Affairs Office, the library staff, and Li shifu and Xu dajie, who capably managed the wild-west dormitory where I lived for two years, and to their children, who brought cheer on the darkest winter days.

My research in Xinjiang would simply not have been possible without the help of the brilliant teacher and linguist Muhäbbät Qasim and her family. She taught me Uyghur in my second year, introduced me to the pleasures of literature and the intricacies of linguistics, fed me many a fine meal, and boosted my spirits with scholarly conversation and good cheer during the long winter months. I owe a great deal to other teachers and friends, including Abdošükür, Ablikim, Ablimit, Abdurišit, Bahargul, Mirsultan, Li Yun, Han Junkui, Niu Ruji, and Mämätjan; a special thanks to Talhat for mountain bike rides and horse sausage. I thank deeply many other friends who unfortunately cannot be named here. Among the "foreign crew" at Xinjiang University, I thank Eric and Ellen Peters, Mike and Victoria Welch. Bill Clark helped me at every turn, providing intellectual exchange, innumerable introductions, and advice on fieldwork. I will always be grateful to the entire Clark family for friendship, field trips, and delicious meals.

Several families provided support through the long years of my graduate career. My grandmother, Isabelle Paterson, generously funded my first trips to Asia while I was an undergraduate and unknowingly launched me on this path. Betsy Judson, Margaret Bovingdon, and Peter Bovingdon have stood by me for so many years, as did my father George Bovingdon; I dearly wish he had lived to see this day. My mother and Henry Judson have taken me in during my dizzying trips back and forth, never complaining about how seldom they see me. Bill and Ellin Friedman and the extended Friedman-Weiner family embraced me as one of their own. The same is true of our Ithaca "parents," Barbara and Jerry Nosanchuk, who became ideal fictive kin, treating us as well as any child has a right to expect; better, in fact.

At Indiana I have been fortunate to find a community of scholars offering expertise, counsel, and camaraderie. I cannot imagine a more congenial academic home than the Department of Central Eurasian Studies for someone trying simultaneously to research Xinjiang and to leaven that tight geographical focus with insights into its broader regions of Central Asia and China, as well as the disciplines of political science, sociology, history, literary criticism, and legal studies. I thank especially Chris Atwood, Erdem Cipa, Bob Eno, Bill Fierman, Ray Hedin, Jeff Isaac, Scott Kennedy, Ed Lazzerini, Josh Malitsky, Ethan Michelson, Scott O'Bryan, Toivo Raun, Jean Robinson, Mark Roseman, Heidi Ross, Nazif Shahrani, Elliot Sperling, Sue Tuohy, Jeff Wasserstrom, and Tim Waters. My writers' group at Indiana University, Konstantin Dierks, Lauren Morris-Maclean, and Marissa Moorman, helped me reshape the book manuscript and prune the wildly overgrown introduction into a more readable form. My graduate students have inspired, challenged, and taught me more than they can know. It is a special pleasure to see so many focusing on Xinjiang and preparing to shape the field. April Younger and Karen Niggle, CEUS's superbly capable administrators, helped me in too many ways to count.

The Institute of Ethnology and the Institute of Political Science at Academia Sinica gave me the time and space to research and revise parts of the book. I am grateful to Huang Shu-min and Yu-shan Wu for extending the invitations. In Taiwan I was fortunate to come to know, and learn from, Liu Shao-Hua, Fred Chiu, Chou Hui-min, Allen Chun, Lin Kai-shi, and Chih-yu Shih.

The field of "Xinjiang studies," once small enough to fit in a broom closet, can now boast a community of excellent scholars. At various times I have benefited from the insights and bibliographic assistance of Kara Abramson, Nicolas

Becquelin, Ildiko Beller-Hann, Linda Benson, David Brophy, Cristina Cesaro, Bill Clark, Jay Dautcher, Rahilä Dawut, Michael Dillon, Arienne Dwyer, Mark Elliott, Joanne Smith Finley, Dru Gladney, Rachel Harris, Jun Sugawara, Ablet Kamalov, Nathan Light, Jonathan Lipman, Colin Mackerras, Jim Millward, Laura Newby, Kurban Niyaz, Abliz Orkhun, Peter Perdue, Sean Roberts, Justin Rudelson, Yitzhak Shichor, Jim Seymour, Äsäd Suläyman, Konstantin Syroezhkin, Stan Toops, Näbijan Tursun, Edmund Waite, Calla Wiemer, and Yang Shengmin. To Nathan Light I owe special thanks not only for discussions about research and his great Central Asia Web site, but also for providing me with a crucial text. I am deeply grateful to Näbijan Tursun for countless hours of stimulating discussions, instruction, and materials of incomparable value.

Other scholars who have advised or commented on work that found its way into the book include Marc Abramson, Arun Agrawal, Muthiah Alagappa, Steve Averill, Sara Davis, June Teufel Dreyer, Prasenjit Duara, Valerie Hansen, Steve Harrell, Kate Kaup, Scott Kennedy, Morris Rossabi, Barry Sautman, Jim Scott, Mark Selden, Fred Starr, Stefan Tanaka, Sue Tuohy, and Jeff Wasserstrom. Naturally, none of these scholars is responsible for the content of the book. Remaining errors of fact or judgment are mine alone.

Many of the ideas and findings in the book were first presented as talks at Academia Sinica, Berkeley, Cornell, Harvard, University of Illinois at Urbana-Champaign, Indiana University, Oxford, University of Washington, Xinjiang University, and Yale. I learned a great deal from the discussions that followed.

Three friends have played especially important roles in my academic career. Elizabeth Remick, one of my oldest friends, helped me choose China and Cornell, and convinced me to persevere at many difficult moments. I met Jay Dautcher in 1995 after three fruitless trips to his digs in Ürümci. I had all but given up on him. It's fortunate I didn't, as he has been a constant friend and mentor since the day we met. Jim Millward has helped enormously over the years, with guidance, criticism, helpful nudges, and musical inspiration. His ode to Iparkhan, to the tune of "The Girl from Ipanema," is not to be missed.

I now understand why so many authors thank editors for a mixture of support and forbearance. Anne Routon has been marvelous at every point, supporting the book from the first, enduring my ponderous pace with good grace, and giving vital encouragement at just the right moments. With a sensitive eye and a restrained pen, Margaret B. Yamashita improved the manuscript in many places. Vin Dang did a wonderful job with the tables, charts, and maps.

I cannot say that Maddie's arrival made my writing any easier or that she pretended to understand my long disappearances into my office, but she has brought me more joy than I imagined possible. Words cannot express my gratitude to Sara, who has enriched my life beyond description. She has read nearly every word I have written and tested and improved all my ill-formed notions. I like to think that the compatibility of our ideas about cultural politics is testament to the way our lives have grown together. I dedicate this book to her and Maddie.

NOTE ON ROMANIZATION

Chinese terms in the text are romanized according to the now-standard *pinyin* system. Uyghur is a Turkic language currently written in the Arabic script. Because there is no one generally agreed-upon system of romanization, I have largely followed the scheme in Reinhard Hahn's *Spoken Uyghur* (1991), with the following exceptions: for the alveo-palatal affricate, I have used "c" rather than "č"; for the voiced uvular fricative, I have used "gh" instead of "ğ"; for the voiceless fricative, I have preferred "kh" to "x"; and for the velar nasal, I have used "ng" instead of "ṇ."

For names, I have generally followed these rules except for widely used variants and for Turkic rather than Chinese (or Arabic) spellings of Turki names. Thus it is Muhämmäd Imin Bughra, rather than Memtimin, Muhammed Imin, Mehmet Emin, or Maimaitiming; and Säypidin Äzizi rather than Seypidin, Seyfettin, Saif al-Din, or Saifudin(g). At the same time, I refer to Chiang Kai-shek instead of Jiang Jieshi and Sun Yat-sen rather than Sun Zhongshan (or Sun Yixian). For Uyghur place-names,

I have generally followed the orthography indicated earlier; hence Ürümci, rather than Ürümchi or Urumqi. But I have followed older convention in referring to two of Xinjiang's cities best known in English as Kashgar and Yarkand, instead of Qäšqär and Yäkän.

ABBREVIATIONS

AR	Autonomous Region
CCP	Chinese Communist Party
CECC	(United States) Congressional–Executive Commission on China
ETGIE	Eastern Turkestan Government in Exile
ETIC	Eastern Turkestan Information Center, Munich
ETIM	Eastern Turkestan Islamic Movement (not Eastern Turkestan *Independence* Movement)
ETIP	Eastern Turkestan Islamic Party
ETIPA	Eastern Turkestan Islamic Party of Allah
ETLO	Eastern Turkestan Liberation Organization; see also SHAT
ETNC	Eastern Turkestan National Center, Ankara; later National Congress
ETPRP	Eastern Turkestan People's Revolutionary Party

ETR	Eastern Turkestan Republic (1944–1949)
ET(U)NC	Eastern Turkestan (Uyghurstan) National Congress
ETUNRF	Eastern Turkestan United National Revolutionary Front; see also URFET
GMD	Chinese Nationalist Party (Guomindang)
IMU	Islamic Movement of Uzbekistan; now renamed Islamic Movement of Turkestan
INA	Ili National Army (military force of the ETR)
PAP	People's Armed Police (Wuzhuang jingcha)
PCC	Production and Construction Corps (Shengchan jianshe bingtuan)
PLA	People's Liberation Army
PRC	People's Republic of China
PSB	Public Security Bureau (Gong'anju)
SCO	Shanghai Cooperation Organization
ShAT	(Uyghur) Šärqiy Türkistan Azadliq Täškilati; see also ETLO
SSB	State Security Bureau (Guojia anquan ju)
TGIE	Tibetan Government in Exile
TIRET	Turkish Islamic Republic of Eastern Turkestan (1933–1934)
UAA	Uyghur American Association
UCA	Uyghur Canadian Association
ULO	Uyghurstan Liberation Organization
URFET	United Revolutionary Front of Eastern Turkestan; see also ETUNRF
USCIRF	United States Committee on International Religious Freedom
WUC	World Uyghur Congress
WUYC	World Uyghur Youth Congress
XUAR	Xinjiang Uyghur Autonomous Region

The
UYGHURS

China, with Xinjiang in the northwest. (Perry–Castaneda map collection, University of Texas, available at http://www.lib.utexas.edu/maps/middle_east_and_asia/china_polo1.jpg)

INTRODUCTION

A quarter century ago, many scholars believed that nationalism was no longer a major force in world politics. Although several highly influential books on the subject emerged in the 1980s, even their authors seemed to agree that they could finally get a clear view of the phenomenon because it was receding into the past (Anderson 1983; Gellner 1983; Hobsbawm 1990). Eric Hobsbawm echoed Hegel's comment that the "owl of Minerva flies at dusk," noting hopefully that nationalism's importance had waned irreversibly (1990:183).

Events in the two years from 1989 to 1991, however, demonstrated that reports of nationalism's demise were premature. The fall of communism in Eastern Europe, the unification of the two Germanys, the peaceful fission of Czechoslovakia, and the breakup of the Soviet Union and Yugoslavia illustrated the enduring power of the national idea, as well as the brittleness of the socialist project. Hobsbawm rewrote the final chapter of his book for a revised 1992 edition, ruefully acknowledging that more new states had emerged in the two years since its first publication than in all the prior decades of the twentieth century combined (Hobsbawm 1992:163).

As the importance of nations and nationalism changed so dramatically, the status of sovereignty fluctuated as well. During the 1990s a series of humanitarian interventions by high-profile multilateral organizations buffeted the delicate armature that balanced competing values in international affairs, including the foundational principle of state sovereignty and the equally foundational, though more nebulous, principles of individual and collective human rights (Benhabib 2002). By the end of the decade, the balance appeared to have shifted substantially in favor of the latter two, to the detriment of sovereignty. High officials grumbled, and academics marveled, that governments could no longer shield their policies and populations behind sovereignty's protective carapace. The very bedrock of the international system of states appeared to have rather serious fissures and, in fact, appeared to be a form of "organized hypocrisy" (Krasner 1999).

These parallel developments in the 1990s reinforced each other. The recrudescence of nationalism made it more plausible for international organizations to intervene on behalf of whole peoples, and the possibility of international intervention gave even numerically small nationalist movements much greater influence. If the leaders of nationalist movements believed it likely that powerful actors would lend a hand, they were likely to think and act more boldly; likewise, governments were likely to be more circumspect in countering such movements. Each of these consequences fed the other. Bosnia and Herzegovina broke off from Yugoslavia. Chechens twice mounted military challenges to Russian rule, and Quebec arranged a referendum on independence from Canada. At the end of the decade East Timor slipped from Jakarta's control with the help of a UN military mission and a UN-sponsored plebiscite. And not too much later, Kosovo separated from rump Yugoslavia under a hail of NATO smart bombs.[1] The message that national self-determination was again possible and that it might enjoy international support spread to other parts of the world. The fact that the Chechen and Quebec movements were less successful than those of the Timorese or Kosovars did not deter their participants—or the populations watching from other parts of the globe.

The September 11, 2001, attacks and subsequent attacks in Spain, Britain, and Indonesia gave yet another global phenomenon new (though not unprecedented) prominence. Suddenly, people were widely aware of political Islam and the threat that deep political disagreements rooted in religious values posed to world peace. Al-Qaeda and the Taliban gained more publicity than their leaders had ever dreamed of, and much of the non-Muslim world launched earnest and terrified discussions of the "problem of Islam" and "global terrorism."

All these issues come together in China's northwest. Just as the Soviet Union had been formed from the heterogeneous territories of the Russian czarist empire, the People's Republic of China (PRC) had inherited most of the lands conquered by the Manchu Qing empire before its collapse in 1911. In the course of abandoning socialism, the Soviet Union disintegrated, finally disgorging many of the former imperial territories. In 1979 China's leaders in Beijing embarked on ambitious reforms of the socialist system, and many foreign observers wondered whether China's transition to postsocialism, if that was indeed what was taking place, would be similarly cataclysmic.

In 1759, Qing generals conquered the vast territory of what is today China's northwestern region of Xinjiang and incorporated it into the empire. Even 190 years later when the PRC was founded, it remained culturally distinct and geographically remote from China proper. The substantial population of Muslim, Turkic-speaking Uyghurs, gave Xinjiang its full name: the Xinjiang Uyghur Autonomous Region. Beijing claims Uyghurs as part of the "great family of the Chinese nation" and asserts that Xinjiang has been an integral piece of Chinese national territory "since ancient times." Many Uyghurs, by contrast, believe themselves to be part of a distinct Uyghur nation, with its own rightful homeland, history, culture, and language. Having seen their Turkic-speaking, Muslim neighbors to the west—Kazakhs, Uzbeks, Qirghiz (Kyrgyz), Turkmens, and others—secede from the "eternal" Soviet Union and found independent states bearing their own names, many Uyghurs sought, and some still seek, to turn Xinjiang into a sovereign state. Learning of NATO's intervention in Kosovo, many Uyghurs hoped that foreign assistance would make this possible, since they could not achieve independence on their own.

It is not surprising that well into the 1990s, few people in the wider world were aware that Uyghurs were Muslims, since very few people had even heard of Uyghurs. Within two years of the September 11 attacks and the subsequent incarceration of twenty-two Uyghurs in Guantánamo, anyone in the United States who knew of the Uyghurs also knew that they were Muslim. One lamentable consequence of the Uyghurs' coming to international prominence during the "war on terror" has been that they have been fit into a ready-made grand narrative of culture clash, terrorism, and global Islamic threat. In fact, though, there is scant evidence that more than a few hundred Uyghurs, if that many, ever had any connection with al Qaeda or the Taliban.

One aim of this book is to demonstrate that most Uyghur resistance to Chinese rule is prompted by nationalism, not Islamism. But a wider purpose is to explore, first, how and why large numbers of Uyghurs have resisted their incorporation into the Chinese nation-state and, second, how and why the Chinese government has attempted to overcome that resistance. Finally, my main aim is to elucidate how the global currents just described—the renewed significance of nationalism, the tension between sovereignty and self-determination, the possibility of humanitarian intervention, and the heightened perception of an Islamic threat in the non-Muslim world—have combined to make the contention between Uyghurs and the Chinese state an international, rather than a merely national, problem.

THE "CHINESE NATION" DENIED

Although for more than eighty years Chinese leaders have been telling the Uyghurs living in Xinjiang that they are an indissoluble part of the Chinese nation, many Uyghurs today disagree.[2] A visitor to that contentious territory, known since 1955 as the Xinjiang Uyghur Autonomous Region, is likely to be initiated into the conflict there through stories. I heard one such account on a winter afternoon in 1995. I was speaking with a young man whose parents had immigrated to Xinjiang from China's interior but who himself had grown up in a small city in Xinjiang, speaking Uyghur so well, he claimed, that "without looking no one could tell I was Han" (that is, a member of China's ethnonational majority). Remembering the harmonious relations between the groups in his childhood, he told me about a recent event that had left a deep impression on him.

> As I rode the commuter bus one day, two Uyghurs and two Hans[3] began yelling at each other. At first it wasn't clear what the dispute was about. Listening more closely to what they were shouting, I pieced together the story: one Uyghur claimed that one of the Hans had knocked his stereo to the floor of the bus and demanded that they pay for it. The two Hans denied having touched the stereo. Another Han on the bus, trying to smooth things over, said, "Hey, we're all Chinese, eh?" One of the Uyghurs responded venomously, "You Hans are Hans. We Uyghurs are Xinjiang people. We're not one family."[4]

That so seemingly trivial an event as a fight over a radio could elicit such an outburst indicates that a deep disagreement about the shape and membership of the Chinese nation lurks just beneath the surface of social life in Xinjiang. And while the Chinese Communist Party (CCP) has gone to great lengths, and made substantial material investments, to persuade the Uyghurs of the benefits of being part of the People's Republic of China, a considerable proportion remain deeply dissatisfied. Historians of China have argued for decades that the Communists forged a strongly united nation out of the heterogeneous peoples and lands conquered by the Qing empire (1644–1911). This book casts doubt on that proposition. CCP leaders claim to have completed the task of building the Chinese nation more than forty years ago. But in fact, they are still working strenuously on that project today, and in China's far west they have not succeeded.

Nation building has unquestionably succeeded in China's core provinces, often called "China proper." The Hans who comprise more than nine-tenths of the population firmly believe in and strongly support the idea of the Chinese nation (Zhao 2004). Resistance to incorporation into that nation, and to the very idea of the nation, is most visible in Xinjiang and Tibet (see, for example, Goldstein 1997; Schwartz 1994), the two regions farthest from Beijing and in which Hans are a minority, and also in Inner Mongolia (Bulag 2000, 2002).[5]

Beijing also has incorporated Xinjiang into the state (Mackerras 2004a, 2004b; McMillen 1979; Shichor 2005). The People's Liberation Army (PLA) has maintained an uneasy peace in Xinjiang, as in Tibet, for much of the period from the late 1950s to the present. Yet Uyghurs have raised substantial challenges to the Chinese state in the past and may do so again. For several years after what Beijing afterward called the "peaceful liberation" of the region in 1949, PLA units remained hard at work fighting various insurgent groups that sought independence. The formation of several underground parties in the 1950s and 1960s and again in the post-Mao era, as well as the episodic bombings, riots, and protests since the 1980s, suggests that the government has often preserved the appearance of peace at the cost of heavy coercion. As Vivienne Shue points out, while a state must monopolize coercion to be successful, "constant reliance upon coercion to ensure popular compliance is not only an inefficient and expensive strategy, but probably ultimately a self-defeating one" (Shue 1991:218). The CCP has thus tuned its nation-building efforts precisely to the goal of reducing its dependence on military and bureaucratic coercion. At the same time, most Uyghurs lack the resources or gumption to openly defy the heavy hand of the state. Instead, they have challenged the CCP's attempts to incorporate them into the nation by means of "everyday resistance" (Scott 1990; Scott and Kerkvliet 1986).

Whereas earlier scholarship focused on everyday resistance to economic exploitation and uncontroversially oppressive institutions such as slavery, here I broaden the categories of both domination and resistance to include contestation over the "nation." Even though ethnonational and economic cleavages may overlap (see, for example, the classic work by Hechter 1975), nation building by states need not be exploitative or involve outright subjugation for sub- or nonnational groups to chafe under their rule. One of my aims is to explore exactly how and why such groups contest state efforts to incorporate them into the nation.

By invoking nation building here, I move beyond the sense of the term employed by modernization theorists in the 1950s. At that point, a positivist conception of nations and states, combined with the staggering proliferation of new states in the period of decolonization following World War II, predicted the need and the possibility for governments to construct nations by design. Both government officials and scholars believed that states could, through the construction of roads and communications networks, bureaucratic recruitment, and the extension of the market economy into the hinterlands, draw peripheral and heterogeneous peoples into the dominant culture and thus build homogeneous nations.[6] In retrospect, such work had several conspicuous problems: it was teleological, assuming that there was an identifiable end point and that nations actually "got built" in the end.[7] Officials and scholars proved to have been overoptimistic about the capacity of states to reorient citizens' identities at will. Finally, the government plan and its academic theorization were internally incoherent. If nations objectively existed, how could nationalities be altered? If identity was malleable, how could a stable identity ever be "built"?

Now the broad scholarly consensus is that nations are constructed, but not under conditions or with outcomes of states' choosing. One direct implication is that the construction process never ends, that nations are never finished but are always in the making (Beissinger 1995; Brubaker 1996; Kolstø 2000; Suny 1995). Some scholars even suggest that "there is nothing to prevent homogenized nations from separating out into different peoples, and raising new claims of nationhood . . . [which] threatens even apparently successful nation-states with a recurring crisis of legitimation" (Suny 1995:190).

The peoples "raising new claims of nationhood" are engaging in nation building as well. Nationalist activists disputing their membership in existing states attempt at the same time to constitute cohesive, politically mobilized nations through their labors. Uyghur intellectuals have sought to build a collective identity embracing all Uyghurs (Rudelson 1997), and I argue that ordinary Uyghurs have also participated in constituting the nation through acts of individual resistance. I therefore focus on both the CCP's nation-building strategies and the Uyghurs' counterstrategies, capturing in a single framework both the Chinese state's bid to incorporate Uyghurs into the Chinese nation and the Uyghurs' attempts to resist it.[8] In this contest, the state is neither entirely helpless nor so strong that it can simply impose its will on Uyghurs and others, restructuring society according to a national blueprint, as the modernization school once predicted. Similarly, while Uyghurs lack the power to separate from China at will and found a new state, many have found ways to challenge the Chinese nation-building project, to Beijing's immense frustration. Both the Chinese state and defiant Uyghurs engage in representational politics.

REPRESENTATIONAL POLITICS

This book is centrally concerned with the role of narrative in politics and narratives of a particular kind. I contend that narratives of what is going on in Xinjiang play a leading role in Xinjiang's politics. Like many other observers, I am interested in the determinants of both the conflict in Xinjiang and the Uyghurs' collective identity. Of the many important factors, I concentrate on a particular class of them. "Representational politics" is implicated in both the emergence and the hardening of the Uyghurs' collective identity and in the conduct of the contention among the Chinese party-state, the Uyghurs in Xinjiang, and the Uyghur diaspora. Various actors have engaged in representational politics to conjure certain identities or thwart the emergence of others, and to strengthen or protect the identities so conjured against external assaults and internal conflicts. Other actors have employed these strategies to galvanize the groups for political purposes. Indeed, focusing on representational politics helps us trace processes crucial to the emergence and survival of distinct identities, and the conflicts that ensue as entrepreneurial actors mobilize them for diverse ends.

I am not arguing that identities are *just* narrative constructions or that conflicts might easily be resolved by the expedient of changing representations. It is clear that differences of physiognomy, *habitus*, religion, and socioeconomic status distinguish Uyghurs from Hans and that the differential treatment of these groups by the party-state has contributed to the gulf between them; this is one of the main points of chapter 2. I also recognize the importance of political organizations, political action, and episodes of violence and brutality that members of each group have visited on the other, as chapters 4 and 5 show. Nevertheless, to put it the other way around, were we to focus only on those matters, we would miss a crucial realm of political action and contention.

The various actors in the book narrate such matters as what the government is doing, what the "splittists" are up to, what the broad masses really believe, which "hostile foreign powers" are plotting to carve up China, and how Xinjiang's present squares with its "true" past. Narrative representations are not figments we need to peel away, false leads we need to eschew in our quest to understand the goings-on in this contentious region. They are not mere *misrepresentations* (although they often are also that); they are the very stuff of politics in Xinjiang. All the main actors are consciously engaged in representing their own actions and those of their opponents as they pursue their political aims. For many actors, principally Uyghurs, this is the only means they have to do so.

State actors, like the political organs in Beijing and their counterparts in Xinjiang, deploy representation as a vital supplement to other tools at their disposal. They can call in military and police forces, initiate campaigns with the force of law, mobilize party cadres, turn on or off the spigot of state largesse, and offer or withhold jobs, schooling, or other social goods. These tools endow officials' representational strategies with consequences. One example is that after a series of large-scale student demonstrations that began on December 12, 1985, officials concluded that "Xinjiang's principal threat comes from *minzu* splittism at home and abroad."[9] No mere analytical judgment, this decision quickly became an official "set phrase" (*tifa*) and thus the obligatory frame of interpretation for subsequent disturbances (Dang Yulin and Zhang Yuxi 2003:357; Schoenhals 1992). In other words, when students and other groups held protests in later years, regardless of the slogans shouted or the likely provocations, government and public security officials were instructed to interpret—and treat—the protests as separatist actions, inviting harsh responses.

Other groups have far fewer options as they contend with the state. Ordinary Han citizens have very few avenues available for influencing politics or even expressing their discontent. Uyghurs in Xinjiang have fewer still. They have no legitimate political parties outside the CCP that they may join.[10] Elections are limited to the village level, and reports from around the country indicate that party officials still have an influential hand in selecting (and excluding) candidates, so contestation is limited. Higher offices are filled by appointment, and the few Uyghurs selected for prominent positions have been carefully vetted for their tractability after decades of service in the bureaucracy. Demonstrations are formally legal but suppressed in practice; until July 2009, no major organized protest had taken place in Xinjiang since 1997. Even recorded expressions of criticism, dissent, or discontent are thwarted. All mass media, including electronic media, newspapers, magazines, and even books and pamphlets, are censored. Every poem, every song, every short story, essay, and novel must pass through a battery of censors before being published. Even those items that succeed in passing the censors can later be judged harmful because of their "social effects" and be banned.

Because other forms of political participation are closed off and the open expression of dissent is punished by the state, ordinary Uyghurs have been forced to speak and write obliquely—in the margins and interstitially—to represent their views and share them with others. A Uyghur scholar discussing the novels of Zunun Qadir, a famous Uyghur novelist, aptly cited Edward Said (1993:xiii, quoted in Walia 2001:21), to the effect that "stories . . . become the method colonized peoples use to assert their own identity and the existence of their own history" (Thwaites 2005:24).

I use the phrase *representational politics* to denote these practices, having in mind two distinct but related senses. The first is the use of mimetic representations in politics—narratives of history and contemporary politics, the labeling of groups, particular explications of historical relationships, and trends—and as a tool of politics. The second is what is more commonly called *representative politics*, the selection of an individual or a party to represent the views and press for the aims of a group. The central problematic uniting the two is the assumption that something can stand for something else, simply and without distortion.

The discursive sense of representational politics focuses on the shaky premise that words stand simply for reality and capture political reality without distortion. All official studies of modern Xinjiang published in China (and unofficial studies have been extraordinarily rare) espouse this premise implicitly or explicitly. Many of the texts I use purport to express the views of Uyghurs and the "people of various *minzu*" or to explain what the CCP has done for the peoples of Xinjiang. In several chapters I illustrate that skeptical consumers of such works—many Uyghurs and some Hans as well—skillfully pick them apart.

The political arrangement in Xinjiang also rests uneasily on the assumption that a small number of people, identified as political representatives, can stand for many more people and articulate their wishes faithfully (Bourdieu 1991; Williams 1998). This is exemplified in the state's claim that the top Uyghur (and other non-Han) leaders in various government bodies were selected and promoted democratically and that thus they are legitimate representatives of the peoples from which they sprang. Curiously, although such leaders are explicitly chosen and raised through the ranks on the basis of *minzu* affiliation—a Uyghur must head the Xinjiang Uyghur autonomous regional government; a Qazaq, the Ili prefectural government; and so on—the state also maintains that such leaders are able and expected to represent the common interests of all. Leaders who focus on the interests of their respective *minzu* have frequently been condemned as "narrow nationalists" by the party-state and stripped of their offices. A third important facet of the problem of political representation in Xinjiang concerns the place of the party and party officials in politics. Top party officials at all levels in Xinjiang have been overwhelmingly Han, and yet it is forbidden to suggest that the selection of Hans over Uyghurs and others vitiates the system of autonomy. Chapter 2 takes up this problem in the discussion of how government and party leaders are recruited and promoted and, more broadly, in the construction of the system of "*minzu* regional autonomy."

Several common themes emerge from the study of both forms of representational politics. The first is selection: Hans outside Xinjiang, or brought in from outside the region, have the power to choose which individuals will represent the wider population, which texts will depict social realities, and with what "formulations" (*tifa*) they will do so. The second common theme is the consistency of the selectors' aims and preferences in choosing individuals or narrative frames. This consistency is reflected in intentional elisions or gaps. In discursive representation, this includes topics not raised, interpretive frames excluded or condemned, and voices not heard. With regard to the selection of political representatives, we find individuals who are not promoted or are moved to less threatening positions, striking imbalances in the proportion of officials chosen from different *minzu*, and the extreme rarity of officials who speak out about these elisions and exclusions.

Although I use the concept of representational politics to illuminate politics in modern Xinjiang, I believe it can be applied far beyond this relatively little known region in Central Asia. Because antistate movements often lack military or organizational resources that would facilitate their struggles, stronger states can successfully deny these tools to all but the most fearless and motivated. The more ruthless and autocratic states seek to strip separatists even of rhetorical weapons, but no actual state has yet succeeded in squelching dissidence completely. Even George Orwell's nightmare vision of a socialist polity with a chicken in every pot and a surveillance camera in every wall allowed that citizens might organize themselves against the state in the interstices of the invigilatory system.[11]

CHINA'S NORTHWEST

The Xinjiang Uyghur Autonomous Region (also referred to as Xinjiang or the XUAR), as it is officially known to the Chinese (most Uyghur nationalists call it Eastern Turkestan or Uyghurstan), is a vast swath of territory on the inland border of today's People's Republic of China. Occupying one-sixth the total area of China, it holds only a fraction more than 1 percent of China's population (see map of China).[12] Lying as it does near the center of the Eurasian landmass, most of the land area of Xinjiang is desert or extremely arid, so most of the population is concentrated in oases dotting the region. Compounding the isolating effects of distance are the four mountain ranges dividing the province itself and separating it from Tibet, the countries to its southwest, and those to the north (Rudelson 1992). The northern part of the autonomous region is wedged between Kazakhstan and Mongolia, and the southwestern part abuts on Kyrgyzstan, Tajikistan, Afghanistan, Pakistan, and a sliver of India. Within China it touches Gansu and Qinghai provinces and the Tibet Autonomous Region, themselves largely arid and sparsely populated. As recently as 1935, the journey from Beijing to the region's capital, Ürümci, took two months by car (Teichman 1937), and in 1951, it still took a month to drive to the rail spur in Xi'an.[13] Until the late 1950s, the northern rail line from Beijing extended only into Gansu (with an initial gap of more than six hundred miles to Ürümci) and reached Ürümci only in 1962. Today the trip from the capital takes two days by train or five hours by plane. Even though modern transportation and communication networks have narrowed the distance considerably, Xinjiang remains remote in the popular Chinese imagination.

Nevertheless, several of Xinjiang's features make it "integral" to China in the eyes of the leadership. It possesses rich reserves of natural gas and oil, estimated by Beijing to be one-third of the country's total. China has been a net oil importer of oil since 1993, and Xinjiang's production can satisfy only part of domestic demand, but the region remains vital to the country's economic security (Downs 2004). Other mineral resources include substantial quantities of gold, other nonferrous metals, and uranium. Xinjiang's climate makes it attractive for cotton cultivation, and the CCP intends to turn it into the country's "cotton basket," despite the scarcity of water and the obvious environmental devastation around the Central Asian Aral Sea caused by cotton farming (Toops 2004b). The vastness of Xinjiang has long impressed party planners as a potential solution to overcrowding in China's heartland. The region was chosen, for instance, for the relocation of a portion of the villagers displaced by the Three Gorges Dam project. Finally, owing to its location, the region has been seen, by turns, as a bulwark against the Soviet threat during the decades of Sino-Soviet tension, a gateway to the markets of Central Asia since rapprochement (and especially since 1991), and a corridor for shipping energy resources. The region now boasts an oil pipeline and will soon have a gas pipeline connecting Central Asia's and Siberia's far richer resources with China's energy-hungry coast (Asiaport Daily 2008; Xinhua 2005).

Uyghurs predominate in the Tarim Basin oases of southern Xinjiang. According to official figures, 9.65 million Uyghurs lived in the XUAR in 2007.[14] Sixty years ago they constituted the vast majority of the population, three-quarters of the region's 1944 population of less than four million. Hans then were a tiny minority, barely exceeding 200,000, and that only after several decades of Han immigration with the support of successive warlords and later China's Nationalist government.

What the Nationalists had only encouraged, the Communists compelled for almost two decades: state-directed immigration beginning in 1950 that increased the Han population to nearly five million by 1975. From the mid-1980s on, state policies to lure more immigrants brought that figure to roughly 8.2 million in 2007.[15] Thus while Uyghurs are still officially the most numerous non-Han group in Xinjiang, they now constitute only a plurality. There is little doubt that in recent decades the vast Han population has done as much as the military and the party to counterbalance Uyghurs' political aspirations. Nevertheless, the persistence and depth of the Uyghurs' alienation and Xinjiang's substantial strategic value to the CCP have kept the "Uyghur problem" high on Beijing officials' agenda since the founding of the PRC. While the government frames the problem practically in terms of the conditions and aspirations of a known population, we should not. Rather, we must inquire into the "Uyghur problem" by asking about the constitution of the population itself. When and how did the people now known as Uyghur come to think of themselves as such?

WHEN WERE UYGHURS?

For a long time, scholarship on Xinjiang appeared to be caught in a time warp, insulated from developments in social science theory. This limitation was, of course, common to work focused on geographical regions rather than academic disciplines. Early studies of politics in Xinjiang shared the assumption that the Uyghurs' ethnic origins and current identities were clear (McMillen 1979; Norins 1944; Whiting and Sheng Shih-ts'ai [Sheng Shicai] 1958).[16] Scholars typically read political implications directly from the *minzu* categories of Uyghurs and others, using the identity of individuals and groups to explain their actions. Later work influenced by the constructivist turn in the social sciences transformed the study of Xinjiang by demonstrating that the Uyghur, Hui, and Han identities had emerged comparatively recently, were mobilized and shaped by political elites, and remained fluid and contested (Gladney 1990, 1991, 1996; Millward 1998, 2007; Rudelson 1997). Several scholars have argued controversially that despite the well-attested history of the powerful eighth-century Uyghur Empire (744–840) and the Uyghur Qoco Kingdom (850–1250), both the ethnonym "Uyghur" and its associated identity are in some sense modern inventions (Gladney 1990; Rudelson 1997). Gladney argues that the emergence of a Uyghur ethnonational identity in the twentieth century was the indirect result of a conference convened by Josef Stalin in 1921 at which participants proposed the official adoption of "Uyghur" as an ethnonym in the Soviet Union.[17] The term later spread to Xinjiang and was institutionalized in 1935 by the government of the warlord Sheng Shicai (Bao'erhan [Burhan Shahidi] 1994:244). Though once debated, the thesis that Uyghur identity was a modern invention or reinvention has gained wide acceptance in Uyghur studies. Yet in presuming the sudden reemergence and speedy spread of a new category of identity, this thesis begs the question of why the Uyghurs did not mount a cohesive nationalist challenge to either Republican or Communist Chinese rule.

Three scholars have answered the question in slightly different ways. The historian Andrew Forbes contends that the very expectation of concerted Uyghur action betrayed a fundamental misprision regarding the history of the region and people. Xinjiang was not a single territory inhabited by a people with a common identity. Instead, it remained separated into three distinct regions before the Qing conquest, and the disorganization of warlord rule in Republican-era Xinjiang again brought these differences to the fore.[18] Forbes (1986:230–31) suggests that these distinct regions and regional identities persisted through midcentury.[19] Justin Rudelson argues that historically there had been four distinct zones within the territory and four corresponding regionalized identities. By closing the region to its western neighbors for several decades after 1949, the CCP actually contributed to the formation of a cohesive Uyghur identity, but the reopening of the region to the outside world in the reform era revived the four regional orientations. According to Rudelson (1997), Uyghur nationalist intellectuals reinforced the old divisions by vying to constitute authentic Uyghur identity according to regional dictates. Like Rudelson, Joanne Smith writes as if the emergence of a unitary Uyghur identity ought to be expected and its tardy arrival lamented. She contends that Uyghur unity has been thwarted not by oasis differences but by distinctions of age, gender, and occupation. Smith speculates that the passage of elder generations from the political elite (Smith 2000:195) or the renewed emphasis on religious and cultural identity (Smith 1999:128) might foster greater cohesiveness, and at the same time she concludes that city dwellers and rural folk differ enough in outlook that a single Uyghur-wide political platform, based on shared identity and interest, is unlikely to emerge any time soon.

Many Uyghurs themselves bemoan their disunity, seemingly confirming the theses of Forbes, Rudelson, and Smith. Some blame *yurtwazliq*, or "localism," as the root of the problem (Abdurehim Ötkür 1996 [1985]). Others criticize what they regard as disloyal behavior, such as toadying to Hans and spying for the government. Many particularly regret the infighting among intellectuals, whom they expected to take the lead in promoting ethnonational unity.[20] Indeed, while many of my informants felt that all Uyghurs should foster unity and act in concert with Uyghur-wide interests, few believed this was happening, and fewer still could specify what behaviors and attitudes this abstract wish for unity demanded of them and their friends. Not surprisingly, this divisiveness has not been confined to Uyghurs in Xinjiang. Chapter 5 discusses calls for both unity and factional behavior among Uyghurs in organizations abroad. What the Uyghurs' laments and the scholars' more dispassionate diagnoses of Uyghur disunity miss, I believe, is the distinction between identity and intention. They have somehow expected national identity to overcome quotidian politics (Roberts 1998a).

Following Anderson (1991), I suggest that educational and employment "pilgrimages" to Ürümci (and, to a lesser extent, regional educational centers such as Kashgar or Ghulja) have effaced the regional and professional differences among Uyghur elites, inculcating in them a strong sense of collective identity (Bovingdon 1998; see also Naby 1986). The trend of traveling to the regional capital for education or to find work has not abated, and travelers returning to their homes all over Xinjiang have spread widely the vision of a Pan-Uyghur identity and shared interests. The comparative rarity of Uyghurs' traveling to China proper and the still greater rarity of their settling there have also contributed to the preservation of a Xinjiang- and Uyghur-focused rather than a Pan-Chinese identity.[21]

Furthermore, as a number of scholars have argued, both the Soviet Union and the PRC strengthened novel or weakly rooted identities in many groups by institutionalizing them, assigning people to discrete ethnonational categories and distributing goods or authority on the basis of those categorizations (Brubaker 1996; Gladney 1990, 1991; Pipes 1968; Roeder 1991; Roy 2000). Yet those identities have not extinguished or supplanted all others. Olivier Roy showed, for instance, that clan identities preceded ethnonational identities in Central Asia and have survived alongside them. To assert that identities remain plural is not to deny their power or substance, however. Uyghurs cleave deeply to the idea that they, as a group, are essentially different from Hans, which is a view that the vast majority of Hans share. The belief in a basic and universal difference between Hans and Uyghurs is predicated on the assumption of essential sameness among Uyghurs and among Hans. But what that essence entails in terms of language, practice, dress, or deportment is still, and will remain, contested. While nationalists imagine the irreversible "awakening" of a unitary and stable identity, we must recognize this as an aspiration rather than a description of reality. Even groups sharing a collective sense of belonging may display different levels of "groupness" over time and in different contexts (Brubaker 2002; Gladney 1996; Roy 2000).

The party-state has cleverly exploited internal distinctions among Uyghurs and other non-Hans. By the late 1950s, while recognizing and institutionalizing ethnonational categories, officials increasingly emphasized class, and by the mid-

1960s they placed class above all else. During the Cultural Revolution, the Gang of Four promulgated the notion that all group conflicts ultimately boiled down to problems of class. Officials worked to further weaken ethnonational loyalties by inviting women from all groups to join women's associations. During the high socialist era, bureaus and work units tried to replace solidary with political ties by rewarding individuals willing to show enthusiasm for the regime (Oi 1989; Walder 1986); this certainly was true of party and government administrations in Xinjiang (McMillen 1979; Toops 1992). Having expropriated and marginalized Muslim clerics after 1949, officials then sought to loosen the hold of religion on the rest of the population while simultaneously working to transform Uyghur Islam into a state-supporting institution.[22]

Strengthening one identity in competition with others (and under patient government assault) requires work. It is partly through resisting party initiatives that Uyghurs have constituted themselves as a group. As we will see, the consumption and dissemination of heterodox popular culture link Uyghurs in circuits of transmission and identification.[23] Thus to interpret "everyday resistance" as merely the consequence or expression of Uyghur nationalism is to miss one of its principal effects. In resisting, Uyghurs invoke the nation and claim membership in it, even if they have different conceptions of and interests in that nation.

I argue that a subtler institutional legacy also contributed substantially to the formation of Uyghur national consciousness: the very language the CCP used to denote the Chinese nation and the non-Han groups it supposedly encompassed. Officials employed a single term, *minzu*, to refer to both the nation and its subgroups. In so doing, they unintentionally opened a rhetorical and ideological space in which Uyghur identity and nationalism could flourish.

By using the same word to denote subnational and national groups, Chinese officials departed from earlier European and Soviet examples. In the latter half of the nineteenth century, as the ideas of the nation and national self-determination spread throughout Europe, the leaders of several states anticipated a problem in acknowledging substantial unassimilated populations while simultaneously attempting to construct unified nations. They sought to avert this problem through careful distinctions in nomenclature. The aim was to establish rhetorical bulwarks against demands for autonomy or separation. Between 1848 and 1868, Austrian and Hungarian bureaucrats developed the lexical strategies on which all subsequent multinational states would depend to manage intrastate cultural difference, using the term *nationality* (*nationalität*) to denote cultural communities without acknowledging them as nations (Seton-Watson 1977:147). The Russians would have *natsionalnost* to *natsia*; the Americans, *ethnic groups* and *nation*; and so forth. Walker Connor is quite right to point out that in the Soviet system, "being classified as a *nationality* rather than as a *nation* [could] have political implications," the crucial one being the kind of autonomous unit to which a particular group was allocated. The hierarchy of republics, *okrugs*, and so on, indicated, on a territorial level, the status of each titular group in the great chain of peoples.[24] But Connor gets it wrong when he asserts that "Peking, by referring to all peoples within China, other than the Han, as nationalities, justifies its refusal to create republics on the Soviet pattern" (Connor 1984:xv).[25] In fact, after China's officially sponsored ethnologists determined in the 1950s that there were fifty-odd distinct groups according to Stalin's criteria, the party formally placed everyone, including the Han, on an equal footing by labeling them *minzu*.[26] The party then placed above them the abstract category of the "Chinese nation" (*zhonghua minzu*), which, it emphasized, was not reducible to the Han but encompassed all groups.[27] Thus despite the vastly different political rights assigned them by the party, both the putatively "minority" groups and the "Chinese nation" were given the same nomenclature, *minzu*. Official boosting of the *zhonghua minzu* is complicated by constant official reminders that China is a "multi-*minzu* state" (*duo minzu guojia*). If the *zhonghua minzu* alone possesses the state, as the party claims, the principle of transitivity suggests it is a "multi-*minzu minzu*." The decision not to follow the example of the Soviet Union and other states, which underscored the political hierarchy of categories with careful linguistic distinctions, has contributed to the party-state's difficulties with Uyghurs and others. It is for this reason that I leave the term *minzu* untranslated throughout this book.

In other work I have provided extensive evidence (Bovingdon 2002b) that the instability of the term *minzu* has, from the vantage of the state, dangerously exposed it to political manipulation from below. Here I cite only two examples. The CCP has made "*minzu* solidarity" (*minzu tuanjie*) the centerpiece of its yearly propaganda drives to combat separatism. The slogan is intended to advocate solidarity *among* the various *minzu*. Yet Dru Gladney discovered during field research in the late 1980s that some Huis used it in quite a different sense. Several people told him, "Our Hui *minzu* has deep solidarity." Gladney observed that "without changing the Chinese phrase, they [had] radically altered its meaning." Whereas it originally had been promulgated by party elites to strengthen solidarity among all the groups making up the "Chinese nation," his Hui informants used it to describe their strong collective identity *distinct* from that of other groups in China (Gladney 1991:313).[28] In 1995 Beijing University professor Ning Sao published a massive theoretical work that sought to nail down the complex relationship between *minzu* and state (*guojia*) in China, and to do so by distinguishing the various meanings of the term *minzu*. Seeking to contain the very semantic leakage just described, Ning wrote sententiously that "in China there is only one *minzu* that can be called a *minzu* (nation)"[29]—that being the "Chinese nation" (*zhonghua minzu*) (Ning Sao 1995:13). In recent years, the official English name of the State Council's *minzu shiwu wei-yuanhui* was quietly changed from "Nationality Affairs Commission" to the "Ethnic Affairs Commission."[30] Officials also changed the English title of its mass periodical *Minzu tuanjie* from *Nationality Unity* to *Ethnic Unity* (Bulag 2000:196). The decision of bureaucrats in Beijing to make these changes can be seen as part of a drive to eliminate ambiguity and close the door on unwanted international interpretations of Beijing's contention with Uyghurs and Tibetans as national rather than ethnic conflicts. But bureaucrats and scholars in Beijing have not yet agreed. China's premier postsecondary institution dedicated to the education of non-Hans, the Zhongyang minzu daxue, retained the English name Central Institute for Nationalities until February 2009, when its title changed, intriguingly, to the Minzu University of China.[31] The flagship scholarly journal of the Minzu Research Institute at the Chinese Academy of Social Sciences now claims the English title *Ethno-national Studies*.[32] These divergent translations of a single vexed term, and the disagreements among various agents who use the term, illustrate in microcosm the political importance of linguistic strategies of representation.

METHODOLOGY

I conducted twenty months of field research over three years between 1994 and 1997 and followed up with two months in the summer of 2002 and a short trip in 2005. The bulk of my interviews were unstructured and open-ended and involved one or more meetings with more than 160 individuals, among them ninety-five Uyghurs, fifty Hans, and a small number of Xibos, Huis, Uzbeks, Mongols, and Qazaqs. I encountered many more people through informal interactions, participation in everyday activities, and attendance at ritual celebrations. I interviewed the Uyghurs and Uzbeks in Uyghur, and the others in Mandarin. My informants included clerks, service workers, students, teachers, professors, lawyers, judges, doctors, businesspeople, office workers, police, bureaucrats, local government officials, editors, reporters, writers, and farmers. The group was weighted heavily toward educated urbanites aged nineteen to fifty. As a young male in a society with fairly strict restrictions on cross-gender socializing, I had easier access to men than to women, and men therefore constituted roughly two-thirds of my interview sample. Social groups underrepresented among my informants included farmers and very religious people.

I spent much of my time in Xinjiang's capital city of Ürümci, where I was formally registered as an advanced postgraduate student at Xinjiang University for several months in 1994 and again for the academic years 1995/1996 and 1996/1997. During those periods I studied oral and written Uyghur more or less daily for several hours with a single instructor. Personnel in the university's Foreign Affairs Office (*waishi bangongshi*) made clear from the start that they were responsible for me and, in that capacity, offered strong advice about where I could travel and with whom I could interact. I lived in a student dormitory, and although I moved about quite freely during the day when not in language classes, I was expected to return home every night by 10 P.M. local time (midnight Beijing time) during the semester, which placed obvious (and obviously intentional) constraints on how far I could travel.[33] I was able to make day trips to the suburbs and exurbs of Ürümci, as well as to the more distant towns of Changji and Hutubi. During weekends, long holidays, and when school was not in session, I traveled to other parts Xinjiang. I lived for short periods in private homes in periurban neighborhoods of Kashgar and Qumul and moved about those towns unimpeded. At one time, I was stopped by Public Security personnel, asked where I was staying, informed it was illegal for a foreigner to stay in a private home, and made to move into a hotel.[34] Finally, I made other week-long trips to Kashgar and Turpan, as well as subsequent, shorter visits to Ürümci in 2002 and 2005.

The atmosphere in Xinjiang was sufficiently tense and my informants cautious enough, given the topics of my research, that I had to rely on informal and often impromptu, rather than formal, interviews. Even though I had brought a tape recorder with me on my first research trip, it became clear within days that pulling it out in interviews would immediately end most interactions.[35] Indeed, as I learned in the initial days of my first stay, taking out a notepad and showing signs of writing down what my informants said caused most of them to fall silent or flee immediately—or, equally disastrous, to lapse into mere platitudes. After trial and error, I developed the technique of bringing a notebook and jotting down "grammatically interesting" sentences or "unfamiliar" vocabulary for future language study, to jog my memory about crucial moments in the interviews. As soon as possible after such interactions—sometimes half an hour, sometimes half a day—I would return home and type detailed field notes into my computer, often for several hours. For those conversations lasting an hour or more, except the quotations for which I had jotted notes, I could record only the general flow of ideas. Accordingly, when I use direct quotations in this book, I base them on those verbatim (or shorthand) records in my notebooks.

In addition to interviews with one person or several in various settings, I employed the technique of participant observation. When invited, I attended weddings and funerals, circumcision ceremonies, holiday celebrations, and other social gatherings. These large events were particularly valuable, for several reasons. First, they enabled me to interact with multiple people without fear of being overheard and without the stiffness of a formal research encounter. Second, I could observe conversations directed by others and determine what topics emerged without my intervention. Third, I became known to a large number of people in various communities, which facilitated later contacts.

In sum, all my interviews in Xinjiang were conducted under conditions that were far from ideal. Even though my sample contained more than 160 informants, it was very small compared with the total population of the region, and given the combination of logistical challenges and my research goals, it could not have been a random sample. Instead, I used the "snowball" method, seeking out individuals of interest and encouraging them to introduce me to family or friends. The advantages of this method included the ability to gain the trust of and learn about the social networks of a large number of people. The most obvious disadvantage is that the complexion of my sample was influenced by the first people I met or sought out in each site. I never allowed officials to suggest interviewees, and I ignored strong hints that I cease meeting with some of my informants. Only on very rare occasions was I aware of individuals trailing me, although I cannot exclude the possibility that some of my acquaintances had been instructed by the government to watch me and provide information to officials. Scholars conducting research in Xinjiang then or since have faced similar constraints.[36]

I supplemented my interviews with constant attention to print and broadcast media in both Chinese and Uyghur. I regularly listened to the radio and watched television programs, focusing attention on news and programs about China's cultural diversity. During my research stays, I subscribed to and read several local newspapers and nearly a dozen scholarly journals. From the Statistical Bureau and several Gazetteer offices, I bought statistical yearbooks, narrative yearbooks, and other such compendia. I acquired nearly one hundred audiotapes, videotapes, and compact discs with performances of music or poetry.

I also drew on interviews with many Uyghurs abroad, conducted between 2000 and 2006. One clear advantage of émigré interviews is that they can be conducted more freely and the respondents do not worry nearly as much about the consequences of frankness. At the same time, there is the problem of bias in the sample, since émigrés clearly "voted with their feet" by leaving Xinjiang. Social scientists studying the PRC in the 1960s and 1970s, when field research inside China was impossible, confronted the same problem when they interviewed émigrés in Hong Kong (Chan, Madsen, and Unger 1984; Madsen and Center for Chinese Studies 1984; Parish 1978; Whyte 1974; Whyte and Parish 1984).

In order to strengthen confidence in my interviews and my interpretations of them, as well as published sources from China, I set them carefully alongside the writings of foreign journalists and researchers. Wherever possible, I juxtapose different versions of the same events both to arrive at a most likely version and, reflexively, to judge the reliability of those versions or their authors. My conclusions are based on these combined resources. This is the first work in English to make extensive use of Uyghur-language sources produced by transnational organizations abroad. These materials provide crucial information about political activities and representational politics in the Uyghur diaspora, and many of them also offer descriptions of historical events affecting Uyghurs inside and outside Xinjiang. This book is also the first to pay sustained attention to the important internal-circulation work *Guojia liyi gaoyu yiqie* (*The National Interest Above All Else*, 2003) by the Beijing-based researcher Ma Dazheng. Ma's importance as both a researcher and a policy adviser on Xinjiang cannot be overestimated. The research that he and his assistants conducted for the book was commissioned by top party leaders in Beijing and written in consultation with the highest officials in Xinjiang. Equally important, two of the most powerful officials in Xinjiang, Wang Lequan, the party secretary, and Feng Dazhen, head of the Propaganda Department, claimed, in the prefaces they wrote for it, to have read most or all the book (Feng Dazhen 2003; Wang Lequan 2003). This text is an indispensable guide to official strategies of representation. It offers extensive advice on how to respond to Uyghurs' heterodox speech and media and how to handle international scrutiny of human rights problems.

When not in Xinjiang, I have kept abreast of developments there through a continuous review of various news sources, including foreign, Chinese, and Uyghur media. Over the last decade, the growth in the amount of information about Xinjiang has been staggering. National and local newspapers, various government organs down to the county level, and a number of research organizations all have extensive and regularly updated Web sites (though nearly all sites in Xinjiang were shut down in July 2009 and have not reopened as this book went to press). Uyghur transnational organizations have also developed sophisticated sites for the dissemination of news, polemics, and communiqués. In addition, since the late 1990s, human rights organizations such as Amnesty International, Human Rights Watch, and Human Rights in China have produced carefully researched studies of affairs in Xinjiang. The April 2005 work "Devastating Blows: Religious Repression of Uighurs in Xinjiang" (Human Rights Watch 2005) and the many reports by the Congressional-Executive Commission on China are of particularly high scholarly value. It goes without saying that all publications from Chinese government organs, Uyghur transnational groups, and human rights organizations have been crafted with political purposes in mind; I have read them critically and cross-referenced them extensively, treating none as a sole authoritative source.

PLAN OF THE BOOK

Chapter 1 describes how both Uyghur and Han nationalists (including officials in the Chinese state) strategically concocted histories to serve political purposes. It also illustrates how Uyghurs could have come to the conclusion that Chinese rule over them and Xinjiang is imperial. I briefly describe the Qing rule over Xinjiang as a colony, how Chinese nationalists at the turn of the twentieth century sought to retain Qing territories while jettisoning the baggage of empire, and how some officials in the Nationalist government acknowledged that Xinjiang was a colony and might be due for decolonization on the model of India or the Philippines.

Having defeated the Nationalists and consolidated authority over China's interior, the leaders of the Chinese Communist Party squelched talk of decolonization soon after Red Army forces occupied the strategic cities and towns in Xinjiang. In lieu of independence or a Soviet-style republic, they offered the Uyghurs a system of "*minzu* regional autonomy," a truncated version of the one they had set up in Inner Mongolia in 1947. Chapter 2 analyzes the system that the party established in Xinjiang. I first evaluate the actual system according to international legal standards for autonomy and then examine the particular components or consequences of that system, showing how each has contributed to the Uyghurs' discontent. Han academics and policy advisers have proposed various changes to that system since the late 1990s, and in the concluding section of the chapter, I argue that far from accommodating the demands of Uyghur protestors and critics, these proposed changes portend the further consolidation of power by Han party officials, more policy-driven Han immigration, and the perpetuation of policies that many Uyghurs oppose.

Officials and public security personnel have kept a tight lid on public protest in Xinjiang. As a consequence, most protest has been individual or private. In chapter 3 I describe many Uyghurs' everyday strategies for criticizing and defying the system of governance they find so objectionable. I contend that while these strategies have done little to change the region's system of governance, they have nonetheless strengthened the Uyghurs' collective identity and widely disseminated information about the nature and depth of popular discontent.

In chapter 4 I turn to the comparatively rare occasions when that discontent burst onto the public stage, in the form of protests and violent episodes that brought Xinjiang and the Uyghurs some notoriety in the 1990s. I point out that such protests in fact took place decades earlier, indicating that opposition to rule from Beijing emerged immediately after the revolution and continued, openly or secretly, through the end of the twentieth century. Second, I show that the incidence of violence and protest in that region was falling precisely during the period that Beijing began to publicize the idea of a "violent Xinjiang" harassed by terrorism. Equally important, the frequency was declining just as protests were on a dramatic rise in the rest of China.

Few Uyghurs inside Xinjiang have dared to organize politically, and as explained earlier, Chinese officials have dealt harshly with open expressions of discontent. Uyghurs in the diaspora have been far more successful at establishing organizations and working to direct international attention to Xinjiang's contentious politics. In chapter 5 I look outside Xinjiang to that substantial diaspora community, with a focus on Uyghur transnational organizations. I address the decision of the United States to label the Eastern Turkestan Islamic Movement a terrorist organization in August 2002, and Beijing's politically adroit use of this identification to argue that Uyghur separatist organizations were part of a global terrorist network. I cast doubt on Beijing's claim that such organizations have been the principal cause of unrest inside Xinjiang and show that there is very little evidence of terrorist activity or affiliations among the vast majority of the organizations.

In the conclusion I discuss the implications of the current deadlock, given that a sizable proportion of Uyghurs will not be satisfied with anything less than a substantial expansion of autonomy in Xinjiang, even though China's leaders show no willingness to compromise and, in fact, appear to plan further diminutions of the autonomy provided by the current administrative arrangements.

USING THE PAST TO SERVE THE PRESENT

POLITICIZED HISTORY

Groups embroiled in political conflicts often appeal to history to strengthen their cases. They invoke historical records to prove the location of a boundary, specify the historical population of a region, refer to battles fought, or underscore the validity of agreements signed. But as historians well know, history has never been the impartial arbiter that partisans depict. A Uyghur professor told me one blustery November day in 1996 that in his view, "history is like the Taklamakan Desert. Everything is past; it's all covered with sand. The historian simply pulls out of the sand the things he needs."[1] He might have added that the clever scholar or activist also takes care to leave buried what he does not wish to have appear.[2] Even more problematic, the enterprising person might take advantage of the remoteness of the desert from most people's homes by constructing new artifacts and pretending to have found them beneath the sand.

The writing of history is a central domain of representational politics. Yet if there cannot be, strictly speaking, truly unbiased historiography, neither is it helpful to object that all history is fiction, representation without any real referent. There is nothing to be gained from denying that there is a Taklamakan Desert, that there is a meaningful distinction between "planted" or factitious artifacts and those actually dug out of the sand, or that there are better and worse ways of uncovering the things that are buried. Careful scholarly history requires the review of as many sources as possible without prejudice as to their origin. No serious historian would refuse to consider Chinese documents merely because they are Chinese or dismiss Russian records because they are "foreign" to Xinjiang, as partisans on one side or the other have done. By the same token, serious historical research requires the scholar to evaluate the reliability of sources—to question not only the authenticity of documents and artifacts but also the motives of their writers or fashioners. Finally, responsible historical study requires that the researcher not begin with a preference for having the story come out one way rather than another.[3]

The very name of the region is a bone of contention. Uyghurs point out acerbically that Xinjiang means "new boundaries" or "new dominions" in Chinese, unambiguously acknowledging the territory's late incorporation into a Chinese-speaking polity.[4] Many Uyghurs revile the name as a Chinese imposition and prefer Eastern Turkestan or Uyghurstan, toponyms whose use the government forbids today.[5] For nearly two thousand years, Chinese-language historical records used the term Xiyu (Western Regions) to denote a region of shifting size and shape in the general vicinity of today's Xinjiang.[6] Strictly speaking, the history of "Xinjiang" extends no further back than the eighteenth century when the name came into currency among literati and bureaucrats, or even more narrowly to the period beginning in 1884 when the region was formally established as a province. In a deliberate anachronism for the sake of simplicity, I generally use Xinjiang in this chapter when referring to historical territories more or less contiguous with today's territory of that name. I do so without intending either to ratify the Chinese use of that toponym or to challenge the use of Eastern Turkestan or Uyghurstan by Uyghurs. When I refer to a historical territory significantly different in size or shape from the current Xinjiang Uyghur Autonomous Region, I will say so.

All the parties involved in the contestation over Xinjiang have used history as a tool to serve political ends. This is true of nationalist historians, officials, and intellectuals who write or disseminate historical narratives and equally true of the many others who consume them. Chinese state actors have manipulated the historiography of Xinjiang to strengthen the state's hold on the region.[7] They have written the story of the place and its peoples to make them parts of China from a very early date. Virtually every text concerning Xinjiang published in China since 1959 begins with the obligatory statement that "Xinjiang has since ancient times been an inseparable part of China," and some texts claim the relationship dates back five thousand years.[8] As two judicious historians wrote, such claims "have only rhetoric on their side" (Millward and Perdue 2004:48), but that rhetoric has been employed by a powerful, autocratic state with very little tolerance for answering challenges, whether by dissident historians or skeptical high school students. In concocting this formula, the officials were trying to extinguish the Uyghurs' claims to independent states in the past and thereby to undercut calls for independence in the future (Bovingdon 2001; Bovingdon and Näbijan Tursun 2004).

Uyghur nationalists have written histories claiming that Uyghurs have lived in what is now Xinjiang for six thousand years and that they founded many powerful independent states in or near that territory. They constructed these histories, as creative and often as unreliable as their Chinese counterparts, with two audiences in mind: the Uyghurs and the international community. In the face of challenges from official Chinese history, they have tried to restore the Uyghurs' collective belief in a proud and independent past and so impart new vigor to their resistance to Chinese rule. They succeeded in this aim in the 1980s, and as a consequence, the Chinese government ended the publication of Uyghur nationalist historiography inside China by 1991. The histories that had been published were burned in the public square, their claims officially contradicted, and their authors vilified (Benson 1996; Bovingdon and Näbijan Tursun 2004; Rudelson 1991, 1997).

Members of the wider Uyghur community have not merely been passive consumers of the ideas promulgated by intellectual elites. Instead they have played an active role in interpreting and disseminating those ideas. Hence even after the publishing crackdown and despite public criticism, the central claims of Uyghur nationalist history have continued to circulate in Uyghur society. These historians' aim with respect to the international community has been to strengthen the case for Uyghurs' self-determination, and their history is intended to persuade skeptics that Uyghurs are a historical nation by providing evidence of Uyghurs' independent states in the past.

Viewed dispassionately, the historical record of the region and its peoples reconstructed by non-nationalists has features discomfiting to both Chinese and Uyghur nationalists. The relations between states on the Central Plains of Asia (I explain later why it is inappropriate to call those states China) and those in or around what is today Xinjiang changed often and complexly. So did the states themselves, sometimes growing, sometimes shrinking, sometimes fusing, and occasionally being incorporated into much larger states located elsewhere. Complexity is the bane of nationalist simplification. The relations between the Central Plains states and parts of Xinjiang began much earlier than Uyghur nationalists would like to acknowledge. Through military colonies (*tuntian*) first established in 120 B.C.E. and commanderies (*duhufu*) first set up in 60 B.C.E., the Han dynasty (206 B.C.E.–220 C.E.) exercised military and political control over a significant portion of Xinjiang for more than one hundred years, more than two millennia ago. The Tang dynasty (618–907), too, controlled much of Xinjiang for roughly one hundred years until the An Lushan rebellion in the mid-eighth century. After that date, no Central Plains dynasty ruled Xinjiang until generals of the Qing dynasty (1644–1911) conquered its northern and southern parts in 1759 (Millward and Perdue 2004: 35–39). It is beyond question that the first two periods of rule far antedated not only the Russian Empire's first forays into the Qazaq steppe but also the very emergence of the Russian Empire itself. Even the Qing conquest of Xinjiang preceded by a full century Russia's subjugating Central Asia proper in the 1860s or the British Empire's taking formal control of India in 1858.

In contrast, contemporary Chinese nationalists prefer not to admit that the various Central Plains dynasties were not, properly speaking, "China." There is a record of the continuous habitation of the Central Plains by Chinese-speaking and -writing people from before the common era, and a series of states governed by Chinese-speakers ruled many of those people for much of the intervening two thousand years. Yet as the historian Victor Mair pointed out, there were no state names or names for human groups that outlasted a single dynasty in the Central Plains (Mair 2005:52). William Kirby argues that "there was no 'China' in a formal sense under dynastic rule," nor was there an idea of the nation (Kirby 2005:107; see also Millward and Perdue 2004:29). Ironically, an early Chinese nationalist acknowledged this inconvenient fact. The well-known intellectual Liang Qichao lamented in 1900 that his people had no name for their country. The term that later generations adopted, Zhongguo (central state or states), he dismissed as a foreign imposition, something "people of other races call us" (Fitzgerald 1996b:67). The "Chinese nation" was a modern invention dating to no earlier than the late nineteenth century, although just as their counterparts around the world had done, Chinese nationalists concocted an ancient origin and a linear history of their "self-same, national subject" moving through time (Chow 1997; Duara 1995:4 and chap. 1 passim; Leibold 2007).[9]

In sum, we must view skeptically the parallel claims of Chinese nationalist historians that "Xinjiang has been part of China since ancient times" and that Uyghurs have been part of China's "great family of *minzu*" for an even longer time. We similarly must scrutinize Uyghurs' nationalist claims that Uyghurs have always been distinct from Chinese and have established many independent states, only to be colonized by the Chinese in the comparatively recent past.

HISTORICAL QUESTIONS

The nationalist claims of Hans and Uyghurs rest on the answers to four questions: Who were the Uyghurs historically? What was the land? What was the relationship between the people and the land? And what was the relationship between Xinjiang and the core of the state (meaning both the ruling elite and the heartlands) in the Qing dynasty and afterward? The answers to these questions are of more than merely scholarly interest. Uyghur nationalist histories written or promulgated in Xinjiang provide answers that have strengthened the Uyghurs' collective identity and rekindled dreams of an independent state. Meanwhile, Uyghur organizations abroad have used similar answers to build a case for self-determination and thus to gain support from the international community. Conversely, Chinese historians and officials have sought to extinguish Uyghurs' dreams of independence and to dismiss the case for self-determination by insisting on very different answers.

First, who were the Uyghurs historically, and when did they first emerge historically? Uyghur nationalists posit that Uyghurs emerged very early, possibly some six thousand years ago (Qurban Wäli 1988; Turghun Almas 1989).[10] Aside from the problem that there are no written records sufficiently old to support this claim, and archeological evidence cannot do so, there is the difficulty that the term Uyghur (variously Weihe, Yuanhe, and Huihe in Chinese sources) is found no earlier than the fifth century (Golden 1992:95, 157). Some Uyghur nationalists claim more recent descent from the Xiongnu, a confederation of peoples who engaged in a "tug of war" with the Han dynasty for control of Xinjiang (Millward and Perdue 2004:36).[11] They place a special emphasis on this lineage because the Xiongnu appear in Chinese-language histories as the mortal enemies of the Han dynasty. Although the topic of ethnogenesis is still contentious, few serious scholars would follow Uyghur nationalists in making the leap from the existence of Xiongnu in the Tarim Basin to the assertion that they were Uyghurs. However that question might ultimately be resolved, the Uyghurs described in Chinese sources several hundred years later were allied with the Tang dynasty for a time in the seventh century before revolting against it (Mackerras 1972:8; Pulleyblank 1956:37). The Uyghurs grew stronger over time until they founded an empire (744–840) in what is today Inner Mongolia, Mongolia, and Siberia. The Qirghiz ultimately crushed the Uyghur Empire and forced the emigration of many of its subjects into Gansu and Xinjiang. Thus, only in the ninth century did peoples bearing the collective name Uyghur settle in the Tarim Basin (Golden 1992; Mackerras 1990).

A second major problem for the history of Uyghurs as a continuously "selfsame, national subject" is that when the Qarakhanid Empire moved south into the

Tarim and began to Islamicize the predominantly Buddhist Uyghur population, it set in motion the gradual disappearance of the name Uyghur, along with the Buddhist religion, until, by the fifteenth century, there were no recorded usages in the region.[12] The name Uyghur reappeared in popular discourse only in the twentieth century. Some scholars have argued that it was a Soviet conference in Tashkent in 1921 that led Turkis in Xinjiang to adopt the name. Soviet officials had revived the historical term Uyghur when they divided Turkic-speaking Central Asians into various "national" groups to ward off the threat of a Pan-Turkist revolt. The strategic adoption of the name after centuries of disuse and as a result of government policies strikes some as prima facie evidence of national invention (Gladney 1990; Rudelson 1997). Several scholars have subsequently challenged this argument, however, providing evidence that the name had already been in wide use by Turkis in the late nineteenth century (Brophy 2005; Näbijan Tursun 2008).[13] Historiographic problems notwithstanding, many Uyghur nationalists believe that the Uyghur nation emerged very early in history and that it has remained distinct from the Chinese nation ever since. As the Web site of the World Uyghur Congress puts it, "East Turkistan's people are not Chinese; they are Turks of Central Asia" (World Uyghur Congress 2006a).

If Uyghur nationalists had to overcome (and thus conceal) a number of gaps and significant changes of place, religion, and political stance in the story of Uyghur "national becoming," Chinese historians confronted a similar challenge. They, too, had to assign Uyghurs a clear date of ethnogenesis and a continuous existence since that date,[14] and they also needed to demonstrate that Uyghurs' history was a component part of the history of the multinational "Chinese nation" (*zhonghua minzu*). To accomplish this, they adopted two strategies. First, they applied the frame of class analysis in interpreting the past, insisting that in all periods the affinities of all exploited peoples, regardless of language and culture, were stronger than those of any one group for its corresponding exploiting class—within the boundaries of the "Chinese nation," of course.[15] Second, in order to manage countervailing evidence, they developed the notion of "main currents" and "countercurrents" in history. The "unification" of many peoples under the rule of powerful dynasties and harmonious relations among the laboring ranks of those peoples were the main currents of Chinese history. Internecine battles among peoples they labeled *countercurrents*.[16] Official Chinese histories of the Uyghurs used these narrative strategies to prove that Uyghurs had been part of China's "great family of *minzu*" from the moment of their emergence and never ceased to be so (Liu Zhixiao 1985, 1986; "Weiwu'erzu jianshi" bianxiezu 1991). In asserting that Uyghurs *had* never separated from the "Chinese nation" in the past, they sought to demonstrate that they *could* never do so in the future.

The second important historical question was, what was the land of Xinjiang? Was it the western part of China? The eastern part of Turkestan? The center of something else? Chinese historians have taken the first position; Uyghurs, the second or third. The first premise of Chinese nationalist historiography, as discussed earlier, is that all dynasties and the lands they ruled were "China."[17] In exact parallel with the gathering and splitting of peoples, historians made the conquest of large territories by powerful dynasties the main current of history, whereas shrunken states ruling only part of the Central Plains belonged to historical countercurrents. The claim of official Chinese histories that Xinjiang has been part of China since ancient times creates serious problems, in that many dynasties did not rule even a part of that region. Chinese historians have resolved the difficulty by regarding diplomatic relations with states in the region, tribute missions originating there, marital alliances with princes and princesses hailing from the Tarim Basin, and encampments of Chinese soldiers or merchants all as proof that each successive dynasty did in fact rule Xinjiang (Xinjiang shehui kexueyuan lishi yanjiusuo 1987; XUAR jiaoyu weiyuanhui gaoxiao lishi jiaocai bianxiezu 1992).[18]

There were and remain Turkis who identify what is now Xinjiang as the eastern part of Turkestan. Muhämmäd Imin Bughra, an Islamic scholar in Xinjiang's southern city of Khotän, founded there the Committee for National Revolution in 1932 and helped establish the short-lived first Eastern Turkestan Republic (1933–1934) in southern Xinjiang (Forbes 1986:83–89; Millward 2007:201–6). The organization has been described as both "Uyghur nationalist" and "Turkic nationalist," but Muhämmäd Imin's later writings and actions showed him to be inclined toward the latter. He hoped to free Uyghurs from Chinese control as a first step toward establishing a broader Turkic state (Forbes 1986:83–84).[19] A decade later he became close to the Nationalist government under Chiang Kai-shek and served along with Isa Yusuf Alptekin as a delegate in the Constituent Assembly in Chongqing. While there, the two managed to publish a series of articles asserting that Uyghurs, Qazaqs, and others were part of a more embracing "Turkic" (Tujue) nation that Chinese governors sought to subjugate by dividing it into smaller groups and sowing discord among them (Bovingdon 2001). Muhämmäd Imin and Alptekin fled Xinjiang in 1949 and later settled in Turkey, where both wrote books, edited journals, and gave speeches identifying their former home as Eastern Turkestan and calling on Muslims and Turks to support its liberation (I. Alptekin 1981; Bughra 1946; Landau 1995:118, 124–25, 150).[20] There was and remains manifest support among Pan-Turkists in Turkey for the cause of an independent "Eastern Turkestan," and quite a few Uyghurs in the diaspora refer to their homeland by that name. Many of those who do so, however, are prompted not by Pan-Turkism but by a recognition that given the presence of several Turkic-speaking peoples in Xinjiang, it cannot be defined as exclusively Uyghur.[21]

Finally, many Uyghur nationalists have rejected the depiction of Xinjiang as either the western edge of China or the eastern edge of the Turkic world, instead identifying it as a center in its own right. Scholars of nationalism will not be at all surprised to learn this; after all, the nation—and the national territory—must be the center of any persuasive national story. Thus in his famous history *Uyghurlar* (*The Uyghurs*), the poet and historian Turghun Almas insisted that the "Uyghur homeland" was Central Asia and characterized the Tarim Basin as the "golden cradle" of culture in the region, as well as one of the world's few such cultural founts (Bovingdon and Nebijan Tursun 2004; Turghun Almas 1989).[22] Many Uyghurs in Xinjiang regard the region as belonging uniquely to them, particularly after Qazaqs, Qirghiz, Uzbeks, and Tajiks all gained recognition in 1991 as proprietors of states bearing their ethnonyms. For the same reason, some Uyghurs in the diaspora, particularly those in Central Asia, have insisted the region be called Uyghurstan.[23]

The third question concerns the relationship between the people of Xinjiang and the land. Several Uyghur nationalist historians, including Turghun Almas, insisted that Uyghurs were indigenous to the territory, inhabiting it for all their claimed six thousand years (Qurban Wäli 1988; Turghun Almas 1986, 1989). The view that Uyghurs were autochthonous in Xinjiang is widely if quietly shared by many Uyghurs inside the region and is more or less universal in the Uyghur diaspora. Some have made the still more sweeping, and clearly insupportable, claim that Uyghurs were the *sole* indigenes—in other words, that all other peoples later found in the territory were immigrants to a place already belonging to them.[24]

Chinese historians have explicitly denied this claim. All the official histories of Uyghurs and of Xinjiang published in China since 1949 state flatly that the territory was multicultural (and multi-*minzu*) from prehistorical times. They couple this argument with detailed retellings of the story of the Uyghur Empire in Mongolia and the subsequent exodus, endlessly underscoring the point that Uyghurs were "late" arrivals in Xinjiang, entering only in the ninth century.[25] Recent Chinese histories have boldly added that Hans were among the first inhabitants of the region and in fact arrived long before Uyghurs (He Jihong 1996; Ji Dachun 1993:149, 606).[26] A recent journalistic piece announced that Hans "have been settled in Xinjiang for over 2000 years, preceding not only the Mongols, Qazaqs, Uzbeks, Manchu, Hui and Xibo, but also the western migration of the Huigu [Uyghurs]" (China Radio International 2006). Such arguments are clearly intended to simultaneously defeat Uyghur assertions of indigeneity and establish China's claim to the region through its prior occupation by Hans. In turn, these assertions rest on the intertwined assumptions that Hans existed *as Hans* two millennia ago and that they represented "China." In fact, as Zhao Suisheng argues, the idea of Han ethno-national identity, like that of the Chinese nation, dates only to the late nineteenth century (Zhao 2004:21–22; see also Chow 1997).[27]

Uyghur intellectuals are aware that demonstrating indigeneity in Xinjiang might be one of their only resources for contesting Beijing's actual political control of the region, which has not been legally challenged by any foreign state or international organization since 1949. It is precisely for this reason that Beijing has adamantly refused to recognize any "minority *minzu*" in China as indigenous, fearing that international organizations might codify rights for indigenous peoples that it does not consider "appropriate" for those non-Hans (Hannum 1988:655–56, quoted in Corntassel and Primeau 1995:n. 77). Party officials' recognition that history is a bulwark (or threat) to China's rule over Xinjiang can be discerned from the construction of the most significant documents on the region prepared for international consumption since 2002. Both the State Council's brief on "Eastern Turkestan terrorism" (Guowuyuan xinwen bangongshi 2002), and its white paper touting the virtues of Xinjiang's system of governance (Guowuyuan xinwen bangongshi 2003) begin with lengthy—and carefully manipulated—historical summaries.[28]

The fourth question concerns the relationship between the imperial heartland and the periphery following the Qing conquest. Was the relationship between country and province or between empire and colony? The importance of the answer to this question lies in the relationship between the pair of binaries discussed in the introduction: nation-state versus empire and sovereignty versus self-determination. For if Xinjiang was simply a province in a nation-state from the Qing period on, then its status must be governed by the principle of sovereignty and the emphasis on territorial integrity in international law. But if the Qing conquest and rule of Xinjiang prove to have been colonial and if that relationship was not materially altered in the Republican period, then Uyghurs would have a correspondingly stronger case for independence from China today.

QING CONQUEST

Despite contemporary Chinese claims, it was only with the Qing conquest of Xinjiang in the mid-eighteenth century that the territory was firmly bound to a Central Plains state. The conquest began not as a land grab but as a punitive expedition against the Zunghars, whom three successive Qing emperors had tried to crush. The conquest was sanguinary and ruthless: under the orders of Emperor Qianlong, the Qing troops were not to stop until they had killed or routed nearly the entire population of Zungharia (Perdue 2005a).

Having won the campaign, the Manchu emperor and his administrators found themselves in charge of an enormous territory. The northern part had largely been depopulated by the bloodbath, and the southern region was a distinct unit often ruled indirectly by nomads in the northern region who supported themselves on the agricultural wealth of the oasis towns but were content to leave administration to the locals. Qing rulers elected to continue the practice of indirect rule, giving the top military and political posts to Manchus and Chinese but leaving the daily administration of local affairs around the Tarim Basin in the hands of the *begs*, or Turkic notables. Under Qing control, Xinjiang remained distinct from China proper and was frankly ruled as a colony. The imperial administration hoped that the colony could eventually be made to pay for itself (Millward 1998:76–112, 153; Millward and Perdue 2004:57–58).

This proved a vain hope. Sustaining the garrisons and officials controlling the region proved to be expensive and was beset by numerous challenges. Turkis rose repeatedly against Qing rule, most notably in the late 1820s and 1830s and again in the mid-1860s. In 1820 the literatus Gong Zizhen memorialized the emperor by urging that the colony be transformed into a province. Gong argued that by opening the region to immigration, the state could serve two goals at once: it could relieve the population pressures on the heartland provinces, and it could stabilize the volatile border region by colonizing it with industrious, tractable farmers. The emperor ignored the first of Gong's proposals but found the second sensible in the wake of the Turki uprisings, and so the immigration of Chinese increased (Millward 1998:241–46). In the 1860s, an uprising by the Chinese Muslims of Gansu cut off Xinjiang from China proper and facilitated the emergence of an independent state in Xinjiang (1864–1877) led by Ya'qub Beg, a canny operator from Kokand who styled himself as emir and began diplomatic negotiations with the Russian, British, and Ottoman empires (Kim 2004). Russian generals in Central Asia took advantage of the state's weak control of northern Xinjiang to conquer a strategically crucial chunk of the Ili Valley region, which they managed to hold for a decade, from 1871 to 1881.

Both Ya'qub Beg's emirate and the Russian incursion contributed to a major crisis in the Qing administration. While the Qing general Zuo Zongtang was battling the Gansu uprising, Japan invaded Taiwan in 1874, an event compounding the shock from the Qing's devastating losses in the Opium Wars. Facing military challenges at opposite ends of the empire, the emperor and his advisers felt incapable of responding effectively to both and uncertain which was the more important. Xinjiang had consistently been a drain on Qing resources and was proving increasingly difficult to defend (Borei 1991). Maritime administrator Li Hongzhang argued that the coastal threat was more pressing and urged the Qing to abandon Xinjiang in order to marshal resources for a naval response. General Zuo, influenced by Gong Zizhen's earlier writings, asserted, on the contrary, that the inland threat mattered more, since Xinjiang was the bulwark protecting Mongolia and Mongolia, in turn, was the buffer protecting the capital. In the end Zuo was victorious in the "great policy debate" and won permission to launch a very expensive campaign to crush Ya'qub Beg's emirate and reconquer Xinjiang for the Qing, which he did by 1877. Only in 1884, after a Qing diplomat induced St. Petersburg to give up the land in Ili—without which the region would have been indefensible—did the emperor finally act on Gong's suggestion of sixty years earlier and transform the colony of Xinjiang into a province (Hsu 1964–1965, 1965; Wright 1994:660–61).

Three features of the Qing conquest and subsequent administration of Xinjiang are important. First, the acquisition of territory was a by-product of the emperor's attempt to rid himself of a troublesome foe. During the military campaign, there was not a word about "unification" or "reunification"; it was later Qing historians who painted the conquest as a fulfillment of imperial destiny, a legacy left by the Han and Tang dynasties but overtopped by the Manchus (Perdue 2005a:500–501, 509).[29] Second, the Qing imperial house regarded Xinjiang as a colony and saw its Muslim inhabitants as a discrete population in an empire of culturally distinct parts (Millward 1998:197–203; see also Crossley 1999). Third, far from thinking of it as an "inseparable" part of the empire, on numerous occasions both the imperial house and much of the Qing policy elite seriously contemplated abandoning the colony before finally deciding to make it a province. Both the events in Xinjiang during the Qing period and the Qing Empire itself ill fit the national frame that was later imposed on them (see, e.g., Esherick 2006).

CHINESE NATIONALISM: TALK OF THE NATION

These difficulties did not stop people from trying to stretch a Chinese national skin over the Qing imperial body (Anderson 1991:86). It is generally agreed that Chinese nationalism emerged in the late nineteenth century, though as in the case of nationalisms everywhere in the world, its progenitors set the movement in motion by invoking a hoary history of the "Chinese nation." They felt called to the task by the widespread perception that the Qing was on the verge of collapse and that its territory might be carved up "like a melon." The wholly unexpected naval defeat by Japan in 1894 incited near panic. The birth of Chinese nationalism saw the odd conjunction of announcements that the Chinese nation was awakening and dire warnings that it might soon disappear from the earth (Zhao 2004:17).

There were two principal and conflicting strands of Chinese nationalism in the 1890s, exemplified in the work of near contemporaries Zhang Binglin and Liang Qichao. The distinguished literatus Zhang Binglin envisioned a Chinese nation that was both racially and culturally unified. He argued that its members could rescue the nation from its crisis only by jettisoning non-Hans and, with them, all the territory that had not been part of the Ming (Zhao 2004:66). His rationale was that mutually hostile groups would not consent to stay together. Zhang bitterly hated the Manchus and, during a stay in Japan, had himself photographed in Ming-era garb (punishable by death in the Qing) to indicate his absolute rejection of the Qing dynasty. He acknowledged in his writings that the Muslims of Xinjiang felt toward Hans precisely the antipathy Hans felt toward Manchus (Zhang Binglin 1907:18; cited in Perdue 2005b:189; see also Gasster 1969:206). There is little doubt that he expected Xinjiang to separate from a future "purified" China, although he also apparently believed that it might ultimately be reabsorbed, since it did not "belong to anyone else."[30] Liang Qichao, also an accomplished and very influential literatus, shared Zhang's belief that race defined the nation but asserted it could be culturally plural. Liang saw all the various peoples of the Qing as belonging to the "yellow race" and differing only in culture. He was led to envision a culturally heterogeneous nation by the practical concern that abandoning territory would weaken the state still further. Liang rejected anti-Manchuism and advocated a "broad nationalism" (*da minzu zhuyi*) that would awaken a sense of belonging to "China" in all the peoples of the Qing Empire (Chow 1997:42; Esherick 2006:235; Fitzgerald 1996a:86–87).[31]

Sun Yat-sen, a humble Cantonese farmer's son who emigrated to Hawaii as a youth and later studied medicine in Hong Kong, could not claim the intellectual distinction of either Zhang or Liang, but he was a far more astute politician. Radicalized by the mid-1890s, he shared Zhang's fiery anti-Manchuism and staged an abortive revolt in 1895, as a consequence of which he had to flee to Japan. When the Wuchang uprising brought down the Qing dynasty in 1911, Sun was on a fundraising trip in the United States, yet he was subsequently credited with leading the Republican revolution and dubbed the "father of the Republic." After returning to China to serve as the first president, Sun soon recognized the incompatibility between anti-Manchuism and the desire to keep all Qing territories, and he adopted the kind of "broad nationalism" that Liang Qichao had advocated (Zhao 2004:22). In 1919 he urged that Hans "sacrifice the separate nationality, history, and identity that they are so proud of and merge in all sincerity with the Manchus,

Mongols, Muslims, and Tibetans" (Sun Yat-sen [Sun Zhongshan] 1919/1994:225). In his famous series of lectures, the *Sanmin zhuyi* (Three Principles of the People), Sun imagined that while European nations had been forged in violence, the Chinese nation had grown peacefully through the immense attractive power of its culture, thereby neatly erasing the history of conquest that had made the Qing (Sun Wen [Sun Zhongshan] 1985). Sun's Three Principles became the official doctrine of the GMD, or Nationalist Party, and despite their obvious historiographic inaccuracy, his lectures were published as a book and widely disseminated. Chiang Kai-shek, Sun's successor as head of the GMD, proposed an even more fantastic ethnological theory in his *Zhongguo zhi mingyun* (*China's Fate*): the various peoples in China came from a single racial stock, and their cultural differences stemmed entirely from regional disparities in soil and water (Jiang Zhongzheng [Chiang Kai-shek] 1943/1962). The doctrines of Sun and Chiang were transparently intended to deny that any of the peoples ruled by the republic had a right to secede.[32] If Xinjiang had become a province and the Qing had turned into the Chinese nation, Xinjiang and its peoples must necessarily remain part of that nation.

XINJIANG IN THE REPUBLICAN PERIOD: COLONIAL RULE IN NATIONAL GUISE

As is widely known, between 1917 and 1927, the rule of China's various regions devolved on a number of warlords.[33] Chiang eliminated most of them during his Northern Expedition and recentralized authority in Nanjing by 1927. Yet Xinjiang remained largely beyond the reach of that central authority until well into the 1940s.[34] The province's first governor after 1911, Yang Zengxin, maintained autocratic control untrammeled by Beijing from 1911 until his death in 1928. Having installed a network of relatives and associates in various administrative positions and enacted policies intended to "isolate, divide, and maintain in enforced ignorance" the peoples of the region, keeping the single key to the only telegraph office in Dihua (Ürümci) in his own pocket, Yang ruled the province as a virtual feudatory kingdom.[35] He responded to political uprisings with unflinching brutality, once famously ordering rebellious underlings to be beheaded at a banquet, and reportedly ran Xinjiang's economy "largely for his own benefit" (Forbes 1986:13–15, 29). Yang's successor, Jin Shuren, was no more sensitive, though considerably less adroit politically. Jin reportedly had people executed for injudicious remarks made in ordinary conversation and emulated his predecessor in seeking to exclude all external influences, whether from Nanjing or Central Asia. When the king of the still-autonomous khanate of Qumul died in 1930, Jin moved to eliminate the khanate and open the region to Han immigration. Even more provocatively, he forced

Turkis off their land to make room for the immigrants and exempted the latter from land taxes, which the displaced Turkis were still obliged to pay, even though they had been displaced to much poorer land. It is not surprising that in the 1930s, Turkis in several parts of Xinjiang rebelled against the misrule of Jin and his regional subordinates (Forbes 1986:38–62).[36] The most successful of the uprisings established the Eastern Turkestan Republic (ETR, 1933–1934) in the south. Although the short-lived republic was a fully elaborated state, with a flag, currency, and government, it failed to win diplomatic recognition from either Middle Eastern states or Britain, which had a firm policy of supporting the Nanjing government. The Soviet Union offered military assistance to Jin Shuren's de facto successor, Sheng Shicai, but in the end it was a Hui warlord from Gansu, Ma Zhongying, who crushed the republic (Forbes 1986:112–27; Millward 2007:200–206).

Sheng Shicai then ruled Xinjiang, largely as a Soviet puppet, through 1944. While his reversal of Jin's pro-immigration policy and initiatives to build roads and schools seemed to suggest that he would be more responsive to the population's wishes, he proved to be just as corrupt and nearly as brutal as Yang and Jin. While governor, he reportedly imprisoned some 100,000 people, most of them Turkis. During his tenure, Huis from Gansu founded a more or less independent polity in the southern Tarim Basin (1934–1937), and former participants in the first ETR revolted again in 1937. Once more, the Russians assisted Sheng militarily, incensed at the staunchly anti-Soviet doctrine of ETR members, and, after helping crush the uprising, Moscow deployed Russian troops in several Xinjiang cities. By the late 1930s the province had become economically and politically a dependent of the Soviet Union. In 1942 Sheng decided to break with the Soviets and go over to the GMD, before thinking better of his decision and trying to reverse it in 1944, at which point Nationalist leaders unceremoniously relieved him of his position and installed the Chiang loyalist Wu Zhongxin (Forbes 1986:148, 152, 161, and chap. 5 passim; Millward 2007:213).

An unabashed Han chauvinist like his mentor Chiang Kai-shek, Wu followed the example of Jin Shuren in opening Xinjiang to Han immigration. The Chinese government supplied funds to finance the migration, which was clearly aimed at "permanently altering the ethnic balance" in the province and predictably angered Turkis. The combination of renewed Han immigration, economic chaos, and official corruption turned most of the Turkic population against Wu's government (Forbes 1986:163–69). At this point, Uyghurs, Qazaqs, and others established the Eastern Turkestan Republic (ETR) in what had been Xinjiang's three northwestern districts. From 1944 until 1949 the ETR maintained an independent government in Ghulja, though scholars disagree on the degree of Soviet involvement and whether anti-Chinese or socialist elements played a stronger role in the government (Benson 1990; Forbes 1986; Millward 2004:chap. 5; Wang 1999).

In August 1945 the Nationalists dispatched General Zhang Zhizhong to negotiate with the ETR government, and with Soviet encouragement, the latter agreed to negotiations. Within a year, the two sides had formed a coalition government in Ürümci with representatives from Ghulja. A year later in 1947 the coalition had frayed considerably, and Turkis staged several large demonstrations in the widely separated cities of Ghulja, Dihua (Ürümci), and Kashgar. In that year, Zhang traveled around Xinjiang making speeches and seeking common ground with locals. Strikingly, in his speeches, he regularly compared Xinjiang with British India and the former American colony of the Philippines, recognizing that there was a global "tide of decolonization," and acknowledged that Xinjiang, too, might someday become independent. Nonetheless, he often expressed doubts that the region could achieve *true* independence, fearing that instead it would fall under the control of another state, understood to be the Soviet Union (Bovingdon 2001; Forbes 1986:207–9; Millward 2007:216–18; Zhang 1947).[37]

This was not the last time a GMD official openly spoke of the possibility that Xinjiang might become independent. In 1947, Wu Qiyu, an adviser to the Nationalist Ministry of Foreign Affairs, wrote an article analyzing the "Xinjiang problem" for the new journal *Tianwentai* (*The Observatory*).[38] In the article he posed the question of whether China should abandon the unruly province. Both his entertaining this question in 1947 and some of his reasons are of interest to us here. First, as had Zhang Binglin before him, Wu represented Xinjiang as being outside the territory of China, writing that "the roads going from China's territory [*Zhongguo lingtu*] to Xinjiang" were very poor and far inferior to those from India and the Soviet Union. Second, he estimated that garrisoning the soldiers required to bring the restive province under control would consume vast resources and still necessitate buying off local leaders. Betraying his low opinion of non-Hans, Wu likened such a course to "exhausting the Central Plains to serve the four barbarian tribes" (*pi bi zhongyuan yi shi si yi*). As Zhang Zhizhong had done, Wu acknowledged a global trend that seemed to favor Xinjiang's separation from China:

> Given the tide of national self-determination (*minzu zijue*) in today's world, we seemingly have reason to let go of Xinjiang. After all, Britain has already let go of Ireland [so he thought] and India. America has given up the Philippines. What, then, is wrong with our dispensing with Xinjiang? Especially considering we've already given up Outer Mongolia. (Wu 1947:6)

Wu's explanation of the difference between Xinjiang and the other colonies will be eerily familiar to students of colonial rhetoric: India and the Philippines "had undergone years of training by Britain and the U.S., and were therefore eminently qualified for independence." The various peoples of "our" Xinjiang, by contrast, "were very far from qualified" (Wu 1947:7). The tropes of "training" and "political maturation," basic components of the European *mission civilisatrice*, had been deployed by Britain, the United States, and France to stave off decolonization in the face of popular pressures. Beyond the question of Xinjiang's people's lack of qualifications for independence, Wu decided that China could not abandon Xinjiang, for the same reason that Zuo Zongtang had stated seventy years earlier. To do so would leave the heartland vulnerable to attack.

Wu's and Zhang Zhizhong's reasoning was manifestly far from that of nationalist historians. Instead, it echoed, by turns, the pragmatic calculations of Gong Zizhen, the impatient fiscal and military conservatism of Li Hongzhang, or the ethnocultural realism of Zhang Binglin. In comparing Xinjiang with India and the Philippines, they made plain that they considered it a colonial possession and therefore a candidate for self-determination as part of the global tide of decolonizations. Such talk ceased immediately with the founding of the People's Republic in 1949.

■

Uyghur and Chinese nationalists have staked competing territorial and political claims by answering these four historical questions very differently. The former rest their case on the assertions that Uyghurs have existed as a people for millennia, that Xinjiang was not historically part of China but instead the seat of several Uyghur states, and that Uyghurs were indigenous to the region, whereas Hans were not. They underscore the violent conquest and colonial rule of Xinjiang under the Qing and argue that Republican rule was similarly colonial. They point to the emergence of three independent states in the region between 1864 and 1949 as evidence that locals did not wish to be ruled by Manchus or Hans. They also invoke both colonial rule and the independent states in support of their right to self-determination. Chinese nationalists have countered Uyghur claims by postulating, first, that Uyghurs were historically part of the "Chinese nation" and that Xinjiang was part of a transhistorical "China" from earliest times and, second, that the Hans were early inhabitants and the Uyghurs were later immigrants to the region. By separately binding Uyghurs to the Chinese nation and Xinjiang to China, they sought to dismiss Uyghurs' assertions of an independent relationship with the land. I believe that several of the claims on both sides founder on the historical evidence. The charge that Qing Xinjiang was a colony and the implications of that charge are not so easily dismissed.

If officials and authors could casually refer to Xinjiang as a colony in public before the revolution, Chinese historians after 1949 would busy themselves erasing any such reference. They tried to obscure the Qing's having been an empire by emphasizing that it was the victim of other imperialist powers, such as Russia and Britain. Second, by reframing the Qing as "China," they could depict its conquest of Xinjiang as the "reunion" of the nation with a long-alienated part. They worked tirelessly to strengthen the Chinese "national narrative" and undermine Uyghurs' counternarrative. Their colleagues in the field of "*minzu* theory" (*minzu lilun*) grappled with the problem of self-determination, not only because the continuing spate of decolonizations in Africa (often enjoying Chinese moral and military support) demonstrated the continuing vitality of the principle, but also because Lenin had argued forcefully that all Marxists were obligated to recognize an absolute right of national self-determination (Lenin 1914/1975).[39] Finally, they worked for decades to make a persuasive case that the Chinese Communist Party's rejection of Lenin's principle of self-determination was doctrinally sound and to provide theoretical justifications for the system of "*minzu* regional autonomy" (*minzu quyu zizhi*) that Beijing established instead in Xinjiang and other peripheral territories.

HETERONOMY AND ITS DISCONTENTS

HETERONOMY

The political history of Xinjiang prior to 1949 was tumultuous and often violent. The substantial number of public protests and deadly clashes taking place there over the last quarter century have not been contemporary manifestations of an enduring culture of violence. Nor have they been the product of foreign intrigues. While there have been several contributory factors, Xinjiang's very political structure is one root cause of the unrest.[1] The full name of the territorial unit, the Xinjiang Uyghur Autonomous Region, suggests that Uyghurs largely govern themselves. But in fact, they do not. The system officially touted as providing autonomy in Xinjiang instead enacts heteronomy, or rule by others. Furthermore, the system of governance has not only denied Uyghurs the freedom to make some political decisions according to their own interests; it has also deprived them of the capacity to articulate and debate those interests in public or even to protest that deprivation. I argue in this chapter that this political system has exacerbated conflict and deepened Uyghur discontent.

The promise of autonomy arrangements around the world has lain in their capacity to protect both states' territorial integrity and the fragile rights of minorities. Government advisers and scholars have proposed autonomy to avoid discord or, in some cases, to resolve it. Indeed, a major study of "minorities at risk" advocates autonomy as the sole solution acceptable to all sides in otherwise insoluble conflicts (Gurr 1993). Socialist states were among the first to adopt institutions of formal autonomy, and many claimed thereby to have "solved their national question" (Connor 1984:xvi).

Such abstract claims should not blind us to the fact that autonomy regimes emerged from a particular period in the history of nation-states. Nongovernmental organizations first mooted the establishment of formal legal and governmental institutions to protect minorities in discussions during World War I, and the League of Nations oversaw the writing of legal charters in the wake of the war's resolution. Those states emerging victorious from the war saw the "protection of minorities [as] the means to achieve their end," that end being not humanitarian but strategic: the preservation of international peace. It is important to recall that these charters were imposed on defeated states—or, rather, the successor states that replaced former imperial powers—by the victors in the war. As such, the charters were clear examples of victor's justice. Italy, faced with the demand that it accept legal protection of its minorities, claimed to be "too great a Power to submit to such a derogation of [its] sovereignty." This naturally made other states on whom such laws had been forced bridle at the imposition (Macartney 1934:252, 274). Decades later, many states still vehemently deny the right of outside actors to insist that they adopt autonomy regimes or to tinker with those regimes once installed.

All autonomy regimes privilege territorial integrity over absolute responsiveness to the demands of the autonomous group: they are a compromise between states that want unabridged sovereignty and homogeneous populations and peoples that want self-determination, generally meaning independence. Such compromises often leave neither side satisfied. Thus we should not be surprised to find both state actors and autonomous groups pressing for renegotiation. Yet there are dramatic differences in the degree to which states honor their formal commitments and the amount of pressure for change from the nominally self-ruling groups.

A foundational text on the law of autonomy regimes observes that "autonomy is understood to refer to independence of action on the internal or domestic level" (Hannum and Lillich 1980:860). Thus construed, the term ill fits the system of governance in Xinjiang. As I show, Beijing has allowed Uyghurs very little independence of action.[2] The party-state has actively and with careful forethought thwarted the emergence of an autonomous political elite able to press for Uyghur collective interests, and it has similarly squelched ordinary Uyghurs' attempts to respond to or influence policies in Xinjiang. For those silenced voices, it has substituted an official story that most Uyghurs are quite satisfied with the way Xinjiang is ruled. It has thus intervened in representational politics in both senses, actively selecting and managing the Uyghurs (and other non-Hans) charged with representing the Uyghur population, and carefully regulating the narrative representation of the region's politics.

To be sure, the defects in the system are related to larger systemic problems in Chinese politics. The People's Republic of China (PRC) remains a single-party state and has prevented various groups from articulating demands and from organizing to pursue their interests. Beijing employs propaganda, silences dissent, punishes transgressions with violence, and extirpates independent organizations throughout the country. All these practices are amplified in the political system in Xinjiang. Although desperate not to lose any territory, Chinese leaders attribute particular strategic significance to Xinjiang as both a source of energy and a conduit for still more from Central Asia, energy crucial to China's continued economic growth. Concern about ethnic conflict and the fear that many Uyghurs aspire to independence has made party officials in Xinjiang much more sensitive, and often more brutal, than their counterparts elsewhere. The lodging of so much power in the hands of Han officials has only increased the region's fractiousness.

THE ARGUMENT

To charge that China's autonomous regions, prefectures, and counties do not enjoy the self-rule that Beijing claims is not particularly controversial. An early observer derided the system as "regional detention" (Moseley 1965:16, quoted in Shakya 1999:306). Many scholars have argued that the PRC's system of "*minzu* regional autonomy" in fact provides little political autonomy (Dreyer 1976; Heberer 1989; Mackerras 1994). Zhao Suisheng noted, "Regional autonomy . . . by no means meant that the communist state would let minorities govern themselves" (Zhao 2004:183), and several scholars have made this argument with specific reference to Xinjiang (McMillen 1979; Moneyhon 2002; Stein 2003). Two scholars suggested that far from granting the locals self-rule, Xinjiang's administration is colonial (Bachman 2004; Gladney 1998). In this chapter I move beyond formal critique to causal analysis, linking problems with the political system to consequences.

Some have argued that Xinjiang's instability is the product of the system of autonomy and has little to do with Uyghurs' grievances. On the basis of comparative study,

Svante Cornell (2002) claims that systems of autonomy can themselves cause conflict rather than resolve it. In fact, in many cases they facilitate the emergence of secessionist movements. Cornell draws on the substantial literature (Brubaker 1996; Roeder 1991) to contend that the Soviet Union's federal system of union republics contributed to the disintegration of the state. But he argues that the authors were wrong to ignore the institutions below the republic level. In subrepublican autonomous units, as in the republics, Cornell finds, the institutionalization and fostering of distinct identities increase autonomous groups' "cohesion and *willingness* to act"; the institutions themselves enhance the "*capacity* of [groups] to act." In general, a state establishing an autonomous region formally acknowledges the territorial boundaries of that region and the identity of the group or groups exercising autonomy. The state further allots resources to help protect the distinct identity of the titular group. In so doing, the state both strengthens group solidarity and sanctions a territorial frame for its political aspirations. Autonomy arrangements often allow for the establishment of distinct political institutions, the cultivation of leaders to run those institutions, and the local control of media and educational organs. Together, these institutions increase rather than reduce the likelihood of conflict and, therefore, of secession. Finally, a state's formal recognition of an autonomous group may increase that group's international visibility and thus raise the probability of international intervention in any resultant conflict (Cornell 2002:251–56, italics in original).

Three factors that Cornell identifies have been of undoubted importance in Xinjiang politics. First, formalizing the boundaries of Xinjiang and naming it the Uyghur Autonomous Region gave a convenient territorial shape to Uyghur political imaginings (Bovingdon 2002b). Second, institutionalizing *minzu* identities and assigning privileges on the basis of those identities strengthened them considerably.[3] Finally, the formal assignment of one-sixth the territory of China to the Uyghurs has almost certainly given them greater international prominence than they would otherwise have enjoyed, although the violent protests of the 1990s played a role as well. Judging from the number of formal governmental inquiries about and international academic conferences on the Uyghurs and Xinjiang since 1997, they claim more attention than any others in China except Tibet and the Tibetans.

Although formally compelling, Cornell's argument cannot explain the vastly different outcomes in China's various autonomous regions. The PRC's other provincial-level autonomous regions, Mongolia, Guangxi, Ningxia, and even Tibet in the 1990s, have been far quieter than Xinjiang.[4] Nor does his model capture well the system actually operating in Xinjiang. Most of the features that Cornell considers as standard in systems of autonomy are absent or present only in truncated form in that region. The government institutions have been heavily colonized by Hans and have been subordinated at all levels to the heavily Han party structure. Uyghur (and other non-Han) leaders have been carefully chosen and forced to act as apologists, even boosters, for unpopular policies, to ensure they do not develop a popular constituency. The media and educational institutions have remained under tight state control in all periods except the 1980s. Indeed, it can be argued that political controls on these institutions now are tighter than they were at the beginning of the reform era. Thus while Chinese policies in Xinjiang might be credited with strengthening the Uyghurs' sense of collective identity—in Cornell's terms, their cohesiveness and inclination to act together—those policies have actually reduced their capacity to act collectively.

In sum, a purely systemic argument cannot fully account for unrest in Xinjiang. The institutions of autonomy have indeed contributed in various ways to the conflict, but we cannot fully understand how they have done so without considering the Uyghurs' grievances. The manipulation of authority, violent policy swings, and state actions never given legal specification, all of which must be considered features of the system of *minzu* regional autonomy in Xinjiang, have provoked the Uyghurs' discontent. Like other socialist regimes, the Chinese government has continued to boast that the system of autonomy solved China's "*minzu* problems." Instead, however, that system virtually guarantees there will be discontent and conflict for years hence.

INSTITUTIONS

The Xinjiang Uyghur Autonomous Region (XUAR) was established with great fanfare in October 1955. While in principle, the Uyghurs thereby received title to the property,[5] what they confronted was in fact a condominium of nested autonomies, leaving them a patchwork of territories—principally Qumul and Turpan, Aqsu, Kashgar, and Khotän districts—divided and surrounded by the others (figure 2.1) and further overlaid by the overwhelmingly Han military–agricultural garrisons of the Production and Construction Corps (PCC) (McMillen 1981:70–71). The territory had been parceled out in a series of steps over the previous eighteen months and was presented to the Uyghurs as a fait accompli when the XUAR was established. It has recently come to light that in 1953, Xinjiang party officials proposed setting up autonomies "from the top down," but the Central Committee in Beijing decreed that the order instead proceed from "small to large" (Wang Shuanqian 1999:249).

The division of Xinjiang into a number of smaller autonomies was a stroke of administrative genius. In parceling out "subautonomies," the Chinese Communist

FIGURE 2.1 Autonomous prefectures in Xinjiang. (Based on Yuan Qing-li 1990)

Party (CCP) simultaneously satisfied the goals of embodying the idea that Xinjiang belonged to thirteen different *minzu* and of counterbalancing the Uyghurs' overwhelming political and demographic weight.[6] To a certain extent, the political and material interests of each of the other constituted groups were therefore aligned with the central government and against the Uyghurs. By the end of 1954, more than 50 percent of the area of the province had been allotted to autonomous townships, districts, counties, and prefectures.[7] In fifteen out of twenty-seven units established, the titular *minzu* constituted less than half the population; in Tacheng and Emin county autonomous districts, the titular *minzu* (Daghuor and Mongol) made up, respectively, less than 17 percent and 12 percent of the population. Bayangol was made a Mongol autonomous prefecture, even though Mongols constituted only 35 percent of its population. Even more extraordinary, in 1960 the government annexed to it an "almost purely" Uyghur region, after which Bayangol Prefecture occupied fully one-third of Xinjiang's area (Atwood 2004:39).[8] As a result, in 2004 some 48,000 Mongols nominally exercised autonomy in a region with more than 370,000 Uyghurs (and, due to steady immigration, more than 660,000 Hans) (Xinjiang Weiwu'er zizhiqu tongjiju 2005:112–13).[9] In a study on *minzu* relations in Xinjiang, government analysts Mao Yongfu[10] and Li Ling observed that

> Qirghiz, Tajik, and other *minzu*, despite the small size of their populations, nevertheless have autonomous prefectures and counties belonging to their own *minzu*; in those areas, they belong to the self-governing *minzu*. By contrast, in [those places] Uyghurs have once again become non-self-governing *minzu*. ... This is something we must look into diligently. (Yin Zhuguang and Mao Yongfu 1996:173)

The authors' apparent surprise at this situation was rather disingenuous, as the order of establishment of the autonomies demonstrated that this had been precisely the intention forty years earlier.[11] The intention endures today. According to 2000 figures, in none of the five autonomous districts in Xinjiang does the titular population exceed 25 percent of the total, and Bayangol Mongol District is only 4 percent Mongols. Nonetheless, a recent work cautioned that these figures "must not shake our determination to the exercise of *minzu* regional autonomy." While administrative reform is all the rage in China proper, with localities becoming cities and some cities gaining provincial-level status, the boundaries and system of autonomous units will not change, the authors announced (Zhu Peimin, Chen Hong, and Yang Hong 2004:356–57).[12] These odd circumstances then lead us to ask, in what sense are the various *minzu* "self-governing"?

Every official account of "*minzu* regional autonomy" (*minzu quyu zizhi*) makes liberal use of the expression "masters in their own house" (*dang jia zuo zhu*). The system of autonomies, advocated by theorists and enacted by the Chinese Communist Party (CCP) since 1949, is said to have transformed non-Hans from exploited others to rulers of their own domains. In Xinjiang, rather than making non-Hans heads of the house, the purpose of this system has been, above, all to keep them in the house. Granting to Uyghurs any influence over affairs in the Xinjiang Uyghur Autonomous Region (XUAR) has taken a back seat to consolidating the CCP's control and crushing any movements advocating independence, or even the more modest goal of "real autonomy."

Despite maintaining publicly that power stems from the people, the party leadership has always taken pains to extend authority from the top down and has therefore given no quarter to power organized locally. Second, party leaders have regarded the Uyghurs as a group to be politically untrustworthy and thus have allotted very little power to them. Instead, they have selected and promoted officials who exercise power only in a fashion consonant with the CCP's goals and have reserved the decisive authority at virtually all levels for trusted Hans imported from posts in China proper.[13] The system has failed to serve Uyghurs in a variety of ways. Vaunted as a means to lessen interethnic conflict and gain Uyghurs' loyalties, it has instead contributed to their generalized dissatisfaction. To understand how, we must begin with the legal framework of autonomy.

Successive PRC constitutions and associated organic laws have codified a national plan for *minzu* regional autonomy in a set of institutions, cultural and linguistic rights that the institutions were intended to secure, and a carefully specified relationship between those institutions and the central government. Xinjiang's distinctive features and political history notwithstanding, its "autonomous" government institutions emerged from that national plan and therefore strongly resemble those in China's other autonomous regions.

Both the 1952 Program for Implementing *Minzu* Regional Autonomy and the 1954 constitution made clear the expectation that autonomous units at county, prefectural, and provincial levels would have governmental organs broadly similar to those at the corresponding levels in China proper. Stipulated elements included the standard branches of government, a people's congress with elected representatives chosen from the titular group or groups as well as Hans, and obedience to higher-level government organs.[14] Both documents provided that actual institutional forms could be determined by the wishes of the "great majority of the people and leading figures with links to the people" of the titular group or groups.[15] Military organization was not left to local discretion. Although the program allowed for the establishment of local police cadres, all security personnel, including soldiers, fell under the "unified national military system." Between 1950 and 1955, troops in the predominantly Uyghur and Qazaq Ili National Army (INA), formerly the military arm of the Eastern Turkestan Republic (ETR), were folded into the People's Liberation Army (PLA) or demobilized and settled on paramilitary farms. In both cases, they fell under direct CCP control (McMillen 1979:53; Shichor 2004:127–29, 132).

The first constitution also committed the government to drawing up a national autonomy law. Even though the Government Administration Council had passed the program in 1952, a formal law was promulgated only in 1984 and then amended in 2001. In addition to these organizational principles, the 1984 autonomy law affirmed in general terms what had been practices of long duration in the autonomous regions: "affirmative action" in the recruitment of college students, the hiring of employees at state enterprises, and the training of base-level government cadres.

The articles of the autonomy law reveal the limitations built into the system.[16] Article 15 indicates that all autonomous government organs are under the leadership of the State Council and all must "obey the state council." Article 20 grants organs of autonomy the right to "alter or suspend" policies or orders promulgated by higher-level government units but makes such actions subject to approval by those superior units. And while it acknowledges the right of autonomous regional governments to draw up locally appropriate "statutes on autonomy and specific regulations," article 19 also grants the National People's Congress the authority to approve or reject such statutes.[17]

After studying the original law and its 2001 revision, Chinese legal scholar Yu Xingzhong concluded that the political system it specifies "certainly does not correspond to what is usually understood [by] the term 'autonomy'" (Yu Xingzhong n.d.). Studies of the system with special reference to Xinjiang reached much the same conclusion (Moneyhon 2002; Sautman 1999; Stein 2003). The legal scholar Matthew Moneyhon (2002:137) argued that whatever rights the state constitution and autonomy law grant in principle to local decision-making bodies, by requiring that central government organs approve all local decisions, the national laws withdraw most of those rights in practice.

Indeed, the system of governance established in Xinjiang fails to satisfy a single one of five criteria that a pair of expert jurists have determined are fundamental to autonomy. In a widely cited article, Hannum and Lillich insist that legal autonomy requires, at minimum, an independent local legislature not subject to central veto power, a locally chosen executive, an independent judiciary, local decision making not compromised by the center's "reservation . . . of general discretionary powers," and binding power-sharing arrangements (Hannum and Lillich 1980:886–87). Beijing nonetheless retains veto power over the decisions of Xinjiang's People's Congress. The center has chosen each of Xinjiang's successive executives, and the Supreme People's Court retains supervisory power over Xinjiang's courts. Furthermore, Beijing reserves broad discretionary power over

Xinjiang's affairs, including how autonomy is implemented; and the center allocates power over resource exploitation, policing, and other matters on its own initiative, rather than being bound by power-sharing arrangements (Moneyhon 2002:137, 142–44).[18] Despite its dramatic departure from the Soviet model in many particulars, on this last point the PRC system clearly followed Moscow's example. In relations with the union republics before 1991, Moscow "both define[d] the sphere of authority and exercise[d] it" (Gleason 1990:65).

As confining as the legal framework has proved, actual political practice in Beijing and Ürümci has made still greater incursions into the region's hypothetical autonomy. In Yu Xingzhong's estimation, rather than providing a new legal framework for the system, both the 1984 and 2001 versions of the autonomy law simply recorded in statutory form what already were features of established practice. Legal revisions followed policy changes, and not vice versa, and Beijing still governs by policy rather than by law (Yu Xingzhong n.d.).[19] A full account of the workings of *minzu* regional autonomy in Xinjiang must therefore include not only structural limitations of the system but also a brief history of political developments and actual political practice.

XINJIANG POLICY AND PRACTICE
CAMPAIGNS AND POLICY SWINGS, 1949-2000

Two features of the social climate of Republican-era Xinjiang figured prominently in Communist Party leaders' calculations of strategy. As discussed in chapter 1, anti-Han sentiment was deep and widespread among the Uyghurs, partly as a consequence of decades of harsh, exploitative rule by Han warlords and local officials. At the same time, general antipathy to Hans, which might have drawn Uyghurs and other Turkic peoples together, was counterbalanced by religious, political, and cultural differences of long duration. The Turkic peoples had cooperated in founding the first (1933–1934) and second (1944–1949) Eastern Turkistan Republics. In the Ili National Army (INA), the military force raised by the latter republic, Uyghurs, Qazaqs, and members of other groups fought side by side. Yet those governments controlled only small parts of the vast territory of Xinjiang and fell apart as much from internal disagreements as from external attacks (Forbes 1986:229–34 and passim). Resentment of Hans posed a challenge to CCP strategists, but antagonisms within the Turkic population gave the party an opportunity to pit the groups against one another and thus to manage that challenge.

The political history of post-1949 Xinjiang reveals even more about governance in Xinjiang than does the study of autonomy law. If Xinjiang had truly been autonomous, it would have had its own political cycles and campaigns over the last fifty-odd years. Even a quick summary of major political events since the revolution shows that Xinjiang's policies and campaigns closely followed those in China proper.

After leading the People's Liberation Army into Xinjiang in 1949, General Wang Zhen demobilized thousands of soldiers and redeployed them on a network of paramilitary farms throughout the province, subsequently naming them the Production and Construction Corps (PCC).[20] Having installed a tractable government leadership headed by the Tatar Burhan Shähidi and the Uyghur Säypidin (Saifudin) Äzizi, Wang and other party officials set about establishing strategies for managing non-Han groups.

In the early 1950s, those strategies were relatively tolerant. The CCP's "united front" (*tongyi zhanxian*) policy counseled the establishment of links with "progressive members" of social and religious elites, which in turn required minimal interference in business, religious practice, and social norms. The party did, however, gradually take control of religious institutions through the China Islamic Association, as well as through the confiscation of mosque lands and the forcible replacement of religious courts with "People's Courts" (McMillen 1979:113–14).[21]

By the mid-1950s, as Mao pressed regional leaders to make more sweeping economic changes throughout the country in the so-called socialist tide, the Xinjiang leadership faced resistance to such initiatives. Collectivization required antagonizing the "progressive elites" with which the party had previously cooperated. And again, the cadres' attempts to mobilize the exploited classes (mostly peasants, in the overwhelmingly agrarian region) against the elites instead drove many Uyghurs and others together against the party. In China proper, Mao invited criticism of CCP policies from the masses in his 1956 Hundred Flowers campaign. The vehemence and volume of protest shocked the leadership, which then unleashed the antirightist movement in 1957 to silence the opposition. In Xinjiang, Uyghurs, Qazaqs, and others denounced the system of autonomy as a sham and demanded a far greater role in local governance. Party hard-liners swiftly redirected the antirightist movement into a movement against "local nationalism," accusing such critics of seeking to "rule Xinjiang as an independent country" or of resisting CCP rule.[22] Officials were especially irked by the charge that PCC soldier-farmers were "Han colonialists." Faced with such challenges, the party redoubled its efforts to mobilize class against *minzu* interests (Dreyer 1976:150–57; McMillen 1979:116, 117).

Mao's radical voluntarist Great Leap Forward, begun in 1958, led in Xinjiang to calls for rapid cultural homogenization to accompany and facilitate the Leap. This naturally meant much less tolerance of difference. Even ethnicity itself became an "obstacle to progress," and party leaders stepped up their attacks on Islam and other "backward customs" (Dreyer 1976:157–63; McMillen 1979:118). As is now widely known, the combination of Great Leap policies, bad weather, and the central government's ill-chosen decision to export grain to meet its debts to the Soviet Union brought on a terrible famine. Party leaders temporarily prevailed on Mao to restore a more moderate economic course in the early 1960s. Cultural policies in Xinjiang relaxed slightly during this period, as officials acknowledged that linguistic and cultural differences would persist over the long term. Muslims were again allowed to celebrate religious festivals, which had much subdued since 1957 (Benson and Svanberg 1998:139). Talk of speedy assimilation subsided.

Despite the policy retrenchment, widespread starvation in China's interior intensified the Great Leap's impact on Xinjiang. In addition to party-mandated population flows, vast numbers of hungry migrants poured into Xinjiang on their own initiative. This "surplus" flow drove Han immigration to more than 800,000, its highest level ever, in both 1959 and 1960 (Hannum and Xie 1998:324; Li Yuanqing 1990:52). PCC farms welcomed many of the refugees to settle and claim land, provoking increased resentment by Uyghurs and others. In 1962, more than 60,000 Uyghurs and Qazaqs fled across the border into the Soviet Union, exasperated with CCP policies and lured by ceaseless radio propaganda advertising far superior living conditions on the Soviet side of the border. The deepening Sino-Soviet split played a role in this exodus: Soviet consular officials had apparently connived in the mass migration by distributing previously prepared travel papers. For officials in Xinjiang and Beijing, the sheer numbers of emigrants raised the frightening prospect of hostile former citizens receiving military training abroad, then assisting in the cause of "Soviet social imperialism" by helping take Xinjiang by force. In response, the government sealed the border and forcibly relocated thousands of non-Han families away from the border zone, replacing them with Han PCC members (Dreyer 1976:169–70; McMillen 1979:120–23).[23]

Minzu policies changed course again in the mid-1960s, as renewed radicalization at the highest level of the party led to the Cultural Revolution (1966–1976). Officials appointed to the Cultural Revolutionary Small Group, which replaced the XUAR Party Committee for several years, and the initially mostly Han Red Guards raised demands for cultural conformity to a new extreme. While in China's heartland, Red Guards collected and destroyed artifacts of the past, in Xinjiang (as in Tibet and other non-Han regions) they targeted non-Han culture. Difference once again became a sign of backwardness. Activists frightened the various Turkic peoples into shedding their habitual clothes, adornments, scarves, and hats for Mao suits. Activists also destroyed mosques and even forced many religious leaders and ordinary Muslims to raise pigs, apparently in an attempt to engineer rapid and thorough assimilation.[24]

The punishments that the Cultural Revolutionaries visited on intellectuals particularly targeted Uyghur culture. The famous linguist Ibrahim Muttä'i was tortured by having the huge volumes of a multilingual dictionary he had helped edit (with full CCP support at the time) dropped on his head (Clark forthcoming, 17). Ordinary citizens were not exempt. Residents who lived through the period describe witnessing men being subjected to shaving in the streets, for even beards were interpreted as signs of defiance. A Qazaq woman raising a towheaded Uyghur boy dyed his hair black and shaved his eyebrows to avoid persecution. Uyghurs meeting each other in the street learned to initiate every greeting with "Long live Chairman Mao" in Chinese.[25] But in 1975, many Muslims finally lost patience and staged a protest when forced to work on Muslim holidays.[26]

In retrospect, it is clear that policies toward non-Hans were the most assimilationist and intolerant during the Cultural Revolution. After Mao's death in 1976 and the fall of the Gang of Four, party leaders faced a crisis. The Cultural Revolution had alienated a large segment of the population throughout China. Resentment was particularly grave among Uyghurs and other non-Hans because for them, it had been not merely a political and social assault but an attack on their identities. The continuation of hard-line policies seemed certain to provoke increasing discontent and thus instability. But officials worried that more tolerant policies, allowing cultural exploration and freer religious practice, might similarly open the door to unrest. Nagged by these concerns, policymakers charted a zigzagging but narrowing course between openness and control.

In 1980 Hu Yaobang, one of the younger leaders in the Central Committee and soon to be promoted to CCP secretary general, traveled to Tibet to investigate local conditions. Appalled by the poverty and despair he found there, Hu urged that hard-line policies toward non-Hans be relaxed. To remedy Tibet's situation, he advocated "genuine autonomy," economic initiatives appropriate to local conditions, the renewal of cultural and scientific projects, and the gradual transfer of Han officials back to China proper. He made similar proposals for Xinjiang in July 1980.[27] At the time, Hu felt that Xinjiang presented less of a separatist threat than Tibet because it lacked exiled religious or political leaders like the Dalai Lama and had no support abroad for independence (Dillon 2004:36). The archconservative Central Committee member Deng Liqun claimed to have heard that Hu had even proposed devolving nearly all political authority to Xinjiang, reserving power only over national defense and foreign relations and a veto over domestic politics to

Beijing. Deng recalled asking Hu at the time, incredulously, "How can you propose such a resolution in a *minzu* autonomous region? How can it be OK ... to let the autonomous region to exercise [all other powers] itself?" (Deng Liqun 2006:206–7). In the event, the XUAR Party Committee adopted Hu's suggestions on cultural policies and economic reforms and announced in August 1980 that large numbers of Han cadres would be transferred out of Xinjiang, over the objections of such hard-liners.

Held responsible for the increasing number of student and popular demonstrations that convulsed Beijing and other major cities in 1986, Hu Yaobang was purged in 1987. Former Xinjiang Military Commander Wang Zhen, who had fought openly with Hu over his proposed changes, then ordered that the more accommodating policies be scrapped. A Han official siding with Wang is reported to have asserted, "You give [Uyghurs] autonomy and they will only turn around and create an East Turkistan." The official was disgusted with the proposal to send Hans back to the interior and insisted that only tough-minded officials in the mold of Wang Zhen could keep Xinjiang stable.[28] An official report produced for internal circulation a few years later concurred in this view. The dismissal of Han cadres had "made it impossible," the report stated, "for Han cadres to work in Xinjiang with a sense of security, and it also sowed serious ideological chaos among minority *minzu* cadres. [It] was extremely harmful to *minzu* solidarity" (Zhang Yuxi 1993:358).

Over the previous decade, Deng Xiaoping's economic reforms had brought unprecedented prosperity to China's interior. The conservative leadership of Xinjiang initially sought to block the local implementation of reforms, fearing that they would destabilize the region. To many, the pace of the reforms that did come was frustratingly slow. In the mid-1990s, people continued to joke that while China proper had wholeheartedly embraced capitalism, socialism was still being pursued, if not realized, in Xinjiang. Nevertheless, by 1992 the XUAR leadership had come to an agreement that reform was inevitable. The popular Uyghur official Ismayil Ähmäd announced the same year that the central government would cede more autonomy to Xinjiang. He suggested that this would include local authority over foreign trade, control of the border, and administration. At least one analyst saw this move as an attempt to counter the appeal of separatists in the wake of the Soviet Union's collapse (Cheung Po-ling 1992).

But the party complemented the loosening of economic policy with political tightening, a practice that has continued up to the present.[29] There have been two central components of that tightening. The yearly "strike hard" (*yan da*) campaigns, like their counterparts in the interior, aim to capture large numbers of suspected criminals in massive dragnets and then prosecute them on an accelerated schedule.

As in China proper, these campaigns target violent property crimes, drug rings, and the like; in Xinjiang, they also focus on political crimes.[30] Second, public security personnel arrange periodic sweeps to shore up control in each locality, called "comprehensive management" (*zonghe zhili*).[31] A number of my Uyghur informants received orders from their work units to take part in these sweeps in 1997 when the party was fretting about the return of Hong Kong. One ardently anticommunist man told me he was simply notified a week in advance that he would be traveling to the south to spend two months praising CCP policies. He was to go from house to house within "suspect" villages, chaperoned by two Hans, patiently correcting people's misconceptions and erroneous political views. It was, he observed, like being forced to eat a steaming plateful of pork. Another informant told of being sent more regularly on short trips to areas around Ürümci, again without any choice in the matter. Interviews with a doctor revealed that the strategy did not involve surveillance and propaganda alone. With only a few days' advance notice, she was dispatched for several months to several poor rural areas to treat patients and to pass on the party line while doing so.[32]

SPECIFIC POLICIES AND POPULAR RESPONSES
POPULATION

One of the party's most effective tactics for counteracting political pressure from Uyghurs has been, in effect, to subcontract security work, by importing a Han constituency loyal to Beijing. Government-sponsored immigration of Hans into the region has been a central component of CCP policy in Xinjiang. It also has provided compelling evidence that officials in Beijing and Ürümci felt they could never persuade the majority of Uyghurs to be satisfied with their political status in China.[33] Ma Dazheng finally expressed this premise in his internal-circulation report in 1999: "Hans are the most reliable force for stability in Xinjiang" (Ma Dazheng 2003:123). Local officials clearly understood this point, referring colloquially to the settlement of Han immigrants as "mixing sand" (Becquelin 2000:74).[34]

But this was never the government's official rationale for encouraging Han immigration. The public story was that Hans were needed to spur development. In the mid-1950s the British journalist Basil Davidson, who had already published a paean to the first three postrevolutionary years in China, was invited on the strength of that work to travel to Xinjiang to see for himself the boons of the region's "peaceful liberation" and then to broadcast them to the world.[35] As the title of his popular travelogue, *Turkestan Alive*, suggests, it depicts a Xinjiang revivified by Chinese policies. Davidson nevertheless felt obliged to note that the great flow of Han immigration could be seen as in "flagrant contradiction to the fostering of home rule and minority development."[36] To compensate, he pointed out that the region desperately needed rapid economic development and lacked both the skilled workforce and able administrators vital to that task. Davidson thus reported sympathetically the comment of one of his Chinese hosts that "we need another ten million in the next fifteen years" (Davidson 1957:234–35). Soon after the PRC's founding, the State Council prepared a plan to transfer some two million citizens from China's interior. Though far below the figure proposed by Davidson's interlocutor, it was extraordinarily ambitious given the difficulties of both mobilizing Han migrants and finding places for them in a largely arid region.[37] Yet in the end, officials overfulfilled the plan. Between 1950 and 1978 the party induced roughly three million Hans to move to Xinjiang to help "build the borderlands" (Qiu Yuanyao 1994:223–40; Wang 1998:37–38).[38] Many settled on PCC farms, and in the early years PCC cadres traveled to major population centers to recruit more volunteers directly (McMillen 1979:61). Massive and sustained immigration increased the Han proportion of the population from roughly 5 percent in 1949 to more than 40 percent in 1978. But while moving Hans into Xinjiang was relatively easy before 1978, making them stay after that time became increasingly difficult, and beginning in 1977 there was a net outflow of population (Li Yuanqing 1989:124).

The first major disturbances in Xinjiang during the reform era involved not Uyghurs but Hans agitating to return to the interior. Many Han youths had been "rusticated" (*xiafang*) from Shanghai and other major urban centers in China proper during the Cultural Revolution. Some had already returned home clandestinely, discovering to their dismay that local authorities refused to find them jobs or housing. Their residence permits had been permanently transferred to Xinjiang. In February 1979, in Shanghai, Han youths unwilling to return to Xinjiang and other "remote" areas rioted, and in Aqsu, Han youths staged a series of actions petitioning in April and July for the right to return home. Seeing their petitions ignored, four thousand gathered to demonstrate in January 1980 (Zhu Peimin 2000:353–54).[39] The government's initial policy responses were rather tepid and clearly not directed to Aqsu. In July 1979 the government convened a meeting in the northern city of Shihezi to "make a plan to resolve the problem of educated youths." In mid-November the government announced that it had taken out an interest-free loan of 2 million *yuan* to boost the economy and help find jobs for unemployed Ürümci youths. Later that month the government generously announced that workers in Xinjiang would henceforth be allowed to return home for a family visit once every five years (Chen Chao 1990:221, 27).

These steps clearly did not satisfy the Shanghai youth. In November 1980 they staged a demonstration in Aqsu twice as large as that in January. The party responded by dispatching former regional military leader Wang Zhen, aged and sick though he was, to stifle the disturbance, "requesting" that local units improve conditions for young Han settlers and stepping up propaganda stressing how important the youths were to countering Soviet designs on the region. Wang was dispatched to Xinjiang again in January 1981 after the Uyghurs staged a political protest, and in May after an armed uprising. In August he returned with Deng Xiaoping himself, an indication of the top leadership's concern about recrudescent opposition in the region (Dreyer 1986:736). Despite their efforts, emigrants continued to outnumber immigrants. Increasingly desperate at the upsurge in violence and continued Han flight, Beijing recalled Wang Zhen's old comrade Wang Enmao from retirement in October 1981 to serve once again as Xinjiang's first party secretary. The latter proposed a compromise to keep the bulk of the former Shanghai youths in Xinjiang: a small number judged to have "qualifications" would be allowed to return to Shanghai, while the majority, though required to remain in Xinjiang, would be permitted to have one child resettled in Shanghai by the state (McMillen 1984:574–76; Zhu Peimin 2000:356). The most significant and far-reaching decision was made in Beijing. In June 1982 Deng Xiaoping announced the reinstatement of the Production and Construction Corps. This move meant renewed subsidies from Beijing, an expanded paramilitary force to respond to local uprisings, and an institutional framework for the recruitment and absorption of more Han immigrants (McMillen 1984:585–86; Zhu Peimin 2000:337–40).[40]

Despite the efforts of the two Wangs, not until 1990 was there again a net inflow of Hans, when a new wave of immigrants moved to Xinjiang by choice rather than compulsion. This inflow was the result of a combination of market forces and the declining significance of the national household registration system (*hukou*), which had been established in the 1950s precisely to stanch migration.[41] Deng Xiaoping's economic reforms had enabled farmers to lease land, individuals to strike out in private business, and underemployed rural and urban workers to seek jobs in new enterprises. Both geography and central policies initially favored the coastal regions, but by the early 1990s the government announced favorable land lease rates and tax abatements in China's western hinterlands—the so-called west-leaning policies—to lure labor and capital to the west. Finally, burgeoning markets in food, land, and labor greatly diminished the power of the household registration system to fix people in one place. By the late 1990s, the combined effects were plain to see in the thousands of simply dressed, heavily burdened people pouring out of the Ürümci train station each day, drawn by rumors of land and jobs in the "great northwest." Nicolas Becquelin noted that the 2000 census proved what Uyghurs had suspected but local officials had adamantly denied for a decade: Han immigration had risen enormously in the 1990s. The Han population in Xinjiang grew an astonishing 31.6 percent between 1990 and 2000, a pace almost exactly double that of non-Hans. And as Becquelin pointed out further, this figure would not have counted summer seasonal laborers because canvassing for the census took place in November (Becquelin 2002:61).[42]

Since 2000, while clearly aiming to maintain the inflow of large numbers of Hans, the party has given special attention to the scarcity of particularly desirable kinds of immigrants: educated youths, technical workers, and committed, politically reliable cadres.[43] It has tried a variety of stratagems to remedy those deficiencies, including subsidies to college graduates willing to immigrate and temporary "swaps" of cadres from the interior with groups in Xinjiang. Strikingly, the party announced quietly in April 2000 that it was reassigning one hundred demobilized army officers from China proper to head local CCP branches responsible for "political, legal, military, and recruitment affairs" (Agence France-Presse 2000). In March 2001, the Xinjiang government acknowledged that of the 12,000 students from the region who traveled to the interior for schooling each year, only 20 percent returned. Over twenty years, the "brain drain" amounted to 210,000. The head of the Law and Regulations Office in the XUAR Personnel Department announced the division's intention to put together a package of high salaries and subsidies to lure and keep talented people ("Xinjiang 20 nian liushi rencai 21 wan" 2001). A year later, an expanded version of the same article appeared on another government news site. This time the department's party secretary announced a "human resources emergency" and called on the national government to set aside monies to support high salaries, subsidies, communications infrastructure, and other perks to tempt talented people to "happily put down roots in the borderlands." He urged that long-term settlers receive even higher salaries and retain their subsidies even in retirement. Implicitly acknowledging that few talented people (understood to be Hans) were willing to stay in Xinjiang permanently, he suggested that individuals working there for more than twenty years should receive a "really eye-catching relocation allowance" to help them return to their home towns ("Rencai gaoji! Xinjiang 20 nian liushi rencai 21 wan" 2002). Xinjiang First Party Secretary Wang Lequan even made recruitment trips, observing pointedly during an inspection tour of Shanghai that Xinjiang was short on "qualified personnel" and its workers were of "poor overall quality." One of China's top newspapers interviewed him during the trip and broadcast his plea for "talented people of all types" to immigrate to Xinjiang to serve as party and government cadres, managers, or technicians (Xing Zhaoyuan and Wang Se 2003).[44]

Officials in Xinjiang have never been shy about calling openly for skilled and talented immigrants to come to the region. Such solicitations conformed to the public story that immigration was necessary to spur development. In 1999 the government began to speak openly about immigration as an end in itself. Ma Dazheng's comment that Hans were the main force for stability in Xinjiang was originally written in 1993 and intended for only internal circulation. Nicolas Becquelin argued that by the end of the 1990s Beijing had taken Xinjiang fully in hand, so there was no need to "proceed with caution and coded double-speak any more" (Becquelin 2004b:374). This change was visible in an article in the very public venue of the *Ta kung pao*, a CCP-controlled newspaper in Hong Kong.[45] Alarmed by NATO's intervention in Kosovo and rumors that Tibet or Xinjiang might be a future target, the author argued that the government should "appropriately increase immigrants" to Xinjiang and settle them on PCC farms. The aim, the author continued, was "to adjust the proportions of the populations of different ethnic groups in this region, especially in its southern part" (Ai Yu 1999). In 2000, Li Dezhu, the leader of the State *Minzu* Affairs Commission (Minzu shiwu weiyuanhui) stated outright that the government expected a larger number of immigrants to flow to western China in response to its "open the west" (*xibu da kaifa*) campaign begun that year. He also made clear that Beijing intended this augmented influx of Hans to counter the threat of separatism by altering population ratios, although he acknowledged that in the short run, this alteration might actually "increase contradictions and friction" (Li Dezhu 2000:705–6, cited in Becquelin 2004b:373–74). This last admission directly contradicted officials' earlier repeated assurances that Han immigration served the interest of all peoples in Xinjiang and would bring peace and prosperity to all (see, for example, Xinjiang jiushi ti bianji weiyuanhui 1993:16–8). As provocative as such announcements might have been decades earlier, by 2000 they merely acknowledged publicly what Uyghurs had been saying in private for years.

Uyghurs' fears about the political implications of Han immigration were compounded when the party began to apply family-planning policies to non-Hans in Xinjiang. Knowing this action would be explosive, officials implemented them gradually.[46] Even though Hans throughout China had been subject to birth limits since the early 1980s, Uyghurs and other non-Hans had been exempt. The government began to publish the new periodical *Xinjiang Family Planning* in Chinese in February 1985 and to post notices (presumably in Chinese), where Hans would be likely to see them, observing that all *minzu* had an "obligation to limit family size." The family-planning periodical came out in its first Uyghur-language edition in December, and on December 12, students took to the streets in a demonstration that one observer called the "most serious political event" in Xinjiang since 1949 (Li

Yuanqing 1990:71). The students shouted their firm opposition to birth limits for Uyghurs and raised other complaints as well; the eruption of the protest so soon after the periodical came out suggests that it was the triggering spark. No doubt dismayed by the violent response, party leaders maintained their measured pace, waiting two years before requiring Uyghur party officials to limit their fertility, another year before promulgating "temporary regulations" on minority *minzu* birth planning, and yet another year before enforcing limits of three children for rural Uyghurs and two for those in cities. In 1992 the State Council issued "strict ceilings" for Xinjiang's population in 1995 and 2000 (Xu Xifa 1995:171, 173).[47] As the decade wore on, the combination of a strict limit on Xinjiang's total population growth and policies not just allowing but encouraging Han immigration lent considerable weight to the suspicion that Uyghurs were being made to limit their procreation to make room for more Hans.

My Uyghur informants condemned birth restrictions for at least three reasons. First, it was a clear external imposition by a government they regarded as alien. They argued that no other category of social life was more clearly part of "their own affairs," to be carefully sheltered by the principle of autonomy. Second, many Uyghurs objected on religious grounds that the party-state was arrogating to itself an authority it had no right to wield. Third, an overwhelming number of Uyghurs felt that had millions of Hans not immigrated to Xinjiang, there would be no ecological case for birth planning.[48] Uyghurs protested against Han immigration beginning in the 1950s ("Zizhiqu dangwei kuoda huiyi henhen de fandui difang minzu zhuyi" 1958). The influx of Hans and family-planning policies figured in student protests in 1985, 1988, and 1989 and continued to be a theme of demonstrations in the 1990s (see chapter 4 and appendix). When a Uyghur official in the Ürümci government told a BBC reporter in 2005, "There's very little difference in the ethnic balance between now and the early 1950s," his comment reflected the vast gulf—whether in perception or in honesty—between officialdom and the populace (Sommerville 2005).

THE PRODUCTION AND CONSTRUCTION CORPS (PCC)

Officials in Beijing and Ürümci deployed many Han immigrants in a manner that neatly complemented the division of Xinjiang into subregional autonomies. Redeployment of demobilized Guomindang (GMD), Ili National Army, and Red Army soldiers in the PCC, or *bingtuan*, at strategic points throughout the region enacted a subtler parcelization of the territory.[49] PCC units set up along the margins of "troubled" regions, along key transport arteries, and around hubs

provided the potential to control travel and isolate regions with very few enforc-
ers. Heavy concentrations of PCC farms in Kashgar, Aqsu, and Qumul districts
were intended to counterbalance the overwhelmingly Uyghur population in
those areas. The *bingtuan* was initially billed as a force to protect Chinese sovereignty from external threat in sensitive border regions, but the pattern of its
units' deployment makes plain that defense against foreign invasions was never
the planners' primary worry. The concern of first importance was and would continue to be Uyghur agitation for an independent Xinjiang. The complexion of the
PCC underscores this point: it has been overwhelmingly Han since its establishment. A recent publication praises the *bingtuan* not only for quelling the 1990
Baren uprising and similar disturbances but also for "preventing more than 8,600
people from leaving" during the mass exodus of more than 60,000 Uyghurs and
Qazaqs in 1962 (Yang Zhenhua 1997:15). After the event, the government forcibly
evicted farmers and pastoralists from a fifteen-mile-wide swath of territory along
the entire border with the Soviet Union and set up new PCC camps there. Jiang
Zemin's explicit statement in 1990 that the PCC's primary mission had changed
from guarding against foreign threats to quelling domestic ones marked a change
much less in function than in rhetoric (Becquelin 2002:63). Indeed, Deng Xiaoping had privately described the *bingtuan* as an "an important force in maintaining local stability" to Wang Zhen when authorizing him to reinstate it in 1981
(Seymour 2000:182).

It is a supreme irony that the PCC boasts more of the trappings of autonomy
than any other entity in Xinjiang. According to a professor at the XUAR Party
School, it "administers its own internal affairs," claiming its own public security
apparatus, courts, procuratorate, judiciary, and jails (Zhu Peimin 2000:423, 422).
With regard to those powers it does not exercise itself, it is answerable not to the
party organization or the government of Xinjiang but instead directly to the State
Council in Beijing. A former Uyghur official commented that the PCC consti-
tutes Xinjiang's "second provincial authority," and an expert on China's military
described it as "an independent government within a government and Beijing's real
and reliable power base" in the region. There is a strong case to be made that Beijing
regards the organization as a better counter to the threat of Uyghur nationalism
than the Xinjiang government itself (Becquelin 2004b:367–68; Rahman 2005:87–88;
Seymour 2000:181; Shichor 2006a:144).

The organization's demographic significance in Xinjiang is unmistakable. In
1974, the number of *bingtuan* members reached 2.26 million, or one-fifth of the
total population and two-fifths of the Han population in Xinjiang. Despite being

disbanded in 1975 and receiving no government support for seven years, the network of farms and construction units recovered and grew steadily after 1982, so that by 1994 the PCC again claimed 2.22 million souls, of which 88.3 percent, or 1.96 million, were Han, constituting 35 percent of Xinjiang's total Han population in that year. By 2004 it had far exceeded that previous mark, with 2.56 million members.[50]

Officials and scholars have lately increased calls to expand the organization still further. A 1997 work on the history and function of the *bingtuan* insisted that Beijing "organize the transfer" of Hans from China proper to Xinjiang for the sake of national unity (Fang Yingkai and Li Fusheng 1997:1539, cited in Becquelin 2000:78). In 2001 Ma Dazheng wrote more bluntly still that "Hans are the most reliable force for stability in Xinjiang" and complemented this comment with the pithy statement that "the stronger the PCC, the more stable Xinjiang will be." His text, intended for and read by policymakers, provided a detailed plan for further Han colonization. PCC sites near Qumul must be strengthened to enable full control of the passage from Xinjiang to the interior, and those near Kashgar should be beefed up to isolate Xinjiang from turbulence in Central Asia. Further deployments should "draw a circle" around southern Xinjiang by filling in "blank spaces," one between Aqsu and Korla and another between Khotän and Ruoqiang. The expansion of PCC organizations in the latter region, Ma remarked brightly, "will prove an excellent conduit for changing the *minzu* population ratio in Khotän, which has gotten out of balance" (Ma Dazheng 2003:123, 124, 234–35). A Qing historian by training, Ma knew very well that Turkis had been the absolute majority of Khotän's population for centuries; it is very hard to understand how he could have construed Khotän's still overwhelmingly Uyghur population as "getting out of balance." Yet there is absolutely no doubt that he meant the district needed more Hans.

The PLA and other security forces enjoy a decisive logistical and military advantage over any potentially violent challengers in Xinjiang. Both the system of nested autonomies and the network of strategically located PCC farms have augmented Beijing's capacity to control the region by giving non-Uyghurs in Xinjiang a stake in the current distribution of power. The strategic deployment of immigrants and subprovincial units of autonomy has ensured that even if Uyghurs were to join together in a peaceful demand for independence tomorrow, they would be opposed by the nearly eight million Hans as well as by more than two million members of other Turkic, Xibo, and Mongol groups. To maintain the loyalties of numerically small groups, the party has incorporated members of each into the government through targeted recruitment, which mirrors and reinforces the effects of the territorial parcelization. By appointing members of those groups to offices in a higher proportion than their ratio in the wider population (Benson and Svanberg 1998:121), the system dilutes the already meager influence of Uyghurs and gives other groups disproportionate authority in the system.

RECRUITING CADRES

The second major component of the CCP's representational politics in Xinjiang is the careful selection of non-Han officials. Beijing has successfully co-opted many Uyghurs and members of the other, smaller groups. Through the careful selection, training, and promotion of loyal Uyghur cadres, the CCP has added substantial numbers to the government without compromising its policymaking autonomy. By law and tradition, the head of government of each autonomous unit from provincial down to township level is a member of the titular group; thus every head of Xinjiang's government has been a Uyghur since 1955; each head of Ili Prefecture, a Qazaq; and so on.[51] Uyghurs and other non-Hans in regional and local government are frequently called on to announce the party's unpopular policies, all but guaranteeing that those officials will not develop a local power base and blunting the criticism that Hans alone rule the region.[52] The recruitment has followed a consistent pattern.

Uyghurs and other non-Hans have been best represented at the lowest levels of government. By mid-1961, more than 85 percent of county magistrates and deputy magistrates were non-Han, and more than half the commissioners and deputies at the district, prefectural, and regional levels were non-Han. Yet according to McMillen, "the key departments and organs of Xinjiang administration . . . largely remained in the hands of Han CCP members." In October 1965, non-Han cadres comprised 106,000 of 190,000, or 55.8 percent of the total. The continued (though reduced) preponderance of non-Hans was again tempered by a skewing toward the bottom: fewer than 10 percent of non-Han cadres were leaders at the county level or above (McMillen 1979:48, 75–76).[53] Furthermore, the ratio dropped dramatically during the Cultural Revolution (1966–1976) when tens of thousands of non-Han cadres received damning political "labels" and were dismissed from their positions. The ratios fell most quickly late in the Cultural Revolution not because of purges but because of a massive influx of Hans into government positions. Between 1974 and 1975, the number of Hans in government more than doubled, from 133,000 to 269,000, while the figure for Uyghurs rose from 62,000 to 67,000 (Zhonggong Xinjiang weiwu'er zizhiqu weiyuanhui zuzhibu 1996:730) . Even in 1979, three years after the fall of the Gang of Four, non-Hans held only 29 percent of cadre positions (Benson and Svanberg 1998:109).

Deng Xiaoping's reforms, and in particular the policies advocated by Hu Yaobang, reversed this trend with moves both to reduce Han dominance and to restore non-Hans to their former positions. In July 1980 the Central Committee Secretariat, headed by Hu, heard a report on "Xinjiang work," and in September it convened a symposium on the topic. Wang Zhen was then deputed to convey the sense of the September meeting to Xinjiang's leadership. In November, the Xinjiang Party Committee explicitly stated for the first time that the proportions of minority *minzu* cadres in both party and government ought to reflect the proportions of those non-Han groups in the broader society. This objective was to be reached by a combination of recruiting more non-Han cadres and reducing the number of Han officials. To achieve the latter goal, some Han officials would be retired or furloughed; others would be given advisory roles; and many would be transferred to posts in China proper. Party scholars later described as "one-sided" the decision to make the complexion of officialdom numerically representative and condemned the initiative to remove the Han cadres as based on "an incorrect assessment of relations among *minzu*" (Dang Yulin and Zhang Yuxi 2003:277; Zhang Yuxi 1993:358).[54]

By the end of 1983, tens of thousands of non-Hans, now considered to have been "wrongly labeled," had been reinstated. The combination of reinstatement of old cadres and the hastened training and selection of minority *minzu* stipulated by Hu brought the number of non-Han cadres up to 181,860, a substantial rise. On Hu's orders, the ranks of Han cadres had shrunk dramatically over the same period. In 1982 alone, they were reduced by more than one-fourth, from 320,000 to 230,000. But despite the large increase in non-Han cadres and the departure of so many Hans, the percentage of non-Hans remained, at 43.1 percent, more than ten points lower than it had been in 1965. This reflected the fact that the purge of Han cadres in 1982 had been three-quarters less than the size of their prior influx into officialdom in 1975 ("XUAR gaikuang" bianxiezu 1985:52–54; Zhonggong Xinjiang weiwu'er zizhiqu weiyuanhui zuzhibu 1996:832).[55]

Chinese texts that showcase long series of figures on non-Hans at various levels of government—and all works that discuss the system of autonomy do so—delicately sidestep the key indicator of political authority: party first secretaries. In the Soviet Union, first secretaries in autonomous units were members of titular minority groups, while the top-ranking vice secretary was invariably a Russian. Beijing reversed the Soviet practice, with a Han in the top slot and a member of the titular group in the second position. One observer noted drily that there was "never ... any suggestion" that top party officials in any of China's autonomous units would "need to be members of the relevant nationality" (Mackerras 1994:156).

Another averred that in Mao-era Xinjiang, the party secretary who was found in every government office and every work unit and who was the final authority on all decisions was "normally a Han" (McMillen 1979:48). Careful inspection of party rolls indicates that these observers were much too conservative, as the evidence suggests that there has been a tacit but rigid rule, with a vanishingly small number of exceptions, that the top party secretaries *must* be Han. This pattern has not changed appreciably (Yee 2003:449). Three decades into the reform period, it is exceedingly unusual to find a non-Han first party secretary in a government bureau, state-owned enterprise (SOE) work unit, or private enterprise.[56] Non-Han first secretaries in local or regional government are never found. In 2000, all of the 124 secretaryships at prefectural, municipal, and county levels were occupied by Hans (Becquelin 2004b:363). In 2006, the official government Web site for Xinjiang party affairs displayed the names and photographs of all secretaries at the prefectural level and above, not one indicating an exception to this rule.[57]

Indeed, the percentage of non-Han party members has remained far below the proportions in the population. In 1987 only 38.4 percent of party members in Xinjiang were non-Han, even though non-Hans made up more than 60 percent of the population. By 1994, the percentage of non-Han party members had fallen further, to 36.7 percent, before rising to 40.3 percent in 2004.[58] Despite the calls for "nativization" of government ranks in autonomous regions, there has never been a corresponding initiative in the party. The XUAR's government chairman, Säypidin Äzizi, had warned in 1957 that proposing to increase the proportion of non-Hans in the party was "reactionary" (McMillen 1979:93). Decades later, officials continued to eschew targeted recruitment, claiming that party members had no particularist loyalties and were therefore capable of representing all groups without prejudice. With campaigns on the wane and the idea of "reactionary" political errors increasingly implausible, officials updated the language of justification, calling demands for *minzu* quotas in the party "unscientific" (Guo Zhengli 1992:92).

As with non-Russian groups in the Soviet Union that were underrepresented in the Communist Party of the Soviet Union (CPSU), several explanations were plausible: either the CCP considered non-Hans politically suspect, or they were averse to joining the party, or both (on the Soviet Union, see Armstrong 1992:243). Not only have non-Hans been reluctant to take responsible positions in government or enter the CCP, but many have become acutely frustrated with the political system after doing so. An official Chinese study provides a tantalizing piece of evidence of Uyghur cadres' deep and increasing frustration. Whereas in the 1950s, Uyghur separatist organizations were composed mainly of Guomindang diehards, former officials and soldiers from the Eastern Turkestan Republic, and angry ordinary citizens, by the 1990s the organizations contained a substantial and increasing number of cadres and party members in their ranks (Ma Dazheng 2003:80).[59]

Thus Uyghurs are quite underrepresented in the government apparatus, particularly at the higher levels, and are even less well represented in the party. In a sense, recruitment policies have dovetailed neatly with the policy on immigration. Over time, the increasing numbers of Hans have made it easier to justify the Hans' predominance in government. In interviews, Hans invariably approved of recruitment patterns, whereas those Uyghurs willing to discuss the matter strongly objected.[60] Even those who themselves were not implicated in the Han–Uyghur rivalry felt that the system was skewed. A Xibo man who had once announced proudly to me that he had not suffered any discrimination because "no one knows I'm not Han" admitted months later that he had lost patience with official propaganda contrasting equal opportunity in China with discrimination in the United States: "Our media say the U.S. discriminates, but even so, a black man can become head of the Defense Department. Of Commerce. Of the Supreme Court. In China, does the Supreme Court have a single *minzu*? Does the Military Affairs Commission in Beijing? Damn!"[61]

Such comments cannot be found in newspapers or other media. Indeed, the same system that placed Han party officials in charge of non-Hans at all levels of government has, with the exception of a brief period in the 1980s, prevented the open expression of grievances about that fact.

RELIGION

The rarity of Uyghurs and other Muslims in positions of ultimate authority in Xinjiang has had a clear impact on the handling of religion there. While the government's control of religion was noticeably relaxed during the reform era in many areas of the PRC, as among the Dai in Yunnan, the Hui in the north and southwest, and even to some extent in Tibet, the same cannot be said for Xinjiang.[62] To be sure, the party did loosen control of religion in the early 1980s as part of its overture to Uyghurs and others after the antireligious excesses of the Cultural Revolution. One obvious sign was the great number of mosques that were rebuilt. Before the Cultural Revolution began in 1966, there around 5,500 mosques in Kashgar District in southern Xinjiang, of which 107 were in Kashgar City. The prefectural figure was far below that in 1949, as a "religious investigation team" dispatched from the Xinjiang Academy of Social Science noted with satisfaction.[63] This had been the consequence of the "greatly elevated consciousness of the masses," although the team's report also admitted that quite a few mosques had been taken over by communes during the collectivization movement in 1958. One indication of the Cultural Revolution's devastation can be seen in the further reduction in these figures. Of the original number for the Kashgar District, only 392 mosques remained usable by the 1970s, and only two stayed open in Kashgar City.

Muslims responded vigorously to Deng's broadening of cultural policies at the beginning of the reform period. In 1980 and 1981 alone, communities reclaimed or rebuilt more than two-thirds of the original number, so that by the end of the latter year, there were 4,700 mosques in Kashgar District and 93 in Kashgar City (Zongjiao yanjiusuo Yisilanjiao diaocha zu 1983:21–23). Mosques continued to be built through the 1980s. Many villages had more resources as a consequence of the agricultural reforms of the early Deng era, and they had decided to build mosques with their new wealth.

A violent uprising in the southwestern town of Baren in 1990 caught officialdom by complete surprise. In addition to the uprising's violence and its evident popular support, what most stunned party leaders was the news that the participants had announced openly that Islam would conquer Marxism–Leninism (Liu Zhongkang 1990:50). In the aftermath of Baren and in response to the shocking collapse of the Soviet Union, the government reversed its previous policy of tolerance. Officials prosecuted "illegal religious activities," defrocking suspect clerics, breaking up unauthorized scripture schools (*mädräsä*), and halting the construction of mosques. In 1991, 10 percent of roughly 25,000 clerics examined by officials were stripped of their positions (Harris 1993:120–21). The party instituted new regular political examinations for imams, decreeing that only those judged patriotic and politically sound could continue to serve. Those restrictions, along with the stipulation that all new clerics be trained at Xinjiang's sole religious institute in Ürümci, have continued to the present. After a decade of turning a blind eye to mosque building, officials felt that their construction had exceeded acceptable limits. In 1990, cadres in Akto County (where Baren is located) closed fifty mosques judged to be "superfluous" and canceled the construction of one hundred more out of fear that religion was getting out of control (Dillon 2004:73).

Despite the crackdown, propagandists in Kashgar continued to complain of "indiscriminate (*lan*) construction of mosques" five years later: by 1995, the Kashgar District had some 9,600 mosques, more than twice the number in 1981 and, in the judgment of atheist party members, "already plenty enough to satisfy the needs of normal religious practice by the believing masses."[64] Certain religious personnel, officials warned, engaged in wanton building, with the excuse that the number of religious sites were inadequate.[65] Officials then sought to halt as well as to reverse the trend of mosque construction. Between 1995 and 1999, officials in Ili Prefecture demolished seventy mosques or religious sites, and their counterparts in Ürümci razed twenty-one sites in 1998 alone. Mosques near schools were specially targeted for destruction, lest they continue to exercise a "negative influence" on pupils (Agence France-Presse 2001a; Human Rights Watch 2005:56). In 1996, I observed the flattening of several mosques in the vicinity of Xinjiang University.[66]

Officials were even more concerned about clerics opening private schools and Qur'an study classes without official permission, or taking on religious pupils (*talip*).[67] There were reportedly more than four thousand *talip* in Kashgar District in 1995 (Kashi diwei xuanchuan bu 1995:37). Concern about renewed private religious study and growing popular religiosity led to further repression in the following year. Michael Dillon noted that both national and XUAR governments directed more attention to the influence of religion on regional unrest beginning in the latter half of 1996 than they had since the founding of the PRC (Dillon 2004:90). Officials closed all underground schools and cracked down on both pupils and teachers, labeling all private scriptural study "illegal religious activity." Even so, such schools continued to spring up (Ma Dazheng 2003:99). Alarmed at the emergence of religious networks that were neither organized nor sanctioned by the state, Wang Lequan imposed new restrictions on religious education in December 1999:

> In general, patriotic clerics [should] have two to three students or, in big mosques, three to four; more is unacceptable. The practice of appointing mollas from outside districts is strictly forbidden. We cannot give them the opportunity to link up by forgetting this. Originally, there were no contacts between village and village; once mollas were laterally appointed, it produced a problem.

Wang derived this "lesson" from the activities of Abduqadir Ayum, damolla of Qaghiliq (Yecheng), who had been the teacher of members of an alleged separatist gang in Khotän that officials were trying to "mop up" in December 1999. Equally, if not more, significant, Abduqadir had managed to train some eight hundred students and dispatch them to various parts of Xinjiang, building a network that Wang regarded as deeply threatening. Wang's new rules were plain: "Wherever an *ahong* [a Muslim cleric] is trained, that's the mosque where he serves; there will be no lateral appointments" (Wang Lequan 1999:6). Wang's fiat was later transformed into law. The 2001 revision of the 1994 law on religion, much stricter than its predecessor, included an "on-the-spot" rule, which meant that imams from one town could not preach in another, nor could a mosque receive people from different parts of the XUAR (Human Rights Watch 2005:39 and n. 80).[68]

The treatment of Islam in China's interior has been much more relaxed. Religious schools for young students continue to thrive and enjoy state protection in China proper. It seems clear that Hui Muslims have been granted so much more religious latitude because almost none have challenged secular authorities (Lipman 1997; Savadove 2005; Yardley 2006). The Hui religious leader of a Sufi sect in Ningxia was reportedly allowed to establish a "virtual religious state" with one and a half million followers and a wide network of mosques and religious schools. Remarkably, this leader was able to do so despite openly acknowledging having heard Osama bin Laden speak and meeting many fundamentalist clerics while studying for five years in Pakistan. The price of this freedom was his profession of absolute loyalty to the Chinese state and service in the Ningxia People's Congress (Savadove 2005).[69]

Not only Islamic institutions but Muslims themselves have been treated quite differently across regions. Every version of the PRC's constitution has maintained, and textbooks on religious policy repeat, that all citizens have two freedoms with respect to religious belief: the freedom to believe and the freedom not to believe. Officials have worried for years that continued religious belief threatens party authority and provides a breeding ground for Uyghurs' political mobilization. The Xinjiang government's chosen strategy has been to protect the freedom of people not to believe and to "dilute religious consciousness" in the population (Yin Zhuguang and Mao Yongfu 1996:233). The principal aim of official policy in securing freedom of belief is to make religion a "personal matter" (*sishi*). Officials have clearly grasped that attempting to force people to stop believing in or practicing religion does not work and may in fact provoke a strong backlash. They have come up with a clever second-best strategy that, even if not fully effective, will have a profound impact on Xinjiang's Muslim populations. Over the long term, the party aims at no less than ending the transmission of religiosity from one generation to the next. Interrupting that transmission will in turn serve the larger project of reducing the distinct (and oppositional) identities of Uyghurs and other Turkic Muslims.

The party has placed special emphasis on eliminating the pull of religion on two groups: party members and students, which has been a matter of growing urgency. Since 1978, substantial numbers of Uyghur and other Muslim party officials have become religiously observant. Surveys in 1983 determined that 20 to 30 percent of rural party members believed and practiced and that in some districts the rate was a high as 70 percent (Zhu Peimin, Chen Hong, and Yang Hong 2004:222). The proportions appeared to have held steady or risen further by the end of the decade. In 1989, a survey in Lop County found that more than 58 percent of party members took part in religious activities, and another survey in Qaraqash (Moyu) found that 83 percent took part. To higher officials' horror, even party branch committee members and secretaries prayed daily, and some secretaries even became imams. These outcomes were characterized as a "loss of party and political control" in the bottom rungs of the party (Ma Dazheng 2003:15).

Even though the constitution guarantees these two freedoms, party cadres and students are now openly denied the right to believe. As one text explains,

> Ordinary citizens are permitted two freedoms. Though party members are also citizens, they are first of all members of the party of the proletariat, and therefore *enjoy only one freedom*—the freedom not to believe—and absolutely do not enjoy the freedom to believe. They cannot have a foot in two boats. (XUAR Party Committee Propaganda Bureau 1997:52, italics added)

This novel explication of freedom has not persuaded many people. Many party members continue to believe and pray, even if they rarely dare to attend mosques. In at least one documented instance, one group responded to this difficult situation by simply removing their foot from the party boat, and in a very public setting. In 1999 in a village outside Kashgar, twenty-eight party members, including some village leaders, mounted a stage in front of more than a thousand locals and announced that they were quitting the party, whereupon they were embraced as Muslims by local religious authorities (Ma Dazheng 2003:117–18). In June of the following year in another village not far from Kashgar, eleven party cadres openly entered a mosque together, and fully one-half the party members in the village were religious, according to an official report. A month later, authorities in Qaghiliq, the site of frequent unrest since the beginning of the reform era, punished seven party members for various offenses related to religion (Kashi diqu shizhi ban 2001:318). There is little doubt that these scattered reports reflect a broader pattern of defiance by Muslim party members. The mere fact that in 2006, officials placed signs over the gates of mosques forbidding party members and government officials to enter suggests that the prohibition had not been entirely successful (RFA 2006a).

While in theory, students also are citizens, they now also are limited to a single religious freedom. Official explanations stress both the vital role of education in ensuring the future prosperity of the nation and the importance of allowing youths, once old enough to choose, to make a free, informed choice to believe or not to believe. For example,

> youths and children are in the growing-up stage; their worldviews have not yet formed. They lack scientific knowledge and life experience. They cannot yet make responsible and scientific choices appropriate to their goals. To irrigate the minds of immature youths with religious thought is to allow someone to impose belief in a particular religion on them. (Luo Yingfu 1992:171)

The author pointedly ignores the fact that to prevent youths from practicing religion and others from teaching them about it is to allow another agent to impose unbelief. But such intervention has proven ineffectual. Prosecuting religious activity and expressly forbidding the teaching of religion on school campuses have not eliminated belief. A scholar noted with alarm in the mid-1990s that when asked which was greater, the "strength of Khuda [Allah] or the strength of science," 71 percent of high school students in Changji Prefecture sided with Allah (Gong Yong 1997:4). Party strategists also have placed hopes on mandatory classes in atheism.

An Amnesty International report on Xinjiang claimed that the CCP began the "education in atheism" campaign in 1997 (Amnesty International 1999:n. 52), but a textbook published in 1992 that I purchased in Kashgar shows that the campaign began earlier. The text of the book makes clear that students no longer enjoyed "freedom of religious belief," and the fifth lesson is devoted entirely to the bald assertion that "teenagers must become atheists" (Li Ailing et al. 1992:144 ff.). A reporter's visit to a middle school in the central city of Korla in 1999 shows that the message did not remain inside books. An educational poster on the wall of the school listed "two musts," the first being the obligation to fight "splittism" and the second, the obligation to "believe in Marxist atheism and not attend religious activities" (Marquand 2003). By 2000, academics in China were writing openly that atheism education was the way to "gradually reduce religious consciousness among the masses." They urged that the government "try every conceivable stratagem to lighten the influence of religion and shrink the terrain held by religion." The authors' hostility to religious belief and practice was quite plain in the language they chose: the term "terrain" (*zhendi*) connotes territory held by the enemy in a military conflict (Long Qun and Guo Ning 2000:78). During interviews in 1996–1997 and again in 2002, secular Uyghur intellectuals, even actively antireligious ones who bemoaned the conservatizing influence of Islam on Uyghurs, criticized the party's putting so much pressure on believers.[70]

The party-state has taken the more aggressive step of forbidding anyone under the age of eighteen to enter a mosque. Although signs excluding minors are not visible outside the major city mosques in the capital city of Ürümci, they can be seen elsewhere in the region (Fuller and Lipman 2004:335; Mackerras 2004b). The placard warning party members and government officials not to enter also includes youths under eighteen. Questioned in 2006 about who was permitted to pray in mosques, the imam of the Idkah mosque in Kashgar, the largest in Xinjiang, initially responded that every Muslim could do so. Then, after being reminded about the rules in other mosques, he admitted that the same restrictions applied in Idkah (RFA 2006a).[71]

In the mid-1990s, students at Xinjiang University were fully aware of the increasingly stringent official policy. They observed privately that many classmates continued to pray five times a day and to participate secretly in study groups. But the costs of doing so were readily apparent. For instance, in the spring of 1997, at the entrance to the campus computer building, a series of posters with gaudy vermillion stamps indicated that six students from Khotän had been expelled and arrested for attending religious study groups and that they had received substantial prison sentences. In 1999, parents of students at another postsecondary school received letters warning them their children had been caught praying or fasting and threatening expulsion if they were caught again. Two years later, a female student in Kashgar was in fact expelled for performing *namaz* (Human Rights Watch 2005:62, 110). In 2005 Xinjiang University distributed a 142-page student handbook with specific rules against students' religious observance, although they are somewhat inconsistent. Some articles forbid students to participate in "illegal religious activities," while others prohibit participation in religious activities of any kind. One even bars students from activities with a "religious coloring." One regulation (dated 2001) specifically forbids fasting at Ramadan and mandates penalties for students who do.[72] Another states that students will be given a disciplinary warning the first time they are caught taking part in religious activities, a demerit in their dossiers for a second occurrence, and expulsion if caught a third time (*Xinjiang daxue xuesheng shouce* 2005:57, 88, 124–25).

If students have been subject to particularly severe religious restrictions since the 1990s, the wider religious community felt a palpable and immediate effect in the aftermath of the September 11 attacks. In October 2001, authorities in Ürümci announced that they would increase the intensity of the "strike hard" campaign against "separatists and terrorists," with particular emphasis on punishing "illegal religious activities." In November the police closed down thirteen "illegal religious centers" in Kashgar and arrested more than fifty people they found praying there. In December the police arrested nine people in Bayangol for translating the Qur'an into local languages and "illegally preaching" to locals; they were accused of using religion to incite separatism. In the same month, police in Khotän detained a man and a woman, each accused of teaching young pupils privately about the Qur'an (Amnesty International 2002).[73] Since that time, the restrictions have only increased. In 2001 the national government promulgated a revised form of the 1994 law on religion, with a subtle change in wording that indicated a major change in policy. Whereas the 1994 law had listed among its purposes the "protection of normal religious activities," the 2001 law spoke instead of "regulating religious activities according to law" and "inducing religion to conform to socialist society." As researchers at Human Rights Watch pointed out, even though the party-state had always been the sole arbiter of the distinction between "normal" and "illegal" religious activities, the 2001 law left the pious in even greater doubt about where the distinction lay. The law also enacted another subtle but significant change in applying to all believers the loyalty requirement originally applied only to clerics. This made the practice of religion by private citizens "conditional on support for government and Party leaders" (Human Rights Watch 2005:33–34, 37).

Further restrictions on religion came into force in March 2005, and again the effects could easily be seen. In July 2005, three Uyghurs waiting at a bus stop had their bags searched and were detained for holding "unauthorized" religious texts. In August of the same year, police burst unannounced into the home of a religious teacher and arrested her along with thirty-seven pupils for studying the Qur'an privately (Hoo 2005; Human Rights Watch 2006). Over time, the official rubric of "freedom of religious belief" has worn quite thin indeed.

PRESSURES FOR CHANGE

The Uyghurs' dissatisfaction with the political system in Xinjiang has been clear since the founding of the People's Republic of China. Demands for "real" or expanded autonomy figured in most of the organized protests in the 1980s, and Uyghur informants privately expressed their wishes for greater collective autonomy to many researchers in the 1980s and 1990s (Beller-Hann 1997, 2002; Bovingdon 2002a; Smith 2000, 2002). Pressures to change the legal framework or the policies on autonomy have also come from other sources: Soviet-bloc writers and officials, more liberal Xinjiang officials urging the expansion of autonomy, and hardliners demanding its reduction. In the last decade, the United States, some European Union members, and international organizations have also begun to criticize the system.

From very early on, Marxists inside and outside China condemned the framework of autonomy. Following the Sino-Soviet split, Soviet authors scornfully denounced China's system of autonomous regions as a betrayal of socialist principles. One argued that Beijing was denying non-Hans their "legal right to self-determination," while another complained that in its place, the government was offering "only a truncated territorial autonomy" (Connor 1984:236).

Deng Xiaoping showed he was aware that this was still a live issue in the 1980s, as a comment that came to light much later revealed: "Xinjiang's fundamental question is [whether it should be] a republic or an autonomous region." Echoing Zhou Enlai's 1957 remarks, Deng asserted that "we're different from the Soviet Union. We can't have a republic; we are an autonomous region."[74] Also like Zhou, he defended the Chinese system against Soviet-bloc criticisms. In 1987, Deng admitted to Hungary's János Kádár that the Chinese government had consciously chosen not to have a Soviet-style federation of republics; yet he boasted that the system of autonomous regions was one of the best points of China's socialist system and must not be abandoned (Zhu Peimin 2000:334, 337).

Party theorists attempted to lay the matter to rest in lengthy treatises. For instance, in a work billed as the first account of China's system of regional autonomy integrating Marxist–Leninist theory and Chinese practice, the author acknowledged the CCP's gradual abandonment of the principle of self-determination but claimed that it was entirely justified. The CCP did indeed "emphasize many times and over a long period the principle of the right to *minzu* self-determination," though it ceased to do so after the victory over the Japanese in 1945. The CCP's supporting the principle of self-determination in the 1930s and 1940s was "understandable" given its membership in the Communist Third International; so was its "use of the slogan of *minzu* self-determination" to motivate non-Hans to fight against imperialism. So, finally, was its decision to abandon the principle entirely in September 1949 as the Chinese People's Political Consultative Conference deliberated the shape of New China. At that point, the repudiation of self-determination was "correct" and "a matter of course" because acknowledging it any longer would simply have served imperialist plans to split up China (Zhang Erju 1988:33–36).[75] Officially supported scholars adopted a still firmer line in 1999, declaring that in contemporary Xinjiang, "to pursue 'self-determination' is to engage in splittism" (Pan Zhiping 1999:178–81).

These official comments and theoretical works have clearly been intended to answer Marxist critiques of the political-legal framework of autonomy. While neither silenced those critiques, Chinese officials can observe with bittersweet satisfaction that many of the critics lost their jobs and, in several cases, their countries.

CCP officials often point to the disintegration of the Soviet Union and Yugoslavia as proof that Mao and his cohort made prudent choices in 1949 (Zhu Peimin, Chen Hong, and Yang Hong 2004:357). In the meantime, Uyghurs have continued to clamor for more autonomy (Becquelin 2000; Bovingdon 2002b; Gladney 2002, 2004b; Rudelson 1997; Smith 2000).

Already at the beginning of the reform era, a few officials and scholars had acknowledged the limitations, even the failures, of the system's implementation. This is revealed, for example, in the recently published report of a group of specialists on *minzu* problems (which would have included a large number of non-Hans), trading ideas at a symposium on that topic in Beijing in 1980. Despite the party's proclivity for "emphasizing the positive," an occasional critical note slipped through. It was the consensus of the conferees that

> the principal problem at present is that the powers of self-government and decision-making powers pertaining to the policy of *minzu* regional autonomy have not yet really been implemented (*wei neng zhizheng de luoshi*). . . . Some comrades noted that *minzu* equality has not yet been successfully established in people's minds, compromising the implementation of decision-making authority. There are those who see *minzu* regions purely as "materials supply sites" and seldom concern themselves with the economic development of [those regions]; they infringe on the legitimate interests of *minzu* regions. The problem of nativization of organs of self-government has for quite a few years now, and especially during the time of the "gang of four," become a virtual taboo. The proportion of *minzu* cadres in organs of self-government has fallen drastically, producing a situation in which "minority *minzu* manage household affairs (*dangjia*), Hans make the decisions" (*zuozhu*).

Public acknowledgment of the problem did not bring about much change over the ensuing decade, in spite of Hu Yaobang's reforms. In 1988 the author of an officially supported national study admitted with concern that most non-Han groups continued to be underrepresented in government in the autonomous regions, as reflected in the gap between cadre ratios and population ratios. He argued that this was a critical problem for the system's implementation. Without a substantial body of non-Han cadres, he wrote, "the true realization of . . . autonomy is impossible." The only solution was to train non-Han cadres in large numbers (Zhang Erju 1988:287). Yet after another twenty years, the gap had not changed appreciably.

A dominant group of high officials viewed with suspicion the renewed calls for nativization. As previously noted, many believed that rather than satisfying the demands of disgruntled Uyghurs, the looser and more tolerant policies enacted under Hu Yaobang had only whetted their appetite for more and thus *caused* the demonstrations and violence of the 1980s and 1990s. Many contended that the criticism of the Cultural Revolution's leftist excesses had provided cover for the emergence of ethnonationalist extremism. Ma Dazheng cited as evidence a letter submitted to the Xinjiang government in 1980. The letter's author, understood to be Uyghur, complained that "in Xinjiang, the leadership of the party has always meant leadership by Han cadres." To remedy the situation, the Uyghur author proposed setting ratios for cadres:

> Xinjiang is the Uyghur autonomous region. This point absolutely must not be forgotten or overlooked. Therefore … Uyghur cadres should constitute no less than 45 percent of the total (not less than 60 percent in southern Xinjiang), and cadres from the autonomous region's other minority *minzu* should make up not less than 15 percent.

Reading the letter almost two decades later, in 1998, Ma was disturbed by two aspects. First, its call for "full autonomy" smacked of "serious *minzu* attitude" (*qianglie de minzu qingxu*) and appeared to him to conceal a wish for independence. This concerned him particularly because Kosovar Albanians had recently raised the standard of full autonomy to cloak their quest to secede from Serbia. Second, in the two decades since the letter was written, its spirit had not only developed into an "erroneous intellectual current" but also spread widely among the Uyghur masses, making them susceptible to incitement and organization by separatists (Ma Dazheng 2003:185–86).

Facing pressures for more autonomy, hard-liners instead have pushed measures to diminish its scope. These include stimulating increased Han immigration and *reducing* the proportion of non-Han cadres by recruiting more Hans: "Hanization" instead of nativization. Policy advisers on *minzu* affairs to the Xinjiang government argued in the mid-1990s that Han flight and more relaxed family-planning controls on non-Hans had damaged the balance of populations in the region. They urged the government to adopt targeted policies to remedy the "out-of-balance population ratio" by luring Han cadres and members of the masses to Xinjiang, although they noted pessimistically that no policies could swiftly bring about radical change in population ratios (Mao Yongfu and Li Ling 1996:180).

Ma Dazheng made a more searching critique. It was not just the ratios them-selves that were troubling, but non-Hans' focus on them. Directly contradicting the policy analysts of a decade earlier, he opposed equating cadre ratios with auton-omy, hammering away at a fundamental premise of representational politics. To do so carried a grave risk: "The minute one raises 'autonomy' in Xinjiang, people, and especially comrades from minority *minzu*, think immediately of the question of ratios of cadres and civil servants. The two have practically become synonyms. This has become a 'big and intractable problem' difficult for local governments to resolve." In fact, it has become fertile "soil for 'ethnocentrism.'" Ma repeatedly pro-posed recruiting still more Han cadres, though he urged that local Hans be chosen in preference to those from China proper.[76] He also put into words the principle that had governed cadre recruitment over decades but had never previously been stated openly: The government preferred Hans over non-Hans as cadres in Xin-jiang. "We should," he announced, "see the special usefulness of Han cadres from the lofty strategic vantage of Xinjiang's stability" (Ma Dazheng 2003:21, 124, 188–89). In his policy proposals for counteracting the growing *minzu* consciousness and assertiveness of Uyghurs, Ma candidly urged that the government "weaken the '*minzu* ratio system' for appointing cadres, changing over to a '*minzu* inheritance system' for cadre positions" (Ma Dazheng 2003:201).[77] To eliminate the "ratio sys-tem" would mean decisively repudiating the principle of political representation. There is no discernible doctrinal justification for switching to "inheritance" of cadre positions, but such a change would have two practical consequences. First, assum-ing that the Han population will continue to outstrip that of non-Hans, it would not just perpetuate but increase the underrepresentation of Uyghurs. Second, it would justify the permanent adoption of the now fifty-year-old practice of assign-ing Hans to all party first secretary positions at all levels.

Although Ma's study was supported by the highest levels in Beijing and Ürümci, it is not always clear whether his policy suggestions were true proposals or scholarly justifications for existing practices. Given that two of the top officials in Xinjiang acknowledged having read the chapters of his book in the prefaces they wrote for it, we can be certain that had his policy suggestions not been officially approved, they would not have been published. In either case, we can detect high officials' inclina-tion to move in this direction in their retreat from the language of definite ratios. By the late 1990s, in calling for the training of "politically aware minority *minzu* cadres" who could implement party policies correctly, Jiang Zemin announced sim-ply that China must have "a group" (*yi pi*) of them (Huang Guangxue 2001).

Scholar-officials have attempted to endow these changes, which might otherwise be seen as manifestations of hypocrisy or blatant chauvinism, with the sanctity of

Marxist principle. In a work earning the imprimatur of the XUAR Party Committee, a professor at Xinjiang's Party School wrote that "it is no longer permissible, as in 1957 or 1980, to raise demands for 'nativization.'" He went on to argue that nativization and ensuring that various *minzu* were masters of their own house were fundamentally different matters. *Korenizatsiia*, once slavishly copied from the Soviet Union, was inappropriate for China's national conditions, and "judging from the present vantage, one cannot even say it was appropriate for the Soviet Union" (Zhu Peimin, Chen Hong, and Yang Hong 2004:357).

Some scholars have even obliquely proposed abandoning the commitment to autonomy altogether, almost certainly with official support. In the reform era, academics and low-level functionaries frequently publish theoretical essays that float ideas being contemplated in the government. This provides what Americans now refer to wryly as "plausible deniability" for potentially unpopular actions. Thus the young scholar Zhu Lun, a researcher in the *Minzu* Institute of the Chinese Academy of Social Sciences, asserted in 2002 that the idea of autonomy was obsolete and no longer suited to global realities. Collective rule (*gongzhi*) is now the "basic tenet of *minzu* politics in contemporary multi-*minzu* states." He therefore proposed that policymakers begin to think about "postautonomy" (*hou zizhi*) (Zhu Lun 2002:4, 6).

The appearance of a similar article later in the same year strengthened the supposition that the idea had official support. Commenting several months later on Zhu's article, legal scholar Du Wenzhong argued that "China's praxis for resolving problems of *minzu* relations should be understood as ... 'collective rule'" (*gongzhi*). Chinese jurisprudential scholars' continued use of the term "autonomy" (*zizhi*) to describe *minzu* policies was both unwise and "inaccurate." In reality, Du maintained, the newly amended law on regional autonomy stipulated "collective rule" by the state and local autonomous organs (Du Wenzhong 2002:8). This idea was echoed in policy proposals made specifically for Xinjiang, once again by Ma Dazheng. Prior work on the theory of *minzu* policies, Ma contended, had "put too great an emphasis" on *minzu* autonomy. This ought to be balanced by a greater stress on "collective rule" (Ma Dazheng 2003:188–89).

CONCLUSION

This chapter began by suggesting that Chinese policies in Xinjiang have been a key source of discontent and conflict, thereby implying that different policies might have produced less contentious outcomes. Historical counterfactuals are notoriously shaky ground for comparison. Furthermore, the frequency of ethnic conflict and violence in Xinjiang during the Republican era might have been expected to continue after 1949. The argument here is not that some set of ideal policies would have eliminated discontent and friction entirely. Instead, it is, first, that had the CCP hewed more closely to what Hannum and Lillich described as the minimal principles of autonomy, there would have been less friction. Second, the specific departures of Chinese practice from that minimal model exacerbated discontent in particular ways.

The large discrepancy between the promise of autonomy and the reality of Xinjiang's governance did not originate at the regional level. As Pei Minxin (2002:319) pointed out, two features of China's national political system have "in reality allowed almost no genuine local autonomy." First, Beijing has kept power strongly centralized and resisted the devolution of much authority to regions, and second, party leaders have adamantly opposed substantial democratization, which might have allowed the articulation of, and bargaining over, local demands. Both features remain obstacles to beneficial changes, and they demonstrate the perspicacity of Hannum and Lillich's argument that democracy and federalism are crucial guarantors of robust autonomy (Hannum and Lillich 1980:885, 887).[78]

Pei suggested that China's system of *minzu* regional autonomy faced a crisis in the mid-1990s. The country's market transition had dramatically reduced Beijing's capacity to redistribute resources and therefore to subsidize the less-developed border regions. Second, both international criticism and domestic opposition placed greater restraints on Beijing's capacity to use Han migration as a tool of control. Finally, in recent years, repression has proved to be less effective and more explosive in regions like Xinjiang and Tibet. Pei argued that the crisis would have to be resolved by strengthening institutions to protect the "rights and political representation" of non-Hans (Pei Minxin 2002:319–21, 323, 327).

Since Pei made this argument, changes in the international climate and China's economic situation have reduced pressures to enhance autonomy in Xinjiang and other peripheral regions. In the 1990s, international scrutiny and the specter of humanitarian intervention gave repressive states pause, particularly in the wake of NATO's intervention in Kosovo (Finnemore 2003). For a time, Beijing was gravely concerned that the United States or international organizations might use human rights abuses as a pretext for intervening in Xinjiang or Tibet (Dreyer 2000; Lawrence 2000; Ma Dazheng 2003:106–24). Then the attacks on September 11 gave Beijing the cover it needed to further reduce the scope of autonomy and step up political pressure in Xinjiang from 2001 on (Amnesty International 2002; Human Rights Watch 2005).

This chapter has argued that the system officially billed as providing Uyghurs "*minzu* regional autonomy" has in fact enforced heteronomy, as illustrated by the

Hans' monopoly on the most powerful party offices. The system of heteronomy has in turn enforced a series of policies that Uyghurs would not have chosen had they been able to govern themselves. The response of party officials to Uyghurs' complaints has been to further concentrate power in the hands of Hans and to enact even less popular policies. The new proposals to do away with the very rubric of autonomy are unlikely to reduce the discontent, even if they help silence its expression. I have suggested that the configuration of power and the unpopular policies have been key sources of discontent and therefore conflict in the region.

EVERYDAY RESISTANCE
GUERRILLA ACTIONS IN THE BATTLE OVER
PUBLIC OPINION

Xinjiang's main radio station broadcast a curious announcement in mid-January 2002:

> At the end of a singing concert at the Xinjiang People's Hall on 1 January, Tu'erxinjiang Aimaiti [Tursunjan Ämät], who was out of work, recited a poem written by him. The poem attacks social reality by innuendo, advocates ideas of ethnic separatism, and shows a strong tendency of opposing the society, the reality, and the government. It is really inflammatory and has produced a very bad influence on the society. The regional Party Committee paid great attention to the incident and immediately held a meeting of its Standing Committee to study the matter. . . . It instructed relevant departments to conduct an investigation . . . and to seriously mete out punishment. It also asked them to use the incident to conduct anti-separatism re-education. (BBC Monitoring Asia Pacific 2002)[1]

In the same broadcast Ablät Abdurišit, chairman of the XUAR government, professed characteristic amazement that "that such [an] incident has occurred in the most favourable situation of ethnic unity and social and political stability across the region."[2] The report should provoke a number of questions. First, how could a single poem recited at the end of a concert have caused such a stir? Second, what was so threatening about attacking social reality "by innuendo"? Third, even if government officials found the poem disturbing, why leap to the extreme of convening the Standing Committee and contacting other "relevant departments"? Fourth, if Xinjiang was so politically stable and intergroup relations were so "favourable," how could the poem have caused "a very bad influence on society"?

These questions, couched more broadly, animate this chapter. Given the extraordinary range of powers and controls described in the last chapter, why does the regime fear Uyghur dissidence? Does the party-state intend ordinary citizens to conclude that the regime is so weak and brittle that oblique criticism and subversive ideas pose a grave threat, even in the most favorable of circumstances? Do officials really seek to inhibit—and can they possibly hope to stop—the use of innuendo, symbolism, allegory, and other stratagems common to artists and gossips alike? Does this not risk setting the bar for political offenses so low that great numbers of people end up behaving "criminally," seemingly undermining the authority of the party-state?

THE BOUNDARIES OF DISSENT: WHAT IS AT STAKE

In the summer of 2002 Professor Wang, a Han scholar I had known for years, shared his thoughts on why the party-state has put so much effort into ideological battles. He first hewed to the official line that only a small number of extremists pursued independence and that they spared no means. Then he changed his argument significantly:

> In fact all *minzu* want independence. But it's not just ordinary people doing this. It's intellectuals. Some of them write history. Now [since the clampdown on historiography] they write novels and poems. And never directly. They always write indirectly, so that if you confront them, they can deny that they meant what you think they did. What they write is nonsense, but people believe it. So it must be corrected.

Revealing his intention to dedicate his scholarship to the task of correction, Wang told me that his target audience was Uyghur cadres. When I asked him whether scholarly work might reach ordinary people and banish their misconceptions, he threw up his hands and exclaimed, "Ordinary people are beyond our reach."[3]

The poet Tursunjan's performance clearly troubled officials. Perhaps they worried that he was able to reach ordinary people in a way that Professor Wang never could. In the summer of 2002, Bahargül, a service worker in her thirties employed in downtown Ürümci, spontaneously brought up Tursunjan's recitation during an interview. She said he had chosen as his theme the expressive music of the very popular *tambur* player Nurmuhämmät Tursun: "Tursunjan decided to write a poem about his playing, about how the mournful quality of his playing expressed the spirit of the Uyghur people. Tursunjan wields a fierce pen (*uning qälimi ötkür*)! The poem was great. . . . All the Uyghur officials attended the meeting, and plenty of Han officials as well."

Bahargül told me that because her friends privately shared their appreciation of Tursunjan's small triumph, they also exchanged the news that within a week of his performance, officials filed a report saying his poem had "unacceptable content."[4] She had heard that either the poet or the musician—she wasn't sure which—was confined to his home soon afterward. Foreign sources later announced that the poet had indeed been formally arrested, but released some time later (Amnesty International 2002, 2004).

As I argued in chapter 2, the key purpose of the Chinese Communist Party (CCP)'s system of *minzu* regional autonomy initially was to avoid territorial loss by winning the political acquiescence of large, non-Han groups. It has been neither the aim nor the effect of the system to allow those groups substantial authority over their own affairs, however narrowly construed. From the beginning, aside from matters such as language use, folk custom, and limited religious practice, the political institutions of autonomy left most decisions in the hands of party secretaries, who were almost exclusively Han and answered to Beijing.

As it became clear in the 1950s that this was the design and not a distortion of the center's policies, prominent Uyghur leaders and others in Xinjiang repeatedly raised increasingly vehement complaints. At a 1951 conference in Ghulja, the former seat of government of the Eastern Turkestan Republic, a group of Uyghur leaders proposed the establishment of a "republic of Uyghurstan" with the capacity to regulate all its internal affairs. On instructions from Beijing, Xinjiang's CCP officials hastily convened a meeting to condemn the proposal and ensure that this "incorrect idea" not be spread widely. At the meeting, newly appointed minority *minzu* officials, who had graduated from a political training course that Wang Zhen referred to as a "factory for producing the people's cadres," reportedly "used the Marxist perspective they had just mastered" to oppose the erroneous proposal and side with the party (Zhu Peimin 2000:335).[5] But the idea did not disappear. A speech by Zhou Enlai at a 1957 conference in Qingdao, released only in 1980, shows Beijing was aware that many Uyghurs continued to hope for a federal system and self-determination. At different points in his speech, Zhou told the assembled officials that China "could not" establish and "had no need" to establish a federal system on the Soviet model (Zhou Enlai 1980 [1957]). In an attempt to silence such proposals and the people making them, party officials initiated a "campaign against local nationalism," which lasted from December 1957 through April 1958. Newspaper reports at the time announced that Ziya Sämädi, head of the Xinjiang Culture Bureau, and a number of other prominent Uyghurs had formed an "anti-party group."[6] They stood accused of proposing yet again the establishment of a "Uyghurstan republic "and of "insulting Hans by suggesting they were 'rulers' just like the GMD [Guomindang]." They also were charged with saying that too many Hans had immigrated and should be sent home and with claiming that "we could build our economy even without Hans" ("Gezu renmin fennu shengtao difang minzu zhuyi fenzi zuixing" 1958; Zhong Yu 1958; "Zizhiqu dangwei kuoda huiyi henhen de fandui difang minzu zhuyi; chedi fensui yi Ziya wei shou de dandang jituan" 1958; "Zizhiqu dangwei kuoda huiyi zuochu jueyi—Kaichu youpai fenzi" 1958). The massive campaign slapped "local nationalist" labels on more than 1,600 people and sent many to jail. It also conveyed the powerful message that criticisms of Xinjiang's governance or the importation of Hans from the interior were forms of "incorrect speech" (*cuowu de yanlun*) subject to severe punishment (Dang Yulin and Zhang Yuxi 2003:190–92).[7]

The campaign did not eliminate Uyghur discontent with the way that Xinjiang was being governed but only drove it underground. Since then, organized and public resistance has sporadically reemerged, several times in the 1960s, once in 1975, again beginning in the 1980s and lasting through 2000, and, most recently, beginning in July 2009 (see chapter 4 and appendix). Given the difficulties of organizing opposition under the incursive single-party state and the harsh punishments dealt to open protestors, it makes little sense to argue, as party officials have, that the episodes of public unrest were paroxysms of baseless mob hysteria.

It is simply not plausible to reduce major protests to the work of a "handful of splittists" (and, since the winter of 2001, "terrorists") who, aided by hostile foreign powers, repeatedly lured thousands of gullible people out into the streets to serve their own purposes. Rather, the sporadic protests reflected deep and enduring discontent among Uyghurs. Official pronouncements have insisted that most Uyghurs oppose separatism and also have implied that they reject political protests of any sort and that the party will triumph because it enjoys the firm support of the people. This depiction has grossly misrepresented the attitudes and actions of a sizable proportion of the population. In fact, while explicitly denying it in public, officials have acknowledged in internal circulation speeches and documents that disaffection for the party and hostility toward Hans have long pervaded the Uyghur community. In 1999, for instance, XUAR Party Secretary Wang Lequan told other party cadres in a secret speech that separatists had "immediate appeal" among Uyghurs in Khotän and admitted that the cadres had "no place in the hearts of the people" (Wang Lequan 1999:11, 17).[8]

We might argue that Beijing had completed its quest to establish unchallenged administrative and military control of Xinjiang by 2004 or so (Becquelin 2004b:374). Yet it has met continual defeat in its attempt to transform all Uyghurs into willing and loyal Chinese citizens. While officials have sought to eliminate not just troublemakers but even troublesome ideas, Uyghurs have refused to give them up. The mere fact of widespread dissent—expressed in acts of "everyday resistance" by ordinary citizens—is important because it gives the lie to the official story. But such resistance also has had political effects. Intellectuals and farmers, musicians and their fans, joke tellers and cooks, have collaborated in constructing and promulgating heterodox visions of Xinjiang's past, present, and future. They have played an active role in shaping and transmitting Uyghur nationalism, and in that way they have affected the trajectory of politics in Xinjiang.

Uyghurs' everyday resistance has targeted both ideas and policies. Religious Uyghurs have fought official attempts to fit religious practice and Qur'anic interpretation to party needs, by defying efforts to eliminate religiosity among the young. The vast majority of Uyghurs privately condemn, since they cannot hope to stop, policies governing immigration and resource exploitation. They have derided the system of *minzu* regional autonomy as a sham.[9] Uyghurs have rejected the party-state's insistent claims that they are Chinese. As discussed in chapter 1, they have rejected the imposition of a history that denies them a legacy of independent states or a claim to Xinjiang based on indigeneity. Furthermore, a substantial number have spurned the notion that their interests and their future are indissolubly bound with those of China as a whole.

THE MEANING AND FORMS OF EVERYDAY RESISTANCE

James Scott (1985, 1990) introduced the concept of "everyday resistance" to capture the ways individuals privately defy authority when open, organized resistance is too dangerous or too difficult to arrange. He focused on acts of individual noncompliance and the use of private speech to transmit coded subversive messages out of the hearing of the powerful. Quite a few political scientists accustomed to looking for organized and public resistance have considered private grumbling and secret intransigence unworthy of attention. They have treated these behaviors as merely "prepolitical" or "epiphenomenal," having no appreciable political effect and implying a resigned acceptance of the order of things (Scott 1986:23–24). But as Scott pointed out, the most oppressive or exploitative states often severely proscribe the kinds of collective action we would expect them to provoke. Because protest is sure to draw punishment, few dare to engage in it. To explain the apparent paradox of highly oppressive social systems that are outwardly placid, Scott posited that many ordinary people bow to authority in public yet mock it in private. He challenged the received notion that autocratic regimes enjoy hegemony by comparing the "public transcript," consisting of people's behavior in public settings, with the "hidden transcript," recording their actions when they think themselves beyond the reach of surveillance (Scott 1985, 1990). Scott's analytical and research methods are well suited to analyzing Uyghur resistance in Xinjiang, for both practical and intellectual reasons. On the one hand, the extreme limitations placed on all research conducted in Xinjiang have made obligatory a departure from the standard model of structured, official interviews. On the other hand, Scott's distinction between public and private transcripts demonstrates quite well the jarringly different modes of expression encountered in Xinjiang, as well as the modes of domination and resistance they illustrate.[10]

Scott's method helps us recognize the forms of everyday resistance, but determining the significance of that resistance is more difficult. What do people intend by resisting party stratagems? What are the consequences of acts of peaceful and individual resistance? Although I am a great admirer of Scott's method, I believe we need to acknowledge and remedy an artificial assumption at its core. He posits a realm of resistance beyond the reach of oppressive or exploitative authority, a realm that may be as big as a coffeehouse or a plantation field, or as small as the inviolable interior space of an individual's mind. Scott does not give sufficient attention to the ways that power can structure those physical spaces and even mold the mind. "Where there is power, there is resistance," Michel Foucault once remarked, yet "resistance is never in a relationship of exteriority to power" (Foucault 1990:95).[11] As a consequence, resistance takes particular forms under particular structures of domination, to use Scott's expression, or what Foucault describes as relations of power. The nature of the CCP's power has influenced both the form and the meaning of resistance. Beijing has, to a substantial degree, been able to structure the realm of dissent and even to influence the conceptual categories with which Uyghurs resist. Pierre Bourdieu observed that "the specifically symbolic power to impose the principles of the construction of reality—in particular, social reality—is a major dimension of political power" (Bourdieu 1977:165). Because the construction of social reality is such a nebulous concept, political scientists have generally been leery of using it. As I have been at pains to argue, however, Uyghurs, Hans, and the party-state have been vying in precisely this domain, seeking to define and shape social reality to serve political ends. Thus to elaborate on Bourdieu's phrase, successfully altering the construction of social reality may in turn confer power on those resisting the party-state's version of reality—and it is for this reason that CCP officials have cracked down so consistently on "challenges in the ideological sphere" (Adila Baikere [Adalät Bäkri?] 2002; Feng Dazhen 1992; He Fulin 2002; Xiaokaiti Yiming 2002; "Xinjiang shouci pilu minzu fenlie shili zai yishi xingtai lingyu pohuai huodong de liu zhong xingshi" 2002).

The second aspect of Scott's theory that needs further exploration is its discussion of political effects. Scott and others have proposed that by engaging in "everyday resistance," actors can preserve their dignity and sense of personal efficacy by puncturing the narratives justifying their subordination to elites.[12] He also has suggested that they can challenge institutionalized discrimination or exploitation as well as insulate themselves against its harshest consequences. Scott has at least implied that such forms of resistance better serve the needs of the exploited and oppressed than some social revolutions have, but he allows that such strategies of resistance "are unlikely to do more than marginally affect . . . various forms of exploitation" (Scott 1985:29).

These assertions provoke further questions. What is the lower threshold of "everyday resistance"? There is a wide range between absolute noncooperation and happy compliance with the demands of power. If most behavior is a mixture of grumbling and obliging, at what point can it be considered resistance? Is it true, as one skeptic claims, that in their "zeal to uncover seeds of hope and traces of freedom in the mundane business of everyday life," devotees of Scott have focused on a range of "discourses and dispositions that range from expressions of alienated resentment to rueful complicity" (Maddox 1997:275–76)? If "everyday resistance" consists only of "discourses and dispositions," its political significance must surely be negligible. Does it, in fact, amount to nothing more than chatter and attitude? Theoretical debate will continue; here I seek to answer these questions concretely. On one hand, as I described in chapter 2, the Uyghurs' quiet struggles have had little perceptible impact on Beijing's policies in Xinjiang: what many of them regard (in the Scottian mode) as modes of domination and exploitation. On the other hand, these acts of defiance have been efficacious in a subtler but perhaps no less important way. The various forms of everyday resistance have, I believe, strengthened Uyghurs' collective identity and resolve to remain distinct from the "Chinese nation."

KEEPING THE LID ON: THE STATE'S ATTEMPTS
TO COMBAT ERRONEOUS THOUGHT

The previous chapter described the various ways party officials in Beijing and Ürümci have limited Uyghurs' capacity to exercise effective political authority and develop policies to protect their perceived collective interests in Xinjiang. Since 1957, officials also have tried to prevent Uyghurs and others from publicly discussing the absence of these crucial features of autonomy or from organizing to demand them. People's congresses at the provincial level and below remain largely ceremonial bodies and do not question the guidelines handed down by the party.[13] Never since the 1950s have there been institutions for freely airing, aggregating, and acting on the wishes of ordinary citizens, a fact about which Uyghurs have long been angry; nor are there any signs that party leaders intend to establish them. In the absence of such institutions, therefore, we must turn to the hidden transcript to find out Uyghurs' political views.

One of the few state-sponsored surveys of political attitudes in Xinjiang makes clear that social scientists employed by the state felt bound to inculcate proper ideas rather than impartially report opinions.[14] In 1990, researchers at the Xinjiang Academy of Social Sciences canvassed the views of some two hundred Uyghurs on the exploitation of resources, one of the most contentious matters in Xinjiang. Despite the risks of doing so, a handful of respondents admitted that they felt Xinjiang's oil and cotton belonged to "a particular group." The report heaped criticism on these people, contending that their views were mistaken and violated the constitution. When some respondents remarked that too many resources flowed out of Xinjiang and too few into the region, the authors observed that this "did not conform to reality." Finally, confronted with a substantial number of respondents who said that resource exploitation had caused intergroup relations to deteriorate (fully one-third of teachers polled, for instance), the researchers observed that such views were temporary and superficial and would be resolved by the proper execution of existing policies. The text indicates that the researchers closely questioned those offering "incorrect" responses and then remonstrated with them. The researchers thus concluded that "the 'resource psychology' of the vast majority of Uyghurs and other fraternal *minzu* is correct" (Liu Yongqian 1992).[15]

For years, peasants and workers in China's interior have sought to influence, by staging public protests, state policies that they opposed and have done so out of a deep conviction they were expressing legitimate objections. Social scientists have begun to give to this quest to register "rightful resistance" the attention it merits. Kevin O'Brien suggests that these groups have successfully articulated criticisms "couched in the language of loyal intentions" (O'Brien 1996:32). When actual practice has strayed from the state's explicit commitments, some groups have pressed successfully for redress, a point that I address further in chapter 4.

Uyghurs have long known that it is dangerous both to criticize publicly the party-state's policies and to speak publicly about the danger of speaking in public. Indeed, when the Han editors of the *Xinjiang Daily*, the party mouthpiece, published articles complaining that speech in Xinjiang was more restricted than in other parts of China and passed other articles along to the more widely read *Wenhui bao* in Shanghai, they were purged for doing so in the 1957 party "rectification" (McMillen 1979:90). A quarter century later, officials reversed the stifling repression of the Cultural Revolution and gave Uyghurs comparative freedom to assemble and speak in public in the 1980s (Rudelson 1997), but restrictions on speech clamped down again in the 1990s. The renewed restrictions both closed a possible outlet for discontent and further alienated many citizens.

Retaining some of the most strident language of the Mao era, the government has continued to speak of drawing a firm line between the people and their enemies in Xinjiang. It has shifted the line so dramatically and, at the same time, left it so ill defined that many peaceful people cannot help finding themselves on the wrong side. The atmosphere has become even more restrictive since September 11. In direct response to the imbroglio over Tursunjan Ämät with which this chapter began, Party Secretary Wang Lequan promulgated a document in February 2002 purporting to expose Uyghur separatists' "six forms of splittist activities." In condemning texts or performances that expressed or spread "dissatisfaction," the document referred to the open expression of discontent as a form of "separatist thought" and linked it to terrorist organizations (Becquelin 2004a: 44; "Xinjiang shouci pilu minzu fenlie shili zai yishi xingtai lingyu pohuai huodong de liu zhong xingshi" 2002).

RESISTANCE THROUGH CRITIQUE

In their quest to eliminate Uyghur separatism and bind Xinjiang fully to China, officials have depended heavily on ideological work (*sixiang zhengzhi gongzuo*), conducted in schools and workplaces and reinforced by regular messages in various media. For decades, teachers and officials have attempted to inculcate in Uyghurs the idea that they are integral members of a culturally plural "Chinese nation." They have relentlessly pressed the message of "*minzu* solidarity," arguing that Uyghurs and Hans are bound together by strong ties of mutual affection, class, and patriotism. Building on both ideas, these authorities have insisted that Uyghurs' highest interests are served by living in a united China and would be harmed by Xinjiang's separation. Officials and the media have constantly repeated the claim that most Uyghurs are patriots deeply committed to China, while the separatists number only a tiny handful. Despite decades of official efforts, however, these ideas have not become deeply or widely rooted in the Uyghur community.

Signs that Uyghurs and Hans did not share strong ties of either affect or identity could be found everywhere in the 1990s and 2000s, casting doubt on the slogan of "*minzu* solidarity."[16] Both Hans and Uyghurs habitually distinguished members of the other group in speech. Hans frequently referred to Uyghurs colloquially—and without further explanation—as *tamen* (them), by cultural category as *minzu* (implying that Hans are not also *minzu*), or by the offensive term *chantou* (head wrapper). Uyghurs used such terms as *mušu häqlär* (these people), the sarcastic phrase *bu akam* (this big brother of mine—mocking the implicit ranking of groups), the slur Qitay (Chinese),[17] or the religious expression *kapir* (infidel).

My Uyghur informants regularly emphasized the immutable differences between the groups in daily discourse or action. They often scolded one another for speaking Chinese or adopting the habits of Han, saying, for instance, "Kapir! Xänzu bop kätmä!" (Infidel! Don't go turning Chinese!).[18] A college teacher from southern Xinjiang reported that because Uyghur children in the south were taught from an early age to look down on Hans and to follow their parents in calling them Qitay and *kapir*, whole classes of students in the south simply refused to study Chinese.[19]

Uyghurs frequently remarked on the visible physical differences between Hans and Uyghurs. A Uyghur policeman sitting in a Han stylist's shop observed aloud to me that certain haircuts did not suit Hans because the "infidels had no noses to speak of"; he did not hesitate to say this openly because he knew the stylist understood no Uyghur.[20] Pious Uyghurs overlaid cultural differences with religious ones. On one occasion I witnessed a *muäzzin* refusing to enter a dental clinic run by Uyghurs and insisting on remaining outside while his prosthesis was adjusted because there were Hans inside. The dentist who treated him explained to me later that the cleric always refused, regarding sitting with Hans or speaking Chinese as sins.[21] Some held the difference between the groups to be racial as well as cultural.[22] A Uyghur college teacher told me one day, "I think the Han race is an inferior race. I know it's bad to say, but I think the whole race is a bad people."[23] People even spoke of Hans and Uyghurs as different species. An older Uyghur man on a crowded minibus told me the fundamental problem in Xinjiang was that "sheep and pigs are forced to live together in one pen" (sheep representing Uyghurs, pigs Hans), a line that elicited uproarious laughter from the other Uyghurs on the bus.[24]

On numerous occasions I heard Uyghurs insist that the fusion of the two groups was inconceivable, a point concretely reflected in the extremely low rates of intermarriage. A dissident intellectual living outside Qumul and distributing nationalist manifestos to friends in the 1990s told one of them that Uyghurs would never follow the example of the Hui and assimilate into Han culture because they "are stronger psychologically."[25] In 2002, on the heels of a discussion about Zordun Sabir's nationalist novel, a Uyghur reporter said to me, "Uyghurs and Hans are totally different. This is this and that is that. They will never come together. Despite all the talk, there's no way we're ever going to blend into one. We're absolutely unwilling to do so. This is impossible. So all this talk about *minzu* solidarity is nonsense."[26]

The talk about belonging and difference, whether of the fusion of groups or a distinct Uyghur identity, should not be read as only chatter. It also is performative. Han or Uyghur, peasant or party historian, "*invoked*" solidary groups in order to "*evoke* them, summon them, call them into being" (Brubaker 2002:166, italics in original). And by calling some groups into being, they often sought thereby to banish or erase others. For instance, Uyghurs rejected the idea that they belonged to the officially multicultural "Chinese nation" (*zhonghua minzu*). The term had been promulgated by the victorious integralist Chinese nationalists early in the century to justify the retention of the five large culturally distinct groupings (Han, Manchu, Mongol, Tibetan, and Muslim)—and their territories—after the Qing collapse, as discussed in chapter 1 (and see Leibold 2007). After 1949, party propagandists preserved the term but attempted to purge it of Han chauvinist connotations. Scholars produced a small mountain of books on the *zhonghua minzu* beginning in the late 1980s, clearly with the government's imprimatur, seeking to shore up national cohesiveness in the face of antistate protests in Xinjiang and Tibet and the fissiparous tendencies unleashed by China's uneven capitalist development (see, for example, Chen Linguo 1994; Chen Yuning 1994; Fei Xiaotong 1989; Li Kangping 1994; Wu Xiongwu 1994).[27]

The tension between scholars' and propagandists' attempts to fill the term with cultural content and their endeavors to avoid alienating any cultural group was not resolved. Without cultural content, the term was unlikely to evoke the slightest loyalty in China's citizens and thus to provide any cohesive force. If defined solely by attributes of Han culture, it would repel instead of attract the peripheral groups such as Tibetans and Uyghurs, thereby defeating its whole purpose. If propagandists delved too deeply into the cultural symbols and practices of non-Han groups, it would offend Hans, the crucial core constituency. The resultant hodgepodge had little power to attract the Uyghurs that I interviewed.

When asked the meaning of this concept, a high school teacher in Ürümci answered, "The term *zhonghua minzu* means Han; it has nothing to do with us."[28]

On another occasion, a broadcast journalist analyzed the parts of the term: "*Zhong* means *zhongguo*; *hua* refers to *huaxia*."[29] He noted that party propagandists casting about for widely resonant symbols had hit upon Yan Huang *zisun* (the progeny of emperors Yan and Huang) or *long zhi chuan* (descendants of the dragon). "It makes it obvious we're not included," he continued; "If that's China, we're on the outside."[30] A graduate student explained that the government's obvious intention in using the term was to assimilate non-Han groups into the Han, like an enormous grinding wheel. He was aware that Beijing had clearly set its sights on Uyghurs, yet he firmly believed they would not be drawn in.[31]

If scoffing at "*minzu* solidarity" and rejecting the idea of the *zhonghua minzu* were hazardous, advocating independence for Xinjiang was clearly much riskier. A number of my informants had spent time in jail either on suspicion of being separatists or for associating with those who were. Even so, they and others found moments while alone with me or among trusted friends to talk about the forbidden topic.[32] I was taken by surprise the first time this happened. In December 1995 I met an editor in an Ürümci press for the first time through a mutual friend. As we looked over some rare historical materials in his possession, he began to speak about the history of the Uyghur independence movement beginning in the 1930s. Minutes later, he mentioned what would happen when China "disintegrated" (*jieti*), using the very term that had been applied to the Soviet breakup. Taking my lack of expression for skepticism, he assured me that China would follow the Soviet example. He went on to say that Xinjiang University, where he knew I was studying, was a hotbed of independence-minded teachers and students, the epicenter of most popular protests in the 1980s.[33] While my later encounters confirmed his description, it was some time before I met anyone else as bold as he had been. A few months later, at a party in another section of Ürümci, a group of Uyghur intellectuals who were close friends shared their dissatisfaction with the lack of human rights in Xinjiang. One turned to me and observed that while there surely could not be electronic bugs everywhere, phone lines were definitely bugged; he regularly heard odd clicks on the line. "When someone talks about Xinjiang's independence on the phone," he said to me, "it's best just to say 'oh, hmm, I see.' To respond is to invite trouble."[34]

In October 1996, a student from Kashgar, herself an ardent advocate of independence in private settings, told me about three of her friends from that city, all top students, who had recently suffered for their outspokenness. One stayed in Kashgar for college, and his two friends went to universities in China proper. He wrote them both a letter complaining about the political situation in Xinjiang and imagining that if the region were independent, the three of them would be high officials. A classmate of one of the other students saw the letter, became alarmed, and turned the student in. Eventually all three were brought back to Ürümci and sentenced to eight years in prison.[35]

In the spring of 1997, many Uyghurs brought up the wish for independence as Hong Kong's retrocession approached. It seems quaint more than a decade later, but there was a widespread belief, despite the constant barrage of triumphal messages emanating from Beijing and the gigantic clock ticking down the seconds in Tian'anmen Square, that Britain would not relinquish its colony without a fight. Xinjiang was rife with rumors that Uyghur organizations were preparing to take advantage of the ensuing chaos to stage a military uprising. At various points that spring, a baker told me cheerfully as I bought my daily bread that Xinjiang would soon be independent; a hotel guest assured me the cause would receive God's help; a group of taxi drivers predicted to me at curbside that July would bring independence; and a gathering of police spent several hours alternately lamenting Xinjiang's colonization by China instead of the Soviet Union and speaking hopefully about the possibility that the rumors of a planned uprising were true. At the end of April, a student quietly asked me, "How much time do Uyghurs have?" Mistaking this for a question about their eventual assimilation, I began to speak about language preservation and so on when he cut me off impatiently. He was sure that Uyghurs *would* become independent; he simply wanted my judgment of whether it would take ten years or fifty. In May a broadcast reporter told me privately that "all Uyghurs want independence," even if the majority were too afraid to admit it.[36]

Hong Kong's peaceful retrocession seemed to take many people by surprise. The morning after Hong Kong's return, on July 1, I sat with a group of students utterly sick at heart that nothing had happened the night before. They explained that a significant portion of their university's student body had been herded to a nearby park under the watchful eye of police to prevent them from participating in any potential uprising.[37]

It also was clear that more practical Uyghurs believed they would need outside help to bring about changes in Xinjiang and that they hoped it would come from the United States.[38] At an evening party in January 1997, a Uyghur intellectual stated, "Every time Clinton criticizes the human rights situation in China, human rights improve. The United States really is the policeman of the world, and Uyghurs like that," a sentiment readily confirmed by the other young men at the party.[39] In early May of that year a rural cadre said to me at a gathering near Turpan, "We have no freedom. We place a lot of hope in Clinton and America," only to be shushed by his colleagues for discussing politics with a foreigner.[40] Several years later, NATO's intervention in Kosovo inspired new hope of foreign support. In August 1999 a group of Uyghurs attacked the Public Security Bureau in Lop County after the sentencing of accused separatists. While attacking the bureau, the protestors are reported to have shouted, "We'll invite the U.S. and NATO to come, and we'll blow up Xinjiang" (J K P Š U A R komiteti täšwiqat bölümi 2000?:49). Such hopes would, of course, be dashed a few years later when Washington listed the obscure Uyghur independence group "Eastern Turkestan Islamic Movement" (ETIM) as a terrorist organization (see chapters 5 and 6).

On a return trip in the summer of 2002, only months before that announcement, I heard from a number of new informants about their hopes for independence, although both they and acquaintances from previous trips with whom I had reconnected were quite pessimistic. Two young professionals in Ürümci, speaking under the cover of crowd noise in a restaurant, used a formula I would hear on many occasions: that all or nearly all Uyghurs hoped for independence but that the government had successfully co-opted members of the elite with jobs and other perks.[41] A short time later, as we spoke in a park, a soft-spoken young teacher brought up the gulf between very religious Uyghurs and others. Some people had responded to the call of proselytes and placed all their hope in religious salvation, giving up any interest in independence, but they were a small minority, he claimed. Asked whether people not drawn to reinvigorated Islam spoke of independence, he replied, "Of course, we all do. All of us Uyghur teachers talk about it privately among ourselves, when we know no one is listening. We all wish for it, but we never say anything publicly."[42]

These anecdotes are illustrative in that they show that some Uyghurs sharply distinguish themselves from Hans, reject their inclusion in the Chinese nation, and wish for independence. They cannot, of course, tell us how widespread these views are or what their consequences might be. Two important surveys conducted in Xinjiang by Herbert Yee supplement these ethnographic findings, although the researcher himself acknowledged that the results must be regarded with some skepticism. Based on studies carried out in Ürümci in 2000 (with 393 respondents) and in five other Xinjiang cities in 2001 (with 367 respondents), Yee concluded that the relations between Uyghurs and Hans were tense and that Uyghurs identified very strongly with their group and with the territory of the XUAR.[43] Yee also found in the first survey that whereas more than 70 percent of Hans strongly believed Xinjiang had been part of China since ancient times, only about 40 percent of Uyghurs said they did, and he speculated that because of the sensitivity of the question, many of the Uyghurs responding affirmatively were not being candid. In the same survey, only 36 percent of Uyghurs strongly agreed that separatist activities harmed everyone (compared with 64 percent of Hans), and fewer than half of the Uyghurs polled agreed *at all* with the government's claim that separatism was the main threat to Xinjiang's stability, while 80 percent of Hans supported that claim.[44] While conducting the second survey, Yee and his collaborators met with intransigence from many local cadres. Officials eliminated some questions and changed others to look "like propaganda slogans," prevented the random selection of informants, urged the researchers to abandon the study altogether, and actually withheld all the survey responses from two field sites. Under the circumstances, Yee was not surprised that 40 percent of those polled declined to respond at all, and he assumed that many of the remaining respondents gave "politically correct" responses. Yee therefore began his article with the caveat that the results should be read "with great caution." Again, though, he found that Uyghurs identified more strongly with Xinjiang than did their Han counterparts and that the two groups were mutually hostile and mistrustful. Yee regarded as "inconceivable" the survey's finding that 87 percent of Uyghurs were proud of being Chinese citizens (Yee 2003:35–36, 44, 50; 2005:438–39, 445).

Thus far we have considered individuals' comments on politics in Xinjiang, captured in ethnographic interviews that may not be representative, and broad survey samples that may not be reliable. We can complement those findings by scrutinizing the messages in published music, poems, and novels. Because they require the collaboration of many individuals for their production and dissemination and because they circulate widely, such works offer a particularly valuable window into popular attitudes.

POPULAR CULTURE: CONSUMING AND SPREADING RESISTANCE

Many scholars have studied songs, poems, jokes, and literature in attempting to understand popular politics in Xinjiang.[45] They have looked at these sources because so many other avenues for political speech or resistance have been closed off. The progressive confinement of public speech and action, combined with the administrative and economic policies described in the previous chapter, has increased popular resentment. By the late 1990s, popular culture was one of the only avenues for the public display of discontent.

Publicly circulating audiotapes are particularly rich resources for studying that discontent. Early in the reform era, several tapes containing veiled or oblique critiques of life and politics in Xinjiang made it through the gauntlet of censors and were published by officially sanctioned media organizations. In addition, street-side duplication stands in both northern and southern Xinjiang enabled the dissemination of songs, poems, and jokes, some recorded in private homes, away from state surveillance (Dautcher 2000; Harris 2001). If individual acts of everyday resistance sent ripples only among a circle of friends, songs and other performances could call a larger community into being. While listening to and sharing popular songs and poetry, Uyghurs could imagine that those in other neighborhoods and other towns were listening and seething or laughing, just as they were (Anderson 1991).

Furthermore, whereas private conversations remained firmly part of James Scott's "hidden transcript," taped performances provided more concrete, tangible tokens of resistance. Several features of the tapes caused them to occupy an ambiguous space in Scott's schema. First, because officials abandoned policies strongly encouraging Hans to develop proficiency in Uyghur in the 1950s and the number who chose to learn the language thereafter was vanishingly small, performances in Uyghur were incomprehensible to the vast majority of Hans. We might describe them as private Uyghur conversations concealed in Han public space.[46] Second, as the exasperated Professor Wang indicated, their imagery was allusive and ambiguous rather than direct. He expressed frustration that the authors and performers could always deny any secret meaning in their words. Uyghurs who were found with subversive recorded or printed materials could protect themselves by pointing out the words were not their own. They could also claim not to detect any hidden messages imputed to them.

Uyghur musicians in the 1980s and early 1990s made a specialty of allegorical jeremiads. For instance, in a 1993 recording, the hugely popular male vocalist Abdulla Abdurehim sang, "I stand by the waterside, longing for a drink, but when I lick my lips, they smack my mouth / . . . As I lie on the riverbank, the stones prick me; the unjust ones throw more stones at me." After describing each form of abuse, Abdulla moaned, "I said thanks, I said a thousand thanks." Another popular singer, Mähmud Sulayman, lamented that "I can't go where I want / they've chained my neck and I can't move / . . . these mountains are tall / I want to ascend them / but my wings are bound, so I can't."[47] In language that was necessarily vague and allegorical, these singers described a life of suffering and confinement. Prevented from slaking thirst, stoned without cause, immobilized in full sight of their goal, they could do nothing but sing of defeat and frustration.[48] These songs quickly achieved wide currency. Concerts were mobbed. Shop speakers inundated bazaars with their refrains, and groups of college students still sang them with great feeling in the mid-1990s.

But by that time, the period of relative openness ushered in by Deng Xiaoping and Hu Yaobang a decade earlier was already coming to a close. Some of the tapes approved for distribution were later banned or taken out of the market. *Pighan* (*Rooster's Cry*), a widely circulated tape of allegorical poems all legally published in the 1980s, includes one that describes the anger of a generous host whose guest occupies the best seat at the table and never leaves. In another poem, a Uyghur narrator speaks caustically to a statue of a Han soldier of how comradely cooperation had turned into domination and promises of abundant meals had been followed by a Barmecide feast. Another tape collected poems by Rozi Sayit entitled *Dehqan bolmaq täs* (*It's Hard to Be a Peasant*) and described the excruciating labor and grinding poverty of peasants, understood to symbolize Uyghurs. *Pärwayim peläk* (*Destiny Is My Concern*), a tape by the popular musician Ömärjan Alim, contains another song about a guest who never left, but it was banned after its release.[49]

The singers also faced censorship of their public performances. Abdulla Abdurehim was forbidden by 1996 to sing either of the songs just described. Another singer, Küräš Sultan, given to laments about the plight of peasants, had his music banned and his equipment taken away in 1993, and indeed could not perform at all until he left the country in 1996 (Hoh 2004).[50] Enforcement has not always been consistent, nor have the guidelines been clear.[51] Two writers in Ürümci said in 1997 that they had heard "pro-independence" songs performed at weddings on several occasions, but one also said he had seen a singer led away from a wedding in handcuffs.[52] In 1996, the popular singer Abdurehim Häyit was not allowed to tour and had difficulty releasing his recordings (Smith 2007). Yet in 1999 he was unsure what the government would do about his political songs, like "Stubborn Guest," another song about a guest who would not leave, or "Rooster," which described awakening the people—a classic nationalist trope (Fitzgerald 1996a).[53] Abdurehim Häyit told a foreign reporter that officials had not yet said anything about the songs that he acknowledged were political, "so I don't know if I have a problem" (Strauss 1999). Within three years he had a problem. Censors had forbidden him to record or perform many of his songs. In March 2002 he reported that he "hadn't performed for months" and was permitted to play only previously approved songs as part of an officially sponsored musical troupe (Forney 2002b).

Evidence from the early 2000s indicates that the government had changed its tactics. Rather than waiting to determine the "social impact" of songs, Ürümci officials required professional singers to submit their lyrics to a censorship committee before performing them in public or recording them. Censors could instruct artists to change gloomy images into more positive ones—for instance, replacing regret at the approach of winter with hopeful anticipation of spring—and song lists for concerts also faced official scrutiny to guard against too negative a performance (Taynen 2004:33).

The censorship of humbler musicians had stepped up as well. The very tunes forbidden by the government remained the ones that people wanted hired musicians to play at weddings. Bahargül, the Ürümci service worker introduced at the beginning of this chapter, told me that by the end of the 1990s when she and her friends negotiated with wedding musicians, they were given long lists of proscribed songs. She complained that "whenever a good song comes along, they ban it."[54]

The party's forbidding the publication or performance of songs was not unexpected. The year 1991 had begun with the public vilification of poet and historian Turghun Almas, who had published a series of articles and books limning a "national" history for Uyghurs completely distinct from those of Hans and China.[55] In a week-long conference, officials and scholars condemned his work for factual and political errors. As party secretaries led criticisms of Turghun in work units throughout Xinjiang, agents of the News and Publications Bureau cleared his books from shops and later ostentatiously burned them along with other offending texts.[56]

A decade later, officials launched several new rounds of clampdowns on publications. In April 1998, officials in Xinjiang seized the opportunity of the tenth annual national campaign against pornography to round up "illegal publications" with suspect political and religious content ("China: Xinjiang Confiscates Publications Which Undermine Unity" 1998). In March 2002, the government announced a new phase in the "struggle against splittists on the terrain of ideology."[57] Officials burned thousands of books in late March, and in April police and other bureaucrats again made the rounds of bookstalls to "clean up the market in printed matter." The campaign officially aimed at eliminating pornography and illegal reproductions of copyright books. A news story at the time explained the plan to close down 52 of 118 periodicals in Xinjiang because of their low circulation and "poor quality" (Agence France-Presse 2002b). Uyghurs understood the principal targets to be religious texts published outside state supervision and other works that might foment antiparty feelings. Informants reported in 2002 that these included more copies of Turghun Almas's work, which up until then had apparently evaded the braziers, as well as works of history and fiction by the younger author Abduwäli Äli. Officials reportedly took the trouble to locate and destroy the printer's plates. Yet as one Kashgar resident remarked with pleasure, "copies remain in private hands."[58]

The successful posthumous release of Zordun Sabir's trilogy *Ana yurt* (*Motherland*) might well have been one of the provocations for this new official initiative. As with the highly popular novels of Abdurehim Ötkür, Zordun's final book was a broadly drawn historical novel, but one about a subject that no previous author had dared touch: the Ghulja Revolution of 1944 that established the independent Eastern Turkestan Republic (1944–1949). The historical setting allowed Zordun to insert critical passages appealing to Uyghurs—and later appalling to state censors, even though they had gone over it many times. A professional with inside knowledge of the publishing industry claimed that the book had been scrutinized at twenty official meetings, revised at least sixteen times, retracted soon after its first printing, divested of two pages in the third volume, and only then released to the public.[59] Another informant pointed to the publisher's introduction, which observed that the revolution achieved "glorious victory after accepting the correct leadership of the CCP" and had properly been labeled a part of the Chinese people's revolution by Mao (Zordun Sabir 2000:1).[60] "They had to put this in to get the thing published," she said.

I was lent a copy of the novel that had fortunately been annotated by one of its previous readers, described by the lender as "really nationalist" (*bäk millätci*). The annotations pointed me to the passages that reader had found most provocative. As expected, the underlined sections exploited the ambiguity of the novel form: in context they addressed matters of the time, but out of context they could have been written about the present, as the reader's marginalia made clear. Next I discuss three of the twelve heavily annotated passages in the nearly six-hundred-page first volume.

Early in the book, the narrator admires the verdant Ili River valley, seat of the Ghulja Revolution, and soliloquizes about Xinjiang's violent history:

> Hey Uyghur, you're just a sheep feeding in the pastures. Even when a wolf or bear comes, you think that any animal is a sheep just like you, you just think it, too, should graze in the fields. Its target is not green grass, but you. It plans to make a meal of you, to wipe away your pastures. You don't know this. (Zordun Sabir 2000:99)

A few pages later, the narrator silently curses the driver of the cart he rides:

> This guy knows nothing but eating and sleeping. What is a people (*xälq*)? What are their burdens, what are their hopes? What is a *millät*,[61] and how is it faring? These kinds of questions he's never thought about; 99.99 percent of the [people] are just like that. It is for this reason that other *millät* rule this people. (103)

The reader heavily underlined these passages, which clearly lament Uyghurs' being ruled by Hans (though the latter word is never used) and attribute this to naïveté or inattention. A third passage questions official claims of equality between Hans and Uyghurs:

> Are there Uyghurs in government positions and among soldiers and police? Even if there are a few here and there, do they have power? None, absolutely none.... Immigrants are esteemed, locals despised. The owner of the house starves while the guest is full, the home's proprietor is the servant while the alley cat is master! ... Whoever bemoans the people's crying dies easily. Whoever sells out the people wins, whoever speaks the truth has his tongue cut out, whoever fixes a glance on dirty dealings has his eyes dug out. (382–83)

The narrator names Sheng Shicai, governor of Xinjiang at the time, as the target of his wrath. But the descriptions of token powerless Uyghur officials, guests who fatten themselves on the host's wealth, truth tellers who are brutally punished, and traitors who are rewarded clearly excited other associations in the reader. He underlined the passage twice and wrote several exclamation points in the margin. The reader gave the same treatment to a passage in the final pages of the first volume. A frustrated Uyghur officer bemoans the lack of strategic knowledge among the populace:

> Anger, resentment, and heroism have ripened within us. But military knowledge is lacking. Younger brother, turn your children into soldiers; they should study firing rifles, fighting battles, vanquishing enemies. Unless we do this, we will always and everywhere be bullied. (577)

In sum, the reader found and marked passages in the long novel that explain why Uyghurs are ruled by others, describe the terrible results, and cry out for a military solution to their problems. It is not a surprise, either, that many Uyghurs read the work voraciously[62] or that the Publications and News Bureau quietly removed the book from the market only a few months after its release.[63]

NEW TACTIC: JAIL FOR DISSIDENT WRITERS

Since the late 1990s the party-state has punished heterodoxy with increasing rigor, advancing from merely banning or censoring works to actually imprisoning their authors. Three more examples from recent years are particularly striking. In 1998, the historian Tokhti Tunyaz returned from Japan, where he was in a PhD program, to his home region to conduct research. State Security officials immediately took him into custody and, after holding him incommunicado for thirty months, sentenced him to eleven years in prison on the charge of "revealing state secrets." All available evidence suggests that the so-called state secrets consisted of a fifty-year old document given to him by a government library employee. A report in a Chinese national security periodical in 2001 further accused Tokhti of "absorbing Western ideas" and engaging in "*minzu* splittism": the first charge is rather laughable on its face, and the second one, intentionally vague (RFA 2006c). Apparently, Tokhti posed a threat only because he was researching Uyghur history, a subject closely regulated by the party-state, as I discussed in chapter 1. His arrest and lengthy sentence offer eloquent testimony to the importance that Beijing and Ürümci attribute to historiography.

The second example is that of Tursunjan Ämät, the poet mentioned at the beginning of the chapter who was arrested in January 2002 for reciting a subversive poem at a public event. A party official in Xinjiang later told a foreign reporter that Tursunjan had challenged government policies toward non-Hans. The official charged that the act of reading critical poetry was "terrorism in the spiritual form" (Marquand 2003). Tursunjan was thrown in jail, and the officials who allowed him to perform were reprimanded. As mentioned earlier, Wang Lequan codified the crime less than a month after, and directly because of, Tursunjan's performance ("Xinjiang shouci pilu minzu fenlie shili zai yishi xingtai lingyu pohuai huodong de liu zhong xingshi" 2002). His offense was airing discontent in public performance. In other words, he was guilty of inviting people to think about their dissatisfaction.

In late 2004, the writer Nurmuhämmät Yasin published a story in *Qäšqär ädäbiyati* (*Kashgar Literature*) entitled "The Wild Pigeon." The protagonist in the story is a young wild pigeon who inadvertently flies into a region inhabited by tame pigeons living among humans who fed, captured, and sometimes ate them. The undomesticated bird quizzes his tame counterparts about their souls, only to find to his amazement that they don't know the word. Fed and watered by their keepers, the birds neither know nor seek freedom. Puzzled and frightened by the things the locals tell him and his father's prior warnings against straying into the region, he tries to fly home, only to find himself trapped by the keepers; he clearly was betrayed by one of the local pigeons. Tortured and broken while in captivity, he decides in the end to eat a poisoned strawberry provided by a thoughtful friend and thus escape his condition by dying (Nurmuhämmät Yasin 2004).

Caught flat-footed again, the censors must have realized in retrospect that the allegory was stuffed full of political barbs.[64] The wild pigeon could represent a rebellious Uyghur youth born locally and unbowed by local pressures, although it seems likelier that he stood for an activist from Central Asia who had succeeded in, or blundered into, crossing the border. The tame pigeons with no concept of the soul clearly represented the majority of Xinjiang's Uyghurs, lulled by state jobs or material comforts into an illusory sense of contentment. Their lack of understanding of the soul might be a reference to the consequences of atheism education and the crackdown on religious practice. No longer allowed to study the Qur'an or receive private religious instruction and subjected to years of education in atheism, ordinary Uyghurs might be seen as having been stripped of appreciation for spiritual life and thus divested of spirit. The soul might also have represented the inclination to live independently rather than under the keepers' control. The pigeon keepers clearly were Hans, and this had two implications. First, it made Uyghurs and Hans different species. Second, it cast Hans as their jailers and exploiters, and Uyghurs as beasts living eternally separate lives, literally fattened to feed Hans. In a particularly sharp exchange, an old pigeon explains to the young pigeon that "it is a necessity for mankind to be able to catch us and eat us.... No pigeon among us is permitted to object to this arrangement." The poisoned strawberry might be one of several things: it could represent open political activity, alluring and satisfying but deadly. It might symbolize a drug, such as alcohol or heroin, which provides a temporary thrill but eventually kills its users. One important feature of the story is the pessimistic conclusion that the protagonist can escape from this intolerable condition only by dying.

In November 2004, when the critical content of the story came to the officials' attention, Nurmuhämmät Yasin was jailed and was sentenced to ten years for splittism in a February 2005 trial (RFA 2005b). In November 2005 it was revealed that the journal's editor, Küräš Husäyin, himself had received a three-year sentence for agreeing to publish the story (RFA 2005a).

TALKING BACK TO THE STATE MEDIA

Uyghurs share their displeasure with the political order in Xinjiang through private talk; they listen to subversive songs and read heterodox literature and share them with their friends. They also find ways to resist by refusing to respond to the official media in the expected way. In 1997, Hans viewed the televised Hong Kong retrocession ceremony with great enthusiasm, while Uyghurs, resenting the outpouring of Han nationalism, waited for a political opportunity that failed to appear (Bovingdon 2002a:67).[65] Five years later, it was the Uyghurs who celebrated while Hans groaned at the results of the 2002 World Cup competition. An otherwise politically circumspect informant described to me watching the Turkish–Chinese match in a room of both Uyghurs and Hans. Uyghurs showed their delight each time Turkey surged ahead, and the Hans became increasingly angry. My informant recalled with amusement that one Han had chastised the Uyghurs in the room, saying, "Since you're Chinese citizens, you should cheer for China. Aren't you loyal to China?"[66] Another participant in the conversation asked, grinning, whether I had appreciated the blue flag of the Uyghur independence movement that someone had contrived to drape behind the Chinese goal and that therefore appeared on the television screen during the Turks' offensive attacks.[67] On another occasion, several teachers reported the disturbing (and, it should be said, suspicious) news that officials at schools in Ürümci had disciplined students for cheering the Turkish team, claiming that three students at the Normal University had even been expelled and arrested.[68]

Uyghurs even defied the regime by selecting radio stations. Immediately following the 1949 revolution, Beijing imposed strict party control of the media in the name of guarding against ideological attack from lingering counterrevolutionary elements. Although the reform era produced an explosion of new popular magazines and presses and some observers have speculated that Beijing is gradually losing (if not willingly relinquishing) its overall control of the media (BBC Monitoring 2006; Lynch 1999), it also is quite clear that party officials have kept a close watch on their political content. Hu Jintao's administration has stepped up pressure on various media, appointing tens of thousands of "Internet cops," closing maverick newspapers, and jailing outspoken journalists (French 2006; Goldman 2006; Hong Yan 2006; RFA 2006b).[69] The job of maintaining a monopoly on the media has always been more difficult on the periphery, whether in the southeast, where residents in coastal Fujian or Guangdong could receive signals from Taiwan and Hong Kong, or in Xinjiang. Radio stations in Central Asia had been beaming programs in Uyghur and Qazaq into Xinjiang since the Sino-Soviet split in the 1960s and stopped doing so only during the rapprochement in the 1980s. In the 1980s and beyond, broadcasts from the BBC and the Voice of America continued to provide outside news. The top secret Document no. 7 promulgated by the Politburo in 1996 proposed that the government greatly expand the construction of broadcast and relays stations in order to extend coverage to the remotest parts of the region. The aim was to "firmly occupy the ideological and cultural stronghold" (Human Rights Watch 1999:11).

Nonetheless, by listening to those foreign radio reports, many Uyghurs have continued to reject the party's attempt to impose a single interpretation of Xinjiang's politics. There is strong evidence that even though the government invested heavily in jamming equipment, many people in Xinjiang not only could receive radio from abroad but went to some lengths to do so. One foreign journalist found in interviews that people tired of propaganda relished news from the outside world, even though some felt the broadcasts raised false hopes. Many were saving up for the best shortwave radios they could buy in order to pull in signals through the jamming (Ingram 2001). A secret XUAR party report revealed officials' concern that citizens were listening to foreign stations. It observed that in southern Xinjiang, cadres and masses "listen one after another to the radio programs, and in Aqto, [Khotän], [Qaraqash], Lop, and other counties and cities, stores have sold out of small radios" (J K P Š U A R komiteti täšwiqat bölümi 2000?:52). Another report from the same year claimed that throughout the 1990s, separatists inside Xinjiang had been listening to broadcasts from "enemy stations" nearby and then distributing the contents in handbills (Yang Faren 2000:243). Citizens have also taken advantage of foreign media outlets to report on local events themselves, making frequent use of the toll-free call-in numbers broadcast by Radio Free Asia. On a 2003 trip to Xinjiang, a foreign reporter agreed to allow a local to use his cellular phone to place a call and then later learned it had been to the Radio Free Asia number (Reuters 2003).[70] Subsequent reports indicate the government has attempted to paralyze the call-in line by attacking it with robot callers (Southerland 2005). The government also reportedly spent $40 million in 2004 to purchase more powerful jamming antennas from France (Agence France-Presse 2004a; Southerland 2005).[71]

There is little doubt that people have kept track of the doings of émigrés through the international media. A young translator from southern Xinjiang told me proudly that his former teacher, now on the faculty of a university in Japan, announced soon after moving there that he opposed the Chinese government.[72] Some Uyghurs have even visited dissident Web sites abroad and disseminated their contents, despite China's blocking system. Enterprising computer users inside Xinjiang were able to work around the Internet police and post pictures and a story about Räbiya Qadir's reunion with her husband, the well-known Uyghur dissident Sidiq Rozi. Her children in Xinjiang later told her that they had seen the pictures (Southerland 2005).[73]

CONCLUSION

What have Uyghurs achieved by engaging in everyday resistance? Have they managed to influence official policy or governance in Xinjiang? Have they marginally improved life in Xinjiang, as James Scott might have predicted? Or have the singing, joking, and chatter in fact had "no practical effect," as a pessimistic dissident official put it to me privately in 1997? The evidence suggests that in the face of Uyghur intransigence, Beijing's regulation of religious and cultural life in Xinjiang has grown tighter over time. Restrictions on religious practice have increased; arrests for suspicious behavior or ideas have gone up; and the government recently all but eliminated the use of Uyghur as a language of instruction in college while simultaneously mandating that Uyghur children begin studying Chinese in kindergarten (Dwyer 2005). It would be hard to say the resistance had slowed, let alone reversed, the tightening rigor of laws and regulations. The CCP has had little incentive to grant greater freedom.

In sum, everyday resistance has availed Uyghurs little in moderating Chinese policies, and there is scant evidence that it has improved the material lot of individual Uyghurs. What the various forms of resistance have done is strengthen and keep in circulation the ideas that Uyghurs are fundamentally distinct from Hans, that they are not part of the Chinese nation but constitute a nation unto themselves, and that they would be best suited by another political order. It is safe to predict that party-state will not eliminate everyday resistance even if it succeeds in blanketing the airwaves of Xinjiang with its own messages, blocking unwanted messages from outside with jammers, arresting writers, burning books, silencing singers, and confiscating tapes. Uyghurs have engaged in everyday resistance even when they had no opportunity or did not dare to take part in open and organized resistance, and they have continued to resist even after state security organs have virtually eliminated acts of organized public defiance anywhere in Xinjiang. Under conditions of extreme repression, it may be the only index of the depth and breadth of Uyghur discontent.

COLLECTIVE ACTION AND VIOLENCE

OPEN RESISTANCE IN XINJIANG

The last chapter focused on "everyday resistance," on the premise that most Uyghurs usually have been deterred from resisting openly by the threat of harsh punishments. Newspaper reports in the 1990s revealed to the outside world for the first time since the 1940s that Xinjiang was occasionally rocked by serious political violence or mass protests. These reports, coming on the heels of demonstrations in Tibet in the late 1980s and the collapse of the Soviet Union in 1991, fed speculation that China faced a looming crisis and might disintegrate along the lines of its former neighbor. Not until the end of the decade did new information emanating from China make it apparent that unrest in Xinjiang had occurred with some regularity over the previous fifty years.

This chapter turns to the evidence of open and organized resistance in the region and to the representation of that resistance. Rather than describing every reported major organized uprising or violent antistate attack (for that, see Dillon

2004), I focus on the frequency of protests and political violence and on the aims and strategies of the participants. There is no doubt that the events took place, with very few possible exceptions, but to stop at a straightforward accounting of the events and to ignore the ways they have been depicted by the Chinese government, Uyghur organizations, and other entities would be to miss a crucial dimension of the contention in Xinjiang.

The thousands of arrests each year since 2001 suggest that organizations have persisted and new ones are springing up, despite the state's repressive efforts. But they also show that repression has deterred all but the most violent and fearless. Whereas large-scale protests had been largely peaceful from 1979 through the 1980s (which is not to say there were no violent events), by the 1990s small-scale riots or violent attacks had become more common. This shift began long before the "strike hard" campaigns, mentioned in chapter 2, officially emerged in Xinjiang in 1996.[1] Forceful suppression of protests beginning in the late 1980s, the political atmosphere in China following the June 4 massacre in 1989, and the enactment of stricter regulations for demonstrations in 1990 combined to keep off the streets many people who might have joined protests in the more open climate of the 1980s. Repression increased even more dramatically after 2001, and episodes of protest fell further.

Curiously, official Chinese commentary depicted not a fall but an alarming rise in protest in the new millennium. In 2001, the chairman of the XUAR government, Ablät Abdurišit, announced that "the situation of Xinjiang is better than ever in history. . . . [T]here has been no room for national separatists and religious extremists. By no means is Xinjiang a place where violence and terrorist accidents take place very often" (quoted in Bao Lisheng 2001). Nonetheless, in 2005 the XUAR party secretary, Wang Lequan, warned ominously that "in Xinjiang the separatists, religious extremists and violent terrorists are all around us—they're very active" (quoted in Sommerville 2005). Chinese academics suggested, too, that separatist threats and activity had exploded in that four-year period.[2] In other words, there is no obvious relationship between official descriptions of the threat and the actual trends revealed by the independently compiled record of public protests. The depictions answer the exigencies of representational politics, rather than revealing the party-state's perception of the threats.

This chapter makes four points. First, the sheer number of protests in Xinjiang since 1980 reinforces the contention of chapters 2 and 3 that the Uyghurs' dissatisfaction with the region's governance is deep and broad. The quantity of documented protest events also casts doubt on the Chinese government's argument that major demonstrations were the work of a tiny minority of separatists and that the majority of participants took part out of naïveté or simple excitement. In addition, the political content of the demonstrations, as expressed in banners and shouted slogans, leaders' programmatic statements, and handbills circulated secretly, strengthen the case that the specific criticisms raised by informants and artists were representative of widespread complaints and not the unhappiness of an isolated minority. At the same time, the evidence demonstrates that everyday resistance and the comparatively rare episodes of organized protest are part of a continuous political field.

Second, since protests have increased steadily throughout China proper since the 1990s, the dramatic decline in protests in Xinjiang (and Tibet) since 2001 is an anomaly. Whereas Xinjiang was once regarded as the wildest and most violent part of China, it appears to have ceded that reputation to the contentious factories and farmlands of China proper. Third, even though Uyghurs have expressed deep dissatisfaction with governance in Xinjiang and pointedly called for policy changes, Beijing and Ürümci have almost never responded by accommodating those demands or entertaining public discussions of the concerns. Instead, officials have strengthened unpopular policies and cracked down on both political speech and spaces for assembly outside party control. In other words, they have sought to limit as far as possible the further public articulation of discontent with those policies. Such unyielding responses have not resolved Uyghurs' complaints and instead have often exacerbated them. Thus the anomalous drop in unrest in this famously contentious region cannot plausibly be attributed to the Uyghurs' increased political contentment.

Nor is it easy to argue that rising material wealth has eased Uyghurs' concerns with politics, given their high unemployment rate and the dire poverty of the Uyghur countryside in the south. Rather, the fall in protests reflects substantially increased political repression. Central Asian governments' harsher suppression of Uyghur groups beginning in the late 1990s under strong pressure from Beijing also removed external sources of support for antistate activity in Xinjiang.

UNREST AND THE SOVIET EXAMPLE OF STATE DISINTEGRATION

After the fall of communism in Eastern Europe and Moscow and the disintegration of the Soviet Union, Yugoslavia, and Czechoslovakia, many observers wondered whether China would follow suit. One motivation of various studies comparing the Soviet Union and China was surely a desire to avoid being caught flat-footed by sudden cataclysmic political changes, such as had shocked Sovietologists in 1991. Yet as the Chinese Communist Party continued to maintain its firm grip on power and the Chinese state seemed to remain strong year after year, talk of

China's being bound to follow the Soviet example grew progressively quieter. Then the heightened attention to conflict in China's northwestern region of Xinjiang after September 11, and the publication in early 2006 of startling statistics on surging unrest in the Chinese heartland, seemed to make talk of Soviet-style regime and state disintegration plausible again.[3] The figures on the rise and magnitude of protest events throughout China invited renewed comparisons with the revolutions of 1989 to 1991 that ended the reign of communist parties throughout the Soviet bloc. Discussion of violent unrest in Xinjiang again recalled the specter of the Soviet Union's collapse, which began with protest and bloodshed in the Baltics, as well as the bloody departure of Bosnia from Yugoslavia. Reports of possible "Muslim terrorism" in Xinjiang, many of them hastily assembled by intelligence bureaus around the world, called to mind the brutal struggle in Chechnya as well as intrastate conflicts farther afield in Aceh and Mindanao.[4]

Chinese scholars have continued to think and publish about this topic. Academies of social science in Beijing and Ürümci sponsored research on the Soviet Union and Central Asia beginning in the late 1980s and with greater vigor after 1991. Numerous studies compared the Soviet Union and China on the dimensions of demography, *minzu* policies, governance, and economics. As recently as 2005 a book entitled *China's Borders and Minzu Problems* began with a chapter on the "*minzu* problems and the lessons of the Soviet breakup" (Zhang Zhirong 2005:1–7). The second wave of political transitions in Georgia, Ukraine, and the Kyrgyz Republic similarly rattled the Beijing leadership, and now scholars all over China are researching the etiology of the "color revolutions" in hopes of helping the party stave them off. The sheer number of conferences and published articles focusing on the topic and Beijing's decision to place severe legal restrictions on nongovernmental organizations (NGOs) in China belie officials' public confidence that China will avert such an outcome (Xinhua 2006).[5]

Although there is wide agreement that the Chinese state is strong and maintains powerful authority over society, few honest observers deny that social groups have become much more restive in recent years.[6] The transition from a socialist to a quasi-market economy has brought China one of the highest rates of growth ever sustained over two decades. It also has dislodged vast numbers of people from their jobs and farmlands. It has made many individuals rich and displaced an even greater number from the relative security of the socialist work unit into the stormy sea of market competition. Soon after Deng Xiaoping announced that class struggle was officially over in December 1978, real class struggle commenced in earnest. It is not idle to speak of the "unmaking" of the Chinese working class (Hurst 2004) or to conclude pessimistically that today's Chinese laborers have lost everything that Marx promised the world's proletarians had to gain from socialism (Blecher 2002, 2004). This process has provoked increasing waves of protest throughout the country (Tanner 2005).

Most demonstrations in China proper can loosely be called "economic protests." Workers strike because of layoffs or unpaid wages. Farmers surround government offices to complain of land expropriation and exorbitant taxes. Both groups rise up against corruption by the cadres. In a pathbreaking article, William Hurst demonstrated that collective action by laid-off workers in China has varied dramatically by region. The precipitating factors, demands of protestors, and state responses differ among the northern "Stalinist rust belt," booming central coast, and central inland regions, which he called "tentative[ly] transitional" because they have neither been crippled by layoffs by state-owned enterprises, as in the rust belt, nor enjoyed the same market-driven prosperity as the coast (Hurst 2004). Hurst's analysis demonstrates the importance of multisited research in China, illustrating how regional differences in political economy crucially affect the aims and fates of workers' protests. His study was spatially limited in significant ways, however. All three macroregions in his analysis belong to "China proper." We should broaden the study of protest to embrace China's western periphery, and Xinjiang in particular, where we seem to encounter another realm entirely, if not several other realms.[7]

In the thirty years since reform began, only two demonstrations over purely economic issues in Xinjiang have been documented, one urban and one rural. In 2001 in the southern city of Khotän, around a hundred recently laid-off textile workers, mostly Uyghurs, demonstrated out of concern that their employer would not pay their severance. In that case, local government officials promised to make good any debts that the cash-strapped factory could not pay, and the protestors dispersed without any arrests (Dow Jones International News 2001). In 2004 Uyghur farmers and Qazaq pastoralists in Xinjiang's northwestern Ili region protested what they saw as an unfair relocation package. They were angry about the construction of a hydropower plant requiring 18,000 people to relocate and about the gap between the promised compensation for the loss of land and an actual disbursement of only about 5 percent of the stated amount (RFA 2004).

In China's peripheral regions such as Xinjiang and Tibet, most major protest episodes have not concerned economic matters (the pattern of protest in Inner Mongolia, with a more heterogeneous economy and an overwhelmingly Han population, more closely resembles that in China proper), and the political climate facing protestors is decidedly chillier. In fact, however, the two features are directly related. It is precisely because some protests in the peripheral regions do not target industrial firms or local officials but the very state itself that central and regional governments have been so much less tolerant of them. Mongols have protested Chinese attempts to thoroughly domesticate Chinggis Khan or officials' suddenly canceling a performance by a popular band from Mongolia. Since the harsh crackdown in 1989, Tibetan monks have sporadically demonstrated against religious restrictions or the requirement that they openly condemn the Dalai Lama, and individuals have occasionally used bold gestures such as hoisting the Tibetan flag or crying out for Tibetan independence in the public square. Uyghurs have demonstrated against Xinjiang's governors and policies and, in some cases, challenged the very incorporation of Xinjiang into China. What Uyghurs have not been able to do since Hu Yaobang's fall from power is find high officials sympathetic to their claim that particular leaders have "failed to live up to some professed ideal or ... not implemented some beneficial measure" (O'Brien 2003:53). Officials in Xinjiang and Beijing have taken the position that separatist aims lurked behind *every* protest—concerned, perhaps, that tolerating one kind of protest would be perceived as an opening for separatist agitation—and therefore have forbidden all.

Party officials in Beijing and Ürümci have worried that a large unchecked protest in one part of Xinjiang might mushroom into a broader anti-Chinese mobilization. If many Uyghurs are deeply dissatisfied (Bovingdon 2002a; Smith 2000, 2007; Yee 2003, 2005), and most of them refrain from expressing anger only because they fear retaliation, then it is quite plausible that protest would spread quickly were the party-state to stay its hand. The snowballing demonstrations in Eastern Europe and the Soviet Union showed that previously timid citizens could abandon a lifetime of quiescence in a very short time. Time and again in 1989, 1990, and 1991 as people flowed into the streets, more and more of their fellow citizens stripped off their public facade of support for the regimes until it became clear that the majority had joined the opposition and the leaders had no choice but to step down (Beissinger 1998; Kuran 1992). In March 1997, Rozi, a well-paid Uyghur professional with a steady job, told me that if conditions in Xinjiang continued to deteriorate, he might join the organized opposition. "I might decide that living is not worth more than dying," he told me quite seriously.[8] Without broad survey results, we naturally cannot say how broadly such a view was or is shared.[9] But we should note the hedging in Rozi's comment. If citizens living under repressive states remain in doubt about their neighbors' true political views until moments of crisis, they surely also are uncertain of their own "tipping points": that is, how far the situation must deteriorate before they act and what they might be willing to sacrifice for a collective goal in the heat of the moment.

PROTEST TRENDS: CHINA AND XINJIANG HEADED IN OPPOSITE DIRECTIONS

In his article on workers' protests, Hurst calculated that China faced "at least hundreds, and probably thousands," of contentious events each year (Hurst 2004:95). This must have seemed quite a sensible estimate when the article was written, likely in late 2002. Hurst pointed out that the Chinese government had never publicized any figures on the quantity, frequency, or nature of mass protests. Many observers were consequently stunned when, beginning in early 2004, the State Security Ministry released a series of statistics indicating that Hurst's estimate had been low by an order of magnitude.[10] The statistics recorded 58,000 contentious episodes involving more than one hundred people in 2003, 74,000 in 2004, and 87,000 in 2005.[11] The ministry also revealed at the time that there had been an almost monotonic increase in protests since 1997 (Tanner 2005).[12] Because Chinese official statistics are notoriously unreliable, it is quite possible that even these large figures underestimate the number of disturbances. The numbers seem astonishing because of the party's historical intolerance for organized protest and habit of repressing it harshly and because most Chinese citizens have consequently been loath to incur the wrath of the state by demonstrating. The government's willingness to publish the figures was similarly startling.

Some scholars have leaped on these figures as the strongest indication yet that China may be on the verge of a new social revolution (Jiang 2006). But it is possible to read the publication of the figures differently.[13] Beijing may have strategically released this information about unrest with both domestic and international audiences in mind. Domestically, it might have intended to convince the monied and middle classes to support the continued repression and oppose "premature" democratization, by implying that only the party and the thin line of security forces lay between the comfortable lives those people now enjoyed and a political-economic abyss that would make the Cultural Revolution look like a Mardi Gras celebration. The conventional wisdom has long predicted that a burgeoning middle class would press for political reforms in China as it has elsewhere in the world. But ironically, the increasing prosperity in China may have made economically successful citizens more skeptical of reforms and more sympathetic to hard-line party leaders (An Chen 2003; Tsai 2005). Some have argued that Public Security Bureau (PSB) officials publicized the numbers to wring more money for domestic security out of the national budget.[14]

Beijing also might have released the figures to gain sympathy from the international community. Such a move would not have been plausible ten years ago, since many international observers shared the opinion that popular unrest in China expressed deep and justified dissatisfaction with a brutal and unresponsive regime. Yet September 11 dramatically changed the international climate, giving many states the opportunity to recast domestic opposition as "terrorism" and their own efforts to squelch that opposition as contributions to the "global war on terror" (Dwyer 2001; Li Qi 2002; Millward 2004:10–11). Under these conditions, Beijing might well have considered it safe to acknowledge the sharp rise in protests to an international society increasingly intolerant of antistate violence.[15] This has had especially poignant implications for Xinjiang and Uyghurs.

There is an irony to the role that Xinjiang has played in the story of post-1949 politics in the People's Republic of China (PRC). Bloody clashes and bombings in China proper were frequently compared with those in the XUAR, the "really violent" part of the country, and many bombings were initially attributed to Uyghur separatists, only later to be revealed as the work of spurned lovers or laid-off workers.[16] Transnational Uyghur organizations have asserted for years that Xinjiang was on the verge of a crisis and consequently broadcast news of every violent episode in the region. In some cases, they may have claimed responsibility for damage that actually was the result of natural disasters or industrial accidents. Possibly influenced by those claims, many foreign journalists and researchers have speculated that violence and unrest have increased in the region since the late 1990s.[17]

A careful and critical review of the evidence reveals that Xinjiang has been far quieter since 2001 than has any part of China proper. Despite the region's reputation, no scholar has ever attempted to quantify the amount and frequency of violence there. Some have cited official Chinese statistics promulgated since 2001, but there are several problems with these statistics. Officials quickly and dramatically changed their strategy of representing unrest in Xinjiang. In the 1990s they generally suppressed evidence of protests or violence, sometimes even denying foreign reports of unrest (Agence France-Presse 1995, 1997). The rare revelations of episodic violence attributed it to "*minzu* splittists." But the trend was not entirely systematic, and official numbers and attributions varied widely before being fixed by the State Council in 2002 (Guowuyuan xinwen bangongshi 2002). For instance, the XUAR government chairman, Ablät Abdurišit, claimed in a 1999 interview with reporters that "since the start of the 1990s, if you count explosions, assassinations, and other terrorist activities, it comes to a few thousand incidents" (Becquelin 2000:87).

Since September 11 the Xinjiang and national governments have had conflicting incentives in representing the scope and nature of unrest in Xinjiang. On one hand, officials at the regional and central levels seeking investment have habitually underplayed reports of unrest to avoid scaring away capital. On the other hand, regional governors seeking central grants for economic growth and policing, and officials in Beijing seeking global sympathy for China's "plight," have chosen to maximize the threat of separatists or "terrorists."[18] Most Chinese journalists and authors subscribe to the second strategy, touting large numbers of protests even in what had previously been depicted as placid periods and transforming splittists into terrorists and religious extremists. In other words, they first underrepresented and then exaggerated the number of episodes of political violence. I have attempted to replace speculations and distortions with systematic data collection, paying careful attention to content and sources. I have been able to document violent or organized protests or resistance in Xinjiang since 1949, including armed uprisings, peaceful demonstrations, and riots, as well as clearly political violence such as assassinations and bombings.

Figure 4.1 shows that between 1949 and 2005, there were at least 158 episodes of antistate violence or organized protest documented in printed sources, and of these, 142 had clear ethnonational content. The largest events involved 50,000 to 100,000 people, while most had only a few dozen participants. Only the armed resistance raised by various groups in the 1950s seriously challenged the party's political-military control of the region. The period of greatest antistate or ethnonational protest since then was the mid-1990s, with a high point of twenty events in 1998.[19] In addition, an event involving one thousand or more people took place in four of the five years from 1995 to 1999. Figure 4.2 plots events in the autonomous region against those throughout China from 1993 to 2005, showing that episodes in Xinjiang fell off just as they were increasing rapidly in China as a whole.[20]

WHAT COUNTS AS RESISTANCE?

The care with which it was assembled notwithstanding, my database of unrest in Xinjiang is unquestionably incomplete. One might infer its incompleteness from a comparison with the aggregate numbers cited in Chinese sources, even though the comparison would be misleading. For instance, Ma Dazheng, who presumably had access to internally circulated government statistics, cited "authoritative sources" to support the claim that there were 253 "violent terrorist episodes" in just the ten years between 1990 and 2000. Elsewhere he tallied 116 terrorist acts for 1998 alone, but these proved to include, in addition to bombings, assassinations, and arson, also livestock poisonings, kidnappings, and robberies (Ma Dazheng 2003:126–27, 153). These figures are an order of magnitude smaller than the "few thousand" invoked by the XUAR government chairman Ablät Abdurišit in 1999 but are equally out of step with Abdurišit's 2001 comment that Xinjiang was "by no means . . . a place where

Number of events

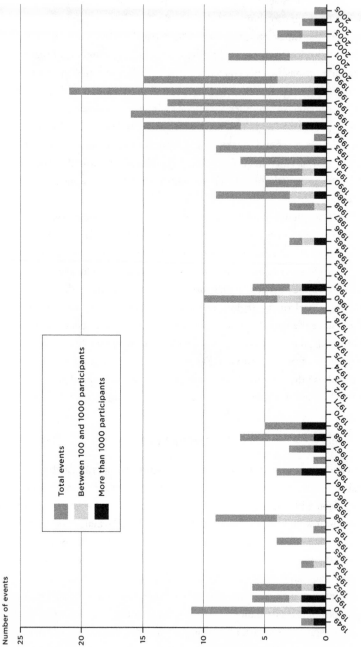

FIGURE 4.1 Organized or violent events in Xinjiang, 1949–2005.

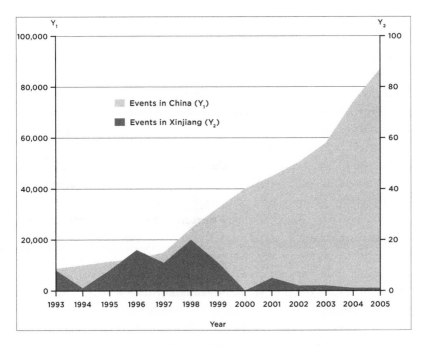

FIGURE 4.2 Protest events in China and Xinjiang, 1993–2005.

violence and terrorist accidents take place very often" (Agence France-Presse 1999c; Bao Lisheng 2001).

The elasticity of official numbers became obvious as the statistics promulgated in the State Council's January 21, 2002, press release on "Eastern Turkestan terrorists" were applied without the slightest modifications to very different periods (Guowuyuan xinwen bangongshi, 2002). That document asserted that more than two hundred "terrorist events" left 162 dead and 440 wounded between 1992 and 2001. Less than two years later, officials assigned precisely the same figures to the period from 1990 to 2001, implying no one had died in violent attacks between 1990 and 1992, which hard to square with the well-attested evidence of casualties in Baren in 1990 and the bus bombings in Ürümci in 1992, among others. In 2005 the deputy director of Xinjiang's Antiterrorism Bureau used the same figures for the "previous decade," and officials continued to use the exact same numbers in 2006. Yitzhak Shichor put the case rather mildly when he observed that this use of an identical set of figures for very different time periods "casts a shadow over the rest of Beijing's arguments" (Shichor 2006b:102).[21]

The numbers I use here are lower because my criteria are more restrictive than those adopted by officially sanctioned Chinese sources. I have not followed their examples in treating attacks on livestock or large robberies as instances of terrorism, or even as political violence, without supporting evidence, although I grant the possibility that some were perpetrated by individuals or organizations with political aims.[22] Furthermore, my graphs and appendix include only those events described in narrative form in some source. Except in rare instances, I have insisted on at least two sources to confirm an event.

By contrast, whether in the State Council's January 2002 document, in subsequent white papers, in the several graphic reports on "Eastern Turkestan terrorism," or in reports for internal circulation, the numbers of violent events cited in statistics always far exceed those described in the narratives. The authors' explicit mention of poisonings, crop burnings, and robberies in those narratives strongly suggests that the much larger figures on terrorism have been padded with figures from police blotters. Officially employed writers and spokespersons instructed to highlight "violent terrorism" in Xinjiang in order to garner international support seem to have elected only to count, and not to describe, episodes whose categorization as terrorist events might provoke skepticism abroad (Millward 2004:12). Since many individual cases claimed to underlie the aggregate numbers cannot be scrutinized, officials need not worry about drawing undue attention to the extraordinary breadth of the government's definitions of terrorism and crimes threatening state security.[23]

Looking beyond the derogatory labels to the individual protest episodes themselves reveals much that is obscured by Chinese statistics. The events that triggered them, the organizations that spurred them, and the issues they raised are far indeed from the themes of global Islamism or transnational terror organizations. Not surprisingly, they are much more closely related to matters of governance and policy shifts in Xinjiang itself.

FRAMING AND SENDING A MESSAGE: REPRESENTATION OF POLITICS IN A COMMAND POLITY

Careful scrutiny of the messages of public protests in Xinjiang reveals substantial overlap with the critiques discussed in the previous chapter. The willingness of large numbers of Uyghurs to march under particular banners or shout specific slogans strengthens our confidence that the criticisms raised by "everyday resisters" reflect broader views in Uyghur society.

In chapter 3 I argued that the myriad forms of everyday resistance in Xinjiang not only expressed dissent but carried out a kind of political work as well. That is, they communicated that dissent widely despite the powerful bans on public expression and organizing. Jokes traveled the breadth of the region in private conversations and via social gatherings of trusted friends. Writers and musicians made strategic use of the Xinhua distribution system itself, one of the party's key tools for spreading propaganda, to broadcast well-hidden but subversive messages in tapes and books across the entire Uyghur-speaking community. Individual books passed through many people's hands, and tapes could be duplicated at roadside stands (Dautcher 2000; Harris 2001). Turghun Almas's historical writings gained a wide readership and an even wider "rumorship" (Bovingdon and Nebijan Tursun 2004). Letters and handwritten manuscripts circulated widely by hand, concealed in bags or clothes. Some textual and audiovisual materials from dissident groups in Central Asia and Turkey were smuggled into Xinjiang by traders or travelers and were passed around through social networks.[24]

Chinese sources provide some information about the Uyghurs' spreading ideas through networks, although in their dogged emphasis on quantifying pieces of paper and documenting smashed organizations, such reports betray a studied uninterest in the messages being passed—or, perhaps more likely, a choice not to risk disseminating their contents any further. The aim has been to vilify separatists without attempting to understand them or make their objectives comprehensible to others.

An internal-circulation report in 1993 suggested that in the latter half of 1988 in the four districts of southern Xinjiang, officials laid hands on 113 "reactionary posters," handbills, or anonymous letters. All the 127 people they caught with these materials were under the age of twenty-five, and the youngest ones were only twelve; the vast majority were elementary and middle school students (Zhang Yuxi 1993:348). Ma Dazheng claims that between 1990 and 2000, the state destroyed 503 splittist or violent terrorist organizations or gangs. He includes under the subheading "violent terrorist incidents," 953 cases of subversive propaganda or incitement, and of these, 458 cases involved "reactionary posters," 107 cases leaflets, 157 letters, and 231 other types. Curiously, another highly placed author cited "incomplete" statistics showing that over the same period, the number of "reactionary" handbills and posters advocating *minzu* splittism averaged 5,000 a year, and reactionary audiotapes, another 1,000 cassettes. There was a marked uptick in 1996, with more than 8,000 handbills and more than 10,000 audiotapes (Yang Faren 2000:243).

This corpus of words and artifacts shaped and disseminated a critique of the political order in the autonomous region. Sociolinguists would recognize in this a kind of "framing": the purposive selection of particular ways to represent social phenomena (Goffman 1974; G. Lakoff 1987; G. Lakoff and Johnson 1980; R. Lakoff

2001). Scholars of contentious politics use "framing" to denote two factors critical to social mobilization: the strategic representation of a sociopolitical situation as objectionable, and the proposal of action to remedy it (Benford and Snow 2000; Snow et al. 1986). Only if activists compose and propagate a frame with wide appeal will large numbers of people decide to join the movement, often a risky choice even in democratic political systems.[25] In authoritarian polities, activists often rely on "mass frames," which cannot be spread openly and are harder to shape, so they may rely much more heavily on already circulating ideas (Hurst 2004:102–5). It is not clear, however, that activists in democratic systems have all the advantages. Popular media are widely read and trusted, as in many liberal polities, whereas movements have only a limited capacity to reframe perceptions already shaped by those media (Tarrow 1994:23). Under authoritarian regimes, the official media—often the only kind—are treated with skepticism, and their influence on popular opinion is correspondingly weaker. Widely disseminated "hidden transcripts" may be more powerful, particularly when suddenly made public during demonstrations. And if suspicion of official media gives dissidents an advantage in China proper, the Uyghurs' far stronger dubiety toward the Chinese media may give even greater power to the dissenters in Xinjiang.

The critiques and other forms of "everyday resistance" described in the previous chapter seldom called people to action. They were broad normative statements, not practical proposals: wealth needs to be distributed more fairly; Uyghurs need truly representative leaders; the government must not impose family-planning policies on non-Hans. As I suggested, in the spring of 1997, large numbers of Uyghurs seemed to trust, or at least hope, that others were taking care of organizing a resistance movement, since they themselves feared to do so.

The comparatively rare episodes of open political resistance in Xinjiang provoke fresh questions about framing. When the demonstrations were spontaneous, why did people join so quickly, and what did they hope to accomplish by doing so? When public protests or actions seemed to have been planned in advance, what messages did the planners propagate, and by what means? How did potential participants decide to take part, even after reflecting on the risks and the low chances of success? We also should ask what purposes or messages can be divined from acts of violence perpetrated by small groups. Were the targets of assassinations or bombings clear? Were the aims easy to understand? These questions are easy to ask but very hard to answer. The available sources of evidence pose particular difficulties for the study of framing in Xinjiang. These problems bear on the amount of information we are able to squeeze out of the available record, and thus on the soundness of interpretations.

For years, those interested in individual episodes of open resistance in Xinjiang—whether collective or violent or both—had no choice but to sift through scattered and sketchy foreign newspaper articles, accounts by human rights groups or transnational Uyghur organizations, and the very occasional Chinese news report. Because Xinjiang has been closed to foreign reporters for long periods, outside media reports have sometimes been hampered by relying on foreign travelers with little local knowledge. An Agence France-Presse report on the June 1988 protest in Ürümci, for instance, relied on the testimony of Western tourists who told the journalist that "the banner carried a lengthy inscription in Arabic script which they could not read" and admitted they had no idea of the point of the protest (Lescot 1988). Reports by human rights organizations frequently relied on the personal testimony of former prisoners (who would have had an incentive to play up their suffering for sympathy or to gain political asylum) or Uyghur organizations. Those groups, in turn, had every reason to maximize, even to embellish, the frequency and gravity of conflicts. As I discuss more fully in chapter 5, many leaders of organizations in Central Asia devoted most of their energies to media presentations as a strategy for keeping their movement alive. Few offered clear sources for their information, and some were serial fabulists. Uyghur news organizations in the diaspora such as the ETIC, the Uyghur Information Agency, and the Uyghur-language section of Radio Free Asia (RFA) have produced more plausible reports, but given their close association with political organizations, these cannot be considered disinterested or absolutely reliable.

After jealously guarding information about individual episodes of unrest (as with the protest numbers) in Xinjiang for decades, Chinese authorities began to release descriptions of that unrest in the late 1990s. Remember that these reports were compiled by officials whose job it is to present the party-state in the best possible light and, at the same time, to depict the protests as unsympathetically as possible. Like Uyghur news agents abroad, they have re-presented those episodes to suit their own purposes.[26] Particular protests explicitly raised such matters as the dismissal of a Uyghur official without popular consultation, continued nuclear testing, perceived disrespect for Islam and Muslims, and the imposition of family planning. Yet in almost every case, the official representations of those events insisted that they openly challenged party rule, proposed the establishment of an Islamic republic, or aimed at secession. In other words, the state's versions of events tarred them all with aspirations ruled unacceptable from the beginning. Next I describe a single example (briefly discussed in chapter 2) of a demonstration in Ürümci by two thousand students on December 12, 1985. An eyewitness reported that the students had protested the government's plan to enforce birth limits on Uyghurs, announced only a short time before, and the continued shipment of criminals from China proper into Xinjiang (Li Yuanqing 1990:71). In a book on the party-state's struggle against Uyghur separatism published nine years later, the "naïve and excitable students" prove to have been manipulated by splittists and so recede into the background. The reader learns only of splittists shouting "Hans get the hell out of Xinjiang" (*Hanren gun chu Xinjiang*), "Xinjiang must be independent, must be free, must have sovereignty," and "Long live independent Xinjiang" (Xu Yuqi 1999:110).[27]

Chinese writers' narratives are full of devious plotters, servants of foreign imperialism, and religious extremists, as well as innocent masses hoodwinked into marching or shouting along with these dangerous people. Reports in the early 1990s made elliptical references to protests by dates: "May 19" for violent protests in Ürümci in 1989, "April 5" for the 1990 Baren uprising, and so on. In offering only cryptic references, the writers intended to convey meaning to those in the know and remain mysterious to others. They had reason to fear that providing more information about major episodes of unrest or violence would backfire. Rather than making Uyghurs more supportive of the party-state and its policies, it would make them more hopeful about the possibility of widespread resistance.[28] The concern was doubtless to avoid disseminating too widely the news of a considerable number of open protests since the mid-1980s. By the end of the 1990s, the events were given short descriptions and years, but finally they were chronicled in great detail.[29] The stories of events have sometimes been subject to several revisions to suit changing political aims. For instance, the 1990 Baren uprising, the 1995 protest in Khotän, and the demonstration in Ghulja in 1997, all blamed for years on "splittists," were transformed in a 2004 article into the work of "terrorists" (Zhu Jun 2004).

Two questions of particular interest in regard to protests in Xinjiang, whether they were organized and whether they had religious content, are also the two matters about which we must be most circumspect when reading the official accounts. Playing up the role of organization and religiosity in particular events, and possibly inventing those attributes where they do not exist, serves particular political aims. Official scholars describe episodes of unrest as planned and organized in order to challenge the idea that they were "natural" and "spontaneous" and expressed popular dissatisfaction. The same writers also may impute religious content (and attribute religious slogans) to uprisings to make them seem irrational, even radical, and the participants backward.

Ma Dazheng's study of protests of the previous decade from the vantage point of 1997 identified growing Islamic belief and practice as critical elements in recent events. Not a single protest lacked some religious content, the author found. Officials noted with alarm that more and more citizens were practicing Muslims, including students and party members. They blamed the influence of missionaries from Central Asia. Islamic missionary groups carrying out *tabligh*,[30] or propagation of faith, reportedly operated throughout Xinjiang, using religious instruction as a cloak for spreading subversive political messages about independence and establishing an Islamic state in Xinjiang. In the first ten months of 1999, *tabligh* groups had reportedly spread from Ghulja in the north to the southern towns of Kashgar, Päyziwat, and Khotän, and officials had rooted out 91 sites and 1,600 practitioners.

Descriptions of protests in Chinese sources imply that if religious slogans were found in many protests in the 1980s, they were ubiquitous in the 1990s (Ma Dazheng 2003:92–105, 118). While some protests were clearly planned in religious settings and raised religious issues, they were not reducible to religious protests; much less can they be regarded as evidence of "Muslim extremism." Uyghurs have often used religion as a vehicle to express wider grievances or have made the state's repression of religiosity examples of broader repressions (Becquelin 2000; Dautcher 1999). Viewed from a distance, the Xinjiang government's multipronged attack on religiosity was clearly intended to eliminate both an alternative source of meaning and a space for organization.

ORGANIZATIONS, VIOLENCE, AND RELIGIOUS INFLUENCE

Students of contentious politics are not surprised to find organizations behind mass protests, even seemingly spontaneous ones. Indeed, Rogers Brubaker argues that the key actors in many ethnonational conflicts are "not ethnic groups as such but various kinds of organizations" (Brubaker 2002:172). If we want to find out whether and which organizations orchestrated protests in Xinjiang, we will face the challenge of extracting usable information from carefully constructed official or dissident narratives of those protests. Officials and academics describing many demonstrations or riots report in scandalized tones that they were planned and organized in advance, assertions sometimes seemingly strengthened when transnational Uyghur groups claim responsibility, though of course both have incentives to see efficacious organizations at work.[31] One finds outraged accusations of "black hands" and "separatist organizations" behind mass events in both academic studies and reportage potboilers (Liu Hantai and Du Xingfu 2003; Ma Dazheng 1990; Xu Yuqi 1999).[32] Such accusations are clearly intended to deny that particular protest episodes were authentic expressions of mass sentiment. For decades, officials broadcast to the citizenry the message that the party alone was allowed to organize people and orchestrate mass demonstrations and that the only legitimate way the masses might express grievances publicly was through purely spontaneous gatherings—

which then had to be dispersed by officials and police in order not to disturb public order.[33]

In China proper, while demonstrations without prior official permission remain illegal and permission is nearly never granted,[34] government officials have become somewhat more indulgent of local protests about economic matters. Peasants and workers have had some luck finding sympathetic officials who recognize their claims as "rightful," thus reducing the chances of harsh repression of demonstrations (O'Brien 1996, 2003). Official treatment of such episodes, however, has varied dramatically by issue and region, as discussed earlier (Hurst 2004; Perry 2001).

By 1997, officials in Xinjiang were alarmed to find organizers drawing participants from across district and even county boundaries and to see demonstrations shifting from remote rural settings to Xinjiang's major cities: Ghulja in early February 1997 and Ürümci at the end of the month.[35] Observers also were disturbed to note that planned actions had grown in scope. Whereas they had previously seen only brief paroxysms of violence, they now faced "armed rebellions." More and more police actions to round up suspects culminated in gun battles with well-armed holdouts. Politically motivated assassins now combined indiscriminate killing of Hans, intended to cause them to flee, with targeted killings of Uyghur officials loyal to the party-state, dubbed "bridge burning" (*chaiqiao*). The expression was a pointed barb directed at the official story that Uyghur, Qazaq, and other non-Han officials would serve as bridges between the party and the population. The most hardened partisans had received military training, at first in camps in rural southern Xinjiang and then, after the PSB closed those camps, in Pakistan or Afghanistan. Armed and battle trained, they now spoke openly of armed secession from China.[36]

The profile of individuals arrested in 1997 challenged a centerpiece of propagandists' brief against separatists. Instead of the uneducated, unemployed, religious *lumpen* described in antiseparatist propaganda, the organization members turned out to be young and well educated—and growing more so over time. Suspects apprehended in connection with a spate of arson attacks in late May 1998, reportedly aimed at turning Ürümci into a "sea of fire" and causing Hans to flee, were found to include female students from two of Xinjiang's top universities, Xinjiang University and the Medical College. Sweeps of suspected members of separatist organizations netted more than three hundred college students from ten postsecondary institutions, hailing from ten different districts.

The earliest reform-era protests appeared to be (even if they were not completely) spontaneous responses to inflammatory events, in much the way that the 1992 Los Angeles riots were touched off by the verdict in the Rodney King trial. Thus when a police officer killed a Uyghur man in PSB custody in April 1990,

Uyghurs who caught wind of this stormed the jail, spirited his body away, and within hours staged a demonstration in which three thousand people marched through the streets demanding that Hans leave Xinjiang (Ma Dazheng 2003:47–48; McMillen 1984:575). Similarly, in October 1981 when a Han youth fatally shot a young Uyghur in Kashgar in a dispute over ditch digging, Uyghurs again marched the body through the streets until the crowd of protestors numbered more than six thousand. This time, the protestors reportedly shouted that they would kill Hans and called for a free "Uyghurstan."[37] In these and other cases, while a proximal cause can be identified, the speed, violence, and scope of the popular response point to pent-up anger that had grown over a long period. Widespread popular grievances at the nature of Chinese rule in Xinjiang and the myriad individual complaints of Uyghurs provided the background conditions. The sparking events seemed at once to capture features of the intolerable system in microcosm and to give the final push to tempers at their limits. In sum, while the precipitating events account for the timing of the protests, they cannot by themselves explain those protests.

In the latter half of the 1980s, students and other citizens in Ürümci organized three major demonstrations, each seizing on a recent happening that offended Uyghurs' sensibilities—the replacement of a popular Uyghur leader, a slur found in a lavatory stall, or the publication of a salacious book—but all raising slogans that responded to matters far beyond the incidents' provocations. Marchers protested the system of autonomy, nuclear weapons testing, Han migration, family-planning policies, and discrimination against Uyghurs or Muslims, among other matters. Officials worried that in each case, the protests lasted several days, and in the latter two instances they spread to (or had spread from) other cities in Xinjiang or elsewhere in China. There was evidence of coordination of both the content and the timing of demonstrations (for more information, see the appendix).

It was two major protests in the 1990s, however, that caused the most alarm in officialdom. Neither was among the largest protests in the reform era. But the two events' organization, violence, and ideological challenge to the regime were without precedent in post-1949 Xinjiang. These were the Baren uprising in 1990 and the Ghulja uprising in 1997.

PROTESTS

Before daylight on the morning of April 5, 1990, in the month of Ramadan, a group of several hundred men set out angrily from a mosque in southern Xinjiang where they had attended services and spoken publicly of their outrage at the Chinese Communist Party (CCP)'s policies on nuclear tests, the extension of family planning to Uyghurs, and the exploitation of Xinjiang's resources for use in the interior.[38] They marched on and surrounded the government offices in Baren, a rural township in Akto County, thirty miles southwest of Kashgar.[39] They chanted the *shahada* in unison and some called for a *jihad*.[40] Later in the day, a larger group of some three hundred returned to mount an armed assault on Baren party and PSB offices. When several carloads of police came to relieve the officials under siege, the insurgents stripped them of their weapons and killed a number of them, taking others hostage. The attack continued into the night, with the insurgents lobbing homemade bombs and firing on the government offices. The next day, much larger troop reinforcements entered the area and chased the remaining insurgents to the marshlands and mountains where they had fled, killing or capturing all of them by the third day. The official death toll was quite low, listing six police, one cadre, and fifteen or sixteen demonstrators or insurgents killed. International sources proposed a much higher figure of more than sixty killed.

Within days, the government displayed on television the weapons and documents seized from the insurgents, including a booklet laying out the purposes and duties of *jihad*, among them killing "infidels," and vaunting the imminent independence of "East Turkestan" ("'Rebellion' Quelling Detailed" 1990). Official sources later announced that years earlier, the leader, Zäydin Yusup, had begun recruiting forces for the uprising. He and his co-conspirators had traveled to several mosques stirring up a religious frenzy and secretly building an "Eastern Turkestan Islamic Party." In each place they had broadcast the message that Islam would soon conquer socialism, that they would drive Hans out of Xinjiang, and that they would found an Eastern Turkestan republic. They also denounced the "colonial" exploitation of the region. Zäydin and others had made extensive preparations, including acquiring weapons and holding four planning meetings, but they were not completely ready to launch the resistance when they learned that the plot had been partially exposed in March 1990, at which point they chose to act in early April.

As soon as security forces had put down the Baren uprising, hard-liners in the government began to crack down on religion much more harshly. This included the questioning of imams, the dismissal of some and the training of the remainder; the closing of new mosques under construction and the halting of repair work on existing mosques; an official policy to find and destroy all private religious schools; and a much broader search for underground political and religious organizations. If the 1980s had provided a brief thaw after decades of anti-*minzu* policies, Baren ushered in a new era of repression and harsh policies.

A month after the Baren uprising, officials quietly promulgated new regulations governing protest in Xinjiang, superseding temporary ones from 1988. In May 1990 the XUAR People's Congress passed the new administrative rule, officially termed a "method for implementing" the national law on protest. It stipulated that all marches or demonstrations must be cleared with the government in advance and must not "threaten the unification of the state, harm *minzu* solidarity, or compromise the interests of state, society, or collective." The application for official approval must contain "the purpose, method, slogans or catchphrases, participant numbers, vehicles, and sound equipment of the assembly, march, or demonstration" and must identify a person responsible. Participants were forbidden to raise banners or shout slogans "incompatible with the aims" of the event. The rules even stated that security organs could set up security cordons protecting party and military offices, courts, jails, PCC offices, and broadcast stations—in other words, precisely those sites that the protests were likely to target (Xinjiang weiwu'er zizhiqu renda changwei 1990). The new rules would prove advantageous to the handling of several episodes of unrest nearly six hundred miles northeast of Baren, in Xinjiang's northern city of Ghulja.

Most journalists' accounts of the 1997 Ghulja protest begin only days before the event, with the sudden arrest of dozens of Uyghur youths in January or the police breaking up a circle of women praying in a private home on what proved to be the eve of the uprising. Chinese versions of the events begin a year earlier with a splittist organization, the "Eastern Turkestan Islamic Party of Allah." The Ghulja uprising was clearly the product of a chain of events that began much earlier and was symptomatic of both the government's repressive methods and the Uyghurs' exasperated responses. As revealed only later in the work of foreign scholars and Amnesty International, this event was distantly connected with government efforts several years earlier to eliminate a popular form of Uyghur social organization (Dautcher 1999:328–29; 2000; Millward 2004:17; Roberts 1998a:686–87).

In 1994 a number of Uyghurs in Ghulja decided to revive a traditional social organization, the *mäšräp*, in order to combat endemic alcoholism and drug abuse in the region. The *mäšräp* met regularly, with memberships of several dozen, to share music and dance, learn more about Islam, and hold one another to account for their public behaviors. Leaders of the gatherings had both ritual and religious authority to punish participants in front of their peers for violating the group code. The groups were quite successful at reducing alcohol and drug use and also at giving Uyghurs a sense of collective capacity to help themselves. They multiplied quickly.[41] In spring of 1995 the heads of all the *mäšräp* in Ili gathered and elected as the leader of all the groups one of the founders of the movement, Abdulhelil. He was detained for questioning soon after, and following this the government banned *mäšräp*, although the organizations continued to operate underground. An anthropologist living in Ghulja during spring 1995 concluded that what the party most feared about the groups was that they were organizations that "it did not initiate, supervise, [or] control" (Dautcher 1999:326).[42]

In July and August, Abdulhelil and other leaders organized a youth soccer league in Ghulja, and many youngsters joined. On August 12, several days before the tournament was to begin, military officials occupied the playing field, parked several tanks there, and announced that it would henceforth be needed for military exercises. Officials also reportedly removed the goalposts from the fields at all schools in the area to ensure that the tournament could not take place. On August 13 Abdulhelil was again taken in for questioning. The following day, hundreds of men marched peacefully through the streets and then dispersed, an event that officials later referred to as the "August 14 illegal march." Remarkably, though there was no hint of violent intent in the march, by noon that day snipers stood conspicuously on the roofs of buildings in the center of town, and the People's Armed Police (PAP) controlled the main intersections with barbed-wire barriers (Amnesty International 1999; Dautcher 1999:325–27; 2004:285–87; Roberts 1998a:686). Abdulhelil and others, angry at the government's heavy-handed action to squelch a very successful social organization, went on to plan and lead the protest in 1997. Chinese sources claim that Abdulhelil and others joined the Eastern Turkestan Islamic Party of Allah (ETIPA) and that its leader, Päyzulla, had begun infiltrating Ghulja in early 1996, planning for the demonstration in January 1997 (Xu Yuqi 1999:177–78).[43] No Chinese source I have seen explains the "August 14 illegal march," and not one connects the Ghulja demonstration with the crackdown on *mäšräp*.

There were more proximal causes. A Uyghur organization in the United States asserted that demonstrators, mostly students, were marching to protest the arrests of thirty youths praying in a mosque on January 27, during the month of Ramadan. Yusupbäk (Yusupbek) Mukhlisi, the long-serving head of the Eastern Turkestan United National Revolutionary Front (in Kazakhstan) and, unfortunately, often not a reliable reporter, claimed that the thirty had been not only arrested but also executed (Hutzler 1997).[44] Many sources agree that a series of raids on the night of February 4, picking up some two hundred worshippers at mosques and in private religious study groups, immediately preceded the peaceful demonstration beginning at around nine in the morning on February 5. There is little doubt that many marchers had religious motivations for taking part. An official Chinese account of the events has students carrying banners saying "It has begun" and "Use the Qur'an as a weapon" (Xu Yuqi 1999:178). A video shot by the Ghulja police shows the students marching under a white banner with the *basmala* and *shahada* handwritten in very large script.[45] They marched speedily to the center of town, shouting "religious slogans" and picking up participants along the way until they numbered at least five hundred.[46] Some sources suggest that demonstrators symbolized their rejection of the Chinese state's authority by burning official documents such as identity cards and residency permits and even report implausibly that they "stripped off their 'Han' clothing" (another version has them removing all their clothing) as they marched, so as to disavow any connection with Hans (Becker 2001; Jiekai Xinjiang 'Dong Tu' fenzi de kongbu miansha 2001).[47] About two hours into the demonstration, the police set upon the protestors in full riot gear and with dogs. Official reports asserted that many protestors were armed with bricks and knives and had begun to attack public security personnel and Han citizens as well as property. The police eventually fired live rounds into the crowd to put down the demonstration (Dillon 2004:96–97).

Chinese officials initially denied there were any casualties from the police action. In fact, a police spokesman in Ghulja refused to acknowledge that the protest and crackdown had even occurred, saying, "Nothing happened here last week."[48] This fit poorly with the autonomous regional government's announcement on the same day that 10 had died and 130 had been arrested.[49] Non-Chinese sources reported up to 130 killed that day and up to 500 arrested. Later reports by human rights organizations indicated that the protestors had been hosed down with cold water and then held outdoors in subzero temperatures for hours, with the result that many developed frostbite and had to have their feet or hands amputated. Some protestors returned to the streets on the following two days, again facing riot police and the PAP. There were further arrests, and some Uyghurs reportedly assaulted Hans they found in the street and destroyed cars. The government enacted a curfew and closed the city to outsiders for two weeks. Unconfirmed reports state that independence activists, some of them from as far away as Kashgar, had planned a major demonstration for February 9, the final day of Ramadan. They were betrayed to the police and arrested, and according to one source, they were among the first group to be executed after the demonstrations. Abdulhelil was reportedly tortured and executed secretly months later (Amnesty International 1999; Campion 1997; Hutzler 1997; Tyler 1997).[50]

Although they were very different events, the Baren and Ghulja uprisings shared certain important features. Both apparently had been planned in advance. In the case of Baren, Zäydin Yusuf, head of the Eastern Turkestan Islamic Party (ETIP), is supposed to have spent the three years from 1987 to 1990 building his organization by inducting members in trips to various mosques. The uprising took place in Baren, but the ETIP reportedly had members in Ürümci, Kashgar, Turpan, and at least ten other major cities in Xinjiang (Zhang Yuxi 1993:349). Investigators reportedly found that the Ghulja uprising had been plotted by the Eastern Turkestan Islamic Party of Allah, an organization founded three years earlier in October 1993.[51] Like Zäydin's ETIP, it had branches and members throughout Xinjiang. Its leaders decided to set the protest in motion at a "Xinjiang-wide congress" of that party on November 27, 1996 (Ma Dazheng 2003:95). Both the Baren and Ghulja uprisings were religiously motivated, and both emphasized public repudiation of the official policy on religion and the party's claim to be the highest authority. The biggest difference is that the Ghulja protest began peacefully, and according to most reports, it became violent only when police began to crack down.

A number of gun battles might be interpreted as armed rebellions that did not come off; this is how Chinese sources generally represent them. Many started when police tried to apprehend individuals suspected of seeking independence through violent means. According to one source, between 1990 and 2000 Chinese forces reportedly fought 57 gun battles, with 26 police or soldiers killed and 74 wounded, with 140 civilians dying and 371 injured. All told, security personnel fatally shot 106 "rebels." Much of the bloodletting took place in the latter half of the decade. In a two-month period in 1996, PSB officials engaged in gunfights six times, with one officer killed, while eighteen suspects were killed and another thirteen injured. In the first half of 1999, the PSB had seven more gun battles. In that period, PSB forces lost one, with sixteen injured. Seven "terrorists" were shot dead and eight injured (Ma Dazheng 2003:73, 126–27, 153).

GOVERNMENT RESPONSES

Between 1980 and 1997, the governments in Beijing and Ürümci made concessions in only four instances to matters raised during demonstrations. After a series of protests by Han former "educated youths" desiring to return to their home cities in the interior in the late 1970s and early 1980s, officials granted them the right to periodic home visits, agreed to resettle some individuals, and allowed for all the individuals who remained in Xinjiang to send one child back to China proper. In response to the Muslims' protests in spring 1989, Beijing halted the publication of the book *Sexual Customs*, which contained offensive (and wildly inaccurate) descriptions of Muslims' sexual behavior, and punished both the authors and publisher of the book. In this case, the government responded before the protests spread to Xinjiang, and although the authorities treated demonstrators in China proper quite leniently, they were much less generous with their counterparts in Ürümci (Glad-ney 1991:3–4; 1992). When 130 uranium mine workers,[52] whose radiation sickness had been ignored by authorities for years, traveled to Ürümci and staged a sit-in on May 13, 1989, officials agreed to address their concerns but then scolded them for the form of their protest, saying that a sit-in was "inappropriate" (Zhang Liang, Nathan, and Link 2001:170). It seems evident that had they not protested, their problems would have continued to be ignored. Finally, in 1996 Beijing ended the testing of nuclear weapons at Lop Nur, although this surely was prompted by the hope of wringing arms control concessions from other countries rather than the many Uyghur protests against the practice (Johnston 1996).

In all other documented cases, the government responded to protestors' demands with either stony silence or even more restrictive policies. When protestors called for greater religious freedom, Ürümci stepped up the repression of religious belief among students and officials, zero tolerance for private religious instruction, and arrests of religious pupils deemed underage or unsuitable (as, for instance, with all children and youths in high school or college or technical schools at equivalent levels). When demonstrators called for increased representation by Uyghur, Qazaq, and other non-Han officials, officials and their advisers pushed for more Han cad-res to preserve stability. When Uyghurs repeatedly insisted that Han immigration stop, the government reinstated the PCC and then enacted a series of policies that dramatically increased the inflow of Hans. Officials expressly targeted those regions of Xinjiang where Hans were the scarcest, lavishing great state largesse on the completion of the Kashgar rail link with this aim in mind.[53] When students asked for greater respect for Uyghur culture, the government chose to phase out bilingual education and has made a bid to eliminate the use of Uyghur (and Qazaq) as a high-prestige language (Dwyer 2005). And when Uyghurs sought local indigenous remedies to social ills such as alcoholism and drug abuse, the government cracked down on these autonomous social organizations (Congressional-Executive Com-mission on China 2009; Dautcher 1999, 2004:286–92).

The party-state has relied heavily on a particular strategy for breaking up exist-ing organizations and thwarting the emergence of new ones. Security officials make a point of targeting the leaders of protests for prosecution and heavy sen-tences as a cautionary example to others. This practice broadcasts the message that potential movement leaders have nothing more to gain than do rank-and-file participants and they also have more to lose (Cai 2002:333; see also Tanner 1999:11). Deterring would-be leaders from taking the initiative has so far been widely effective. One researcher found in interviews with disgruntled workers that many were waiting for someone else to organize a protest, with the excuse that once that happened, "I would definitely participate" (Cai 2002:333). This echoes the comments of the many Uyghurs expecting others to take the initiative in 1997, as described in chapter 3.

Officials in China's inland regions have admitted that they are seeking to convey a "strong signal" to the wider population that "there is nothing to be gained from causing trouble" (Hurst 2004:108). In Xinjiang as in the interior, PSB and other officials have similarly gone after the leaders of movements, ostentatiously singling them out for arrest and harsh punishment while treating most participants in demonstrations leniently. Unlike in the interior, movement leaders in Xinjiang have, on numerous occasions, been publicly executed for the crime of "splittism."

Chinese scholars have attempted to carry out in their descriptions of protest events what police have done on the ground: isolate the leaders from the putatively guileless and therefore blameless masses. The strategy on paper has been to condemn "a few bad people" (Chen Chao 1990:234; XUAR Local Gazetteer Editorial Committee 1997:77) or people with "ulterior motives" (J K P Š U A R komiteti täšwiqat bölümi, 2000?:49; Xu Yuqi 1999:110–12) for fomenting uprisings. In the case of the October 1981 riot after the shooting of a Uyghur youth, official sources identified the "Central Asian Uyghurstan Youth Sparks Party," formed only the month before, as the instigator. Three members of the organization supposedly rushed to the scene within half an hour of the shooting and whipped bystanders into a riotous fury (Zhu Peimin, Chen Hong, and Yang Hong 2004:209). The sources' authors do not try to explain, but instead explain away, the participation of large numbers, asserting that the masses "did not know the true situation" or noting that college students, because of their "ignorance and susceptibility to incitement," could be induced to march in the streets and shout anti-Han and pro-independence slogans (Xu Yuqi 1999:110–12). In other words, they worked hard to find an explanation for large protests safely distant from the far simpler and more straightforward political diagnosis that only because substantial numbers of Uyghurs are deeply disgruntled are they therefore available for, and willing to participate in, protests at the drop of a piece of fruit, the display of an offending slur, or the description of a scurrilous book. But the study of social movements around the world makes it clear that people participate in them for a great variety of reasons, and that variety does not vitiate their participation or the significance of the movement. Quite clearly, this rhetorical gesture by officials and scholars is a panicked attempt to avoid acknowledging the obvious and pervasive problem of Uyghurs' anger at the government.[54] In fact, if we discount the argument that Uyghurs are somehow more excitable and therefore prone to participate in "troublemaking" without inquiring into its purpose or likely outcome, we are led more strongly to the conclusion that ordinary Uyghurs' availability for impromptu protests and organized ones alike is a clear index of that anger.

Government officials in Beijing and Ürümci have, with very few exceptions, shown no tolerance for open protests by Uyghurs, whatever the motivation (Hastings 2005). In other words, no matter what the issue, Uyghurs do not have a right to express their discontent openly. A document promulgated by the XUAR party secretary in February 2002, shortly after the arrest of the poet Tursunjan Ämät, showed that officials in Xinjiang "equate any expression of dissatisfaction ... even metaphorical or ironical, with separatist thought" (Becquelin 2004a:44).[55] In July 2002 Liu Yaohua, vice director of the Xinjiang PSB, told a foreign reporter that "any Uighur who advocated independence for Xinjiang was probably a terrorist" (Pan 2002). In December 2008, administrators squelching a planned protest against the sale of alcohol and cigarettes in shops told the Ürümci college students involved that their demonstration would have been "an act of beating, smashing, and looting ... forbidden by our country's laws." The event, they said, would have broadcast "reactionary speech" and undermined "stability and unity" (Congressional-Executive Commission on China 2009).

Government regulations and governors' comments demonstrate how much more restrictive the political climate is in Xinjiang than in China's interior. The atmosphere in the XUAR has always been more tense precisely because so many Uyghurs resent both the fact and the nature of Chinese control. Despite denials by Ürümci and Beijing, restrictions actually increased over the last decade.

CONCLUSION: THE IMPORTANCE OF REPRESSION

The government has emphasized the message that protest is unacceptable and that any form of public dissent will be regarded as "splittism" and punished severely. There was at least one major political campaign in Xinjiang each year between 1996 and 2004, and every campaign "involved the arrest of hundreds," often followed by expedited convictions under drastically reduced evidentiary standards. The governing principle of the courtroom proceedings, underscored by Wang Lequan in a 2001 speech, has been the so-called two basics: "As long as the basic truth is clear and ... basic evidence is verified," the legal apparatus is obligated to approve arrest, carry out speedy prosecution, and deliver a sentence (Becquelin 2004a:41; Human Rights Watch 2005:57).

The "strike hard" campaigns begun in Xinjiang in 1996 and repeated every year since have substantially raised the level of repression. At the outset, officials in Beijing worried that this move might trigger international disapproval, but they later found that this was not so. Ma Dazheng noted with pleasure that between 1996 and 1998, the "forcefulness of our 'strike hard' [campaign] was massively increased [and yet] there was not a peep from the United States government" and that Western media paid little attention to the matter. Then in 1998, articles "sympathetic to split-tist activities" began to appear in the *International Herald Tribune*.[56] Worse, the U.S. State Department began to cover police action in Xinjiang in its annual report on human rights, and Western countries began to use this as a pretext to make trouble for China (Ma Dazheng 2003:208). In the end, Beijing was able not only to repeat the campaigns every year but even to increase their intensity. September 11 provided an excellent opportunity to ratchet up the force of repression yet again. Shielded by international concern about global terrorism, Beijing launched a "high-pressure strike hard" in 2002, a special "100 days' strike hard" in 2003, and a "high-pressure strike hard" in 2004 with no time limit (Human Rights Watch 2005:67). In interviews with a reporter in 2002, Uyghurs admitted that they feared the police much more than they did terrorists (Pan 2002).[57]

There is abundant evidence of continuing Uyghur discontent, or the party-state's fear of it, since 2001. Han Zhubin, once the top prosecutor in China, revealed in mid-2003 that between 1998 and the end of 2002, the government had arrested 3,400 individuals throughout the country for threatening "state security." Han indicated that there had been a sharp increase in prosecutions since September 11, with 1,600 of those individuals prosecuted after that date. One knowledgeable source calculated that roughly one-quarter of individuals known to have been prosecuted were non-Hans, even though Hans then made up 92 percent of the national population ("A Grim Reminder for the Central Government's Opponents" 2003). Depending on how comprehensive the former prosecutor's figures were, the proportion might have been much higher. A paper released by the Ministry of Justice reflected that 9.2 percent of all Uyghurs convicted in 2001 had received sentences for "state security crimes" (Human Rights Watch 2005:72). Statistics culled from various editions of the *Xinjiang Yearbook* reflect that 2,353 individuals were arrested in Xinjiang alone during the period that Han Zhubin cited, 1998 to 2002 (*Xinjiang yilnamisi*, 1998 through 2002). In the first eight months of 2004, the government had, according to its own reports, exposed and destroyed twenty-two groups carrying out "separatist and terrorist activities" and handed down fifty death sentences to people convicted of separatist activities (Ruwitch 2004). In August 2004, according to Agence France-Presse, "ethnic and religious tensions [were] flaring up again," and an official in Khotän told AFP that eight people had been indicted in the last week of July for "endangering state security." A Uyghur dissident organization reported that seventy-five people, twenty-seven of them children, had been taken into custody in Khotän for "illegal religious activities" (Agence France-Presse 2004a). More recent official statistics count 1,300 people arrested for threatening state security in Xinjiang in the first eleven months of 2008, as against 742 in all of China in 2007, of which roughly half were in Xinjiang. It seems clear that Beijing greatly broadened the definition of a crime threatening state security in the months before the 2008 Summer Olympics. At the same time, the numbers can be read as an index of continuing concern in Beijing and Ürümci about Uyghur discontent.

Officials' deep fears of unrest can be read as well from moves to shore up the region's political stability. In March 2005 the *Ürümci Evening News* reported that police in the region's capital city had been issued heavier weaponry, including submachine guns, and given training in counterterrorism (Congressional-Executive Commission on China 2005b). A month later, officials announced that of seven hundred new government jobs opening in southern Xinjiang, where Uyghurs are the overwhelming majority of the population, five hundred would be open only to Han Chinese (U.S. Department of State 2006). The government-run *Xinjiang Daily* newspaper reported in September 2005 that 947 Hans had been dispatched from China proper to take up various government posts ("947 ming yuan jiang ganbu fen fu Tianshan nan bei" 2005). And in November 2008, the Central Military Commission in Beijing promoted the Xinjiang contingent of the People's Armed Police from deputy to full corps command in order to "safeguard national security and social stability" (Xinhua 2008).

The relative rarity of protest on the periphery since 2001 should not be mistaken for evidence of increasing satisfaction among Uyghurs, Tibetans, and other non-Hans; not even resignation.[58] If the hegemony of market and state partly account for the relative quiescence of labor in China proper (Blecher 2002, 2004), we cannot attribute the rarity of protest by Uyghurs, Tibetans, and Mongols to hegemony of the "Chinese nation," or the state.[59] There is too much evidence of everyday resistance, even in periods with little open protest. Xinjiang Party Secretary Wang Lequan's bitter comment in a private meeting that "our cadres have no place in the hearts of the people" makes this point eloquently (Wang Lequan 1999:17).[60] The small and decreasing number of public protests and acts of violent resistance in Xinjiang since 2001 should not be interpreted as a sign that steady economic growth has made Uyghurs as a whole more materially contented and less concerned with politics and thus less inclined to engage in public resistance. Instead, viewed against the backdrop of increasing protests and violence in China proper and evidence of a pervasive wealth gap between Hans and Uyghurs in Xinjiang, the falling protest numbers indicate the success of the party-state's actions to root out organizations and deter would-be protestors into quiescence—in short, not to resolve Uyghurs' grievances but to deprive them of the resources and opportunities to articulate them publicly. In fact, instead of addressing Uyghurs' dissatisfactions, many of the policy instruments used to quell protests actually exacerbated them.

■

But it would be a mistake to stop with the consideration of domestic effects. Paralleling the domestic crackdown was a regional clampdown on Uyghur individuals and organizations in Central Asia. This reduced or eradicated organizations, sources of weapons, the spread of propaganda, and other sources of support for activities in Xinjiang. More influential still was the dramatic reversal of an international trend toward more frequent humanitarian intervention, indeed, of a seeming revision in the status of state sovereignty, developing in the 1980s and 1990s. Antistate actors who might have won international sympathy and even logistical support, only a year or two earlier now found themselves recast as terrorists. States of all stripes from the most democratic to the brutally authoritarian could now repackage their efforts to squelch challengers as part of the "global war on terror."

UYGHUR TRANSNATIONAL ORGANIZATIONS

Many journalists and government officials throughout the world now routinely depict Uyghur independence activists as terrorists *tout court*. The following passage is representative:

> For the past decade Uighur Islamic militants and nationalists have been waging a guerrilla war against the Chinese authorities, which China, in the spirit of the antiterrorist initiatives [after 9/11], has called upon Washington to condemn. On August 26, 2002, the Bush administration, hoping to engage China's support for its war against Iraq, finally agreed to classify the Uighur militants as terrorists. (Rashid 2003:xiv)

Thus wrote Ahmed Rashid, a noted author well informed about Central Asian affairs, in 2003. His language here is persuasive, and his understanding of the situation is broadly shared by many people aware of the Uyghurs' struggles with the Chinese state. It also is wrong.[1]

In this case, the Chinese government sought to persuade the world of its own view of politics in Xinjiang. As we saw in chapter 4, it did so after dramatically changing its public interpretation, switching from the claim that Xinjiang was untroubled by separatist violence to the assertion that it had long been afflicted by political violence. The document "East Turkestan Terrorist Forces Cannot Escape with Impunity," released on January 21, 2002 (the January 2002 document), purported to demonstrate that years of violent activity in Xinjiang had been the work of terrorists and that those terrorists had links to a global terrorist network run by Osama bin Laden. The document cleverly listed a number of Uyghur organizations, showcased a series of violent events, and cited far larger numbers of events and their casualties, in such a way as to suggest that they all were tightly connected. The document was subsequently shown to be internally inconsistent and unpersuasive in various ways (Clarke 2007; Millward 2004; Shichor 2005, 2006b). Yet as discussed in chapter 4, its principal statistics and the assertion that a single Uyghur Islamist organization had committed many terrorist acts have continued to be reproduced in international media every since, as seen in the preceding quotation from Rashid.

What the U.S. government did seven months later in August, and the UN did on the anniversary of the 9/11 attacks, was to list one *particular* outfit as a terrorist organization. That entity was the previously (and subsequently) obscure "Eastern Turkestan Islamic Movement" (ETIM), headed by Hasan Makhsum.[2] Beijing had hoped that Washington would issue a blanket condemnation of *all* Uyghurs and organizations seeking to challenge Chinese control of Xinjiang. After Washington listed the ETIM, the PRC went on a new media offensive, insinuating that the United States had joined it in condemning Uyghur separatism full stop. Owing to the Chinese efforts and an "acronymic coincidence," many people misunderstood or misrepresented the U.S. decision as having targeted the "Eastern Turkestan *Independence* Movement." Uyghurs and Uyghur organizations have suffered grievously as a consequence.[3]

■

There is no doubt that a large number of Uyghur organizations outside Xinjiang have tried to shape the fate of the region and its peoples. This chapter discusses what the principal organizations have attempted and how the Chinese government has worked to blunt their efforts.[4] Both Chinese officials and a number of Uyghur independence activists have greatly exaggerated the impact of these organizations on Xinjiang's daily politics. In regard to the matter of transborder infiltration, we cannot be too credulous of the claims of either kind of source. The actual authors or sponsors of violence are often hard to establish, and for three obvious reasons: some perpetrators of violence sensibly seek to evade responsibility for their actions to avoid punishment of individuals or sanctions against their organizations. Other individuals may wish to falsely claim credit for documented violent events in order to shore up their claims to be doing something for the cause, particularly in the case of the Central Asian leader Yusupbäk Mukhlisi. For the same reason, they might exaggerate the amount of violence that has occurred. Chinese accusations and Uyghur boasts notwithstanding, there is no independently verifiable evidence that separatist organizations have sent members into Xinjiang, let alone directed antistate attacks in the region.[5] Here the disjuncture revealed in chapter 4 between party officials' talk of frequent and increasing "terrorist violence" in Xinjiang, on one hand, and the suggestive evidence that antistate violence and large-scale protest had fallen to near zero, on the other, is particularly telling.

The groups have succeeded in one enterprise, and on this point, Beijing and members of the Uyghur diaspora are in agreement. By preparing histories and political materials and disseminating them among Uyghurs in Xinjiang and around the world, they have played a role in sustaining both Uyghurs' sense of themselves as a distinct people and their belief in the possibility of independence in the future. Whereas the governments in Ürümci and Beijing have struggled mightily to impose a single vision of Uyghurs' past and future on the region's inhabitants, dissident organizations abroad have managed to smuggle in texts, beam in radio broadcasts, and send ideas across the borders that challenge that vision. Yitzhak Shichor went so far as to argue that while the political struggle for independence was "in a coma inside China, it has been artificially resuscitated outside" (Shichor 2003:284). Shichor is right in the limited sense that there has been no armed and organized opposition inside Xinjiang, although as I demonstrated in chapter 3, broad Uyghur resistance was anything but in a coma.

If Uyghur transnational organizations have not played an obvious role in violent antistate resistance in Xinjiang, neither have they effected much change through diplomacy.[6] No group has yet succeeded in bringing the Chinese government to the negotiating table, let alone wrung policy concessions from it. One reason is that the epicenter of organizing, the region in which Uyghurs had the greatest hope of mounting an effective challenge to Chinese control, has shifted several times. Each geographical shift necessitated changes in strategies and brought new organizational challenges.[7]

MOVING FOR UYGHURSTAN: THE SHIFTING EPICENTER
OF UYGHUR ACTIVISM

The locus of the most significant organizations and activities has shifted twice, first from Turkey to Central Asia in the early 1990s and then to the industrialized democracies by the latter half of the 1990s. This is not to imply either that the organizations ceased operations when the emphasis moved elsewhere or that there were none in Central Asia, Europe, or America before the major shifts. Rather, there was a shift in emphasis and allocation of resources.

The key actors from the 1950s through the 1980s were in Turkey. Muhämmäd Imin Bughra and Isa Yusuf Alptekin, key political figures in Xinjiang before 1949, had settled in Turkey along with more than two thousand Uyghur refugees after the People's Liberation Army (PLA)'s advance into Xinjiang. Muhämmäd Imin's *Šärqi Türkistan tarikhi* (*History of East Turkestan*) became a foundational text for Uyghur independence activists, arguing as it did that Uyghurs had founded many independent states and that East Turkestan was their homeland. Indeed, officials in Ürümci still blamed it as the key ideological inspiration to Uyghur "splittists" in 1991 (Bovingdon and Nebijan Tursun 2004).[8] He and Alptekin wrote a number of popular books in Uyghur and Turkish and also supported the publication of newspapers in Turkey that popularized the cause of Uyghur independence.[9] The two also helped found several organizations, including the Eastern Turkestan Fund, the Eastern Turkestan Refugee Committee, and the National Center for the Liberation of Eastern Turkestan. After Muhämmäd Imin's death in 1965, Alptekin became the uncrowned leader of the Uyghur movement and continued to command enormous influence until his death in 1995 (Shichor 2003:288–89).

Soon after arriving in Turkey Alptekin sought to align his appeal with that of the decolonization movement sweeping Asia and Africa. In 1955 he attended the famous Bandung Conference (the inaugural meeting of the Asian-African Conference), which condemned "colonialism in all of its manifestations." He went to subsequent meetings of the conference in New Delhi in 1960 and Mogadishu in 1965. In addition, Alptekin sought sympathy and assistance from international Islamic organizations, traveling to conferences or congresses in Baghdad in 1961, Mecca in 1963, and Karachi in 1964. Several of these conferences passed resolutions in support of "Turkestan," and Alptekin tried for some time to induce the member states to implement them. Alptekin even worked to make common cause with Tibetans, meeting with the Dalai Lama in 1960 and again in 1970, efforts that finally bore fruit with the establishment of the "Allied Committee of the Peoples of Eastern Turkestan, Inner Mongolia, and Tibet" in 1985 (Shichor 2003:290, 292). In early

1970, Isa Yusuf Alptekin traveled to the United States in hopes of gaining support both in Washington and from the UN for an "independent Turkestan," though without success (Salisbury 1970).

Alptekin sought and received support from the Turkish government, particularly from officials sympathetic to the Pan-Turkist cause. He was close to several Turkish prime ministers, including Süleyman Demirel and his successor Turgut Özal. Özal accepted a Uyghur flag, cap, and clothing from the aged Alptekin in a public ceremony in the 1980s, not demurring when Alptekin announced that he was handing over the "Eastern Turkestani cause" (Tyler 2003:241; Ünal 1995).[10] Owing to the officials' support for Alptekin, Uyghur organizations operated with little interference until the 1980 coup that unseated Demirel, and they were reinstated soon afterward with the understanding that Ankara would have a say in their administration (Besson 1998:170).

Muhämmäd Imin and Alptekin after him were temperate in speech and moderate in their demands, outwardly willing to accept greater autonomy in lieu of independence for Xinjiang, even if their writings (and Alptekin's trip to America) occasionally suggested otherwise. A Uyghur exile claimed that in 1972 Moscow had offered to give Alptekin ten troop divisions with tanks, several of the divisions entirely Uyghur, so that he could take over Xinjiang. Alptekin reportedly declined (Tyler 2003:225). Despite Alptekin's moderate stance, support from the Turkish government, and considerable sympathy from postcolonial states and Islamic organizations, the movement he led wielded no perceptible influence over China. Until the 1970s, Beijing was relatively isolated and thus invulnerable to international sanctions, and the People's Republic of China (PRC) itself had won wide support as a leader of anticolonial struggles in Asia and Africa in the 1960s, making the task of painting it as an imperialist more difficult (Shichor 2003:290–91). The situation did not obviously grow more favorable in the 1980s.

The collapse of the Soviet Union in 1991 and the emergence of independent Central Asian states named for their Turkic-speaking majorities seemed to open up entirely new political vistas. This turn of events led to two final efforts to organize an effective movement centered in Turkey. In 1992 Uyghurs from around the world converged on Istanbul to found the Eastern Turkestan World National Congress. The congress was organized with one eye on Central Asia, in the expectation that the newly independent countries belonging to Turkic-speaking Muslims would support the Uyghurs' quest for independence and finally make coordinated action possible (BBC Monitoring Central Asia 2002). To that end the organizers invited representatives from several new organizations in Kazakhstan and Kyrgyzstan. All those attending agreed on the ultimate goal of an independent Uyghur state, and the congress elected an English-speaking Uyghur writer living in Australia, Ähmät Igämbärdi, as president. But the hopeful atmosphere in which the congress was convened soon dissipated, owing to a lack of funds and internal disputes over leadership and organizational goals. Representatives from different regions differed strongly over who ought to be in charge and whether to advocate peaceful or military methods (Shichor 2003:293–94; Tyler 2003:233).[11]

There were advocates of *jihad* in the Uyghur diaspora at the time. In 1997 a recent immigrant to Turkey from Xinjiang published a book entitled *The Struggle for Independence*. Averring that "tears and suffering will not win independence," the author opened and closed the book insisting that *jihad*, not a quest for human rights protections, was the only path to success and pointing to the Chechens as "models" for the Uyghurs' struggle (Äzimät 1997:1–16, 120–39, 183–222; Roberts 2004:424, n. 45). There is no evidence, however, that jihadists held sway at this or subsequent conferences.

The second major conference in Turkey received not only permission to convene but also material support from Ankara. Uyghurs again gathered in Istanbul in 1998 to found the Eastern Turkestan National Center. They chose as their leader Mehmet Riza Bekin, a Uyghur émigré who had risen to the rank of general in the Turkish army and subsequently served in the cabinet of a Turkish prime minister. As a token of support, the Turkish government "lent" the organization a large building until its members could "go back to their homeland freely." While this organization struck some as an "embryonic . . . government-in-exile," it could not paper over the deep political conflicts among the members (Cao Changqing 1999b).

After this meeting, the epicenter of Uyghur organizing shifted away from Turkey, owing to pressure from both Beijing and Washington.[12] To understand why, and also to see what had made the congresses in 1992 and 1998 so contentious, we need to pick up the story in Central Asia. In the early 1990s it appeared that the newly independent Central Asian states might be ideal sites for a new phase of Uyghur political action. One factor that strengthened this belief was that while there were some 40,000 Uyghurs in Turkey, Kazakhstan alone had a Uyghur community of more than 300,000, with at least 50,000 more in Kyrgyzstan. Uyghurs and outside observers shared a widespread expectation that fraternal feelings among the various Turkic-speaking peoples would induce the states to provide space for, and even actively assist, those groups. Political developments in Central Asia during the 1990s, however, dashed Uyghurs' initial optimism. As a consequence, the focus of organizing did not settle in Bishkek or Almaty but shifted instead to Europe and North America, where far smaller communities lived.

CENTRAL ASIA

Although the disintegration of the Soviet Union turned many Uyghurs' eyes to Central Asia, the history of Uyghur political action in those states begins much earlier, with the widening of the Sino-Soviet split in 1962. It was in the spring of that year that at least sixty thousand Uyghurs and Qazaqs fled from Xinjiang into the Kazakh Soviet Socialist Republic, exasperated with Chinese policies in the region.[13] Seeing the relationship between Moscow and Beijing deteriorate, a group of Uyghurs in Kazakhstan decided to send a letter to Moscow asking for help. Their proposal was that Moscow could harm its rival and simultaneously aid Uyghurs by helping them establish an independent homeland in Xinjiang. Moscow's response is not recorded. The response by Alma-Ata suggested the risks of such a move. When the Kazakh Party Central Committee in Alma-Ata learned that the group had sent the letter without its approval, Hashir Wahidi, one of the letter writers, was hauled in and harshly interrogated. The secretary of the Central Committee reportedly shouted at him, "If you do this again, I'll strap you in an electric chair and burn your body to ash!" (Sabit Abdurakhman 2002:35–36).

Ironically, within a year Moscow had apparently communicated to Alma-Ata the utility of giving Uyghur activists some latitude, allowing the establishment of organizations and a militia supposedly to make Xinjiang independent. But these clearly were foreign policy tools rather than autonomous organizations (Eurasianet 2003).[14] In 1970 Isa Yusuf Alptekin told *New York Times* reporter Harrison Salisbury that Zunun Taipov, a former leader in the Eastern Turkestan Republic, commanded a "liberation army of Eastern Turkestan" in Kazakhstan with fifty thousand soldiers. Zunun had reportedly founded the army in 1963, recruiting former members of Xinjiang's Fifth Corps who had fled in the great 1962 exodus. Ziya Sämädi, a famous Uyghur intellectual and another leader of the republic, was said to be in charge of a "committee for the liberation of East Turkestan," also founded in 1963 (Salisbury 1970; Tyler 2003:233). Chinese sources also speak of both the army and the political organization under Ziya advocating "national liberation," indicating that both had KGB support. One author argues that by the late 1960s Moscow had decided to use the Uyghurs as a "trump card" in any talks with China (Li Qi 2003:83; see also Li Danhui 2003). During his 1982 visit to Xinjiang, Isa's son Erkin Alptekin was told by Chinese officials that Russians were regularly sending agents, weapons, and subversive literature into the region. In fact, they blamed on "Russian spies" the burning of a mosque in Qaghiliq in January 1981, which had provoked a major riot (see appendix) (Alptekin 1983:150).[15]

Moscow also sponsored Uyghur-language propagandizing in Central Asia. As discussed in chapter 2, radio stations in Tashkent and Alma-Ata regularly broadcast programs in Uyghur touting the virtues of Soviet-style titular republics and urging Uyghurs to exercise their right of self-determination. The broadcasts took special pains to emphasize that the Soviet Union was working to help "liberate" Uyghurs, offering Zunun Taipov regular opportunities to advertise the preparations of his military force from 1963 on (Li Qi 2003: 82–83; McMillen 1979:123–24, 227; Zhang Zhirong 2005:269).[16] On the basis of archival records, a Chinese scholar has argued that the broadcasts indeed led many non-Hans in Xinjiang to hope that with Soviet help, the region would soon become independent (Li Danhui 2003:98). In 1979 Moscow permitted the writer Yusupbäk Mukhlisi to begin circulating a newspaper, *Šärqiy Türkistan awazi* (*Voice of East Turkestan*) in handwritten form. Following the example of the radio broadcasts, the paper advocated independence for Eastern Turkestan and invoked UN principles in support of Uyghur national self-determination. Moscow's patronage enabled Mukhlisi not only to circulate the paper around the Central Asian Uyghur community but also to mail copies to correspondents in Turkey, India, Pakistan, Afghanistan, Australia, Europe, and the United States. Soviet leaders clearly saw Mukhlisi's paper, like the political organization and the militia, as useful at some points and inconvenient at others. There was no further news of the latter two by the mid-1970s, and in 1980 Mukhlisi's paper was quietly shut down at the same time that the Soviet Union began new border talks with the PRC (Uighur 1983).[17]

Some Uyghurs living in Kazakhstan saw Mikhail Gorbachev's announcement of *perestroika* as an opportunity to renew their political struggle. In 1990 Hashir Wahidi and several other politically active Uyghurs wrote Gorbachev a letter seeking his support for their cause. He responded, "Because our country signed an agreement with the PRC not to interfere in each other's affairs, I am unable to help you. However, I wish you the best of luck" (Sabit Abdurakhman 2002:38).

As the Soviet Union began to disintegrate in 1991, several Central Asian leaders strongly opposed the dissolution of the union, fearing that separation from Russia would bring financial ruin. Nursultan Nazarbayev finally and reluctantly declared Kazakhstan independent in December of 1991 (Olcott 1997:556). Within a few months two organizations successfully registered with the government in Almaty: the Uyghurstan Liberation Organization (ULO) and the Eastern Turkestan United National Revolutionary Front (ETUNRF) (Besson 1998:178).[18] Most of the members of these organizations were Uyghurs who had emigrated from Xinjiang in the 1950s and 1960s, whereas Uyghurs who had come to Kazakhstan earlier were more concerned with improving their conditions in that country. All faced the challenges of making a life in Central Asia under difficult political and economic conditions while also hoping for an independent homeland elsewhere (Roberts 1998b:517).[19]

Hashir Wahidi, one of the authors of the 1962 letter to Nikita Khrushchev and the 1990 letter to Gorbachev, took the helm of the ULO at its founding. One of his first moves was to attempt a merger with a new organization headed by Ziya Sämädi. After two meetings, though, it became clear that Ziya had changed his tune since the 1960s. His organization did not intend to "struggle for the motherland's independence" but had lowered its sights to petitioning China for democracy in Xinjiang (Sabit Abdurakhman 2002:101–2).[20]

As a political organization, the ULO was explicitly and heavily devoted to propagandizing the Uyghur cause in various media.[21] It produced a number of videos, making documentaries on the teratogenic consequences of China's nuclear tests in Xinjiang and later on the Ghulja uprising, and filming the proceedings of Uyghur political congresses.[22] Members staged numerous commemorative events, including memorials to heroes from the Eastern Turkestan Republic of 1944–1949 (among them the recently deceased Zunun Taipov) and an anniversary celebration for the founding of the republic itself. The organization published books on the ETR and on contemporary politics in Xinjiang. Attempting to reach and frighten a wider audience, it promoted a book entitled *Concerning the Danger of Chinese Aggression in Central Asia* in 1994. The organization's vice chairman also wrote a history of the Uyghurs, which he serialized in the organization's newspaper, *Uyghurstan* (Sabit Abdurakhman 2002:60–62).

The ETUNRF was led from its inception by Yusupbäk Mukhlisi, who claimed for the remainder of his life to be plotting or overseeing violent struggle against Chinese rule in Xinjiang. The evidence suggests more mundanely that like his counterparts in the ULO, he mainly engaged in propaganda, in both print and numerous interviews. He reopened his paper, *Voice of East Turkestan*, sometime in the 1990s. He gave regular interviews to Western journalists in the 1990s, during which time he could be relied on for assurances that Uyghur organizations had been infiltrating Xinjiang and perpetrating all manner of violence and destruction there for years.[23] He bragged that a group under his control, the "Tigers of Lop Nor," had destroyed aircraft and tanks in the Lop Nor nuclear-testing zone in 1993. In 1997 he claimed that he commanded an underground army of thirty thousand, and his newspaper published a story about a heroic "Commander Abdulghappar Shahiyari" reported to command a "division of many thousands of volunteers" inside Xinjiang. In the same year, his son Mukhiddin (Modan) Mukhlisi claimed responsibility for the Ürümci bus bombings on February 25. In 1999, when he was eighty years old, Yusupbäk told a reporter that his organization directed much of the violent resistance in Xinjiang, mentioning prison breaks and the theft of weapons from arsenals, claims credited by Ma Dazheng (BBC Monitoring Asia Pacific 1997; Bransten 1997; Cao Chang-qing 1999a; Grabot 1996; Kushko 1997; Ma Dazheng 2003:193; PRC: Exiled Leader Claims 20 Dead in Street Fighting in Xinjiang" 1996; Sheridan 2000). The evidence suggests the elder Mukhlisi was a habitual storyteller, but journalists seeking scarce information about Uyghur political activities in Central Asia and Xinjiang regularly lent him a credulous ear, as did the authors of at least one intelligence report. Mukhlisi's chronic exaggerations notwithstanding, Ma believed in 1999 that his ETUNRF was the "organization most threatening to China," although Ma focused his concern mainly on the group's political influence on other Uyghur transnational organs (Ma Dazheng 2003:192–93; McNeal 2002:11).[24]

Three days after the Ghulja uprising in February 1997, the three main Uyghur organizations, the ULO, the ETUNRF, and the Uyghur Association of Kazakhstan (UAK), agreed to combine forces (East Turkestan Information Center 1997a). The new umbrella organization announced that because affairs in Xinjiang had reached an intolerable pitch, it would now have to take action. The group was strengthened by the addition of hundreds of refugees from the post-Ghulja crackdown, and members were galvanized by the refugees' eyewitness accounts of that crackdown. But owing to increasing pressure from Almaty, the leaders had to look outside the region for alliances or support. In July 1997 Mukhlisi traveled to Washington with Qähriman Ghojambärdi, head of the UAK, where they met with State Department officials. Hashir Wahidi had planned to travel with them but could not because he was recovering from a beating in his home by unknown assailants.[25] They reportedly pleaded with the government officials for assistance in ending "Chinese colonialism" in Xinjiang and also urged that Radio Free Asia begin service in Uyghur (East Turkestan Information Center 1997b). On returning to Almaty, Mukhlisi was then able to use his paper to assert that the meeting had been a success. In it he announced that the U.S. government supported the Uyghurs and would henceforth "mark a day to commemorate their struggle for freedom." He also reported that there would be supportive programming on the Voice of America and Radio Liberty (BBC Monitoring Asia Pacific 1997).

Ma Dazheng observed with alarm that the union of the three organizations, the Uyghur Association, had augmented their collective power dramatically and extended their influence beyond Central Asia. Uyghur organizations outside the region were looking to the association for leadership. It was urgent, he argued, that China "limit as far as possible splittist organizations' political influence and freedom of action in the countries where they are active" (Ma Dazheng 2003:192–93, 199).

Efforts in this regard in fact began soon after the new Central Asian states emerged. Beijing quickly realized the importance of bringing diplomatic and other pressures to bear on Central Asia as Uyghur organizations there gathered strength and confidence. In mid-1994, Li Peng toured the Central Asian states, promising economic aid to the struggling republics and, in turn, demanding assurances from them that they would provide no assistance to the Uyghur separatists (Dillon 2004:144). In 1995 Nazarbayev signed an agreement with Jiang Zemin, under which security services in Kazakhstan would monitor Uyghurs' activities and share their findings with Beijing (Raman 1999). Document no. 7, promulgated by the CCP Politburo in 1996, ordered officials to use "all means" available to thwart Uyghur organizations' attempts to gain international attention. Beijing's top leaders unhesitatingly proposed complementing diplomacy with power politics. "Take full advantage of our political superiority," they instructed, and "always maintain pressure" on the Central Asian states (Human Rights Watch 1999:12). The Shanghai Cooperation Organization (SCO), originally formed as the "Shanghai Five" in 1996, proved the perfect venue for China both to press the Central Asian states to crack down on Uyghurs and to offer the states benefits for doing so. Despite being advertised as a forum for the discussion of all subjects of interest, from borders to economics to joint military exercises, from its inception the SCO focused heavily on security. The communiqués from its yearly meetings repeatedly stressed military cooperation and reciprocal promises not to give quarter to separatists threatening other member countries' security or territorial integrity. These agreements were widely understood to be directed principally at Uyghurs throughout Central Asia, as well as at religious and dissident groups (Blank 2004; Dillon 2004:142–55; Gladney 2006; Goldsmith 2005; Ong 2005).

Beginning in 1996 Bishkek, Almaty, and Tashkent all stepped up pressure on Uyghur organizations (Grabot 1996; Rashid 2003:70–71, 202). In April 1996, a week before the inaugural meeting of the SCO, the foreign minister of Kazakhstan warned the Uyghurs in that country that Almaty would tolerate no agitation for self-determination, condemning separatism as the "political AIDS" of the late twentieth century (Agence France-Presse 1996). In June the Kazakhstan government formally closed *Uyghurstan*, the paper that the ULO had published clandestinely for three years (Sabit Abdurakhman 2002:62–63). In March of the same year the Ministry of Justice in Bishkek banned, for three months, all activities by the organization Ittipak (Unity), including its publication of the paper of the same name, insisting that the organization's activities went against the "interests of the Chinese people" (BBC Monitoring Service: Former USSR 1996; Dillon 2004:145). All three countries ordered the closing of political organizations that had previously been legally registered. Tashkent went so far as to ban purely cultural organizations (Tarimi 2004).

Soon after the Soviet Union's collapse, the Uyghurs had spoken hopefully of "fraternal loyalties" among Central Asian populations sharing a religion, speaking very similar languages, and claiming intertwined histories. In fact this brotherly feeling proved quite ephemeral. Central Asians indeed had sympathy for Uyghurs, but xenophobes and nationalists proved quite receptive to depictions of Uyghurs not as beleaguered cousins but as dangerous aliens. Nationalist newspapers published dark musings about the demographic threats posed by Uyghurs ("Qazaqstanda Qazaq azayip, Uyghirlar köbeyip zhatir" 2000) or claims that Uyghurs threatened political stability, being violent and terroristic by nature (Imatov 2001). In addition to pleasing China by clamping down on Uyghurs, Central Asian leaders found it quite convenient to blame "outsiders" for domestic political problems.[26] In the latter half of the 1990s, it became increasingly clear that Beijing had made it impossible for an effective movement to survive in Central Asia.[27] In response to this pressure, the focus of Uyghur activism shifted decisively to the industrialized democracies.

THIRD PHASE: INDUSTRIAL DEMOCRACIES

Despite their great distance from the focus of Uyghurs' political aspirations, the countries of Western Europe and North America, as well as Australia, had two very attractive features. First, they had legal systems that protected lawfully registered organizations and political speech, and second, they were sufficiently strong economically and politically to withstand Beijing's demands that those protections be abridged.[28] At the same time, it was an obvious limitation to advocates of armed resistance that their governments frowned on talk of political violence.

Small Uyghur communities had formed in Germany, the Low Countries, and Sweden and were collecting in Australia, Canada, and the United States as well. Many of these communities formed nationally bounded Uyghur organizations such as the Belgium Uyghur Association, the Swedish Uyghur Committee, and the Australian and Uyghur Canadian Association. Uyghurs also founded transnational groups in Europe such as the East Turkestan Union and the Union of East Turkestani Youth (Shichor 2003:293). These groups regularly hosted cultural events aimed at preserving the Uyghur culture and language for émigrés and their children. Like their counterparts in Turkey and Central Asia, they also devoted great energies to publicizing the "Uyghur cause" and disseminating news affecting Uyghurs. This is true of national groups like the Swedish Uyghur Committee, whose stated goals are aiding to refugees, publishing news about Uyghur affairs, creating films to disseminate internationally, and sponsoring cultural events and museums (Svenska Uygur Kommittén n.d.). Transnational organizations have mounted even more ambitious efforts. The Eastern Turkestan Information Center, founded in Munich in 1991, regularly published a widely read bulletin through 1996, and since that time has promulgated the even more widely read *World Uyghur Network News* via the Internet.[29]

Uyghurs from the various states had attended the first Uyghur congress in Istanbul in 1992, and many attended the establishment of the Eastern Turkestan National Center in 1998 as representatives of their national or transnational organizations (Shichor 2003:293–95). As mentioned previously, increasing Chinese pressure on Ankara made it impossible to arrange another such meeting in Turkey. The 1999 conference, held in Munich, was planned to transform the national center into a national congress. The delegates wanted to establish the new congress as a genuine umbrella organization, which recognized the various national and transnational groups but was authorized to act as sole plenipotentiary representative of all, so as to present a much more potent challenge to Beijing. From the moment the congress began, however, there were serious disputes. The delegates fundamentally disagreed on tactics. The European-based Uyghurs insisted that the organization embrace only nonviolent methods, but many of the representatives from Central Asia disagreed, considering violence the sole remaining practical strategy. Yusupbäk Mukhlisi had been so disappointed by the prospectus in advance of the congress that he refused to attend at all. Participants in the congress later referred to the ETUNRF as "the opposition," a detail that casts doubt on Ma Dazheng's high estimate of Mukhlisi's influence on Uyghur transnational organizations.[30] The conflict continued with the selection of leaders, in a contest that clearly pitted the much larger Central Asian Uyghur community, now hamstrung by Beijing's pressure on the various states, against the small European community, which had much greater freedom of movement and activity. In the end, Enver Can, a prominent Uyghur living in Germany, won the election by four votes (BBC Monitoring Service: Former USSR 1999; Cao Changqing 1999b; Shichor 2003:294; Tyler 2003:233–35).

The very first item on the agenda and bone of contention, however, was the name of the organization itself.[31] Sabit Abdurakhman, leader of the ULO after Hashir Wahidi's death, felt that the name should not be the "Eastern Turkestan National Congress" but the "World Uyghur Committee to Save the Motherland" or else the "Uyghurstan National Congress."[32] European delegates insisted that the original name be preserved. In the end, the assembled delegates agreed to a compromise, and the organization was saddled with the unwieldy name "Eastern Turkestan (Uyghurstan) National Congress" (BBC Monitoring Service: Former USSR 1999; Sabit Abdurakhman 2002:220). Yaqub Anat, a poet, proposed "let[ting] the people decide" once independence was achieved (Tyler 2003:235). A reporter who interviewed Anat described this as "one of the exile movement's pettier feuds" (Hoh 2000). But in fact, it was not a trivial matter.

Instead, this conflict concerned different visions of the future homeland and the contest over the right to define that homeland authoritatively. Did "Uyghurstan" imply, by analogy with the other Central Asian states, that this would be the state of and for Uyghurs? Did it suggest a nationalizing state, where Uyghur might be declared the sole state language and non-Uyghurs would enjoy rights only at the sufferance of the government (Brubaker 1993)? Would non-Uyghurs be second-class citizens? The ungainly name chosen for the organization indicates that there was no agreement on these questions.[33] It is not at all surprising that the partisans for a state named for Uyghurs hailed from Central Asia, where they had ample experience of being nontitulars in nationally defined states, while Uyghurs living in the industrialized democracies favored a pluralist, civically defined state.[34]

The ET(U)NC arranged for its third congress, preceded by a conference on the "occupation" of East Turkestan, to be held in the European Parliament in October 2001, on an invitation from the Transnational Radical Party. The opening of the venue to Uyghur independence advocates seemed to confer increased legitimacy on their activities. This was the first in a series of instances in which Uyghur activists cannily arranged meeting sites with high visibility that suggested international recognition of their cause. Yitzhak Shichor is right to observe that Chinese officials' greatest concern was not the practical effects of the congress but its "symbolic context," demonstrating once again the importance of representational politics to the contention between Uyghur activists and the Chinese government.

Beijing complained mightily to Brussels and sought in vain to pressure the European Union to refuse the space to the congress, which it insisted was a terrorist organization. China clearly hoped that this charge, coming less than a month after the September 11 attacks, would be a powerful deterrent. For good measure, the Chinese foreign minister warned that allowing the meeting would "damage Sino-European relations" (BBC News Online 2001). Rebuffed, China sent reporters, who sat through all the sessions but pronounced the meeting "not interesting." From Beijing's perspective, it surely did not help matters that the EU's parliamentary delegate to China acknowledged at the conference that while the European Parliament had a "one China" policy, "we cannot rule the future" (Shichor 2003:309; Tyler 2003:237). To Uyghur activists, the success at staging meetings in Munich and Brussels and garnering international sympathy appeared to confirm the wisdom of the westward shift of organizing, even if it alienated some portion of the large community in Central Asia.

Infuriated at the failure to stop the meeting in Brussels and worried that it augured growing international support for the cause of Uyghur independence, officials in China's State Council and Ministry of Public Security changed tactics. Taking advantage of the opportunity created by the September 11 attacks and the subsequent "war on terror," the State Council promulgated the January 2002 document in the hope of persuading the international community that Uyghur activists were not "freedom fighters" but terrorists. The document gave special emphasis to the charges that Uyghurs had met with Osama bin Laden, fought with the Taliban, and received financial and military support from both (Guowuyuan xinwen bangongshi 2002). When the United States and UN listed the ETIM as a terrorist organization in late 2002, as discussed at the beginning of this chapter, Beijing took it as a hopeful sign. Yet officials remained frustrated at Washington's decision to list only one organization, rather than issuing a blanket condemnation of what it called "ET terrorists." Having received advance notice that Uyghur activists were planning yet another congress in Europe, Chinese officials redoubled their efforts. On December 15, 2003, the Ministry of Public Security issued a second document claiming to offer proof that four Uyghur organizations and eleven Uyghurs associated with them were terrorist. The document listed the World Uyghur Youth Congress and the Eastern Turkestan Information Center and announced that China had submitted "most-wanted" notices for the organizations' leaders, Dolqun Isa and Abduljelil Qaraqaš (Karakash), to Interpol ("Gong'anbu gongbu shoupi rending de 'dongtu' kongbu zuzhi ji chengyuan mingdan" 2003). The ETIC was, as noted earlier, an organization entirely devoted to broadcasting news, and the charge against it was manifestly preposterous. Dolqun Isa issued a scorching rebuttal of the charges against him and the organization he led (Dolkun Isa n.d.).[35] Although Chinese newspapers subsequently asserted that the December 2003 document had elicited strong international support ("China Hails Anti-Terror Progress" 2004), governments outside Central Asia offered nothing of the kind; none made moves to add more organizations or individuals to a watch list.

In April 2004, members of the ET(U)NC and World Uyghur Youth Congress once again converged on Munich with representatives from all major regional Uyghur organizations to found the World Uyghur Congress (WUC). Public Security officials in China remonstrated with their counterparts in Germany, arguing that it would be "very dangerous if 'Eastern Turkistan' terrorists were allowed to operate" there.[36] Once again, Chinese authorities tried to paint the Uyghur separatists as part of a global terrorist network, mentioning the recent March 11 attacks in Spain and suggesting that Uyghur activists threatened not just China's security but "world peace and stability" as well (Xinhua 2004). German police made cursory investigations but were not persuaded. The congress was held as planned.

The selection of leaders showed careful attempts to balance regional constitu-encies. Former ET(U)NC head Riza Bekin, chosen as chairman emeritus, hailed from Turkey. Erkin Alptekin of Germany was chosen as chairman. In a blatant thumbing of the nose at Beijing, the WUYC's Dolqun Isa was appointed head secretary. One of the vice chairmen, Memet Tohti, headed the Uyghur Cana-dian Association. The congress chose as chairman of the Executive Committee Alim Seytoff, president of the Uyghur American Association. The leadership also notably included representatives from Central Asia, Qähriman Ghojambärdi of Kazakhstan, and Rozimämät Abdubaqi from Kyrgyzstan. If officials in Beijing read the notice of the congress closely, they might have found a bit of gratification in one small touch that suggested Uyghurs had absorbed at least one precept from the CCP: the token woman appointed to the leadership was given charge of the "Women's Committee."[37]

While similar in form to previous Uyghur congresses, the WUC achieved a greater degree of consensus in articulating its mission and strategies. Thus its claim to be the highest authority representing Uyghur interests and suborganizations had more substance to it than similar announcements by its predecessors, the two national congresses.

These facts made it all the more extraordinary when a group of Uyghurs assem-bled in Washington only four months later, on September 14, 2004, to announce the formation of the "Eastern Turkestan Government in Exile" (ETGIE).[38] The organization quickly announced its extraordinarily elaborate leadership structure, with a president, prime minister, two vice prime ministers, and ministers of trea-sury, natural resources, justice, commerce, transport, construction, education, health, and even national defense. The delegates chose as their president Ähmät Igämbärdi, who still carried some prestige as the former head of the first international congress in Istanbul in 1992 (and remained chairman of the Australian Turkestani Asso-ciation). Longtime American resident Anwer Yusuf, widely seen as the spearhead of the new organization, was elected prime minister. Particularly conspicuous was the choice of Kazakhstan's Qähriman Ghojambärdi, appointed only a few months earlier as a representative to the WUC, for the weighty position of the ETGIE's minister of national defense. The most striking feature of the event beyond the declaration itself, however, was the site where it was declared: room HC-6 of the US Capitol Building. If Turkish government buildings or the European Parliament had lent a certain gravitas to previous organizations, the ETGIE's access to the Capitol seemed to suggest something more: the direct support of the U.S. govern-ment. A notice in Uyghur two days before the proceedings made maximum use of this symbolism, boasting that the site was "the U.S. Congress building, with a status equivalent to the Chinese Government's Zhongnanhai in Beijing or the Russian Government's Kremlin" (Turani 2004).

Others responded far more angrily to what looked like an embarrassing mockery of the Uyghur movement by the founders of the ETGIE, just when the WUC had achieved unprecedented concord. They worried that the announcement would earn nothing but derision in the international community and harm Uyghurs' chances of being taken seriously in the future.[39] The announcement of a new government-in-exile seemed capable of nullifying in a single stroke the WUC's claim to be the highest representative Uyghur organization.

The ETGIE founders had clearly anticipated this objection. The Constitution of the Republic of Eastern Turkistan, promulgated in paperback form in Uyghur, Turkish, English, Chinese, and Japanese, appealed to popular acclamation as well as to a historical legacy for authority. The government "has been accepted," it announced peremptorily (without noting who had done the accepting), "as the sole organ of the Eastern Turkistan Republic authorized to protect the rights of the people of Eastern Turkistan Republic until our country has been liberated from rule by imperialist Communist China" (Šärqiy Türkistan Jumhuriyiti Sürgündiki Parlamenti wä Hökümiti 2005:42–43). Yao Kuangyi, former ambassador to Turkey, soon announced with delight that the founders of the ETGIE had clearly intended to vie with the WUC (Yao Kuangyi 2005). This unexpected development so obviously served the Chinese government's strategy of sowing divisions within and among organizations that some Uyghurs suspected that Anwer Yusuf had acted on instructions from Beijing.[40]

Less than a month later, leaders of the WUC called an executive committee meeting in Munich on October 9 and 10, at the end of which they debated the proper response to the ETGIE. At the conclusion of the debate, the executive committee released a statement reiterating that the WUC was the sole plenipotentiary representative of Uyghurs inside Xinjiang and in the diaspora. As such, it would cooperate with the ETGIE only after the ETGIE had legally registered in the United States and "received official recognition" from the U.S. government. Within a month of that announcement, a State Department spokesman stated unequivocally that no such recognition had been granted (U.S. Department of State 2004). This statement elicited yet another angry response from the Uyghur American Association's discussion board, accusing the ETGIE participants of "building castles in Spain" and demanding that they explain themselves.[41] Nonetheless, the WUC's canny announcement, combined with the State Department's denial, neatly boxed in the ETGIE. There is no evidence that the organization has successfully registered since that announcement. Instead, its members have settled down to much the same tasks as those at their counterpart organizations: staging demonstrations, writing letters to politicians and international bodies, and issuing regular news reports about matters assumed to be of concern to Uyghurs.[42]

THE PROBLEM OF DISUNITY

The hopeful language of some Uyghur groups' communiqués and the dark fulminations of Chinese officials converge on an important point: the claim that there is a single, unified Uyghur independence movement. Activists name their objective the "cause of the homeland" (*wätän däwäsi*), and many hold the Manichean view that one is either working for this cause or obstructing it. As has been well established by this point, Chinese spokespersons and writers refer constantly to "DongTu" *zuzhi* ('ET' organization[s]) taking advantage of the ambiguity of Chinese nouns as to number. At times, officials make clear that this is an umbrella term for a congeries of different organizations. As we have seen, in the immediate aftermath of Rabiyä Qadir's second Nobel Peace Prize nomination, a prominent newspaper published an article referring to a single "ET organization." Yet neither the propaganda emanating from each side nor the energetic politicking of prominent Uyghurs can paper over the fact that there is no single movement. Uyghur communities and that organizations are still divided by different goals and strategies.

The complaint that Uyghurs are divided among themselves has been a constant refrain in the diaspora for decades. Erkin Alptekin, the presumptive leader of the movement by the late 1990s, said in 2000 that "disunity is a historical problem among the peoples of East Turkestan. . . . If we were a united people, we would not have been under Chinese rule today" (Hoh 2000, 24). Even though Uyghurs regularly lament the divisions within the community and the repeated failure to form a united political organization as their special burden, these weaknesses could have been predicted. Any diaspora community spread over a large number of countries with very different economies, attitudes toward immigrants, and political climates faces obstacles to unified action. This is all the more true when members of the group have been engaged in a decades-long, transnational struggle for independence.

The shifts in geography, goals, and activities have saddled the various organizations with many burdens. Activists face the further difficulty of holding a movement together with exceedingly few resources.[43] The groups are heavily dependent on particular patron-states for material resources and often for political support as well. These states have inevitably used Uyghur organizations to pursue their particular interests and then cast them aside for the same reason. This was true of the Soviet Union, to a lesser extent of Turkey, of the Central Asian states for a time, and then more recently of the United States.

The Uyghur American Association (UAA), though a national organization, has in recent years begun to bear the marks of a transnational one.[44] The National Endowment for Democracy elected to fund the UAA in 2004 and to renew that funding in 2005. This money gave the group new luster and, needless to say, new resources. Although the endowment is a private organization, and its financial largesse does not indicate U.S. government support—a point that the endowment representative Louisa Coan Greve underscored in her address to the UAA congress in 2005 (Greve 2006)—neither could the implication that Washington tacitly approved be lightly dismissed.[45] The endowment is a bipartisan organization (with Republican and Democratic suborganizations) funded with taxpayers' money and directed to sponsor democratic initiatives around the world. Thus the organization's funding of the UAA suggests, at minimum, the support of powerful members of US Congress.[46]

Even more significant in the long run was Washington's decision to join forces with international human rights organizations in pressing Beijing to release Rabiyä Qadir (better known abroad as Rebiya Kadeer). Once famous in China as the richest woman in Xinjiang, later a member of the Autonomous Region's and then the National People's political consultative congresses, Rabiyä had run afoul of the authorities when she began to raise complaints in those representative bodies about the Uyghurs' status in Xinjiang. Rabiyä was on her way to meet a U.S. congressional staff delegation and deliver information about Uyghur political activists in 1999 when she was arrested. She was sentenced to six years in prison for "leaking state secrets" but was ultimately released and allowed to travel to the United States in March 2005 on the pretext of seeking medical treatment. Within months of her arrival, she was elected head of the Uyghur American Association. A few months later, she traveled to Europe and met with both Uyghurs and European officials in various states. By late 2006, she was the presumptive candidate for president of the WUC, and the organization's "second assembly" duly elected her on November 27, 2006 (World Uyghur Congress 2006b). By early 2007, the WUC Web site listed her as its president, with Erkin Alptekin now described as one of two "chief advisers," the other being Sidiq Haji Rozi, a noted Uyghur dissident intellectual and long resident in the United States and, not coincidentally, Rabiyä's husband.[47]

GETTING TO THE TABLE: THE STRUGGLE TO BUILD A POWERFUL ORGANIZATION

Just as the government in Ürümci has steadfastly refused to negotiate with Uyghur demonstrators in Xinjiang, Beijing has never publicly acknowledged that it had a legitimate interlocutor among the transnational Uyghur organizations. Put another way, no Uyghur organization has ever been powerful enough to force Beijing to make such an admission. The lack of an organization politically or militarily capable of bringing Beijing to the negotiating table distinguishes the conflict in Xinjiang (as well as that in Tibet) from many other internal conflicts in Asia, such as those in Indonesia and the Philippines (Aspinall and Crouch 2003; McGibbon 2004; Rood 2005).

Beijing's obdurate insistence that all Uyghur independence organizations abroad (and even some that do not advocate independence) are "terrorist" is the outward face of its strategy of refusing all compromise. This stance neatly complements the demonization of domestic Uyghur critics of Xinjiang's policies as "splittists, terrorists, and religious extremists." Just as those who raise the matters of religious freedom or immigration inside Xinjiang stand accused of harboring secret secessionist aims, party officials condemn Uyghurs in the diaspora for using democracy and human rights as pretexts, concealing their final objective of independence.

There appear to be no firm CCP strictures against holding discussions with prominent Uyghurs abroad, only against doing so in public or formally recognizing them as representatives of organizations. China's top leaders have clearly eschewed the latter option to avoid granting legitimacy to those groups and equally to avoid giving credibility to the idea that talks are necessary.[48] Documents intended only for internal circulation, such as the top secret Document no. 7 (1996) or Ma Dazheng's report, have in fact advocated direct contacts with organizations abroad. Document no. 7 proposed a two-track strategy of "dialogue and struggle." Its authors recommend precisely the same pragmatic strategy for handling dissidents abroad as for managing dissenters at home: "Divide the outside separatist forces; win over most of them; and alienate the remaining small number and fight against them" (Human Rights Watch 1999:12).

Chinese officials have occasionally approached Uyghur leaders abroad, something public sources emanating from China have never acknowledged. In the relatively open atmosphere of the early 1980s, Beijing's leaders may have felt there was something to be gained by speaking directly with such figures. In 1981 a group from the Chinese embassy in Ankara met with Isa Yusuf Alptekin, since 1949 the best-known Uyghur leader abroad and long settled in Turkey. Alptekin reportedly put together a list of thirty-one "requests" to the Chinese government on such matters as accuracy in population figures, addressing economic inequalities between Uyghurs and Hans, and religious freedom. Perhaps predictably, the Chinese officials chose not to respond to the requests in any way following the meeting (Derbyshire 1999). The next year Chinese officials allowed his son Erkin Alptekin to return to

Xinjiang after an exile of thirty-two years. They might have taken heart from the first sentence of his short report on the trip, which pronounced his visit "entirely satisfactory." Alptekin noted that he was able to travel freely and meet with relatives and friends, seemingly without surveillance. He also admitted that economic and cultural conditions in the region had improved since the "holocaust" of the Cultural Revolution. Alptekin concluded on a bitter note, however. "There is no need to point out," he observed, and then went on to point out, that "the people of Eastern Turkistan have no political freedom." He left readers with the assertion that while Uyghurs were cautiously appreciative of the liberalization after Mao's death, they would not be satisfied until Chinese rule of the region ended (Alptekin 1983).

Sixteen years later, a Chinese official again approached a prominent leader, a few months after the Ghulja uprising in 1997. This time Yao Kuangyi, China's ambassador to Turkey, invited Mehmet Riza Bekin to dinner and invited him to return to Xinjiang for a visit. Riza Bekin, a former Turkish general and head of the most powerful Uyghur transnational organization at the time, accepted the invitation in the hope that more formal talks might be in the offing. But over dinner, Yao cautioned Riza Bekin that there was no certainty that Chinese officials would agree to meet him and discuss the status of the region, and so the latter elected not to go. Riza Bekin told a Chinese reporter later that Beijing would have to discuss "real autonomy" (*zhenzheng zizhi*) for Xinjiang and to acknowledge that the ETNC's ultimate objective was independence or any discussion would be a waste of time (Cao Changqing 1999b, 1999c).[49] There have been no known contacts with Uyghur leaders in the diaspora since Riza Bekin's dinner with Yao.

Uyghurs outside Xinjiang have long lamented the lack of a Uyghur counterpart to the Dalai Lama. Uyghur transnational groups' many efforts to establish a single umbrella organization and win broad international recognition of a single charismatic leader are easily understood as efforts to change this stark fact. From 1950 through the late 1960s, Muhämmäd Imin Bughra and Isa Yusuf Alptekin were the main leaders and the objects of most Uyghurs' ambitions for international status and recognition. As pointed out, they ultimately achieved little recognition outside Turkey and the Uyghur diaspora. The establishment of the WUC and the promotion of Erkin Alptekin in the 1990s seemed to fill many Uyghurs around the world with new hope. Rabiyä Qadir's triumphant arrival in the United States, her nomination for the Nobel Peace Prize in 2005 and again in 2006, and her selection for the Norwegian Rafto Prize in 2005 gave her extraordinary name recognition around the world. The ham-handed attempts by Beijing to paint her as a terrorist and to deter the Nobel committee by threatening the Norwegian government only increased her international standing (Deutsche Presse Agentur 2006; Li Jing 2005; Luo Tianliang

2006). There was no mistaking that her emergence on the world stage had raised new hopes by late 2006 that Uyghurs might finally gain strong international support. Rabiyä's selection as the symbolic leader—the "mother of the Uyghurs," as she had taken to calling herself—neatly parried one possible obstacle to that support: in the post-9/11 world, Muslim peoples are widely viewed by non-Muslims as antidemocratic, violent, and atavistically intolerant of women's rights. If the tokenism of the WUC's single woman official in charge of Women's Affairs had seemingly confirmed the last stereotype (even though the organization was avowedly secular), the promotion of Rabiyä swept it away. One might almost posit that in the current climate of anti-Muslim hysteria in the non-Muslim world, only a female Muslim leader could assuage the international community's concerns.

What makes Uyghurs' hopes particularly poignant is that even had Rabiyä received the Nobel Prize, she would have faced an international environment a good deal less favorable than that the Dalai Lama enjoyed both before and after he won the prize in 1989. He and the Tibetan Government in Exile (TGIE) had been internationally known for years, and Beijing has several times met with Tibetan delegations. But despite the notoriety and international popularity of the Tibetan cause, these negotiations have won no concessions from Beijing, not even recognition that it was meeting with legal representatives of the Tibetan community. The Dalai Lama publicly renounced the goal of full Tibetan independence in Strasbourg in 1988 (a stance later rejected by the TGIE in 1991). He gained nothing for his pains, and indeed, in a 2006 interview, the newly appointed party secretary in Tibet, Zhang Qingli, sharply denounced the Tibetan spiritual leader as a consistent separatist, asserting that "he has not spent a single day not trying to split the motherland" (*Spiegel* Interview with Tibet's Communist Party Chief 2006).[50] A few months earlier, Zhang had told officials in the region that the government was still in a "fight to the death" with the Dalai Lama (Macartney 2006). It is widely understood that Beijing now intends to conduct this "fight" by simply waiting for him to die so that it can select his next reincarnation under full Chinese control, as it did the Panchen Lama in 1995, and thus put an end to the irritant he has become. Emissaries from the TGIE traveled to Beijing again for a new round of talks in late October 2008, although the Dalai Lama cautioned in advance that his "faith and trust in the Chinese government is diminishing" (Yardley 2008). At the conclusion of the talks, Vice Minister Zhu Weiqun announced on state television that China would never accept calls for "high-level autonomy" in Tibet and accused the Dalai Lama of plotting "ethnic cleansing" of culturally Tibetan areas (Reuters 2008).

Tibetan youths in Dharamsala and elsewhere have begun to dissent publicly from the TGIE's platform of nonviolence, but the prospects for effective armed challenges to Chinese control of Tibet seem dimmer today than they did when Tibetan guerrillas enjoyed financial and military support from the CIA in the 1960s (Knaus 1999; Mishra 2005; Sheridan 2008). The message for Uyghurs seeking autonomy or independence cannot be much more hopeful.

■

Since 1949, Uyghur activists in the diaspora have attempted in various ways to affect Xinjiang's contentious politics. Despite extravagant claims by both the activists and the Chinese government, they have had little success in intervening directly by smuggling weapons or people into the region. Rumors of Uyghur militias preparing for a secessionist offensive appear in retrospect to have been baseless. Growing Chinese power has essentially eliminated the possibility that Uyghurs might separate Xinjiang from China militarily, a prospect that was already remote by the time the People's Liberation Army had occupied the region's major cities in 1950. Neither was it realistic for Uyghur separatists to expect that the Soviet Union would cease merely needling the territory bordering its Central Asian possessions and rouse itself to offer the military assistance that the separatists needed to achieve their aim. The September 11 attacks shattered the slim hopes raised by the intervention in Kosovo that NATO or the United States might step in to do for Uyghurs what the Soviet Union had declined to do.

Instead, politicized Uyghurs have had to focus on propaganda aimed either at inciting uprisings inside Xinjiang or galvanizing external support. While the Chinese government has naturally not been able to squelch protest and crush organizations abroad to the degree that it has domestically, over time it has largely succeeded in excluding them from its neighboring states in Central Asia and reducing them dramatically in Turkey. As the focus of organizing and activism shifted to the industrialized democracies, it meant giving up the advantage of proximity offered by Central Asian states and the broad sympathies of Pan-Turkists in Turkey. Distance and increased policing of China's borders have made it harder to infiltrate the region than ever before. Radio broadcasts have had a diminished effect since China invested heavily in radio jamming to keep unwanted signals out and in expanding radio and television coverage to beam its own message to Xinjiang's remotest hinterlands. Security software blocks access to dissident Web sites abroad, and tens of thousands of Public Security employees work constantly to shore up the electronic bulwark against contact between Uyghurs in Xinjiang and those in the diaspora. Beijing's decision in 2006 to block any news coverage in China of Rabiyä's second Nobel Peace Prize nomination was quite telling (French 2006).

The geographical shift to Europe and North America has also necessitated changes in tactics. Uyghurs in the diaspora seeking to change the policies in Xinjiang or loosen Beijing's grip on the region have had to pin their hopes entirely on third parties such as transnational organizations and governments, much as Isa Yusuf Alptekin had to do decades ago. Without the heady talk of decolonization and national liberation common in Alptekin's prime years and given China's extraordinary rise in economic and political might, they have had to lower their expectations as well. Given the recent trajectory of policy changes in Xinjiang in the face of everyday resistance and open political protest by Uyghurs in the region, Uyghurs abroad face a serious challenge. The quest for an Archimedean fulcrum that might enable them to move Beijing to respond to more limited calls for political autonomy and human rights protections has thus far proven fruitless.

CONCLUSION

One man's imagined community is another man's political prison.
ARJUN APPADURAI, *Modernity at Large*

The leaders of the Chinese Communist Party (CCP) have spent decades pursuing the dream articulated by Sun Yat-sen and Chiang Kai-shek during the Republican era, that of transforming the heterogeneous peoples and lands previously governed by the Qing empire into a unified nation-state. China's leaders have often behaved as if the government had realized the dream long ago. They have regularly trumpeted the party-state's success before both domestic and international audiences. Yet the work is by no means finished.[1] Uyghurs in Xinjiang and abroad lie athwart the CCP's plans. Earlier in the century, China watchers considered other groups on the periphery, principally the Mongols and Tibetans, to pose greater challenges to the unity of the state. Beijing's worries about Tibetans have not entirely ceased, although the Dalai Lama's advanced age and China's increasing global power allowed the leadership to crush widespread Tibetan rioting in spring 2008 and to flatly reject any further talk of autonomy in November 2008, without fear of international consequences. Today the problem of broad Uyghur disaffection and its implications for China's "territorial integrity" are of graver concern to the country's leaders.

In the broadest terms, the argument of this book has been that despite decades of trying, China's government, one of the strongest and most penetrative states in the world, has not been able to transform all its citizens into conscious and willing members of the "Chinese nation." The evidence furthermore suggests that it will not succeed in doing so in the near term. Many Uyghurs have refused to identify with either the strong and homogenizing version of the "Chinese nation," which tacitly equates it with the Han, or the more pluralist conception of a "multi-*minzu minzu*," in which each constituent group has an important, but only a partial, role to play. Furthermore, many Uyghurs continue to be dissatisfied with the functioning or particulars of the system of *minzu* regional autonomy.

REPRESENTATIONAL POLITICS AND NATIONAL STRUGGLES

As should be clear by now, this book has not proposed to tell the story of the long-running contention between discontented Uyghurs and the Chinese party-state simply by looking beyond the propaganda and posturing. I stated in the introduction and sought to demonstrate in each chapter that the posturing and overblown rhetoric emanating from many sources are not just distractions from the true course of that political struggle. Neither are they merely distortions of the struggle, obscuring layers that must be peeled away to reveal the true story behind it. Instead, these various modes of representational politics are crucial components of the contention.

There is much to be learned from work that tries to establish the facts of politics behind the cant and spin, whether in describing Xinjiang and the Uyghur diaspora (Dillon 2004; McMillen 1979, 1984; Shichor 2005), or Guangxi (Kaup 2000), or China's peripheral areas generally (Dreyer 1976; Mackerras 1994). The authors of many of these works properly admit that the official texts on which they have had to rely cannot be regarded as veridical accounts. Published official reports, scholarly studies, and the testimony of officials in interviews are verbal representations constructed to persuade some audience and so must be read as such. Descriptions of events need to be treated with due skepticism (which may ultimately amount to saying, "possibly true, possibly not"). But in compensation for the potential unreliability of the ostensibly mimetic content, we can derive other crucial information from the representational strategies: the political messages encoded in the stories, the techniques for encoding those messages, and the justificatory apparatus defending them. We can fill out our understanding of politics in Xinjiang by consistently taking rhetoric seriously as a terrain of struggle, a terrain previously largely ignored in the literature.

Throughout the book I have tried to show that Chinese officials and many Uyghurs have used representations to do political work. They have attempted thereby to invoke a community, to unify it against challengers, and to rouse it to action. As we have seen, they also have targeted audiences beyond the community itself. In this conclusion I focus on representational politics aimed at the world outside: the aim of drumming up international sympathy and eventually garnering international support for that community.

Representational politics is and will continue to be important to antistate movements because the international political climate has changed over the last two decades. The international community was never very charitable toward secessionist movements, for the obvious reason that the so-called community was composed of states, many of which faced separatist movements of their own and all of whose leaders could imagine the threat of state disintegration. For decades, states and international organizations followed a standard procedure in dealing with separatist violence. First they publicly condemned it, even (in some cases) when they secretly funded and supported it. In the few cases in which challengers succeeded in wresting away a portion of the state, they feigned surprise and then begrudgingly recognized the new states if they appeared to be durable, all the while warning that others should not take inspiration from the example or interpret it as a new precedent. In other words, they quietly welcomed the very rare polities that succeeded in separating from existing states through armed struggle but then turned around and denied that armed secessionist struggles had any legitimacy.

Consequently, secessions and secessionist violence have been rare. Most politicized ethnonational groups have concentrated on "symbolic and organizational politics" (Gurr 2000:27). But in the 1990s, several events seemed to present not just counterexamples to the principle that states frowned on secession but also the emergence of a new international order and a new principle: the international interventions in Bosnia, East Timor, and Kosovo. Each intervention facilitated the separation of territory from an existing state.[2]

Uyghur activists have believed for some time that if they only could make their case forcefully enough, they would gain such international support. During the 1990s it seemed reasonable for many Uyghurs inside Xinjiang and in the diaspora to hope for international intervention on their behalf, and by the same token, Beijing appeared to have reason to fear such a possibility (Lawrence 2000; Ma Dazheng 2003:106–24, 206–11; Pan Zhiping 1999; Zhang Zhirong 2005). Chinese officials angrily opposed the NATO operation in Kosovo, arguing that only a UN sanction could have made it legal. They betrayed a clear concern that the NATO action might set a precedent for intervention in China's territory. Zhu Bangzao, a spokesman for the Foreign Ministry, revealed this worry at a press conference: "Recently," he said, "I heard some people say that in the future, force should also be used against China to solve the Tibet question, among others" (Agence France-Presse 1999a). Officials also clearly had Xinjiang in mind. As Ma Dazheng wrote with alarm in April 1999, "We believe: the things that happen today in Kosovo might very possibly occur in Xinjiang." Ma pointed a finger at the United States for trying to play the world's policeman (Ma Dazheng 2003:145).[3]

Uyghurs have broadcast the message that they were suffering unacceptably under Chinese rule and that as members of a nation they were entitled to independence. Such entities as the Eastern Turkestan Information Center, the Taklamakan Human Rights Association, and the Uyghur Human Rights Project, as well as the various nationally defined Uyghur political organizations, have devoted the bulk of their energies to making this case. At the same time, Beijing has published a large and growing number of documents, complemented by diplomatic speeches, seeking to persuade the international community that Uyghurs suffer no human rights abuses, do not claim or seek to exercise a collective right of self-determination, and, not being a nation, are not endowed with that right even if they were to claim it.[4] The problem for both Uyghurs and Chinese officials lies in the antinomies of the principle of self-determination itself.

THE RISE AND FALL OF HUMANITARIAN INTERVENTION

The principle of the self-determination of nations or peoples, formally recognized by the UN,[5] is widely acknowledged and is as widely flouted. One problem is the impossibility of arriving at unambiguous, and equally important, universally agreed-upon definitions of key terms. In theory, nations, which enjoy a right of self-determination, meaning independence, are different from national minorities, which merit only autonomy or special protection within the state.[6] What distinguishes them beyond the opinion of the state concerned? How is national decolonization considered an acceptable prospect to be distinguished from secession, which is not? The so-called saltwater test, stipulating that only a territory separated from its colonizer by a large body of water qualifies for self-determination, is patently unconvincing, as one scholar observed caustically:

> International law is ... asked to perceive a distinction between the historical subjugation of an alien population living in a different part of the globe and the historical subjugation of an alien population living on a piece of land abutting that of its oppressors. The former can apparently never be legitimated by the mere passage of time, whereas the latter is eventually transformed into a protected status quo. (Buchheit 1978:18)

Buchheit is concerned specifically with the legal validity of claims of self-determination. The three decades since he wrote this have demonstrated that neither the ethical force nor the legal status of such claims carries much weight in deciding which are gratified and which not.

Rupert Emerson pointed out long ago that the rights of sovereignty and self-determination are in tension because they stem from different sources: "The state has an indisputable prerogative and duty to defend its own existence, and the nation comes likewise to be endowed with a right to overthrow the state" (Emerson 1962:299). The unrestricted universal exercise of the right of national self-determination would have unacceptable implications for the international system. As a British foreign secretary once put it, "If it were to be accepted that people have a right to self-determination whenever they ask for it, it would make nonsense of organized international society" (Emerson 1962:451, n. 21). Moreover, advocates of the right were prone to predictable hypocrisy. Any state could be expected to support self-determination when it threatened enemies but be opposed when it threatened allies or its own territory. Thus, "Lenin and Stalin made clear that self-determination was good where it involved a breach in the imperialist structure, intolerable where it involved a separation from the communist fatherland" (Emerson 1962:306). India, similarly, vigorously supported the right in international forums, but its leaders bristled at the suggestion that groups within India might wish to exercise it.

Furthermore, the possibility of foreign intervention wreaks havoc with the notion of the "self-expression" of a collective wish to employ the right. As we have seen, states are heavily favored in disputes with defiant or secessionist small groups in their population. Therefore, for any hope of success, such groups often must depend on the influence and intervention of other states. In a world of largely settled borders and scarce resources, many states have an incentive to intervene "on behalf of" small peoples, but actually for their own gain. Threatened states thus conjure the specter of foreign intervention to condemn all pushes for self-determination as "foreign plots." And indeed, actual cases of intervention, such as India in Bangladesh, the United States in Tibet, and Pakistan and India in Kashmir, demonstrate that such accusations have not been idle.

The international community has kept Tibet under watch for decades, and Beijing has clearly been influenced by a concern about that international surveillance. By contrast, Beijing has never borne the brunt of heavy international pressure over the governance of Xinjiang (Carlson 2005:25, n. 12), although the Chinese government did take notice when human rights organizations began to publish materials focused on the region, and even more when the U.S. State Department mentioned Xinjiang for the first time in its annual Human Rights Report on China in 1998. Since that time, party leaders have devoted considerable thought and effort to avoiding the "internationalization" of the so-called Xinjiang problem (Ma Dazheng 2003:205–11). It is important to remember, though, that the earlier internationalization of the Tibet problem actually drove party leaders to retrench reforms in Tibet and to cool talks with the Tibetan government in exile (Carlson 2005:105).

Chinese scholars have mounted a multifaceted effort to ward off the threat of self-determination in China's peripheral regions. Academicians at the Center for Research on Chinese Frontier History and Geography (Zhongguo bianjiang shidi yanjiu zhongxin) in Beijing have devoted more than a decade to producing scholarly justifications for China's claims to every square inch of the national territory and, indeed, several large regions no longer under Beijing's rule. In addition to providing ammunition for border negotiations with neighbors, this work has clearly been intended to thwart the claims of Tibetans, Uyghurs, Mongolians, and even Koreans to national territories of their own (Bovingdon 2005; Carlson 2005:55; Millward 1996:118–21). Other scholars have focused on the principle of self-determination itself. Pan Zhiping, a leading social scientist in Xinjiang, wrote in 1999 that old Europe honored self-determination in order to arrive at mononational states but that such a program was "clearly already inappropriate for the highly complex contemporary world" (Pan Zhiping 1999:45).

The Sovietologist S. Frederick Starr suggests that Washington and Beijing outwardly appear to agree on this point. Noting that Washington has done nothing about Beijing's abridgments of "democracy, human rights, and religious freedom" in Xinjiang, Starr concludes acerbically that "the United States, by its very founding, placed itself on the side of national self-determination and those seeking freedom from imperial rule. Now we seem to be supporting the imperial powers" (Congressional-Executive Commission on China 2005b).

Starr is perhaps overcritical of the United States on this score, in that it has not chosen a path different from that of most members of the international community.

The fact remains, however, that hardly any states have given rhetorical support, let alone political or military assistance, to state-seeking groups' quests for self-determination. One of the few states that did offer such open support was China during the Mao era, strongly endorsing independence for East Timor, Angola, and Palestine in the *Xinjiang Daily* newspaper ("Renmin ribao" pinglunyuan 1975; "Tuanjie qilai hanwei duli—Zhuhe Angela renmin jieshu putaoya zhimin tongzhi de shengli" 1975; Xinhua 1975).

Beijing would, of course, object to this analogy, arguing that all those struggles were anticolonial, whereas the people of China ended colonialism once and for all in 1949. During an interview in 2006, China's ambassador to the United Nations justified Japan's exclusion from the Security Council and China's right to a seat by saying, "We didn't occupy other people's territory" (Traub 2006). As we saw in chapter 1, the CCP leadership has arrogated to itself the right to define what territory was "other people's" and what belonged to China.

HUMAN RIGHTS

Although few states have stepped forward to protect the right of self-determination of peoples, international bodies have demonstrated a growing commitment to the protection of human rights. On its face, the carefully circumscribed principle of protecting human rights appears less threatening than that of underwriting self-determination, which, by virtue of being a collective right, at least implies the possibility of secession. Despite seeming to be beyond reproach in moral terms, even intervention to safeguard human rights has quietly been opposed in practice by many states. Many governments have been leery of criticizing others for violations of human rights, fearing the derogation of their own sovereignty as a consequence (Krasner 1993:164). China has been no exception. For years after it gained entrance into the UN in 1971, the delegation from the People's Republic of China compiled a near-perfect record of opposing humanitarian interventions. In defending its position, the delegation stipulated that the principles of human rights "do not apply everywhere in the same manner and that the implementation of these standards should be left to the states concerned" (Kamminga 1992:109–11). The government has signed pacts with other regimes aggressively reaffirming the principle that sovereignty trumps human rights. Thus in 2000, Jiang Zemin and Turkmenistan's president Sapurmurat Niyazov promulgated an official statement that "under no circumstances, even reasons based on a thesis of 'priority of human rights over sovereignty,' does any state have the right to interfere in internal affairs of other sovereign states."[7]

While it has not quite evaded criticism for repressing Uyghurs' political action at home and engineering its suppression abroad, Beijing has banished the specter of a humanitarian intervention in Xinjiang that would lead to the territory's secession. It appears increasingly unlikely that other states or international organizations might commit, and Beijing submit, to a lesser intervention. At the moment, it is difficult to be optimistic about a resolution of the long-brewing contention between the Uyghurs and the Chinese state.

EPILOGUE
ÜRÜMCI'S "HOT SUMMER" OF 2009

As this book was going to print, Ürümci erupted in violence once again. Scholars, officials, activists, and journalists have already begun to debate what happened and how to interpret it. I briefly summarize the events and offer my own, preliminary, interpretation.

As discussed in chapter 4, the frequency of protests fell dramatically in the early 2000s. Nevertheless, Xinjiang remained a contentious place and a political headache for Beijing, even in the absence of overt resistance, as chapter 3 illustrated. China's leaders hoped to avert widespread, sustained protest or violence in the region. And even though Beijing's concerns about the threat of international intervention eased in the wake of September 11, officials still worry about the "internationalization" of affairs in Xinjiang, as we saw in chapter 5. Both these concerns flared again with the outbreak of protests and violence in Ürümci in July 2009.[1]

The complete story of the events of July 5 and after will take some time to emerge. Important aspects of the events remain controversial, such as who organized the initial protests; what the protestors' aims were; whether the government's heavily armed response provoked or followed the violence; how many people were killed, wounded, and arrested; and why bands of armed Han Chinese took to the streets several days later.

Most observers agree that the protest was touched off by a brawl that took place in late June 2009 in Guangdong Province, some two thousand miles away from Ürümci.[2] On June 25, responding to a rumor that several Uyghur men had raped two Han women at the Xuri Toy Factory in the city of Shaoguan—a story later repudiated by one of the women supposedly involved—Han workers stormed a dormitory where Uyghur workers lived. Armed with crude weapons such as iron bars and long knives, the Han workers attacked the occupants indiscriminately. Two Uyghurs were killed and several hundred were injured, according to official reports, whereas Uyghur expatriates claimed the casualties were much higher.

On the afternoon of July 5, hundreds of Uyghurs took to the streets of Ürümci to protest the government's handling of the episode. Even official Chinese sources acknowledge that for some three hours, the protests were peaceful.[3] Party officials in Beijing and Ürümci responded to the demonstration as they had to previous such protests, mobilizing the police with riot gear and paramilitary forces armed with automatic weapons. The police sought to bring the protest to a halt, and People's Armed Police (PAP) forces roamed the streets, trying to stop the violent attacks. But either they arrived too late, or according to some reports, they waited several hours to take decisive action while awaiting instructions from Beijing. On July 6 the government shut down the Internet and cell phone service and continued to bring PAP forces into Ürümci.

Chinese officials quickly claimed to have evidence that Rabiyä Qadir and the World Uyghur Congress had organized and triggered the protest through a series of phone calls to relatives in Ürümci. Official media later repeated the charges that Rabiyä was a terrorist and in league with ETIM, referring to "East Turkestan Islamic Movement (ETIM) organizations, including the W[orld] U[yghur] C[ongress]."[4] News stories asserted that the simultaneous eruption of violence in fifty different sites in the city proved it had been premeditated. They also announced that women in "long Islamic robes and head coverings" had directed the rioters, and that one even distributed clubs (Demick 2009). Initial figures counted 156 dead, 123 of them Han Chinese and 33 Uyghurs, and more than 1,000 wounded. More than 200 shops and 250 vehicles were destroyed (Watts 2009). The breakdowns by *minzu* disappeared soon after, and the final official tally was 197 killed and 1,721 injured, "most of them Han" (Wong 2009).

In a departure from previous practice, Beijing invited a group of foreign reporters to Ürümci to investigate and report on events there firsthand. They all were housed in the Hoi Tak Hotel, which reportedly had the only working Internet connection in the XUAR at the time. At one point, a group of journalists walking down a street were accosted by around two hundred women demanding that the government release their male relatives detained after the protests (Mackey 2009). Other journalists encountered a Han mob attacking a Uyghur man, who then turned on the journalists themselves, shouting that they were biased against China and trying to block their cameras (Lloyd 2009). International journalists wrote numerous stories from Ürümci investigating the extent of the violence and trying to clarify the causes. Although these reports praised the government for being more open to journalists, they also produced graphic evidence of the police handling unarmed protestors very roughly. Furthermore, the police prevented journalists from conducting some interviews, and some were detained (Choi Chi-yuk 2009).

On July 7, bands of Han Chinese roaming the streets with homemade weapons carried out revenge killings. No casualty figures were made available. The Han vigilantes drew considerable attention, with the international media reporting that they did not trust Beijing or local police forces to protect Han residents. The violence and tension were serious enough that on July 8, President Hu Jintao returned early from Italy, where he had been scheduled to take part in the G-8 summit. By Friday, July 10, the violence had reportedly stopped, but in order to avoid further conflict, the government posted placards announcing that all Ürümci mosques would be closed for Friday prayers and ordering men to pray at home. Groups of Uyghurs gathered angrily before a number of mosques, and the government relented, allowing several to open. On the same day, a smaller group of Uyghur protestors took to the streets to demand the release of those who had been detained. Even though the protestors were marching peacefully, riot police set upon them with truncheons and fists, an episode captured memorably by BBC video cameras.[5]

With the heavy police presence, the city reportedly quieted by July 11 but remained extremely tense. Officials referred to more than 1,400 people detained in connection with the events, and a month later the government announced it would try some 200 suspects, noting further that there would be a "drastic increase in security" in preparation for the trials (Cai Ke 2009).

August in Xinjiang was comparatively quiet, but by early September there were rumors of a rash of "syringe attacks" in various locales. When the Public Security Bureau sent a text message to Ürümci residents' cell phones, it set in motion an episode of mass hysteria (Reuters 2009). Of the 513 people claiming to be stabbing victims, only 103 proved to have "signs of jabs, bumps or rashes."[6] The rumors and panic spread quickly to other cities in Xinjiang. Of nine reported attacks in Khotän, BBC News reported that three were actually targeted, while four of five reported attacks in Altay and three of five in Kashgar were judged to be false alarms.

Medical researchers in Beijing dispatched to Ürümci found no evidence of chemical toxins or infections in any cases, leaving open to question whether the remainder had no signs of punctures that had actually occurred or whether they had simply imagined them. On September 3, tens of thousands of people (reportedly mostly Han) marched in the streets of Ürümci protesting the general feeling of insecurity and demanding that the government offer better protection. Li Zhi, Ürümci's party secretary, mounted a truck and addressed a large crowd of protestors with a loudspeaker, urging them to calm down and disperse. When the crowds did not leave, riot police then advanced on them with batons and tear gas. Several days later the government announced a ban on "illegal protests." On September 3 Wang Lequan, the XUAR's party secretary, addressed a large crowd that had gathered to protest the government's handling of the reported syringe attacks. By the afternoon, some three thousand had gathered in Ürümci's People's Square, and according to Xinhua reports, "tens of thousands" protested across the city. The crowd was strikingly disrespectful of Wang, shouting "Resign Wang Lequan, the government is useless!" and tossing plastic bottles in his direction (Hornby 2009). Although Wang kept his job, Li Zhi was relieved of his post. The hard-line police chief, by contrast, was promoted.

■

The framework of this book offers more insight into the summer's events than any attempt simply to reconstruct those events and seek "concrete" causes could do. I offer three observations. First, the scope and violence of the protest on July 5 demonstrate that there is, in fact, extensive Uyghur discontent and that many Uyghurs are willing to brave government reprisals in order to express it publicly. Those reprisals were quick in coming, demonstrating similarly that party officials in Beijing and Ürümci remain intolerant of public Uyghur protest. Second, there has been enormous disagreement about "what actually happened" in July and after, with both sides focusing on representing the events to an international audience. That disagreement has demonstrated the importance of representational politics in contemporary Xinjiang. Uyghur organizations and the Chinese party-state have devoted much energy to promulgating versions of the events useful to their political aims.

Third, Beijing has insisted that the July protests were orchestrated by a small number of splittists inside Xinjiang, in league with international agitators, most prominently Rabiyä Qadir, and that most participants in the riots were members of the masses who "did not know the real situation." Officials have once again insisted the protests were orchestrated in order to vitiate the claim that they were spontaneous, and hence authentic, expressions of popular discontent. In addition, officials have described them as "splittist" and "terrorist" in order to justify the harsh crackdown, as splittist and terrorist activities are unacceptable by law. By continuing to invoke such old chestnuts as "black hands" behind the scenes, "hostile foreign powers," the naïve masses, and "splittist" forces operating locally, officials have shown themselves unwilling, or unable, to move beyond its historical framing of Uyghur protest or to allow others to do so. These officials' refusal to use or permit an alternative vocabulary and explanatory framework indicate the brittleness, and even the obsolescence, of Beijing's vision.

Fourth, in an effort to make its version of events authoritative and to deny Uyghurs or others a space (or details) to propose a counterversion, the party-state has shut down international cell phone service from Xinjiang and has kept Web sites in Xinjiang off-line for more than three months (at this writing). The choice to invite foreign journalists to Ürümci within a day of July 5 contrasts favorably with Beijing's exclusion of journalists from Tibet after the protests there in the spring of 2008. Conversely, the gesture of apparent openness had clear limits: reporters were presented with audiovisual materials on the events and invited to government presentations, but they also were closely tailed when they ventured into the streets of Ürümci and sometimes even were denied access to locals. Furthermore, when Beijing chose to install all the journalists in the Hoi Tak Hotel and provide them with the only working Internet connections in Xinjiang, it was reminiscent of the careful management of information at the time of the 2008 Beijing Olympics, when hotels catering to foreigners had temporarily unfiltered access to the Web while the rest of China did not.

The Chinese government's attempt to pin blame for the July 5 events on Rabiyä and to label her as a terrorist with ties to ETIM and al Qaeda have proved fruitless and, in some cases, counterproductive. When Beijing pressured the Melbourne International Film Festival to exclude a film about Rabiyä's life, the festival organizers refused to do so. The subsequent publicity turned Australian public opinion sharply against Beijing and probably increased sympathy for Rabiyä. She has only gained publicity and wider popular sympathy as a consequence.

From these facts we can infer, sadly, that hard-liners remain dominant at the regional and national levels. Although one prominent party official, Guangdong Party Secretary Wang Yang, suggested a few days later that the violence showed the need for Beijing to change its policies toward minorities, he did not offer specifics of either the policies' defects or his own proposals. Unfortunately, the outbursts of violence between early July and early September 2009 indicated, and surely exacerbated, mutual misunderstanding and hostility between Uyghurs and Hans in Xinjiang.

APPENDIX

ORGANIZED PROTESTS AND VIOLENT EVENTS IN XINJIANG, 1949–2005

Year	Duration	Location	Type	Number Involved	Comments
December 22, 1949	—	Khotän	Armed uprising	3,900	Wang Zhaozhi and other separatists organized a "Great Turkic Republic."[1]
January 13, 1950	—	Jinghua, Dihua (Ürümci)	Attack on PLA cavalry	1,000	Khalibek "compels" Kazakhs to attack the PLA.
March 10, 1950	10 days	Yiwu County	Plotted rebellion		Ábäydulla and others plotted rebellion throughout county; suppressed by PLA 10 days later.
June 10, 1950	—	—	Armed rebellion	160	Sultan Šärif, Janabil, and others organize a second armed rebellion, compelling 160 Qazaq households to join Yolwaz, Osman, and Janimkhan.
July 24, 1950	24 days	Ghulja	Armed rebellion	349	Rakhmanov meets with reactionaries, commences armed rebellion. Pacified August 17 by local PLA forces; 114 captured.
August 3, 1950	4 months	Dihua, Changji, Jinghua, Suilai, Turpan, and Toqsu	Armed rebellion: major	9,000	Orazbay, Sidiq, Weli, and "traitorous soldiers" set up a major rebellion; put down by 1,400 soldiers.
August 18, 1950	Days	Shaosu	Armed rebellion	230	Rebellion of 230 led by Idris. Put down quickly by the PLA

1. Bibliographic references for each of these reported events available on request. As discussed in chapter 4, all but a handful of these events are described in multiple sources. Wherever possible, I compared the Chinese and foreign sources when preparing the descriptions.

Date	Duration	Location	Type	Number	Description
February 5, 1951	42 days (ended here)	Gansu, Qinghai, and Xinjiang	Armed struggle	4,380	Bandits under Osman, Janabil, and Khabas (several confederates Han or Hui), Husayin, Khalibek.
September 1951	Year	Qitai, Fuyuan, Mulei, and Zhenxi	Armed struggle	1,100	Osman Batur's son, Qanatbay, and others ally to raise a force of 1,100.
October 28, 1951	1 month	Toqquztara	Armed struggle	170	Ili Tarim and "Malik" force 170 people to raise a rebellion. The Second Army and 300 members of the masses put down the rebellion, capture 140, and kill 20.
March 3, 1952	—	Ili region: Nilka, Toqquztara, Mongolkure, and Tekes	Plotted armed uprising		A group of Pan-Turkists reportedly set up the "Islamic Alliance Party."
April 17, 1952	—	Turpan, Pican	Armed struggle	90	Local tyrant Aimutu (?) Haji, Abdurakhman assemble 90 to rebel.
May 6, 1952	4 months (surrender September 5)	Qitai, Mulei to Altai Mountains	Armed uprising	2,000	Osman Batur's son and a colleague set up a "religious army" and led members of their tribe to rise up.
November 1, 1952	Days?	Xinyuan, Toqquztara, Takäs	Disturbance	130	Wuli Haji, Ili bandit leader, leads 130+ in a disturbance Put down by Twenty-seventh Division, including artillery unit; 126 captured.
December 31, 1954	—	Khotän District: Moyu; Minfeng, Qaghiliq, Yarkand	Insurgency	300	Islamic Republic organization, led by Abduimit, supposedly under the influence of "Imin" as he fled through southern XJ; well-organized alternative government prepared.

ORGANIZED PROTESTS AND VIOLENT EVENTS IN XINJIANG, 1949–2005 (continued)

Year	Duration	Location	Type	Number Involved	Comments
March 1956	Days?	Moyu	Armed uprising	500	Bahai Damolla led the uprising; took 44 prisoners.
May 4, 1956	—	Lop	Insurgency	800	From December 31, 1954 to May 4, 1956, there were 8 "counterrevolutionary rebellions" planned, 5 exposed and averted; the biggest led by Abdukhayr.
April 1957	Days?	Khotän	Armed uprising	60	Qilic Khan (Heiliqihan) led the uprising; took 37 prisoners.
March 1958	5 months	Qitai, Mulei, Baliken to Fuwen, Qinghe	Armed uprising	800	Jukai led 800 families from the regions listed to Fuwen/Qinghe region. The PLA captured Jukai and foiled the planned rebellion. Jamiśti Khan continued the cause.
September 1958	4 months	Fuwen and other towns	Armed independence	360	Jamiśti Khan led uprising with Dalilkhan and Jukai; reportedly aimed to establish "Islamic Republic"; took 33 prisoners; 285 conspirators surrendered.
October 1958	Days?	Qumul	Armed uprising	80	Eli Qurban led the uprising; took 18 prisoners. 56 conspirators surrendered. More than 150 troops involved.
October 1958	Days?	Wusu	Armed uprising	100	Tenzing Gyamtso (? Dangzeng jiamucuo) led the uprising; took 89 prisoners.
December 1958	Days?	Baicheng	Armed uprising	280	Ayśäm Ayub led the uprising; all 280 conspirators taken prisoner.
January 1962	5 months	Ili	Mass exodus	62,000	Uyghurs and Qazaqs fled to Kazakhstan.
May 29, 1962	—	Ghulja, Khorgos	Riot	20,000	—

Date	Duration	Location	Type	Number	Description
December 25, 1966	—	Shihezi	Armed struggle	—	Cultural Revolution 2-line struggle; the army against Wang Enmao.
1967	Days	Ghulja	Ethnic battle	4,000	Leader Mijit captured by PLA and killed 1,968.
January 26, 1967	3 days	Shihezi, Qaramay, Mosowan, Dushanzi Battles (Han)	—	—	Cultural Revolution "line struggle," probably all Hans.
February 1968	—	Ürümci, Ghulja, Qumul, Shihezi, Kashgar	Armed struggle	—	Cultural Revolution 2-line struggles.
May 27, 1968	(canceled)	Ürümci	Demonstration	10,000	An "anti-Wang Enmao, anti-Han chauvinism" rally canceled by Zhou Enlai.
January 1969	Days	Ghulja	Revolt	4,000	—
August 20, 1969	—	Kashgar, Magit	Insurgency	—	Sought help from Soviet Union; exposed, destroyed. Involved Rozi Hakim, Mämtimin, and others.
1975	—	—	Violent protests	—	Non-Hans protested "being forced to work on Muslim holy days" and to use Latin script. PLA soldiers were reportedly brought in.
1975	—	Shihezi, Qaramay	Violent protests (Han)	—	Han immigrants engaged in violent protest "over economic issues."
April 1979	51 days	Aqsu/Beijing	Petition (Han)	46	Shanghai youths petitioned to return home.
July 1979	—	Aqsu	Petition (Han)	70	Attempted second petition by Shanghai youths thwarted.
January 1980	—	Aqsu	Demonstration (Han)	4,000	Shanghai youths seeking right to return home.

Year	Duration	Location	Type	Number Involved	Comments
April 9, 1980	2 days	Aqsu	Riot, clash	3,000	PSB employee Huang Zhen killed a Uyghur "drunk" in custody; demonstrators paraded with the body, shouted "Down with Hans, Hans go home"; attacked government offices.
June 27, 1980	4 days	Atuš	Clash, riot, demonstration	500	Several hundred Uyghurs attack military organs, make trouble in barracks and on the street. Propaganda and "detaining the leaders of the troublemaking" resolved the problem.
August 2, 1980	Days	Ürümci	Shooting, riot		PCC clerk killed Uyghur farmer's ox, then a Uyghur roadworker. After clerk received a death sentence, other Hans stormed jail and freed him. Later sentenced to manslaughter.
August 20, 1980	—	Qaghiliq	Incident	—	—
November 12, 1980	40 days	Aqsu	Riot (Hans)	8,000	"Sent down" youths seeking to return home; 1,000 staged a hunger strike; martial law in effect through December 26, 1980.
January 13, 1981	4 days	Qaghiliq	Riot	2,000	Talips rioted after a mosque fire, accusing a Uyghur PSB official as arsonist. Slogans: "Follow Allah," "Long live the Islamic Republic," "Kapirs out." Attacked government offices.
May 27, 1981	—	Päyziwat (Jiashi)	Insurgency	150	Insurgents stole weapons, planned to establish an independent ET Republic; led by Hasan Ismayil, Dawut Sawut.

Date	Duration	Location	Type	Number	Description
October 30, 1981	Days	Kashgar	Riot, "racial incidents"	6,000	Riots after Han shot Uyghur youth with a hunting rifle. Rioters stormed the post office, party committee, bank; attacked 600, injured 200; shouted "Long live Uyghurstan/Islamic Republic, "Down with Qitay."
December 12, 1985	4 days	Ürümci, Khotän, Aqsu, Bole	Demonstrations	2,000	Later spread to Nanjing, Beijing, Shanghai; 2,000 students from 7 universities involved. Students shouted separatist slogans: Hans out, Independent XJ sovereign; Yuan Qingli says antibirth planning, transfer of convicts—personal observation.
April 1988	1 day	Ghulja	Demonstration (Qazaq)	—	Protest against "White house in the distance," with Qazaq students from 6 colleges.
June 15, 1988	3 days	Ürümci	Demonstration	300	Racist slogans on toilet door; demonstrations at major universities in Ürümci; organized by "student scientific/cultural association"; Dolqun Isa claims responsibility 2006.
February 8, 1989	Days	Southwest Taklamakan (prison sites not revealed)	Prison riot	80	More than 80 prisoners at a remote labor reform farm used hammers and knives to kill guards, take hostages, and burn buildings. There had reportedly been 11 major riots in 23 camps with 96 escapes in the previous year.
May 13, 1989	1 day	Ürümci	Sit-in (Han)	130	Former uranium mine workers protested problems of radiation sickness and also supported students. Met by government officials and PCC officials (who employed them). They were promised redress but told that their sit-in was "inappropriate."
May 16, 1989	1 day	Ürümci	Demonstration	—	—
May 18, 1989	1 day	Ürümci	Demonstration	—	—

ORGANIZED PROTESTS AND VIOLENT EVENTS IN XINJIANG, 1949–2005 (continued)

Year	Duration	Location	Type	Number Involved	Comments
May 19, 1989	1 day	Ürümci	Riot	3,000	Over the book *Sexual customs*; initially described as "orderly march in support of Beijing democracy movement"; degenerated into a riot; 1,000 PSB, 1,200 PAP dispatched.
June 5, 1989	1 day	Ürümci	Sit-in	100	More than 100 students protested outside a district government office; protest posters "appeared at every university."
January 15, 1990	1 day	Qaghiliq County	Demonstration	200	Some 200 Talips petitioned the county government and "made trouble." Although the trouble was squelched expeditiously, the Uyghur imam was criticized for dereliction of duty.
March 25, 1990	1 day	Moyu County	Arson	—	A small group of people reportedly led by Talips burned the family-planning technology station (where ultrasounds and abortions would be performed).
April 5, 1990	2 days	Baren	Armed uprising	200	Started in a mosque.
September 1990	—	Northwest Xinjiang	Disturbances	—	—
February 28, 1991	1 day	Quca	Bombing		A second bomb failed to detonate.
May 1991	2 days	Cöcäk	Demonstration, gunfight	140	Armed rebellion calling for independence, political parties, *minzu* army; armed demonstrators occupied Tacheng government building, demanded government "hand over power"; gunfight left 140 killed, wounded, arrested.

Date	Duration	Place	Event	Number	Notes
June 11, 1991	2 days	Bole	Demonstration, gunned down	3,000	Demonstration for democratic elections, some called for right to join Soviet Union. Arson, looting, shootings. 500 killed or wounded.
February 1992	—	Ghulja	Bombing	—	—
February 5, 1992	1 day	Ürümci	Bombing	—	A series of bombings reported; January 21 document attributes them to "Islamic Reformers' Party."
March 5, 1992	4 days	Khotän, Kashgar, Quca, Cöcäk, Bortala	Bombings	—	—
March 1993	—	Lop Nor	Demonstration	1,000	Antinuclear.
June 1993	—	Ili region	Kazakhs clash	—	—
June 17, 1993	1 day	Kashgar	Bombing	—	Attack on government; January 21 document claims bombings continued through September; Zhu Bangzao attributes it to the ETDIP.
July 1993	—	(Not specified)	Assassination attempt	—	Targeted Hamudun Niyaz, chairman of the XUAR People's Congress.
August 1, 1993	1 day	Yarkand	Bombing	—	In the video parlor of a trade company.
August 4, 1993	—	Kashgar	Bombing	—	Bombings in a total of 5 cities (other cities not cited).
August 19 1993	1 day	Khotän	Bombing	—	—
August 24, 1993	1 day	Qaghiliq	Assassination attempt	—	Attempt on Abliz Damolla, parliamentary member, head of great mosque.
July 18, 1994	days	Toqsu (Xinhe)	Bombings	—	—

ORGANIZED PROTESTS AND VIOLENT EVENTS IN XINJIANG, 1949-2005 (continued)

Year	Duration	Location	Type	Number Involved	Comments
April 22, 1995	3 days	Ili Zhou Mongolkure, Capcal, Nilqa, Takäs, Kunes	Protest	50,000	Possibly up to 100,000 protestors at climax. Protestors reportedly called for a "Qazaq state," "The end of Communist rule," and "Long live Uyghurstan." Note: Not mentioned in any mainland Chinese sources.[2]
July 7, 1995	1 day	Khotän	Riot	1,000	Protest at the dismissal of the molla of Beytulla Mosque.
April 22, 1995	3 days	Ili Zhou Mongolkure, Capcal, Nilqa, Takäs, Kunes	Protest	50,000	Possibly up to 100,000 protestors at climax. Protestors reportedly called for a "Qazaq state," "The end of Communist rule," and "Long live Uyghurstan." Note: Not mentioned in any Chinese sources.[2]
August 14, 1995	—	Ghulja	Demonstration	—	A protest at the jailing of Abdulhelil, leader of *mäsräp*; described by Chinese sources as "illegal protest."
February 10, 1996	79 days	Aqsu: Onsu, Toqsu (Xinhe), Šayar, Quca	Violent clashes	—	Arsons, assassinations, robbery, bombings
February 13, 1996	—	Ürümci	Bombing, violent uprising	—	Separatists blew up a car at a police substation and committed violence.
February 24, 1996	1 day	Šayar Township	Robbery	4	15,000 *yuan* stolen from vice chairman of the People's Political Consultative Congress, Rehmetulla Hidayet, by 4 masked men.

2. Although scholars such as Linda Benson and Ingvar Svanberg, and Michael Dillon report this event as established fact (Benson and Svanberg 1998:194–95; Dillon 2004, no. 949:68–69), James Millward expresses skepticism, since it was reported only in a Hong Kong magazine that regularly retails stories unflattering to the CCP. Millward raises three important objections: first, if as large as reported, it would have been one of the most serious antigovernment protests since 1949;

Date	Duration	Location	Type	Number	Description
March 22, 1996	1 day	Toqsu (Xinhe)	Assassination	2	Hakim Sidiq Haji, vice chairman of the Islamic committee, mosque head.
March 27, 1996	1 day	Šayar Township	Robbery	4	6,975 *yuan* stolen from Imin Saqi, an imam, by 4 masked men.
April 12, 1996	1 day	Šayar County	Gunfight	—	—
April 16, 1996	1 day	Khorgos	Weapons smuggling	—	ETLO members reportedly imported weapons into Xinjiang.
April 29, 1996	Days	Quca	Bombing spree	10	After April 27, 1996, border agreement by Shanghai Cooperation Organization.
April 30, 1996	Days	Multiple sites	Street fighting	—	Followed SCO border agreement previous day.
May 12, 1996	—	Kashgar	Assassination attempt	3	Attempt on cleric and parliamentary delegate Harunkhan Haji, by 3 "fanatical and inhuman" splittists.
July 1996	—	Šayar	Bombing	—	Chinese Foreign Ministry attributes the bombing to the Islamic Justice Party.
July 15, 1996	days	Šayar	Prison break by "separatists"	12	Splittists broke out of the Tarim Prison, stole weapons, and killed police, army, and civilians; Beijing attributes the break to the ET Islamic Justice Party.
August 27, 1996	—	Qaghiliq	Assault	6	6 base-level cadres and masses injured; 4–5 killed.
October 23, 1996	1 day	Yerkand	Murder	—	Splittists murdered an "innocent Han and two helpers"; there was supposedly a later plot to kill 40 people, but the plan collapsed.
November 20, 1996	1 day	Yerkand (several places)	Murder	9	3 farmers murdered at home.
February 5, 1997	2 days	Ghulja	Riot	5,000	Biggest incident since Baren.
February 23, 1997	1 day	Aqsu	Assassination	—	Killed Ömärjan, head of *bingtuan*

ORGANIZED PROTESTS AND VIOLENT EVENTS IN XINJIANG, 1949–2005 (continued)

Year	Duration	Location	Type	Number Involved	Comments
February 25, 1997	1 day	Ürümci	Bombing	—	PRC consulate website claims it was the work of "ET National Solidarity Union."
March 23, 1997	1 day	Aqsu	Assassination	—	Mämätjan Sadiq, party committee secretary of a *minzu* farm, Bingtuan no. 1 division; Ziley Abdurazaq, a woman encouraging other women to take off their veils and use family planning, assassinated by "splittists and violent terrorists."
April 26, 1997	1 day	Ghulja	Riot at execution	1,000	—
June 4, 1997	1 day	Moyu, Khotän; Qiaqike Township	Assassination	4	Mämätrozi Mämät, cadre.
June 26, 1997	1	Ining County, Fanjin Township	Assassination	—	Qasim Mašir, the chairman of a township village public-order group, was killed by "splittists" at home.
July 1, 1997	1	Poskam County, Gulbagh Township	Assassination	3	Mämät Seyit, party branch secretary, was killed by 3 members of an "illegal religious organization."
July 3, 1997	1 day	Bäšlik, Awat	Assassination	—	Killed Turdiniyaz, village cadre in Beshlik, and wife.
September 22, 1997	6 days	Toqsun, Shawan, Pichan, Khutubi, Hejing, and Khoshut	Armed rebellion and riots	3,200	Multiple rebellions in widely spaced towns with 3,200 involved. 800 staged an armed attack on Hejing and Khoshut party and government buildings. Officials first denied the reports but later acknowledged them.

September 28, 1997	Šayar County, Šayar Township, Yengi Mehelle	1	Assassination	—	Äziz Abbas, imam of the Yängi Mähäta Mosque, helped break a 500,000-*yuan* robbery and capture the head of the bombing on February 5, 1997; assassinated by "splittists and violent terrorists."
November 6, 1997	Bay, Aqsu	1 day	Assassination	—	Killed Yonus Sidiq Damolla, Islamic association, head of Bay mosque; blamed on separatists.
January 27, 1998	Qaghiliq	1 day	Assassination	—	Abliz Haji, head of Qaghiliq mosque; blamed on separatists.
February 1998	Ghulja	1st week	Disturbance	—	1,000 police dispatched.
February 22, 1998	Qaghiliq	37 days	Bombings	—	6 bombings total through March 1998; economic damages of 100 million *yuan*.
April 7, 1998	Qaghiliq	1 day	Bombings	—	8 bombings in one day.
April 20, 1998	Ghulja (Hudiyayuzi)	1 day	Gunfight	—	PSB official Long Fei was killed. PSB blamed it on Mämtimin Häzrät and the ETLO. Not originally attributed to terrorists in 1998.
May 21, 1998	Aqsu	—	Battle	—	PSB officials encircled "violent terrorists" in their Black Hills hideout; the suspects kept up a barrage of hand grenades until all were killed or blown up.
May 23, 1998	Ürümci	3 days	Arson (40)	—	15 successful; no injuries.
May 28, 1998	Ili District	—	Gunfight	—	Reportedly 1 of 4 gunfights in the second quarter of 1998.
June 2, 1998	Khotän District	—	Battle	—	2 "violent terrorists" pursued by PSB fought them with knives, injured police, and took hostages. Outcome not specified.
June 26, 1998	Ili District	—	Gunfight	—	Reportedly 1 of 4 gunfights in the second quarter of 1998.

ORGANIZED PROTESTS AND VIOLENT EVENTS IN XINJIANG, 1949–2005 (continued)

Year	Duration	Location	Type	Number Involved	Comments
July 22, 1998	1	Awat County, Tamtughraq Township	Gunfight	—	Ablät Tayip, chairman of the Ustun Aral village committee, was killed while helping police break up a "violent terrorist gang."
August 1998	—	Northwest Xinjiang	Murder of police	—	—
November 2, 1998	1 day	Yarkand County, Igerci Township	Stabbing	—	Taš Razaq, secretary of Politics and Law Committee, stabbed while apprehending head of "violent terrorist gang."
February 10, 1999	1 day	Ürümci	Gunfight	—	Murat Rustäm was killed while trying to apprehend suspects in a major robbery-murder case; by 2005 they had become "terrorists."
February 16, 1999	1 day	Ürümci	Riot, clash with police	300	Police tried to arrest 30 Uyghur men shouting "independence for XJ" after a night of drinking. Crowd growing to 300 surrounded police, who clashed with 150.
March 17, 1999	1 day	Changji city	Bombing	—	PAP headquarters admitted that 30 officers had died in a motorcade bound for Shihezi; military insiders say it was "definitely" a bomb set by separatists. There also were gunfights with suspected separatists in Hutubi.
July 10, 1999	1 day	Hejing County	Attack and bombing	12	Reported separatists attacked a power station on a military base in Hejing, blowing up, killing or wounding 12; 12 armed separatists were killed in police pursuit afterward.
July 17, 1999	—	Khotän	Armed attack	2,000	2,000 protestors surround and attack the PSB after a fruit

Date	Duration	Type	Location	Number	Description
July 23, 1999	—	Armed attack	Khotän	300	300 people mob the PSB as security personnel try to apprehend Hebibolla, suspected in the Hotan event of July 7, 1995.
August 9, 1999	—	Armed attack (riot at execution)	Lop	6,000	Riot at the execution of Murtaza; Chinese sources describe as "very serious."
August 20, 1999	1 day	Religious incitement	Khotän: "Siditu-wei mosque"	—	The molla of the mosque (and apparently some worshippers) reportedly shouted "Drive out the 'kapirs.'"
August 23, 1999	1 day	Assassination	Poskam County, Poskam Township	10	Khudabärdi Tokhti, head of a patrol station; blamed on separatists.
August 24, 1999	1 day	Assault	Khotän area	—	Uyghurs riding a motorcycle and beating one or more Han(s).
August 27, 1999	1 day	Assault	Khotän area	—	Head of the Nurbagh police substation was attacked and left bleeding from the head, sent to hospital.
September 4, 1999	—	Killing	Khotän area	21	Police shot and killed Küräš, called a "terrorist leader" by the government; 21 others arrested.
October 21, 199	1 day	Killing	Poskam County, Gulbagh Township	—	A government driver, Tursun Qadir, and a township communications specialist, Qadir Mämät, wounded; the killings were blamed on Yasin Mämät.
October 24, 1999	1 day	Assault	Poskam	—	Attack on Sayri Township PSB; described in Chinese sources as being like Baren.
November 8, 1999	1	Assassination	Awat County, Bäš Eriq Township	—	Turghun Aqniyaz, a policeman, was killed by "violent terrorists" on his way home.

ORGANIZED PROTESTS AND VIOLENT EVENTS IN XINJIANG, 1949–2005 (continued)

Year	Duration	Location	Type	Number Involved	Comments
December 15, 1999	1	Khotän County	Arrest battle	4	In trying to arrest suspected separatists, the PAP officer Abduqeyum Jumeniyaz was killed.
September 28, 2000	—	Almaty	Murder	—	Chinese Foreign Ministry claims 2 Qazaq police were murdered by members of the ULO.
February 3, 2001	1 day	Shufu, Kashgar	Assassination	—	Mämätjan Yaqup, cadre.
August 7, 2001	1 day	Ürümci	Riot	200	Started when inspectors challenged an unlicensed fruit vendor; people threw fruit, rocks, bricks at inspector; people surrounded substation after police collared a suspected ringleader, police arrived to break up.
August 7, 2001	1 day	Quca	Gun battle, aborted uprising	—	Police surprised a house full of suspected separatists; 4 died in the gun battle, including the chief, Chen Ping; a cache of weapons was reportedly found; report of a plan to storm a government building and raise the Uyghur flag.
September 2001	—	Zhangmu entry port, Tibet	Weapons smuggling	—	ETLO reportedly imported weapons into Tibet. Reports identified two Uyghurs, Ablet Tursun and Ahmet (family name not specified) as the ones responsible
October 2001	1 day	Qaraqaš	Protest	180	Some 180 people protested the destruction of a mosque deemed too close to a school, thus a "negative influence" on students. A Chinese official said it was the third such mosque destruction that year.
November 2, 2001	1	Atuš City, Ustun	Gunfight	—	Feng Tao, the head of special antiseparatist PSB unit "110,"

Date	Duration	Location	Type	Number	Description
December 24, 2001	1	Khotän	Protest	100	A day-long protest by 100+ workers after 200+ were laid off at a textile factory that originally had 1,300 workers, of which 80% had been Uyghur. Workers were worried they'd get no severance; local government officials assured them they would.
May 2002	1 day	Khotän	Stabbing	2	A teacher, an advocate of an Islamic state, was dismissed during a patriotic education campaign; stabbed the principal.
May 27, 2002	1	Poskam County, Yima Township	Attack	2	Yasin Mamut, party committee vice secretary and head of a police substation, was killed while inspecting stand selling religious texts; Yusupqadir Idris, PAP vice head, was killed "protecting a cadre" in a struggle with "violent terrorists."
March 7, 2003	1 day	Khorgos	Student protest	100	A whole class (*minzu* unspecified) boycotted and staged a sit-in in over "exam immigrants"; said to have "threatened social order."
March 18, 2003	1 day	Manas	Student protest	300	Some 300 students boycotted classes at the peak, reason unknown; said to have "threatened social order."
April 5, 2003	1	Ucturpan County, Aqtoqay	Attack	1	Sa'ätqiz Tokhti, an assistant in the family-planning office, was killed by the husband of a pregnant woman being examined.
March 2, 2004	—	—	Bombing of PAP barracks	—	Wang Lexiang, deputy PSB chief, announced the "successful" 2004 bombings in August 2006, after claiming the PSB had foiled other bombing attacks (suspicious report by Xinjiang government given attempt to prove there are terrorists years later).

ORGANIZED PROTESTS AND VIOLENT EVENTS IN XINJIANG, 1949–2005 (continued)

Year	Duration	Location	Type	Number Involved	Comments
June 11, 2004	1	Qapšaghay (Ili Prefecture)	Protest	1,000	A day-long protest by farmers, foresters, and herdsmen. A hydropower station under construction would require the relocation of 18,000 people; 38,000 *yuan* compensation offered, only 880 was given; 16 people arrested.
September 5, 2004	—	—	Bombing of rail line	—	See entry for March 2, 2004, event.
March 12, 2005	1	Poskam	Fight	22	17 to 18 Uyghur students fought with Hans; all were arrested, and 4 were sentenced; 4 teachers were also arrested.
April 16, 2005	3 days	Korla	Strike	100	Korla taxi drivers stuck over a newly announced tax of 4,000 *yuan* per year; on day 3, scabs were driving with covered license plates; the number of participants is an estimate.

NOTES

1. To be more precise, Kosovo received an international peacekeeping force and became independent de facto, though not de jure. The government of Kosovo declared independence in early 2008, even though only about a quarter of the world's states had recognized it by this writing.

2. As I detail at length, it is impossible to state with confidence what proportion of Uyghurs seek independence, although Chinese officials, Uyghur nationalists, and not a few foreign scholars have claimed the capacity to do so.

3. Some readers may be disconcerted by my use of the plural "Hans" when sinologists conventionally use "Han" for both singular and plural. I refer to Hans, and Uyghurs, and Huis, and Sibes, in order to underscore the point that the ethnonyms denote numbers of individuals rather than groups that think, or act, as blocs (Brubaker 2002).

4.	Field notes, November 21, 1995. According to Joanne Smith (2002:169), "bus stories have become a favorite subject of Uyghur storytelling." Minor disagreements have frequently precipitated fights on buses and streets.

5.	Uradyn Bulag suggests poignantly that Mongols in Inner Mongolia are often held up as cautionary examples of what Uyghurs and Tibetans will someday become. Drastically outnumbered by Hans in the so-called Inner Mongolia Autonomous Region, they seem to have given up on public resistance and "no longer exhibit . . . an independent spirit" (Bulag 2002:2–3). Bulag demonstrates that Mongols have continued to resist full integration into the "Chinese nation" in various ways. His method has been an inspiration for this book. For reports of public protests in Inner Mongolia in the 1980s and 1990s, see Jankowiak (1988) and BBC Monitoring Asia Pacific (1999). The Southern Mongolia Human Rights Information Center (http://www.smhric.org/) has reports of Mongol protests and clashes with Chinese authorities as recent as April 2006.

6.	Most famously, Deutsch 1953 and Pye 1966, but see also Emerson 1962. For work focusing on China, see Solinger 1977 and especially Liu 1971. Eugen Weber's celebrated work *Peasants into Frenchmen* is a particularly nuanced example (1976). The following critique draws on Connor 1994:28–66. For another brief critique of the "nation-building" literature, see Brubaker 1996:80–81.

7.	Brubaker criticizes the model for assuming "development toward 'full' national integration" (Brubaker 1996:81).

8.	For exemplary work on state–society relations, see Migdal 1988 and 2001 and Migdal, Kohli, and Shue 1994.

9.	The term *minzu* has been rendered variously as "nation," "nationality," and "ethnic group." Because its semantic field encompasses all these meanings and their political implications vary so widely, I generally choose not to translate the term. For more on the history and significance of the term *minzu*, see Gladney 1991 and Leibold 2007:8–9 and passim. See also Jin Tianming and Wang Qingren 1981; Li Hongjie 2002; Ma Rong 2004; Naribilige (Naran Bilik) 1995; and Ning Sao 1995.

10.	A number of small parties provide the fig leaf of a functioning democracy, but in no sense do they serve as real opposition parties. The "four fundamental principles" articulated by Deng Xiaoping stand outside, and date ontologically before, the constitution. The most significant of the four is the stipulation that the leadership of the CCP may not be challenged. Perry Link and Andrew Nathan (Zhang Liang 2001:11, n. 12) describe the principles as "minimum standards for ideological rectitude."

11.	James Scott made these points persuasively in several books (Scott 1985, 1990).

12.	Compare Henan Province, which, with one-tenth the area, claims nearly six times as many people (Banister 1987:298–99).

13. The son of former provincial governor Burhan Shahidi remembers traveling the several thousand miles to Xi'an by military truck in 1951, as there was no civilian transport, on his way to the Beijing Oil Institute. The journey took him twenty-nine days (Xinhua 1999).

14. China Data Online, at http://chinadataonline.org/ (accessed February 2, 2009). Population statistics in China have not been considered reliable until the very recent past. Many scholars view figures comparing Han and non-Han populations with particular skepticism (Toops 2004a). Several hundred thousand more Uyghurs scattered among the Central Asian states, with substantial populations in Kazakhstan, Kyrgyzstan, and Uzbekistan. Additional hundreds of thousands of "former Uyghurs" who changed their identities to that of the dominant group are rumored to be in each of those states under assimilationist pressure.

15. The 1975 figure is from the *1996 Xinjiang Statistical Yearbook* (Xinjiang weiwuer zizhiqu tongjiju 1996:47); Geographer Stanley Toops (2004a:249) pointed out that by the turn of the millennium, given the size of the floating population, not fully reflected in official figures, Hans may already have outnumbered Uyghurs in Xinjiang.

16. Owen Lattimore's (1950, 1951, 1962) work was a partial exception.

17. Both David Brophy and Näbijan Tursun argue that elites discussed the Uyghur identity before the 1921 Tashkent conference (Brophy 2005; Näbijan Tursun 2008).

18. Forbes contends that Uyghurstan (the Qumul and Turpan area in eastern Xinjiang) had been willingly and well bound to China, its population accustomed to centuries of intercourse, watched over by its khans, with Central Plains polities. Altishahr (the Tarim Basin) was the seat of regular rebellions, and Zungharia in the north had close ties to czarist and then Soviet Central Asia.

19. The survival of regional identities in France at least through the late nineteenth century (Weber 1976) and the collaboration of "subject nationalities" in the administration of the Russian and Austro-Hungarian empires (Comisso 2006:140) demonstrate that these phenomena in Xinjiang were by no means exceptional.

20. Field notes, June 26, 1997, and July 31, 2002.

21. Justin Rudelson found in the 1980s that Uyghur merchants who regularly traveled to the interior were far more likely than intellectuals or peasants to identify themselves as "Chinese" (*jonggoluq*). The destruction of the "Xinjiang village" in Beijing (Agence France-Presse 1999b) and clashes with police in other inland cities (Agence France-Presse 2002c, 2004b) have made Uyghurs feel considerably less welcome since then.

22. Ildiko Beller-Hann notes that officials' expanded attacks on Islam in the 1990s "inadvertently undermine[d] a force which, in some respects, provide[d] useful underpinnings for the acceptance and respect of secular authorities" (Beller-Hann 1997:90).

23. The idea that increased communication promotes nationalism was originally articulated in rather positivist form by Deutsch (1953). Anderson (1991) can be said to have devel-

oped the notion and given it more nuance by attending to particular forms of communication, focusing on novels and newspapers, and demonstrating the importance of their content.

24. Ernest Gellner puts this point with characteristic clarity. The rulers of the Soviet Union employed a "hierarchy of ethnic concepts: 'nations' deserved their own republics, 'nationalities' had to make do with autonomous regions" (Gellner 1995:252).

25. This is an honest mistake. He gets it wrong for the simple reason that he depends on English translations by either officials in China or Western sinologists, both of whom have tried to make CCP nomenclatures intelligible abroad by using contextual remapping. Thus where the Chinese texts have *zhonghua minzu*, they translate *minzu* as "nation," and in reference to the various non-Han groups, they translate *minzu* as "nationality." In other words, they collaborate in the Chinese state's project of allocating rights to some groups while withholding them from others. For examples from Chinese and Western translations into English, see, respectively, Mao Zedong 1977 (1956); and Zhang Zhiyi 1966 (1956).

26. There is a grain of truth in Connor's argument. While proclaiming that Han and non-Han alike were *minzu*—crucial to the official policy of "*minzu* equality" (*minzu pingdeng*), the party nevertheless made a categorical distinction between them. Because they comprised less than 6 percent of the population in the 1950s, the fifty-five non-Han *minzu* were assigned to the collective category of "minority *minzu*" (*shaoshu minzu*). In practice, the term *minority* is often omitted. Thus the expressions "*minzu* education," "*minzu* cadres," and "*minzu* problems," all seemingly applicable to the entire population, are understood to refer only to the non-Han groups. Herein lies the germ of confusion that non-Hans have artfully manipulated.

27. Historian Xiaoyuan Liu argues to the contrary that "to its Chinese audience, the term literally meant the 'central Hua [Sinitic] nation' [and] carried the full meaning of the ethnocultural stratifications in Chinese history" (Liu 2004:23).

28. The original was *Womende Hui minzu hen tuanjiede*. I have altered Gladney's translation in two ways: I have left *minzu* in Chinese, for the reasons just explained, and I have rendered *tuanjie* as "solidarity" rather than "unity" to avoid confusion with the term *tongyi*, often translated with the same English word. My interpretation remains compatible with Gladney's.

29. The English gloss "(nation)" is in the original. Without it, the sentence would make even less sense.

30. See the Web site of the Minzu shiwu weiyuanhui at www.seac.gov.cn/ (accessed June 4, 2006).

31. Web site at www.cun.edu.cn/ (accessed June 4, 2006).

32. Web site at http://www.mzyj.cn/index-en.html (accessed June 4, 2006).

33. Only a year before my arrival, many foreign teachers and some foreign students had been permitted to live in apartments on or off campus, giving them much more freedom.

34. I asked for a statute book containing the relevant law and, having looked through the book, could find none. A public security official then told me that this prohibition was an "internal regulation" and therefore not published in the materials that I was permitted to see (Bovingdon 2002a:48). Stanley Lubman points out that well into the 1990s, many administrative units still relied on internal rules and regulations (Lubman 1999: 146–47)

35. I later learned from several sources that foreign journalists had used recording equipment during interviews in the recent past, with disastrous consequences for both themselves and their informants (field notes, October 22, 1997). I know of a linguistic anthropologist and a cultural anthropologist who were able to use audio and video recording equipment before or during the time of my research, perhaps because they had convinced their informants and officials that their work was not politically sensitive.

36. For a sense of the change in the research atmosphere over time, see Rudelson 1997; Dautcher 1999; and Smith 2006. Herbert Yee, who carried out two surveys in the region, met with a number of obstacles, which I describe in chapter 3 (Yee 2003, 2005).

1. USING THE PAST TO SERVE THE PRESENT

1. Field notes, November 14, 1996.

2. Ernst Renan once famously wrote that forgetting was as important to the nationalist enterprise as remembering (Renan 1882/1990).

3. Eric Hobsbawm wrote that "no serious historian of nations and nationalism can be a committed political nationalist," continuing archly that "nationalism requires too much belief in what is patently not so" (Hobsbawm 1990:12). James Millward's *Eurasian Crossroads: A History of Xinjiang* (2007) is the first monographic *longue durée* history of the region in English and is a model of evenhanded scholarship.

4. The Chinese historian Gu Bao attempted to silence this charge, arguing that the term actually meant "native lands newly returned" (*gu tu xin gui*) (Gu Bao 1983:25).

5. European and Japanese historians distinguish three geographic regions in Xinjiang that had very different political histories over the centuries and up to the mid-twentieth century: Uyghur(i)stan, the eastern part surrounding the towns of Qumul and Turpan; Zungharia, the area north of the Tianshan mountains; and Kashgaria, the Tarim Basin south of the Tianshan, which includes the Taklamakan Desert and the many oasis towns ringing it. Nationalists use Uyghurstan to refer to all three regions.

6. Scholars acknowledge that the term Xiyu had different senses over time, sometimes applying to only a part of today's Xinjiang and other times embracing parts of Central Asia and extending into the Near East.

7. Unless otherwise noted, when I refer to Chinese officials and historians, I mean those working and writing in China after 1949. On the complex interconnections of scholars and bureaucrats and the role of the party-state in the production of Chinese nationalist history, see Bovingdon and Näbijan Tursun 2004.

8. The statement emerged as an official "formulation" (*tifa*) in 1959 as part of the government's effort to combat "local nationalism" in Xinjiang (Bovingdon and Näbijan Tursun 2004:359). On the party-state's use of "formulations" for political ends, see the brilliant short work of Schoenhals (1992). I discuss local nationalism in chapter 2.

9. For an important partial dissent, see Zhao 2006.

10. The World Uyghur Congress's Web site more modestly claims four thousand years (World Uyghur Congress 2006a). Exponents of the ambitiously named "Eastern Turkestan Government in Exile" boast more expansively that Uyghurs "existed before history" and will exist after it (Šärqiy Türkistan Jumhuriyiti Sürgündiki Parlamenti wä Hökümiti 2005:57).

11. Historians of this stripe have also subscribed to the widespread view that the Xiongnu and the Huns were one and the same; see, for example, Turghun Almas 1989. Denis Sinor points out that the view remains unproven (Sinor 1990:177).

12. As historian Joseph Fletcher contended, the notion that the ninth-century denizens of southern and eastern Xinjiang were culturally homogeneous and, more important, that they were Uyghurs, "is an innovation stemming largely from the needs of twentieth-century nationalism" (Fletcher 1968:364, n. 96). The expression "self-same, national subject" comes from Duara (1995).

13. David Brophy argues that the name—and hence the collective identity—reemerged dialectically, not only as a result of top-down Soviet policies, but also because of popular initiatives by Turkis in Xinjiang and Central Asia (Brophy 2005).

14. The historian Geng Shimin (1984:13) argued that the "modern Uyghur nationality" emerged in the late fifteenth or early sixteenth century.

15. Walker Connor demonstrated persuasively that Marxists in the Soviet Union, China, Yugoslavia, and Vietnam strategically fused Marxism and nationalism. They all used class to deemphasize and defeat cultural categories *within* the "national" frame but, at the same time, emphasized national loyalties over internationalist class affinities to thwart secessionist or irredentist movements (Connor 1984). Feuerwerker (1968) brilliantly illustrated these tactics at work in Chinese communist historiography.

16. Nationalist history is a branch not of historical scholarship but of rhetoric. Still, this division of Chinese history into main and adverse currents can be understood as a particularly bald example of "retrospective analysis," which, as Charles Tilly pointed out, cannot be used for valid explanations of state-building processes (Tilly 1975:14–15).

17. James Millward sympathetically describes one source of pervasive nationalism in post-1949 Chinese historiography. Knowing that China had been ill treated by other states

in the nineteenth century and could have been partitioned among European states and Japan, "few Chinese historians ... would object if the lessons from their research served ... a contemporary diplomatic or strategic purpose" (Millward 1996:120).

18. The first Chinese-language history claiming that "China" had run Xinjiang (more properly the Western Regions, or Xiyu) since the Han dynasty was actually written during the Republican era, in 1936 (Zeng Wenwu 1986). In 1996 Xinjiang People's Press published a collection of historical essays that included the astounding claim that Xinjiang had become part of "China" in the twenty-third century BCE when Xiwangmu pledged fealty to Emperor Shun (He Jihong 1996:3–4). Some historians speculate that the legendary Emperor Shun might have had a real historical analogue, but Xiwangmu was not real, having the same historical status as Zeus.

19. Muhämmäd Imin was dedicated enough to this goal and practical enough that he sought Japanese support while living in exile in Kabul in the mid-1930s. He had reason to hope for such support, as Japanese officials had indeed plotted the establishment of an independent Turkic state in the region, even providing weapons and intelligence to the first ETR (Esenbel 2004:1160–62; Forbes 1986:140; Whiting and Sheng Shih-ts'ai [Sheng Shicai] 1958:36).

20. By convention, Isa Yusuf Alptekin is referred to by his adopted last name rather than by his given name, as are Muhämmäd Imin and the vast majority of Uyghurs. Alptekin also made overtures beyond the Muslim and Turkic communities, soliciting help from the United States and the United Nations as well. The political activities of the two are considered at greater length in chapter 5.

21. This matter was debated as early as the founding of the first ETR in 1933 (Millward 2007).

22. The book was published in Kashgar in 1989 and banned almost immediately afterward by the Chinese authorities.

23. By stopping his conquest at the Pamirs, Qing Emperor Qianlong bequeathed a western border to subsequent generations in Xinjiang that bounded the Uyghurs' territorial imaginings and was therefore a principal factor in their seeing themselves as distinct from other Central Asians (Millward and Perdue 2004:55–56).

24. When they cite the (inaccurate) statistics that only 5 percent of the province's population in 1949 was Han and that Uyghurs made up the remaining 95 percent, Uyghur transnational organizations seek to suggest that Uyghurs were once the sole proprietors of Xinjiang. These figures obscure the long presence of Qazaqs, Sibes, and others in the region. Equally important, they slight the evidence that Hans may have made up as much as one-third of the population when the Qing dynasty was at its height, around 1800, owing to substantial immigration after the Qing conquest (Millward 2000:122–23; see also Wang Shuanqian 1999:26–28).

25.   In an ironic counterpoint, Chinese archeologists announced they had found Chinggis Khan's tomb in Xinjiang in 2000 (Bulag 2004:110).

26.   Uradyn Bulag observed that Beijing had "begun a process to systematically remove the foundations of minority autonomy by assertions of native status for Han everywhere." He reported that a leading Han official at the Inner Mongolia Party School gave a lecture in 1993 claiming that Hans and not Mongols were indigenous to Inner Mongolia, eliciting strong protests from Mongols (Bulag 2000:191–92).

27.   Interest among Chinese officials in demonstrating that Xinjiang had always been Chinese began no later than the Republican period. A European archeologist found in the 1920s that officials in Xinjiang "despised" artifacts connected with Buddhism or inscribed in Turkic or other non-Chinese languages and so welcomed foreigners to cart them away. Only stones inscribed in Chinese aroused their interest, and those stones they required to remain in the region (Le Coq 1986 [1928]:60).

28.   For an excellent discussion of how disputants in territorial struggles rely on originary myths to stake prior claims to land, see Zerubavel 2003:101–10.

29.   As Peter Perdue put it, the Manchus "knew well that these conquests were unprecedented." It was Chinese nationalist historians of the twentieth century who implied that the Qing had "merely fulfilled the mission of its predecessors" (Perdue 2005a:336, 506).

30.   The quoted phrase is Joseph Esherick's gloss on Zhang's text. Esherick notes that a debate about whether to claim all Qing territories or focus nation-building efforts on "China proper" continued through the first year of the Republic (Esherick 2006:237, 243–44).

31.   Liang opposed "broad nationalism" to "small nationalism" (*xiao minzu zhuyi*), which pitted Hans against the other groups (*tazu*) (Zhao 2004:65).

32.   After the Soviet Union declared the independent Mongolian People's Republic in 1924, Sun officially supported Mongols' right of self-determination, though he hoped to avert actual Mongolian secession by negotiating a federal compact. Sun made the concession to gain Soviet military support for the GMD. I am grateful to Chris Atwood for making this point to me. Chiang later demanded unsuccessfully that Stalin rescind Mongolia's independence at the end of World War II and went to his death believing that Mongolia was properly part of China. I return to this matter in chapter 5.

33.   In 1920 an obscure revolutionary inspired by the warlord governing his native province of Hunan argued that the province should become an independent republic and there should be "27 small Chinas." Mao Zedong's views later changed rather dramatically (Duara 1995:189).

34.   The historian Xiaoyuan Liu argues that this was equally true of Mongolia and Tibet (Liu 2004:22).

35. The author of the definitive history of the period refers to Yang's reign as "an ossified version of the Imperial administration extended for seventeen years into the Republican era" (Forbes 1986:37).

36. It is clear that misrule by Chinese overlords permitted, in fact set the tone for, similar maladministration by local Uyghur officials (Forbes 1986; Skrine and Nightingale 1973:22–23).

37. David Wang's book, while generally quite thorough, consistently follows Beijing's line on the pre-1949 history of Xinjiang. It contains no reference to these speeches. For an earlier discussion of them, see Lattimore 1950:83, 91–92.

38. The following paragraphs draw on Wu 1947.

39. Walker Connor justly observes that Lenin and his successors distinguished between the "right to a right and the right to exercise that right" (Connor 1984:52).

1. Herbert Yee comes to a similar conclusion: "At the moment, the major threat to Xinjiang stability is not external but internal, that is, Beijing's own bad and [out]dated policies toward the national minorities" (Yee 2003:452). *Oxford Analytica* argues more starkly still that "Chinese policies, not foreign-sponsored terrorism, are the cause of Uighur unrest" (*Oxford Analytica*, December 20, 2002, 2; cited in Gladney 2006:4).

2. This chapter pays comparatively little attention to political sentiments of the more than one million Qazaqs and the several million members of several other non-Han groups who call Xinjiang home. On Xinjiang's Qazaqs, see Benson and Svanberg 1988, 1998.

3. For discussions of the impact of state policies on Uyghur identity, see Bovingdon 1998, 2002b; Gladney 1990; and Rudelson 1997. Scholars have similarly implicated the state in the formation and strengthening of collective identities among the Hui (Gladney 1991) and Zhuang (Kaup 2000).

4. For concise treatments of politics in Mongolia, Ningxia, and Tibet, see the various chapters in Rossabi 2004; on Guangxi, see Kaup 2000.

5. The former XUAR governor Säypidin recalled that in 1955, leaders in Beijing had initially proposed calling the region simply the "Xinjiang Autonomous Region." Säypidin objected that "autonomy is not given to mountains and rivers. It is given to particular nationalities. I do not think the name . . . is really appropriate." He was gratified to learn, several days later, that Mao had agreed with him, insisting it be the "Xinjiang *Uyghur* Autonomous Region" (FBIS-CHI-95–221, November 16, 1995, 89–90). He did not record his reaction to this 1951 "Uyghurstan" controversy (Zhu Peimin 2000:335).

6. In 1955, according to official statistics, the 3.72 million Uyghurs comprised roughly 73 percent of the total population of 5.11 million.

7. The data in this paragraph come from Yin Zhuguang and Mao Yongfu 1996:132–33.

8. I am grateful to Chris Atwood for the reference. To be sure, Mongols had faced similarly flagrant gerrymandering in their "home districts" long before 1949 and saw the shape of their "autonomous region" manipulated several times in the PRC period. They were vastly outnumbered by Hans from the founding of the Inner Mongolia Autonomous Region in 1947 (Bulag 2004:90–92). For a particularly lucid discussion of territorial manipulations in ethnographic Tibet, see Shakya 1999.

9. In 1947, Xinjiang's Eighth District (roughly coextensive with today's Bayangol) reportedly contained 15,000 Mongols, 89,000 Uyghurs, and 1,682 Hans (Xinjiang weiwu'er zizhiqu minzu shiwu weiyuanhui 1995:878–79).

10. Mao Yongfu was director of the Policy Research Office of the XUAR CCP Committee. See David Wang 1998:52, n. 60.

11. For an explanation of the rationale for establishing nested autonomies, and a description of the process through which the Xinjiang Autonomous Region was established, see Säypidin's recollection in 1995, originally published in the *People's Daily* (Säypidin Äzizi 1995). A recent online article argues that "using Hui, Mongols, and Qazaqs to rule Uyghurs" was the explicit aim of gerrymandering and nested autonomies (Xue Yu 2003).

12. One immediately wonders what Zhu made of the decision in the following year to combine the party committees of Ürümci and the Changji Hui Autonomous District into a single "transadministrative region" organ (Zhang Ya 2005).

13. Residents of Xinjiang refer to all Chinese provinces to the east as "the interior" (*neidi*). To avoid confusion, I render this idea using the once-popular term "China proper" (*Zhongguo ben bu* in Chinese).

14. Unmentioned because obedience to party organs at equivalent and higher levels was beyond question.

15. Here "the people" (*renmin*) was understood to denote only a portion of the total population. The party-state retained the right to determine which citizen belonged to "the people" and who were "nonpeople": class enemies or enemies of the state (Schoenhals 1994). For the program's text, see Li Weihan 1982:521–26.

16. References in this paragraph are to the amended 2001 law, although the relevant articles are almost indistinguishable from those in the 1984 law. The most substantial change of interest here is in article 20, which has added a requirement that the higher-level government organ respond to proposed alterations within sixty days. According to an article in an official journal, the amendment committee made this change because the provision for local modification of national policies had "essentially not been enacted." Superior governments routinely regarded such proposals by autonomous governments by "set[ting] them aside and ignor[ing] them, never providing a response" (Ao Junde 2001).

17. Even though the constitution and autonomy law explicitly allow autonomous regions to pass such statutes, Xinjiang's government has never done so (Ghalip Isma'il 1996).

18. Moneyhon makes these points with specific reference to Xinjiang. The autonomy law he analyzes applies to all autonomous regions in China, from the provincial level down, and since 1949 Beijing has chosen all the executives of the five autonomous regions.

19. On lawmaking by bureaucracies and the executive branch in China, see also Lubman 1999:141–44.

20. I refer to the paramilitary farms interchangeably as *bingtuan* and the Production and Construction Corps (PCC). On the PCC, see Becquelin 2000; Cliff 2009; McMillen 1979, 1981, 1984; Seymour 2000; Shichor 2006a.

21. Allen Whiting notes that Chinese media trumpeted the celebration of Muslim holidays, especially in the northwest, even as the Soviet Union in the mid-1950s denounced Ramadan as a "reactionary vestige of feudal superstition" and a drag on productivity (Whiting 1955:174).

22. Tibet, Inner Mongolia, and other non-Han regions also had campaigns against "local nationalism." In this campaign as in so many others, the PRC recapitulated prior movements in the Soviet Union, in which Stalin targeted "local nationalism" in the Ukraine and Central Asia beginning in 1933 (Martin 2001:7–8, 356–62). The influence also appears to have flowed in the other direction. In 1959 Nikita Khrushchev cashiered many officials in Central Asia for "local nationalism" (Whiting 1960:35).

23. In 1963 a Qazaq who had fled in 1962 claimed to head a Soviet-sponsored guerrilla army of sixty thousand, staffed by refugees from Xinjiang and preparing to attack China (Mackerras 1994:172; McMillen 1979:124).

24. Interview, Ürümci, October 23, 1996; see also Rudelson 1997:104. Dru Gladney learned of forced pig-raising in Hui regions as well and attributes it to socialist enthusiasm. Harder to explain are episodes in which Hui were forced to eat pork or watched in dismay as pork bones were thrown into their wells (Gladney 1991:135, 138).

25. Interviews, Ürümci, October 10, 1996; April 1, 1997.

26. The protest was reportedly serious enough that PLA soldiers were dispatched to put it down. The report was published in Soviet and Hong Kong sources but never confirmed by Chinese sources. Han immigrants to Xinjiang also staged violent protests over "economic issues" in Shihezi and Qaramay in 1975. See Dreyer 1986:728, 729.

27. Hu made these suggestions before traveling to Xinjiang. He later visited the region twice en route to Europe, once in 1983 and again in 1986, and made a formal two-week inspection tour in the summer of 1985 (Zhu Peimin 2000:359–60).

28. This passage quotes from and paraphrases Dillon (2004:36). Dillon in turn cites the official's quotation from Ruan Ming, "Missed Historic Opportunity Recalled," *Minzhu Zhongguo* 8 (February 1992):17–18. Translated in JPRS-CAR-92-039.

29. For another account of Beijing's combined "hard and soft policies" in Xinjiang, see Rudelson and Jankowiak 2004:301–2.

30. Although Beijing initiated the national "strike hard" campaign in 1983 to combat the rising crime rate and periodically repeated these sweeps in the intervening years, including in Xinjiang (Wang Shuanqian 1999:331–32), a special Xinjiang-specific strike hard campaign targeting separatists was announced in April 1996 (Dillon 2004:84–85; Tanner 1999). Amnesty International (1999) and other human rights organizations claim that officials have used strike hard campaigns to arrest suspected separatists, convict them in kangaroo courts, and imprison or execute them at lightning speed.

31. A dictionary of "new Chinese terms" explains it as steps taken "to resolve problems of social order ... using political, economic, ideological, educational, cultural, administrative, legal, and other measures, to attack evil trends, crimes, illegality, and breaches of discipline" (Wen Hui, Wang Peng, and Li Bengang 1992:676). The term has since been replaced with "comprehensive political rectification" (*zonghe zhengzhi*).

32. Field notes, 1997. Antiseparatist propaganda sweeps have continued; see BBC Monitoring Asia Pacific—Political 2000, and a similar report by BBC News Online (May 29, 2000) at http://news.bbc.co.uk/hi/english/world/asia-pacific/newsid_768000/768815.stm (accessed April 22, 2001); see also Becquelin 2004a.

33. Melvyn Goldstein contends that Beijing has chosen similar strategies for Tibet, and for similar reasons. Its plans for economic development and Han immigration are intended to alter Tibet so dramatically that "failure to win over a new generation of Tibetans will not weaken Beijing's control over Tibet" (Goldstein 1997:110). Tsering Shakya suggests that Tibetan officials tacitly agreed to Han immigration despite widespread opposition from ordinary Tibetans (Shakya 1999:438).

34. A Qing official eloquently articulated the political point of Chinese colonization in 1827, writing that "as the numbers of [Chinese] soldiers and people increase over time, the Muslims' strength will gradually weaken, and naturally they will no longer entertain ulterior aspirations" (quoted in Millward 1998:227).

35. One reviewer observed that Davidson's book, sunnily titled *Daybreak in China* (1953), offered "almost unqualified praise" of the CCP's endeavors (Escarra 1954).

36. Forty-five years later, one of Xinjiang's most prominent social scientists struck a slightly apologetic note about the planned population transfers: "bringing the population into conformity [*sic*] inside one's own country should not be too harshly criticized" (*wu ke hou fei*) (Pan Zhiping 2001:92).

37. In 1949 Zhang Zhiyi (Chang Chih-Yi), formerly a professor at Zhejiang University but by that time a fellow at Johns Hopkins University, wrote of southern Xinjiang that "any newly cleared ground should be allocated to the [Uyghur] peasants, who are hungry for

land. . . . To import Chinese would be to invite new conflicts." Zhang calculated on the basis of available arable land in the north and the low productivity of that land in Xinjiang that the region must set a maximum figure of three million for "Chinese colonization" (Chang 1949:74).

38. While recruiters called on youths to "volunteer to help the borderlands" (*zhiyuan bianjiang*), the internal description of the plan was "bring in immigrants to fill in the borderlands" (*yimin shibian*). This phrase had actually originated in the Qing with the noted scholar-official Zhang Zhidong. At the time a tutor in the Imperial Academy, he proposed that the government strengthen the defense of Mongolia against the territorial designs of Russia and Japan by "filling it in" with immigrants, a plan carried out over the strong opposition of many Mongolians (Lu Minghui 1994:115–17; see also Liu Xiaoyuan 2004:20).

39. This must have happened in the first three weeks of January because on the twenty-first, the XUAR government ordered that the "Aqsu reclamation region Shanghai youth liaison headquarters" and the "United Shanghai youth committee" disband immediately (Chen Chao 1990:229).

40. McMillen depicted this as a decision by Deng Xiaoping, "undoubtedly seconded" by the two Wangs. Zhu Peimin, a professor at the Xinjiang Party School, indicates more plausibly that Wang Zhen first raised the idea with Deng. Just back from touring the scene of the "Päyziwat insurgency" of May 27, 1981 (see appendix), and well aware of how many Hans wanted to leave Xinjiang, Wang was acutely concerned that the region was becoming increasingly unstable. In a June 1981 letter to Deng, Wang urged that the PCC be restored in order to protect against secession and local unrest. Deng himself toured Xinjiang in August, with particular attention to Shihezi, the city that the PCC had essentially built from scratch. On returning to Beijing, he announced in a Central Committee meeting that the organization must be revived. The orders went out in September (Zhu Peimin 2000:338–39).

41. The system registered each citizen as a resident of a particular locale and gave urban residents access to ration coupons only in that region. Household registration made it nearly impossible for peasants to move to cities. Urban residents could not change their registration to a new locale without an invitation from a work unit there and a release from the home unit, both extremely hard to obtain. Without a change in registration, they could not obtain ration coupons and therefore faced great difficulty purchasing food and other necessities.

42. Chongqing Municipality announced in August 2006 that it would send 100,000 cotton pickers to Xinjiang in that year, a substantial portion of the roughly 600,000 that had come annually in the recent past, and five times Chongqing's 2005 contingent of 20,000. The PCC was slated to provide free housing and amenities for all cotton pickers, which it has recruited in large numbers since cotton planting expanded in the 1980s ("Chongqing

to Send 100,000 Farmers to Pick Cotton in Xinjiang" 2006). For the 2005 figure, see http://english.big5.cqnews.net/system/2005/09/14/000526676.shtml (accessed September 14, 2005).

43. Sociologist Ji Ping noted that it was already clear by 1990 that the government could no longer control the movement of "the most needed labor" in and out of Xinjiang. In a survey he conducted in 1987, many Han intellectuals complained of the government's "'trap' policy": on arrival decades earlier, they had been promised the right to return to their homes after working in Xinjiang for five to ten years. Later on, no official acknowledged responsibility for the earlier promise. According to Ji, the fear of being "trapped" in Xinjiang inhibited many Hans from moving there (Ji Ping 1990:268).

44. I am grateful to Warren Smith for providing the FBIS reference to this article. The newspaper publishing the interview, the *Guangming Daily*, has always been aimed at educated readers, precisely the kind of "talented people" Wang hoped to recruit.

45. The paper is widely regarded as the CCP's main mouthpiece in Hong Kong, a platform for broadcasting party views like the *People's Daily* rather than a serious purveyor of news (Hutcheon 1998:7).

46. Information in this paragraph not otherwise cited draws on Rudelson 1997:106–7, 130–31; and Xu Xifa 1995:23–24, 170–73. Barry Sautman claims, citing a 1985 Xinhua article with no title, that the XUAR Congress adopted birth restrictions for urban non-Hans in 1983 and that this led to a "riot" in Ürümci within the year. I have found no published reports of a disturbance in Ürümci, or indeed anywhere in Xinjiang, in 1983 or 1984 (see appendix).

47. The XUAR government passed a formal law to replace the temporary regulations only two years later and took another year to put it into effect in 1992. The study providing this information justified the implementation of birth restrictions among non-Hans on economic, eugenic, and ecological grounds. The author did not comment on the implications of allowing continued Han migration while limiting Uyghurs' fertility (Xu Xifa 1995:23–24, 170). For a more recent eugenicist justification of birth planning, see Zheng Pingjian and Dai Erfu 2003.

48. Ma Dazheng remarked that religious Uyghurs in the South had harmed relations between Uyghurs and Hans in 1990 by claiming, "Only because too many Hans have come to Xinjiang are they making minority *minzu* undergo family planning" (Ma Dazheng 2003:15).

49. There were originally PCC regiments in Mongolia and other "border" regions (see, for example, Bulag 2000:182–83; and He Gang and Shi Weimin 1994). All but those in Xinjiang were subsequently disbanded.

50. The 1974 figures are from Zhang Erju (1988:241); the 1994 figures are from the XUAR Local Gazetteer Editorial Committee (1995: 499) and Xinjiang Weiwu'er zizhiqu tongjiju (1995:46), and the 2004 figures are from Xinjiang Weiwu'er zizhiqu tongjiju 2005:121.

51. Anwar Rahman, a former Uyghur government official now living abroad, claims that every Uyghur chairman of the autonomous regional government has had a Han personal secretary, assigned to shadow him nearly constantly and living in the same compound. Anwar suggests that these Han secretaries not only closely supervise the chairmen's actions but occasionally use the authority of the office for their own ends (Rahman 2005:76).

52. XASS researcher Li Shangkai claimed history showed that the government ought to rely on non-Han cadres to announce official policies and defuse conflicts, because they had special psychological effectiveness among other non-Hans by virtue of being "one of them" rather than "outsiders" (Li Shangkai 1992:144). Uradyn Bulag (2004:100) notes that Mongol officials in Inner Mongolia were similarly used to announce unpopular policies. In the Soviet Union, Gregory Gleason observes, Moscow selected "pliant local leaders" to provide an "aura of local representation" in the union republics while staving off the emergence of nationalism (1990:88).

53. Guo Zhengli (1992:89) also acknowledged that the real situation of non-Han cadre recruitment was "quite uneven; [among] its principal manifestations is the scarcity of non-Han core cadres (*gugan ganbu*) at the county level and above."

54. Wang Lixiong (2002) describes a similar course of events in Tibet during the 1980s.

55. Not all cadres hold positions of political authority. One scholar-official notes with concern that in the late 1990s nearly 40 percent of non-Han cadres were elementary and middle school teachers (Yang Faren 2000:160)

56. The assertion about enterprises is based on an extensive survey of business advertisements in the annual *Xinjiang nianjian* (*Xinjiang Yearbook*) from 1988 to 2004.

57. Web site at http://www.jj.xjnews.cn/magazine/100shuji/index.asp (accessed July 10, 2006). We cannot exclude the possibility that some of these officials are from non-Han groups in China proper that use Han-sounding names.

58. Figures calculated from *Xinjiang nianjian* (*Xinjiang Yearbook*), from 1988 and 1995.

59. Ma observed that in 1991 the PSB caught thirty-one state cadres and party members in crackdowns on separatist organizations. In 1992, sweeps netted fourteen party members, thirty-eight Youth League members, and twenty-nine cadres, and in 1993 the situation was "even more terrifying" (Ma Dazheng 2003:80). Arrest figures may, of course, be poor indicators of the numbers in organizations that remained at large.

60. Field notes, 1996, 1997.

61. Interview, December 1996.

62. On the Dai, see Hansen 1999; on the Hui, Gladney 1991; and Lipman 1997. Matthew Kapstein describes in the case of Tibet the "twin phenomena of increasing freedom and continuing repression" (Kapstein 2004:261).

63. By one estimate, in the early 1950s there had been more than 12,000 mosques in Kashgar Prefecture and 126 in Kashgar City (Dillon 2004:28).

64. It is striking that avowedly atheist officials could claim to understand the needs of religious citizens, particularly since 1949 the population of the "believing masses" in Kashgar had nearly doubled, while a decade of reconstruction had restored only three-quarters the original number of mosques (Dillon 2004:28).

65. Officials like to point out that Muslims in Xinjiang enjoy the highest number of mosques per capita of any Muslim population in the world, with 24,000 mosques for some 9 million believers, whereas Iran has 5,400 mosques for 60 million, and Egypt has 17,000 mosques for 43 million (Zhu Peimin, Chen Hong, and Yang Hong 2004:221; see also Ma Dazheng 2003:98). These numbers, of course, take no account of the size of individual mosques or their functions in their respective societies.

66. Field notes, 1996.

67. An Arabic term meaning "religious pupil," now well known in its plural form *taliban*.

68. This rule might also extend to Sufi shrines, which would mean the end of Sufi pilgrimages, a practice common for hundreds of years in Xinjiang. On Sufi practices and sites in Xinjiang, see Doktor Rahilä Dawut 2001; and Papas 2005.

69. A month after the report on the Ningxia Sufi network, it emerged that the Ili prefectural government in Xinjiang had outlawed a Sufi sect and arrested a large number of members in the prefecture (Rotar 2005).

70. Field notes 1996, 1997, 2002. On intellectuals' suspicion of popular Islam, see Rudelson 1997; and Rudelson and Jankowiak 2004.

71. Remote control cameras were installed around the Idkah mosque to monitor those entering, according to a 2000 report (Sheridan 2000).

72. Article 10 states that students caught fasting would, without exception, be considered to have taken part in religious activities and would lose any subsidies they received, be barred from receiving any award for "progressiveness," and be forbidden to serve as student cadres (*Xinjiang daxue xuesheng shouce* 2005:97).

73. The Amnesty report cites stories in AFP and Reuters for the arrests in Kashgar and Bayangol (Agence France-Presse 2001b; Vidaillet 2001) and a report by the Eastern Turkestan Information Center for those in Khotän (East Turkestan Information Center 2002).

74. Deng's remarks from a 1981 conversation with Xinjiang's second party secretary, Gu Jingsheng, were published in the *Xinjiang Daily* newspaper in 1998. Officials probably decided to publish the remarks seventeen years later as part of the plan to win public support for the struggle against separatists.

75. For a theoretical work justifying CCP choices with specific reference to Xinjiang, see Guo Zhengli 1992.

76. Ma even proposed addressing Han cadres' concern that serving in Xinjiang might penalize their families, by recognizing that those children "should at minimum enjoy the same

special treatment afforded the minority *minzu* students in the region" (Ma Dazheng 2003:20). In other words, cadre children should benefit from affirmative action. This suggestion is particularly striking, since near the end of the book Ma urges that leaders abandon the "inappropriate system" of admitting minority *minzu* students with lower scores on college entrance examinations (Ma Dazheng 2003:201). Hence between the covers of one book, he advocates extending affirmative action to some Han children and abolishing it for non-Hans.

77. Ma originally wrote the essay containing this sentence in 1999 and, of course, for internal circulation. A year later, the journal of the Xinjiang Academy of Social Sciences published an article on methods for "adjusting" inter-*minzu* relations in which the author discussed, among other methods, stipulating that the ratio of minority *minzu* cadres be roughly equivalent (*dati xiangdang*) to the ratio in the population at large (Tian Mengqing 2000:72).

78. Democracy offers little protection to autonomy regimes when it is weakly institutionalized, as shown by the reversals and "backsliding" in Jakarta's handling of autonomy in Aceh and Papua (McGibbon 2004:3–5).

3. EVERYDAY RESISTANCE

1. I have slightly interpolated the original translation.

2. Within days, the party announced a broad crackdown on cultural units and media in Xinjiang, targeting those seen as "advocating separatism by means of art." Ablet Abdurisit, chairman of the XUAR government, informed cadres that "politics" was henceforth to be the sole criterion in evaluating literary and artistic works (Chan 2002).

3. Field notes, summer 2002.

4. Field notes, summer 2002.

5. Tursun Islam, the leader of a Uyghur organization in Kyrgyz Republic, claims that in 1951 a group of fifty-one intellectuals calling themselves "the Fifty-one" demanded independence from the Chinese government, notifying other Uyghur intellectuals they had done so, and urging members of the former Ili National Army to prepare for an armed struggle. According to Tursun, the government bloodily suppressed the ensuing movement, jailing and secretly executing many of the intellectuals, thereby enraging the general population and spurring further popular resistance (Tursun Islam 2004:45).

6. After three years in a labor reform camp, Ziya escaped and fled to Kazakhstan, where he went on to have a distinguished career as a writer and fame in the Uyghur diaspora for his political activities. The latter are described in chapter 5.

7. Xinjiang officials reviewed many questionable cases between 1959 and 1964 and lifted the label from some who had been accused. Some cases dragged on until 1985, at which point wrongful accusations had been "basically" rectified (Dang Yulin and Zhang Yuxi 2003:192).

8. In 1993 Ma Dazheng warned that the "negativity and destructiveness" of what he called "*minzu* consciousness" (*minzu yishi*) were growing more prominent daily: "Dissatisfied talk and public opinion about *minzu* rights, status, and interests have clearly intensified, and demands on these scores have increased as well" (Ma Dazheng 2003, no. 939:17).

9. The XUAR Propaganda Department acknowledged that these "incorrect" attitudes were prevalent among both masses and cadres (J K P Š U A R komiteti täšwiqat bölümi, 2000?:47). Both Ma Dazheng (2003:184–88) and Yin Zhuguang and MaoYongfu (1996:260–63) discuss criticisms of the autonomy system that Uyghur cadres circulated inside the government.

10. Both Valerie Bunce (1999:28) and Nancy Bermeo (1992:184) suggest the value of Scott's method for research on popular attitudes in socialist countries. Unfortunately, given the sensitivity of this study, I cannot provide in this chapter the kind of ethnographic richness that is a hallmark of Scott's work. The risk is too great that my informants might be identified if I provided details about their backgrounds, jobs, and the circumstances in which we spoke. I hope in the future to be able to write a companion work that provides that detail.

11. This is a judgment about the spatial extension of power and its role in the constitution of subjects. Scott focuses on *punitive* power and hence on a hypothetical realm autonomous from power's operation: "social spaces insulated from control and surveillance from above" (Scott 1990:118). Foucault asserts that power also can be *productive*: of discourse, of behavior, and even of resistance. In this sense, the structure of domination both frames and shapes resistance. For a critique of Scott that pursues this point, see Moore 1998.

12. See, for instance, his chart schematizing the argument (Scott 1990:198).

13. Interviews with former delegates to congresses in Xinjiang, October 1996 and September 2006. Stanley Lubman observed in 1999 that most laws in China were made by the State Council, the pinnacle of the executive branch, and its more than sixty administrative subunits, rather than by the congresses. Furthermore, administrative offices continue to employ "internal" regulations either partially or completely shielded from public scrutiny (Lubman 1999:141–47).

14. I already have discussed in the difficulties that Hong Kong–based researcher Herbert Yee faced while conducting surveys in Xinjiang in 2000 and 2001. He nevertheless published in English-language journals the findings that there were strong prejudices between Uyghurs and Hans and that Uyghurs did not support the government's policies in Xinjiang, including those toward separatists (Yee 2003, 2005). In 2002 he collaborated on another survey on "*minzu* solidarity" (*minzu tuanjie*) with Guo Zhenglin of Sun Yat-sen University in Guangzhou. The resulting article, published in Chinese in Hong Kong, drew markedly different conclusions. It indicated a strong belief in a shared Chinese national (*zhonghua minzu*) identity and found that most Uyghurs believed the govern-

ment had "basically implemented" (*jiben luoshi*) *minzu* regional autonomy. The authors also noted that the vast majority of Uyghurs believed Xinjiang had been part of China since ancient times and was now an inseparable part of China (Guo Zhenglin and Yu Zhen [Herbert S. Yee], n.d.).

15. CCP propaganda officials in Kashgar tacitly acknowledged in 1995 that "incorrect" views about resource exploitation were widespread (Kashi diwei xuanchuan bu 1995:55). Informal interviews by foreign researchers confirm that such views continued to prevail in 2002 (Smith 2007); field notes, summer 2002.

16. For survey evidence in support of this claim, see Yee 2003, 2005.

17. It is not clear why this is a slur, although there is no doubt that it is one. The term has a very long history, reaching back to the (non-Sinitic) Khitan. It is the unmarked proper name for "China" in Russian. Chinese authorities frown on the use of the term, insisting that Uyghurs instead use a localized form of Hans' Chinese-language autonym, *khänzu*.

18. Field notes, April 25, 1997.

19. Field notes, July 21, 2002.

20. Field notes, March 8, 1997.

21. Field notes, June 13, 1997. The Uyghur dentist did not share the prejudice of the *muäzzin*. He told me, "Han, Uyghur, I fix their teeth just the same." In a previous conversation, however, he had speculated that Uyghurs had grown to hate Hans with a passion in recent years and that the sentiment was growing stronger (field notes, June 1, 1997).

22. I regularly encountered discussions of race (*irq* in Uyghur; *zhongzu* in Chinese) within either Uyghur or Han circles of friends, with many Hans wanting to know whether foreigners regarded Uyghurs as racially white. Uyghur informants who raised the matter of race often claimed scientists had proved that Uyghurs were Europeans, in many cases bringing up the notorious "Xinjiang mummies" (Mallory and Mair 2000). The discussions called to mind Chiang Kai-shek's insistence in the 1940s that all the various *minzu* in China were from the same "racial stock" (Chiang 1947). Both Uyghur and Han informants were disappointed to learn that Western scholars no longer regard race as a scientific category. On the discourse of race in China, see Sautman 1997 and Dikötter 1992, 1997.

23. Field notes, July 21, 2002. Hans were often equally dismissive of Uyghurs, averring that they were primitive and of "low quality" (*suzhi hen di*). The Han hairstylist in whose shop the Uyghur policemen had spoken derogatorily—without her understanding—told me (knowing only that he dressed nattily and spoke Chinese well) that he was a particularly cultivated Uyghur, an exception to the rule. "In general," she told me, "we think of them as, we don't really . . . well, we fairly hate them" (field notes, April 22, 1997).

24. Field notes, June 1, 1997. I also frequently heard Uyghurs refer to Hans as dragons and Uyghurs as wolves. The wolf is a totem of Uyghur and Pan-Turkic nationalism, and its use is severely proscribed in Xinjiang.

25. Field notes, April 23, 1997.

26. Field notes, July 18, 2002.

27. For the twentieth-century career of the term "Zhonghua minzu," see Leibold 2007.

28. Field notes, April 22, 1997.

29. The term *huaxia* was an ancient name for peoples living on the Yellow River, later considered the core of the Han *minzu*. A Uyghur intellectual who had studied at an elite Beijing university reported that he had infuriated one of his Han teachers by saying, "Since Zhonghua really refers to *huaxia*, and *huaxia* were only a tiny part of what is now the Han, why not just say 'Hanzu'? It would be more inclusive" (field notes, June 30, 1997).

30. Field notes, November 9, 1996, and June 1, 1997. Chow (1997, no.707:47–49) argues that the claim that all Hans descended from the Yellow Emperor (Huang di) was an early twentieth-century nationalist innovation.

31. Field notes, June 26, 1997.

32. My informants clearly chose different levels of candor, depending on their perception of the safety of the situation. Informants would speak candidly only around people they knew and trusted, changing the topic when strangers walked by or a new person joined the conversation. Many proposed to meet in noisy public spaces rather than indoor settings that might be bugged or quiet places where neighbors might eavesdrop.

33. Field notes, December 17, 1995.

34. Field notes, January 27, 1996.

35. Field notes, October 25, 1996.

36. Field notes, spring 1997, various dates.

37. Field notes, July 2, 1997.

38. In chapter 5 I discuss the efforts of Uyghurs in Turkey to drum up international support beginning in the 1950s, and Uyghurs in Central Asia to gain the support of Moscow beginning in the 1960s.

39. Field notes, January 27, 1996.

40. Field notes, May 5, 1997.

41. Field notes, July 20, 2002.

42. Field notes, July 31, 2002.

43. Yee cited the earlier 1987 survey of Ji Ping and Gao Bingzhong (1994) also finding that Uyghurs had much stronger collective identities than did the Hans polled (see also Ji Ping 1990).

44. For comparison, it is worth considering a survey on Uyghur–Han relations conducted in 2005 by Yang Shengmin, an anthropologist at the Central University of Nationalities, with Chinese government support. On the one question comparable to Yee's, "Is it true that participating in separatist activities is harmful to most people?" 88 percent of

Uyghurs agreed or strongly agreed, and 93 percent of Hans fell into the same categories (Yang Shengmin 2008:17).

45. Indeed, these works comprise the bulk of published research on popular politics (Bovingdon 2002a; Dautcher 2000; Harris 2001; Naby 1991; Rudelson 1997; Smith 2007).

46. On language policies in Xinjiang, see Dwyer 2005. A 2005 survey revealed that nearly 58 percent of Hans reported no Uyghur proficiency whatsoever, while only 4 percent could speak and write the language well; by contrast, roughly 17 percent of Uyghurs said they knew no Mandarin, and 30 percent said they wrote and spoke proficiently (Yang Shengmin 2008:14).

47. I have transcribed both songs from a bootleg recording of live performances in my possession, though a somewhat expurgated version of the second can be found in Mähmud Sulayman 1994.

48. For analyses of political songs by other musicians, see Dautcher 2000; Harris 2001; and Smith 2007.

49. For the fate of particular tapes, see, for example, Smith 2007 and Bovingdon 2002a. A Uyghur émigré who claimed to have worked in the publishing industry in Xinjiang offered an explanation of how materials might pass the censors and be published, only to be withdrawn months later. He suggested that each work was watched for up to three months after publication by a number of bureaus, including Public Security and the Xinjiang Academy of Social Sciences. If "any problem" emerged within that time, the publisher would cease production, and distributors would pull the work from shelves (Ertughrul Atihan 2002).

50. In 1996, Sultan was arrested after landing in Kyrgyzstan with thousands of tapes he hoped to smuggle into Xinjiang. After nine months, he was released and told to leave the country within twenty days, a sure sign of Chinese influence over Bishkek (Hoh 2004).

51. Perry Link (2002) argues that the CCP inhibits criticism by issuing threats in purposely vague terms, so that people censor themselves. See also the articles by Link and others in a Woodrow Wilson Center special report, "Scholars Under Siege? Academic and Media Freedom in China" (Link et al. 2002).

52. Field notes, April 22, 1997.

53. Performers have reused and embellished many key themes. Note that the earlier tape *Pighan (Rooster's Cry)* contains a poem about a rooster waking people, as well as Abuxaliq Uyghur's celebrated poem "Awakening" (Rudelson 1997:146–49).

54. Field notes, summer 2002.

55. On the Uyghurs' contested historiography and the role of Turghun Almas, see Benson 1996; Bovingdon 2001; Bovingdon and Näbijan Tursun 2004; and Rudelson 1991, 1997: chap. 6.

56. On the content and official treatment of Turghun's work, see Bovingdon 2002b:chap. 5. Red Guards had burned Qur'ans and "nationality historical writings" in 1966, early in the Cultural Revolution (McMillen 1979:196).

57. Xu Yuqi had already used this expression in 1999 to describe the state's response to the work of Turghun Almas (Xu Yuqi 1999:114–28).

58. Field notes, summer 2002. Reporters sans Frontières (2002) reported the crackdown and new book burnings. A 1995 "administrative regulation" on the handling of religious texts forbids the publication of commentaries, recorded sermons, audiovisual materials, and cartoon books on religious subjects, and requires approval from various departments for the publication of permitted materials (Xinjiang weiwu'er zizhiqu minzu zongjiao shiwu weiyuanhui 1999:243–46). In 2002, a reliable source gave me an undated internal-circulation memo (most likely promulgated in 2002), issued jointly by the XUAR Party Committee Propaganda Department and other organs, that repeats and amplifies these regulations.

59. Field notes, summer 2002. There is no way to verify these assertions at present.

60. As discussed in chapter 2, Mao made this pronouncement in 1949 specifically to deny that the leaders of the Eastern Turkestan Republic had sought, or achieved, independence.

61. I have not translated *millät* here for the same reasons that I have not translated the Chinese *minzu* elsewhere.

62. Field notes, summer 2002, four different informants.

63. The book was later re-released in a modified version, with all these passages intact.

64. A knowledgeable informant suggested that the journal's editor, later jailed himself, must have had powerful backers for the story to get past censors in the first place. Interview, September 8, 2006.

65. Hamudun Niyaz, chairman of the Xinjiang People's Congress, claimed that the government had uncovered and stopped a plot to fight for independence on the day of Hong Kong's retrocession (Lim 1997).

66. Field notes, summer 2002.

67. An image of the flag seen through the goal, which appeared on the BBC Web site at http://news.bbc.co.uk/media/images/38072000/jpg/_38072303_suker300.jpg (accessed June 13, 2002), was distributed the same day on Uyghur listservs.

68. On further questioning, they admitted that the students had been accused not merely of clapping at the wrong times but of making contacts with international separatist organizations, a charge that these teachers considered groundless (field notes, summer 2002).

69. The editor of Netease, one of the most popular Internet portals in China, was dismissed in September 2006. Among the mistakes that may have cost him his job was reporting on the nomination of Uyghur dissident Rabiyä Qadir (Kadeer) for the Nobel Prize. Though his source was an official statement by the Chinese Foreign Ministry to for-

eign reporters, Beijing had apparently mandated a domestic news blackout on the topic (French 2006).

70. An RFA reporter in Washington confirmed that Uyghurs regularly call the toll-free number from Kashgar and Khotän to complain that "they're bullying us." Interview, July 11, 2003. In 2002 Shäpqät Imin (Xiaokaiti Yiming), vice party secretary and bureau head of the XUAR Radio, Film, and Television Bureau, complained that "telephone hotline regulation has been too lax, allowing a few bad people to take advantage" (Xiaokaiti Yiming 2002).

71. In 2002, the government announced a crackdown on "illegal television stations" in Ghulja (Agence France-Presse 2002a). In 2005, government censors cut off BBC programming about Xinjiang in mid-broadcast, even though it was transmitted only to hotels and apartments serving foreigners. Just seconds after the announcer said that "the Uighur people have little affection for their Chinese masters," television screens went black ("PA" 2005).

72. Field notes, summer 2002.

73. In late 2006, two of her sons were jailed in Xinjiang on the charge of threatening state security. Both were later sentenced to long prison terms (U.S. Department of State 2007).

4. COLLECTIVE ACTION AND VIOLENCE

1. "Strike hard" campaigns to reduce crime were begun in 1983 in China proper (Tanner 1999). PSB officials in Xinjiang initiated a strike hard campaign against escaped criminals in 1987 (XUAR Local Gazetteer Editorial Committee 1988:138). After Beijing initiated the 1996 national strike hard campaign, Ürümci announced that in Xinjiang it would target splittists, building a "Great Wall of Steel" against their threat (Macartney 1996b). Similar "antisplittist" campaigns were announced in Inner Mongolia and Tibet at the same time (Macartney 1996a, 1996c).

2. A 2005 article by a researcher at the Chinese Academy of Social Sciences, for instance, asserted that the "'ET' problem continues to escalate" (Song Xinwei 2005).

3. Longtime *New York Times* China reporter Nicholas Kristof announced in July 2006 that he saw "more fragility in the system than at almost any time in . . . 23 years" and likened the atmosphere of 2006 to that at the beginning of 1989 (Kristof 2006, 11). He did not speculate whether this analogy extended both to social fractiousness and a party-state still intent on delivering a bloody lesson to quell it.

4. In the English language alone, there are open-source examples from the United States (McNeal 2002), Canada (George 1998), and India (Raman 1999, 2002).

5. For a brief statement, see "Yongding" [pseud.] 2005. For an article specifically urging that China work to prevent "color revolutions" from destabilizing Xinjiang, see Song Tianshui 2005. In October 2005 I attended a conference in Ürümci on "nontraditional security"

in China and Central Asia. Two panels and most of the discussions were devoted to the color revolutions. The speakers emphasized the use of NGOs by Western governments to interfere in other countries' domestic politics (copies of the conference papers in my possession).

6. For examples of early and more recent work predicting that social pressures would lead to democratization in China, see Nathan 1986 and Gilley 2004.

7. James Millward argued, similarly, that Qing and Republican-era Inner Asia differed starkly from the regions of China proper, and its systematic exclusion in major Anglophone studies of those polities allowed conclusions that were artificially narrow and, in some cases, simply wrong (Millward 1998:4–19)

8. Field notes, March 1997.

9. In the introduction I discussed why the surveys conducted by Ji Ping (1990); Ji Ping and Gao Bingzhong (1994) and Herbert Yee (2003, 2005; Guo Zhenglin and Yu Zhen [Herbert S. Yee] n.d.), while quite valuable, almost certainly did not reflect the respondents' heartfelt political attitudes.

10. In fairness, Hurst was speaking only of protests by laid-off workers. The official figures do not break down contentious episodes by type and include rural protests. Nevertheless, given the size of the figures, it seems certain that laid-off workers' protests numbered not in the hundreds or thousands but the tens of thousands.

11. Note that the figures we have are for all episodes of unrest. There have long been many more labor disputes than this number would suggest. Official Labor Ministry statistics showed that labor disputes increased 1400 percent from 1992 to 1999, when the figure was 120,000, and another 12 percent in the subsequent year (Kurlantzick 2003, citing, Forney 2002c; Pomfret 2000). Michael Szonyi (2000) claims, citing no source, that "over 100,000 mass demonstrations were reported to the government in 1999; the real number is surely many times higher."

12. See also the "China Balance Sheet" (http://www.chinabalancesheet.org/Snapshots. html), a project sponsored by the Institute for International Economics and the Center for Strategic and International Studies.

13. The two principal interpretations in these paragraphs can be found, for example, in Frum 2006.

14. See http://www.cfr.org/publication/9425/#6 (accessed June 1, 2006).

15. I thank Jeff Wasserstrom for underscoring this point in comments on an early version of this chapter.

16. A bus explosion in Beijing on March 7, 1997, was first blamed on Uyghurs, partly because of the recent bombing of several buses in Ürümci on February 25. Xinjiang's government chairman later stated flatly that it had no connection to Uyghurs (Svartzman 1997). A bus bombing in Wuhan in February 1998, again initially attributed to Uyghurs (BBC

Monitoring Asia Pacific 1998), proved to be the work of a man whose girlfriend had left him (Associated Press 1998).

17. For Uyghur activists' comments, see Mooney 2004; and "Anti-Chinese Feeling 'Rising' in Xinjiang" 2005. For those of foreign journalists and academics see, for example, Blank 2004; "China's Far West: Under the Thumb" 2005; "China's Growing Problem with Xinjiang" 2000; and Zhao 2004:208.

18. On officials' strategic decisions to broadcast information about unrest in some situations and mute it in others, see the HRW/HRIC document "Devastating Blows" (Human Rights Watch 2005:25). On the sharp reversal of the previous habit of minimizing unrest immediately after September 11, see Millward 2004:11.

19. There was considerable violence in Xinjiang during the Cultural Revolution: at least 1,300 violent clashes among Red Guard factions in 1967 and 1968, some of them protracted armed conflicts (Millward 2007:268–69). Furthermore, as I have already noted, the reporting of violence changed dramatically during the 1990s. Thus the chart certainly overstates the contrast between the Cultural Revolution era and the reform era.

20. Murray Scott Tanner (2005) published the figures on unrest in China.

21. Ma Dazheng cites a different set of figures for the period 1990 to 2000, that "according to authoritative figures," the 253 "violent terrorist events" caused 166 deaths (twenty-six of police or soldiers) and 371 injuries (Ma Dazheng 2003:126).

22. Yitzhak Shichor (2006b:100–101) makes a similar point.

23. Since I have space to cover only a small number of cases here, the complete database of cases of open resistance, whether acts of violence or organize protests, is in the appendix.

24. I saw a number of handwritten manifestos during several trips to Xinjiang, and I heard about many more from trustworthy sources. The risk to informants precludes a more precise specification of texts, times, or locations. In 1999, while exhorting local PSB and PAP to capture the "Küräş gang," Ismayil Tiliwaldi noted that capturing "illegal audiovisual materials and publications" was a crucial component of the mission. "We must dig out the roots, pull out the nails, and kill the leader," he urged (Zhonggong Hetian shiwei bangongshi 1999:6). As we have seen, Küräş Sultan, the Uyghur singer who fled Xinjiang in 1996, was arrested in Kyrgyzstan with thousands of tapes of his songs he hoped to smuggle back into the region (Hoh 2004).

25. There is a seeming tautology in the description: it is precisely the participation of large numbers that proves that the frame has had wide appeal. Yet the "resonance" of a frame is analytically separable from its empirical success, if not often easy to distinguish in practice.

26. These concerns have certainly prompted officials not to advertise some episodes of conflict or unrest. Two XUAR regulations from 1995 declare secret all information about,

analysis of, and state responses to incidents with religious or *minzu* implications (Human Rights Watch 2005:app. III, 101–5).

27. Ma Dazheng's report on the event, written in 1996, attributes the protests to students and includes the two complaints reported by Li, plus opposition to nuclear testing, Han immigration, and "sham autonomy." In Ma's version, the separatist slogans described by Xu "appeared in a few places at the same time as" the student protests (Ma Dazheng 2003:51–52).

28. Several Uyghur students and employees required to participate in public criticisms of splittists reported such conclusions to me.

29. One can see the progression from unexplained "dates as labels" in 1995 (Kashi diwei xuanchuan bu 1995:16), to the categorization of different dated events into "illegal student demonstrations" and "beating smashing looting incidents" in 1996 (He Fulin 1996:3), to chronological ordering of dates (and more events) with an explanatory phrase for each in 1997 (XUAR Party Committee Propaganda Bureau 1997:16–17), to multipage narratives published in a book in 1999 (Xu Yuqi 1999).

30. The Chinese term *taibilike* denotes both the Arabic term *tabligh*, for publicizing one's faith, and the missionary organization active in Pakistan and elsewhere in South Asia, the Tableeghi jamaat. Religious influence evidently began spreading in the early 1980s. In 1986 Olivier Roy saw "hundreds of Uighur pilgrims" supposedly making the *hajj* but in fact staying up to a year in lodgings provided by the Pakistani Jama'at islami (Roy 2002:140). According to Ma Dazheng, in May 1992 Pakistan's Tableeghi jamaat sent eight groups with a total of eighty-seven people to southern Xinjiang, where they reportedly intrigued with separatists hoping to recruit more followers (Ma Dazheng 2003:10). Ahmed Rashid noted that in 1997 Peshawar's madrassas contained "hundreds" of Uyghurs and other Turkic speakers from China (Rashid 2003:141, 204). Sean Roberts argued that religious influence spread both through Pakistani traders in Xinjiang and Uyghurs studying in Pakistan until the crackdown in 1997 (Roberts 2004:226–27). Dewardric McNeal reports that Kyrgyz authorities broke up a sect of Tableeghi Jamaat led by a Chinese-born Uyghur in 1998 (McNeal 2002:12–13)

31. Party officials have used these venerable charges to cut the legs out from under political opponents at least since 1959, when Mao accused Peng Dehuai of an "organized, pre-meditated" attack at the Lushan plenum (Kuang Chen and Pan Liang 2005:131).

32. In 1992 the government issued a secret list of sixty-two secret organizations. There were reports of at least six underground parties in Xinjiang in 1993, including one still formally run by Isa Yusuf Alptekin (who was already blind and frail in that year and died two years later at the age of ninety-four) (Dillon 2004:66). A news story released by Xinhua in 2002, a week after the January 21 document, claimed there were more than fifty organizations at that point. The figure combined domestic organizations with

those abroad, and Xinhua asserted that all had ties to "'ET' terrorist forces" (Xinhua 2002).

33. Although as Elizabeth Perry showed, different kinds of protest have received different treatment. Some forms have been tolerated, while others have been rigidly suppressed. Events that protest unemployment or other economic ills have been grudgingly borne, though often with stern lectures to participants. The multiday riots and protests against the bombing of the PRC embassy in Belgrade in 1999 enjoyed not just sufferance but active support from the government; officials may even have orchestrated the protests. Falun Gong practitioners met with implacable government repression (Perry 2001). Kevin O'Brien (1996, 2003) made a similar argument in discussing righteous resistance and boundary-spanning contention, although his point is that the reception of protest may vary from official to official.

34. Beijing provided a designated space, and procedure, for protests to be held at the Olympics in August 2008—and then denied *every single petition to protest*.

35. The next two paragraphs summarize points in Ma Dazheng 2003:92–105.

36. Chinese sources (which, of course, must be used with caution) assert that the armed participants in the 1990 Baren uprising wanted to secede and set up an independent Islamic state with its capital in that town. On this point, see Dillon 2004:62–63, which draws on Xu Yuqi 1999:130.

37. The three most detailed accounts, which tally quite closely, are in Ma Dazheng 2003:49–51; Xu Yuqi 1999:106–9; and Zhu Peimin, Chen Hong, and Yang Hong 2004:208–9. See also Li Shangkai 1992:131; Zhang Yuxi 1993:347; Dillon 2004:60; and McMillen 1984:581.

38. The following two paragraphs summarize and combine the accounts in Zhang Yuxi 1993:338–41; Xu Yuqi 1999:129–33; Ma Dazheng 2003:57–60; and Dillon 2004:62–65.

39. In 1984 this county had been held up by the autonomous regional government as a model of inter-*minzu* harmony (Zhang Yuxi 1993:360).

40. The *shahada* is the fundamental profession of faith in Islam, acknowledging a single divinity and Muhammed's status as prophet.

41. Artoush Kumul claims there were more than four hundred *mäšräp* in Xinjiang by the end of 1994 but he cites no source, and other figures in his article incline one to skepticism (Artoush Kumul 1998).

42. In December 2008, Xinjiang officials announced that they had thwarted a student demonstration in which college students from several Ürümci campuses planned to urge or force shopkeepers to stop selling tobacco and alcohol. A December 26 report claimed that the handbills advertising the protest were "reactionary" and that the planned "illegal assembly" would threaten "stability and unity" (Congressional-Executive Commission on China 2009).

43. This assertion conflicts with a 2001 report in China's national court newspaper, which claims that Alerken Abula was the leader of the organization until his arrest in January 1997 and that it was not called ETIPA until November 1996 (BBC Monitoring Asia Pacific 2001).

44. In 2001, for example, Mukhlisi boasted creatively that "twenty-two million Uighurs ... even little boys" were ready to rise in arms against the Chinese government (Working 2001).

45. The *basmala* is the phrase that introduces individual *suras* in the Qur'an, invoking the name of Allah (videotape with explanatory notes in my possession). Xu Yuqi claims this banner was raised during the second march of around one thousand people, beginning around noon (Xu Yuqi 1999:178).

46. The Ili prefectural government Web site records that the youths' slogans included "Struggle with *kapirs*," "Don't pay taxes," "We don't want anything from the government," and "There is only one Allah" (*Anla wei yi*). This last is a Chinese translation of the first part of the *shahada* (quoted from mail.xjyl.gov.cn/qy/dys/18.htm [accessed June 28, 2006]). Xu Yuqi has all of these slogans plus "Establish an Islamic caliphate" and "Expel the Hans" (Xu Yuqi 1999:178).

47. This story is hard to believe, for three reasons. First, the marchers would have had to choose to put on the clothing in the morning only to take it off during the march, difficult to imagine given the extremely cold temperatures in Ghulja in February. Second, they would have had to recognize particular items of clothing as "Han," and few such items suggest themselves other than the Mao suit, which at any rate was no longer widely worn by Uyghurs by then. Third, adult Uyghur men and women generally adhere to high standards of sartorial modesty in public. This story seems to have been concocted to depict the demonstrators as irrational religious extremists.

48. This claim is quoted in Campion 1997. Other police in Ghulja told widely divergent stories. On Monday, February 10, one police officer told a reporter that Uyghurs had "demanded independence" and gone on a violent rampage; the police had arrested five hundred. A day later, the director of the same police department rejected this and other versions, asserting instead that some two hundred members of an "illegal religious organization" demonstrated by "[taking] off all their clothes and shout[ing] slogans like 'Don't sleep. Don't eat. Don't work.'" This official said that police arrested five "ringleaders" and that the other protestors melted away after a stern lecture. The reporter to whom the official delivered this version remarked drily that it "could not be immediately reconciled" with others (Hutzler 1997).

49. The Ili Prefecture Political Consultative Committee Web site records that the February 5 demonstration "seriously endangered national security." See http://www.ylzzx.gov.cn/history/ShowArticle.asp?ArticleID=239 (accessed August 9, 2006).

50. The fullest exposition of the Ghulja uprising is in Dillon 2004:92–88.

51. Xu Yuqi had ETIPA active only from 1995 under its leader Peyzulla (Xu Yuqi 1999:177). By 2002, Chinese government spokesman Kong Quan was claiming that ETIPA was the another name for ETIM, the organization declared terrorist by the United States and the United Nations in August 2002 (Xinhuanet 2002, cited in Amnesty International 2004).

52. Because uranium mining is a security matter of the highest priority and because the mines were run by the PCC, it is safe to assume the miners were mainly, if not exclusively, Han.

53. To be fair, officials also made the case that the rail line would facilitate the transport of goods to and from the south, spurring further economic growth. A proposed line through Kyrgyzstan to Uzbekistan, announced as far back as 2000 and still under discussion in 2006, will necessarily begin from the Kashgar spur (RFE/RL 2006).

54. There are occasional acknowledgments of the Uyghurs' estrangement from the party-state and Hans. Zhang Yuxi observed after the Baren uprising that it showed fierce feelings of hatred toward Hans who had thrived in that region (Zhang Yuxi 1993:341). Ma Dazheng cautioned readers in 1997 that the "splittists' ability to stir up the masses must not be underestimated" (Ma Dazheng 2003:100). XUAR Party Secretary Wang Lequan admitted during a 1999 speech in Khotän that locals had no love for government officials (Wang Lequan 1999:17).

55. The document lists periodicals, texts, or artistic performances that "disseminated feelings of dissatisfaction" among the six types of "splittist sabotage" ("Xinjiang shouci pilu minzu fenlie shili zai yishi xingtai lingyu pohuai huodong de liu zhong xingshi" 2002).

56.   Ma might have been referring to an article describing China's "vast human rights problems" in Xinjiang and Tibet (Mirsky 1998) and to another expressing surprise that Beijing was pressing Jakarta to protect Indonesia's Chinese minority from rioters, since the CCP regards foreign criticism of its handling of unrest in Tibet and Xinjiang as "interference" (Richardson 1998).

57. For a scholarly study of Uyghur protest arguing that the strike hard campaign was principally responsible for the downturn from the late 1990s on, see Hierman 2006.

58. Ronald Schwartz counted 140 demonstrations in Tibet between 1987 and 1992 (Schwartz 1994:1). There have been far fewer protests in Tibet since then.

59. Mackerras argues that China's territorial claims enjoy "some legitimacy" in the periphery, although he cautions that they are "much more doubtful" in Tibet than in the other regions. I think he misses the level and pervasiveness of resentment among Uyghurs (Mackerras 2004a:230).

60. A decade earlier, after Tibetans mobbed a delegation from the Tibetan government in exile everywhere it traveled in 1980, Hu Yaobang is said to have concluded pessimistically that they "preferred to report their grievances to the Dalai Lama . . . rather than to

complain to the Party. . . . The Dalai Lama still represented their hopes for freedom and . . . a speedy deliverance from their suffering" (Shakya 1999:378).

5. UYGHUR TRANSNATIONAL ORGANIZATIONS

1. In another 2003 publication, Rashid correctly noted that the United States classified only ETIM as a terrorist organization (Rashid 2003:121–22).

2. In September 2002, foreign diplomats in Beijing queried about ETIM told a reporter that according to their information, the organization was defunct and its activities had always been limited to Afghanistan (Forney 2002a).

3. In a 2006 article, two analysts at a terrorism research center in Singapore pretend to view skeptically the PRC's claim that Uyghur separatists belong to a global terror network and then seem to confirm that claim. As evidence, they rely uncritically on the January 2002 document, a video of unknown provenance, entitled "Jihad in Eastern Turkestan" and posted on a jihadist Web site, and a database maintained by their research center, proved by James Millward to consist entirely of the entries in the January 2002 document. They come to the conclusion that "the Uighur groups [unspecified] are now significantly influenced by the developments in the global jihad arena." They misread the January 2002 document as attributing all violent events to ETIM, and they misleadingly suggest there are many other Uyghur organizations with ties to ETIM. Particularly egregious is their insinuation that the World Uyghur Congress, an explicitly secular organization, inclines toward Islamism (a term whose complexities they do not acknowledge). The 2006 article should not be read as an independent confirmation that Uyghur separatists are Islamists and terrorists, when it is nothing of the kind (Gunaratna and Pereire 2006:57 and passim). For an excellent brief critique, see Clarke 2007:19–20.

4. The most important works on Uyghur organizations abroad include Shichor 2003; Besson 1998; Gladney 2004a:229–59; Dillon 2004; and Millward 2004. In reading Shichor's very thorough and well-documented article, the reader should keep in mind that his abbreviation "ETIM" is his own acronym for the "Eastern Turkestan Independence Movement," a movement that Shichor himself acknowledges is not unified. His acronym must not be confused with that of the "Eastern Turkestan Islamic Movement."

5. The U.S. State Department's report on terrorism claimed that Uyghurs trained by al-Qaeda had returned to China but provided no supporting evidence (U.S. Department of State 2003:16).

6. I refer to Uyghur organizations as transnational for two different reasons. First, some Uyghur organizations have been transnational by nomenclature and design. The Eastern Turkestan National Congress, the Eastern Turkestan Information Center, the Eastern Turkestan European Union, the World Uyghur Youth Congress, and the World Uyghur Congress all share this characteristic. Second, each organization, regardless of the state

in which its members live, is at least partly oriented to Xinjiang. Some organizations focus predominantly on regulating local communities and protecting their interests, but all keep the imagined "Uyghur homeland" in mind. This is true even of those groups that explicitly adopt the name of their host states, as, for instance, the Uyghur American Association, the Uyghur Canadian Association, and the Swedish Uyghur Committee.

7. Note that the geographic shifts and spreading diaspora mean changes in language. The full record of Uyghur organizations in the world includes names in all European languages, Turkish, Arabic, Russian, and Uyghur. It also necessarily includes Chinese, since Chinese officials and scholars have leveled charges at various organizations using translations or transliterations in that language. As a consequence, the names of organizations and their leaders are an extraordinary tangle. When jumping from one language to another, it is a constant challenge to determine which names refer to the same organizations, which to distinct ones (including names that were made up). Except in the case of well-established names (and even then on occasion), I have generally opted for fidelity to Uyghur spelling and chosen a consistent word order for long names. Hence Eastern Turkestan United National Revolutionary Front (ETUNRF) and not United Revolutionary Front of Eastern Turkestan (URFET), Dolqun Isa and not Dolqun Eysa, Qähriman Ghojambärdi and not Kaharman Khojamberdi, and Rabiyä Qadir rather than Räbiya Kadeer. I list the acronyms for most organizations in the abbreviations in the front matter.

8. He published the first edition in Kashmir in the early 1940s and then later revised it in Turkey (Bughra 1942/1987).

9. Muhämmäd Imin had been seeking outside support for the cause for many years. In 1935 he met with the Japanese ambassador to Kabul and proposed that Japan provide money and weapons to help found an independent "Eastern Turkestan Republic." He believed that Japan's reward would be "special economic and political privileges" vis-à-vis the new republic, though it is clear that Japanese officials instead had in mind a client state like that in Manchuria (Esenbel 2004:1161–62; Forbes 1986:140).

10. Tyler's account, based on a Uyghur news source to which I do not have access, has Özal himself announcing his acceptance of the cause.

11. The book was printed in Turkey and was circulating in Central Asia in the late 1990s (Sean Roberts, personal communication, September 29, 2006).

12. Although Uyghur organizations persisted, after Jiang Zemin encountered public protests over Beijing's treatment of Uyghurs during his 2000 visit, Ankara forbade them to engage in "overt political work," in order to avoid jeopardizing its relations with China. Two years later, Zhu Rongji elicited a promise from Prime Minister Bulent Ecevit that Ankara would "curb the Uyghur 'terrorists'" in the country (Hoh 2000; Tyler 2003:241). Ankara also had to worry about annoying the U.S. government, which by that time was deeply concerned with the rise of "Muslim power" (Cheong 1997).

13.   Chinese scholar Li Danhui argues that Moscow had authorized consular officials in Xinjiang to issue large numbers of Soviet passports to would-be emigrants, with the long-term goal of using those émigrés to exert pressure on China (Li Danhui 2003:86).

14.   A retired intelligence official in Kazakhstan explained, in nakedly Machiavellian terms, Moscow's support for one such organization: "We were at odds with China then, and it was of use to us" (Eurasianet 2003).

15.   The story of Russian involvement is quite implausible. Two thousand Uyghur protestors rioted, reportedly shouting religious slogans as they did so. The protestors blamed the arson on a Uyghur PSB official (Alptekin 1983:150; Ma Dazheng 2003:48–49; XUAR Local Gazetteer Editorial Committee 1997:78; Zhang Yuxi 1993:343; Zhu Peimin 2000:334).

16.   The arms race between Moscow and Washington was complemented by a propaganda contest. Judging from volume alone, Moscow was winning the latter handily, according to a U.S. source. In 1980 the Soviet Union produced a total of 2,760 hours of radio broadcasts a week in more than 80 languages; the United States only 1,927 hours in 46 languages, through the Voice of America and Radio Free Europe / Radio Liberty (RFE/RL) (Shultz and Godson 1984:28).

17.   Curiously, a year later Mukhlisi traveled to Istanbul with Moscow's help to pay a visit to Isa Yusuf Alptekin. The person reporting the meeting suggests that it did not go well because Mukhlisi's sponsors had placed limits on what he could offer the Uyghur leader, although it is equally possible that Mukhlisi proposed and Isa declined to support a plan for military action (Uighur 1983).

18.   A former intelligence official in Kazakhstan claimed that the ETUNRF had been founded in Alma-Ata in 1975 with the support of the Soviet Politburo (Eurasianet 2003), a claim echoed by a knowledgeable scholar (Roberts 2004:424–25, n. 47). A Uyghur source records that Yusupbek Mukhlisi founded the ETUNRF only in 1992 (Äkhmät Egämbärdi 2004). It is quite possible that both sources are right, in the sense that the organization operated clandestinely in the Soviet era and was established openly and legally only after the Soviet collapse.

19.   Sean Roberts's fine documentary *Waiting for Uighurstan* captures this tension with great sensitivity (Roberts 1996).

20.   A Uyghur leader in Kyrgyzstan told James Millward in 2003 that young Uyghurs armed and trained themselves in that country's mountainous regions around 1995 and later were arrested. It is not clear whether the youths had grown up in Kyrgyzstan or fled from Xinjiang, and no organization was named (Millward 2007:336, n. 89).

21.   A journalist who interviewed Wahidi in 1992 pronounced him and other ULO leaders "far more interested in history than waging guerrilla warfare" (Higgins 1992).

22.   A CCP scholar-official suggests that some of the thousands of reactionary handbills circulating annually in Xinjiang in the 1990s resulted from Uyghurs' listening to "broad-

casts from enemy stations in countries surrounding Xinjiang, tidying them up, and then distributing them" (Yang Faren 2000:243).

23. Mukhlisi, interviewed by AFP on May 31, 1996, claimed twenty dead in gun battles in Turpan and Qaramay. ("PRC: Exiled Leader Claims 20 Dead in Street Fighting in Xinjiang" 1996; PRC: AFP Reports Further on Clashes in Xinjiang," 1996). At the time, Chinese officials denounced the report as "pure lies" ("PRC: Security Official Says Deaths in Xinjiang 'Pure Lies'" 1996).

24. Sean Roberts, who conducted fieldwork over several years in Kazakhstan, counsels skepticism, pointing out that the elder and younger Mukhlisi were the group's "primary members" and that it was originally set up by the KGB for "propaganda purposes" (Roberts 2004:424–25, n. 47).

25. Wahidi died a year later. Uyghur organizations widely believe this was a political assassination engineered by the Chinese government.

26. James Millward argues that Almaty and Bishkek found it easy to point fingers at Uyghurs for economic and organized crime, both because they were "unpopular minorities" and because it pleased China (Millward 2004:30).

27. Beginning in the late 1990s, Beijing persuaded Central Asian states, Pakistan, and Nepal to extradite Uyghurs accused of separatism back to China and later executed many of them. The extraditions sent a very strong message to refugees that they remained vulnerable to prosecution in China even after leaving the country. The intent was clearly to deter would-be demonstrators inside Xinjiang (who might have imagined they could escape to Central or South Asia and safety) and in Central Asia (Blua 2004; IRINNEWS 2004; "Tighter Security for Chinese Diplomats in Pakistan" 2006). The arrest of Canadian citizen Husäyin Jelil (Huseyincan Celil) in Uzbekistan and his subsequent extradition to China in 2006 was particularly striking. The Uzbek and Chinese governments ignored his Canadian passport and denied Canadian consular officials to him, contravening international law and exemplifying Beijing's view that one cannot discard Chinese citizenship even after acquiring citizenship in another country (York 2006).

28. According to Shichor, it was because Turkey declined to resist Chinese pressure that Uyghur activists shifted their hopes to Europe (Shichor 2003:307).

29. On Uyghur "cyber-separatism," see Gladney 2004a:229–59; and on "virtual transnationalism," see Shichor 2003:esp. 297–311. Both authors see online political participation as less involving, and therefore less effective, than traditional political organizing.

30. There were reports in 2002 that Uyghurs in Central Asia, Europe, and America still disagreed. Central Asian organizations preferred the "radical path" of using force to achieve national independence, while "pro-Western secular nationalists" in Europe instead preferred democratic methods and alliances with Chinese democratic organizations (BBC Monitoring Central Asia 2002). In a 2003 interview with Konstantin Syroezhkin,

a scholar and security analyst in Kazakhstan, the head of the East Turkestan Europa Union stated that the members of the ET(U)NC regarded Mukhlisi's ETUNRF as "opposition" and acknowledged that Mukhlisi had criticized the goals articulated in the congress charter (Syroezhkin 2003). For disputes between the ULO and ETUNRF, and between ULO leaders and Dolqun Isa, see Sabit Abdurakhman 2002:185–90, 232–34.

31. Sabit claims this took place on the third day of the conference, October 12, which would suggest extraordinary deliberation in handling the agenda items. Tursun Islam recalls that the conference lasted from October 11 to 15.

32. For Hashir Wahidi's argument in favor of "Uyghurstan" over "Eastern Turkestan," see http://uyghuramerican.org/about_uyghurs/history/east_turkistan_or_uyghuristan (accessed October 15, 2004). Erkin Sidick actually translated this on January 7, 1998, but it was not posted on the UAA site until August 17, 2004.

33. When Turkis and other Muslims rose against the Xinjiang government in the early 1930s, the rebels debated what to call the new state they had founded. An eyewitness reports that the debate led to the choice of the "Eastern Turkestan Republic" because "there were other Turkic peoples besides Uyghurs in Xinjiang and in the newly established government." Dr. Näbijan Tursun learned this in an interview with Ghulamettin Pahta, one of the earliest Uyghur activists in the United States (Millward and Nabijan Tursun 2004:78, 403, n. 33). Gunnar Jarring suggests that the terms "Uyghur" and "Uyghurstan" first appeared in printed texts in the region in 1935 and attributes the use of the term to increasing Soviet influence. Noting that the very popular "Turkestan calendar/almanac (*taqwim*)" published yearly by the Swedish Mission in Kashgar was renamed the "Uyghurstan calendar/almanac" in 1936, he attributed the change to pressure from "authorities in power" and printed facsimiles from 1909 and 1937 illustrating the name change (Jarring 1991:6, 35, 106).

34. This is an oversimplification, since there also were Pan-Turkists from Turkey who were neither "narrow" Uyghur nationalists nor advocates of a culturally plural state but still envisioned a fusion of Turkic peoples (and possibly of territories).

35. In it, Dolqun declared himself the widely acknowledged former leader of the June 1988 student protests in Ürümci (see appendix) and detailed how he had been hounded out of Xinjiang University as a consequence. He also pointed to the charter of the World Uyghur Youth Congress, which insisted on strictly peaceful methods of challenging China's control of Xinjiang. Dolqun closed his case by noting that the German authorities watched all such organizations and would never have tolerated any suspicious activity. As this book went to press, Dolqun was facing restrictions on his international travel for the second time in three months. In July 2009 he was denied entry to Taiwan, and in mid-September he was held without charge at the Seoul Airport, reportedly because

Beijing had warned the Korean government he was a terrorist (Associated Press 2009:2233; Llopis-Jepsen 2009:2234).

36. Dolqun Isa later reported that Chinese officials had tried to intimidate him by calling him from China with his parents and brother in the room and asking him to cancel the Munich meeting (Cloud and Johnson 2004).

37. See http://www.uygur.org/uygurche/uchur/2004/10_11.htm (accessed October 17, 2004).

38. Original announcement promulgated by the East Turkistan National Freedom Center at http://etnfc.org (accessed November 2, 2004). Site now defunct. The organization now uses the URL http://www.eastturkistangovernmentinexile.us (accessed September 17, 2009).

39. BBS originally found at http://www.uyghuramerican.org/phorum/read.php?f=11&i=1166&t=1166 (accessed October 1, 2004). Link no longer available as of September 1, 2006. Interviews with Uyghur expatriates in the United States in late September 2004 confirmed that this was a widespread concern among politically active members of the community.

40. Interview, August 22, 2005. Speculation in this vein grew rampant when Anwer and his entire family were able to travel back to Ürümci for a family funeral in January 2006 and then return safely to the United States. Critics also pointed out that this trip disqualified him as an officer of the ETGIE. Discussion at http://www.uyghuramerican.org/forum/archive/index.php/t-3029.html (accessed September 1, 2006). Article 13 of its constitution specified that "anyone having a political or economic relationship with China" could not serve in office (Šärqiy Türkistan Jumhuriyiti Sürgündiki Parlamenti wä Hökümiti 2005:7).

41. Blog entry at http://www.uyghuramerican.org/forum/archive/index.php/t-250.html (accessed June 1, 2006).

42. By January 2009, the ETGIE, now with Anwer Yusuf as prime minister and a "parliament" of sixty-one named members, had taken to providing Web links to news stories and issuing press releases. A sampling from 2008 included a communiqué extending recognition to Kosovo and announcements that the ETGIE would boycott the Olympics and had the "legitimate right to wage war" against the PRC (http://www.eastturkistangovernmentinexile.us/press_releases.html [accessed January 31, 2009]).

43. Besson notes that Uyghur organizations in Central Asia and (in the past) the United States have depended heavily on the generosity of wealthy Uyghurs in Saudi Arabia (Besson 1998:170, 187).

44. The organization was founded on May 23, 1998, in Washington, D.C., with Dolkun Kamberi as chair and Ghulamettin Pahta as honorary chair. See http://www.uyghuramerican.org/aboutuaa/uaa.html (accessed March 15, 2003; URL now defunct). Current information about the organization is available at http://www.uyghuramerican.org.

45. The NED's close connections with the U.S. government were exemplified by Washington's withholding development aid from Nepal until its King Gyanendra agreed to open the country to NED in 2005. Many observers also see Washington's hand behind NED's support for the "color revolutions" in post-Soviet states (Maitra 2005).

46. In 2006 the endowment agreed to fund the World Uyghur Congress as well (World Uyghur Congress 2006c).

47. Interview with Rabiyä Qadir, September 25, 2006. In a July 2006 communiqué published on the WUC Web site, President Erkin Alptekin referred to Rabiyä as the "spiritual mother and political leader of the people of Eastern Turkestan" (Alptekin 2006). The WUC leadership is listed at http://www.uyghurcongress.org/En/AboutWUC.asp?mid=1095738888 (accessed March 21, 2007). In 2007 the Web site betrayed a curious sloppiness: while the list of officials prominently identified Rabiyä as president, the accompanying picture showed Alptekin seated front and center behind the official seal, with Räbiya to his right, and the introductory text still described Alptekin as the president.

48. When a *Spiegel* reporter suggested to the recently appointed party secretary of Tibet that Beijing had held talks with representatives of the Dalai Lama, he vehemently denied it. Zhang Qingli responded, "His government-in-exile is illegal. Our central government has never recognized it. No country in the world, including Germany, recognizes it diplomatically. There are no talks between the Chinese and his so-called government-in-exile. The current contacts merely involve a few individuals from his immediate surroundings. The talks revolve around his personal future" (*Spiegel* Interview with Tibet's Communist Party Chief 2006).

49. The article was published simultaneously in English in the *Taipei Times* and in Chinese in the *Ziyou shibao* on October 11, 1999. It is necessary to read both to grasp subtle differences in wording, since Cao notes that he interviewed Riza Bekin in English.

50. For a thorough discussion of the Dalai Lama's changing public statements and the talks between Beijing and Tibetan representatives through 2004, see Rabgey and Sharlho 2004.

CONCLUSION

1. Compare Bennigsen's (1986, 132) appraisal of the situation in the Soviet Union: "It can be stated without exaggeration that the survival of the Soviet empire depends largely on the positive solution of the nationality problem. . . . For the last fifty years, Soviet theorists have been repeating ad nauseam that the problem has already been solved, but there is ample evidence that this is just wishful thinking on their part."

2. To be sure, the final status of Kosovo was still uncertain as of the winter of 2008, with only a minority of the world's states recognizing its independence.

3. On another occasion, Ma wrote more optimistically that the example of Chechnya showed the "Kosovo model is not absolute." He pointed out that to avert such an outcome, Beijing needed to make sure that China's "comprehensive national power" continued to grow. The implication was that because it was strong, Russia could fend off interference, whereas weak Yugoslavia could not (Ma Dazheng 2003:120). On the subject, see also Carlson 2005:146–83.

4. See, for example, "Gong'anbu gongbu shoupi rending de 'dongtu' kongbu zuzhi ji chengyuan mingdan" 2003; Guowuyuan xinwen bangongshi 2002, 2003; and Pan Zhiping 1999.

5. The 1970 Declaration on Principles of International Law Concerning Friendly Relations and Co-operation Among States in Accordance with the Charter of the United Nations observes, in part, that "all peoples have the right freely to determine, without external interference, their political status . . . and every State has the duty to respect this right" (quoted in Buchheit 1978:247). See also Raič 2002.

6. In the introduction I suggested that the use of the single term *minzu* to refer to both entities elides the normative distinction and thus renders the conceptual apparatus of China's system of autonomy vulnerable to immanent critique.

7. RFE/RL 2000. A 1999 *China Daily* article warned that Western diplomats were "peddling ideologies" placing human rights above sovereignty ("UN Has a Mission to Build New World Order" 2001). A professor at the China Institute of International Studies argued that no international body agreed to this ranking (Yang Chuang 2005).

EPILOGUE

1. There is not space here to discuss a protest in Khotän on March 23, 2008, or a reported attack on police in Kashgar on August 4 of the same year. For preliminary accounts, see French (2008) and Foreman (2008), respectively.

2. My chronology hews closely to that offered on the BBC Web site (http://news.bbc .co.uk/2/hi/asia-pacific/8249848.stm), although it incorporates information from numerous other sources. For a thorough and carefully prepared analysis of the events and reportage on them, see the Congressional-Executive Commission on China report, "Xinjiang Authorities Forcefully Suppress Demonstration, Restrict Free Flow of Information" at http://www.cecc.gov/pages/virtualAcad/index.phpd?showsingle=125582 (accessed August 10, 2009).

3. The chairman of the XUAR government, Nur Bäkri, announced that some 200 protestors assembled in the People's Square around 5:00 P.M. Beijing time, then a larger number gathered in Uyghur areas south of Nanmen and "shouted slogans." The violence began, he continued, at "approximately 8:18 P.M." ("Xinjiang pilu" 2009).

4. An article in the party newspaper *Global Times* asserted that in 2007 the National Endowment for Democracy had funded various "ETIM organizations," including the World Uyghur Congress ("Rebiya Kadeer's Funding Sources" 2009).

5. See, for example, BBC reporter Quentin Somerville's report at http://www.youtube .com/watch?v=k7FcBVpUlSk (cited August 1, 2009).

6. Xinhua (2009) produced figures of 531 victims, 171 with "obvious signs" of stabbings, on the same day.

REFERENCES

Abdurehim Ötkür. 1996 (1985). "Towa, Däymän, Towa! [My God, I Say, My God!]." In *Ömür Män-zilliri (Destinations in Life)*, ed. Abdurehim Ötkür, 104–7. Ürümci: Shinjang Yashlar-Ösmürlär Näshriyati.

Adila Baikere (Adalät Bäkri). 2002. "Fazhan shengchanli, cujin xianjin wenhua jianshe, tong yishi xingtai lingyu minzu fenlie shili zuo douzheng [Develop Productive Forces, Promote the Construction of Advanced Culture, Do Battle with *Minzu* Splittist Forces in the Realm of Ideology]." *Xinjiang daxue xuebao (shehui kexue ban)* 30 (suppl.):93–95.

Agence France-Presse. 1995. "China Denies Bloody Uprising in Far-Northwestern Xinjiang." June 16. Available from Factiva (accessed June 4, 2006).

———. 1996. "Kazakhstan Warns Uighurs Against Trying to Secede from China" [newswire]. April 19. Available from Factiva (accessed June 30, 2004).

———. 1997. "Local Police Deny Bomb Attacks Killed 22 in Xinjiang" [newswire], October 10. Available from Factiva (accessed August 2, 2006).

———. 1999a. "Beijing Warns US Against Using Force Against China" [newswire], June 3. Available from Factiva (accessed June 4, 2006).

———. 1999b. "Demolition of Beijing Moslem Minority 'Village' Sparks Anger" [newswire], February 4. Available from http://www.uygur.org/enorg/wunn99/wunn990204.htm (accessed March 1, 1999).

———. 1999c. "Governor Says Xinjiang Suffering Separatist Violence," March 11. FBIS-CHI-1999-0311.

———. 2000. "China to Deploy Demobilized Officers in Xinjiang Region" [newswire], March 31. Available from Factiva (accessed April 2, 2000).

———. 2001a. "Authorities in West China Demolish Mosque, Arrest 180 Protestors," October 12. Available from LexisNexis (accessed July 1, 2006).

———. 2001b. "China Conducts Anti-Crime and 'Education' Campaign in Xinjiang" [newswire], November 14. Available from Factiva (accessed September 1, 2006).

———. 2002a. "China's Xinjiang Province Launches Campaign Against Illegal TV" [newswire], January 29. Available from Factiva (accessed December 9, 2004).

———. 2002b. "Chinese Officials to Close Down Several State-Owned Publications in Xinjiang" [newswire], March 28. Available from World News Connection (accessed December 5, 2004).

———. 2002c. "Traders from Muslim Xinjiang Protest in Southern China City: Report" [newswire], November 19. Available from Factiva (accessed May 11).

———. 2004a. "French Antennae Blocking Foreign Radio Broadcasts to China: Media Group" [newswire], October 9. Available from Factiva (accessed June 1, 2006).

———. 2004b. "Riot Police in Brawl with Uighur Muslims in South China" [newswire], November 9. Available from Factiva (accessed May 11).

Ai, Yu. 1999. "Kosovo Crisis and Stability in China's Tibet and Xinjiang," June 2. FBIS-CHI-1999-0624.

Äkhmät Egämbärdi (Ahmet Igemberdi). 2004. "Yüsüpbeg Muhlisi akini esleymen!" [I Remember Brother Yusupbek Mukhlisi!] [online news]. East Turkestan Information Center, August 10. Available from http://www.uygur.org/uygurche/uchur/2004/08_10a.htm (accessed June 10, 2005).

Alptekin, Erkin. 1983. "Eastern Turkistan After 32 Years of Exile." *Central Asian Survey* 1 (4):149–53.

———. 2006. "DUQ ning 'Uyghur rehberlirini terbilesh programmisi' heqidiki bildirgisi" [WUC Declaration Concerning the "Uyghur Leader Training Program"]. World Uyghur Congress, July 7. Available from http://www.uyghurcongress.org/Uy/pressrelease.asp?ItemID=-2131385241 (accessed September 28, 2006).

Alptekin, Isa Yusuf. 1981. *Dogu Türkistan dävasi*. Istanbul: Marifet Yayinlari.

Amnesty International. 1999. "People's Republic of China. Gross Violations of Human Rights in the Xinjiang Uighur Autonomous Region." London: Amnesty International.

————. 2002. "People's Republic of China: China's Anti-Terrorism Legislation and Repression in the Xinjiang Uighur Autonomous Region." London: Amnesty International.

————. 2004. "People's Republic of China: Uighurs Fleeing Persecution as China Wages Its 'War on Terror.'" London: Amnesty International.

An, Chen. 2003. "China's Changing of the Guard: The New Inequality." *Journal of Democracy* 14, no. 1:51–59.

Anderson, Benedict. 1991. *Imagined Communities: Reflections on the Origin and Spread of Nationalism.* Rev. ed. London: Verso.

Anderson, Benedict R. O. 1983. *Imagined Communities: Reflections on the Origin and Spread of Nationalism.* London: Verso Editions / NLB.

"Anti-Chinese Feeling 'Rising' in Xinjiang." 2005. *Gulf Times,* October 2. Available from http://www.gulf-times.com/site/topics/article.asp?cu_no=2&item_no=54883&version=1&template_id=45&parent_id=25 (accessed October 7, 2005).

Ao Junde. 2001. "Minzu quyu zizhifa shi zenyang xiugai de" [How the Law on *Minzu* Regional Autonomy Was Amended]. *Zhongguo minzu [China Ethnicity]* (4):5–7.

Appadurai, Arjun. 1996. *Modernity at Large: Cultural Dimensions of Globalization.* Minneapolis: University of Minnesota Press.

Armstrong, John A. 1992. "The Ethnic Scene in the Soviet Union: The View of the Dictatorship." In *The Soviet Nationality Reader: The Disintegration in Context,* edited by Rachel Denber, 227–56. Boulder, Colo.: Westview Press.

Artoush Kumul. 1998. "Témoignage—Le 'séparatisme' ouïghour au xxème siècle: Histoire et actualité." *Cahiers d'études sur la Méditeranée orientale et le monde turco-iranien* 25:83–91.

Asiaport Daily, News. 2008. "Central Asia–China Gas Pipeline to Start Service Next Year." Available from http://www.downstreamtoday.com/news/article.aspx?a_id=11700 (accessed February 2, 2009).

Aspinall, Edward, and Harold Crouch. 2003. " The Aceh Peace Process: Why It Failed." *Policy Studies* (1):1–74.

Associated Press. 1998. "Report: Two Villagers Planted Bomb on Bus That Killed 16 People" [newswire], February 27. Available from Factiva (accessed August 7, 2006).

————. 2009. "South Korea Holding Uighur Activist at Airport." *New York Times,* September 17. Available from http://www.nytimes.com/aponline/2009/09/17/world/AP-AS-SKorea-Uighur-Activist.html?sq=dolkun%20isa&st=cse&scp=1&pagewanted=print (accessed September 18, 2009).

Atwood, Christopher P. 2004. *Encyclopedia of Mongolia and the Mongol Empire.* New York: Facts on File.

Äzimät (pen name). 1997. *Mustäqilliq küriši [Struggle for Independence].* Istanbul: Bayrak Mat. San. ve Tic.

Bachman, David. 2004. "Making Xinjiang Safe for the Han? Contradictions and Ironies of Chinese Governance in China's Northwest." In *Governing China's Multiethnic Frontiers*, edited by Morris Rossabi, 155–85. Seattle: University of Washington Press.

Banister, Judith. 1987. *China's Changing Population*. Stanford, Calif.: Stanford University Press.

Bao, Lisheng. 2001. "PRC Officials Say Not Much Terrorism in Xinjiang," September 2. FBIS-CHI-2001-0903.

Bao'erhan [Burhan Shähidi]. 1994. *Xinjiang 50 nian—Bao'erhan huiyi lu [50 Years in Xinjiang—The Reminiscences of Burhan]*. 2nd ed. Beijing: Zhongguo wenshi chubanshe.

BBC. 2009. "Timeline: Xinjiang Unrest," June 9 [cited June 10, 2009]. Available from http://news.bbc.co.uk/2/hi/asia-pacific/8138866.stm (accessed October 30, 2009).

BBC Monitoring. 2006. "China: Central Propaganda Chief Admits Losing Control over Media," May 9. Available from Factiva (accessed May 10, 2006).

BBC Monitoring Asia Pacific. 1997. "Anti-Chinese Uighur Military Leader Speaks" ["Golos Vostochnogo Turkestana," September 28, 1997, 3], October 8, 1997. Available from Factiva (accessed August 2, 2006).

———. 1998. "Xinjiang Separatists Suspected in Wuhan Bus Bombing" [newspaper article, Ming Pao online, February 15], February 17. Available from Factiva (accessed August 4, 2006).

———. 1999. "Over 300 Dead After Rebellions in Xinjiang and Inner Mongolia, Hong Kong Journal Says" [*Tung hsiang*, October 15, 1997, 14], December 24. Available from Factiva (accessed August 4, 2006).

———. 2001. "People's Court Web Site Reports Death Sentence for Islamic Figure" [*Renmin fayuan bao*, January 12, 2001], January 13. Available from Factiva (accessed August 4, 2006).

———. 2002. "Xinjiang Government Chairman on Incident of Reciting Anti-Government Poem" [radio broadcast, Xinjiang People's Broadcasting Station], January 13. Available from Factiva (accessed December 9, 2004).

BBC Monitoring Asia Pacific—Political. 2000. "China Reports Popular Support for Propaganda Work in Xinjiang's Ili Region," February 17. Available from Factiva (accessed August 2, 2005).

BBC Monitoring Central Asia. 2002. "Uighur Movement Lacks Coordination, Unity—Kazakh Paper." *Vremya po*, Almaty, March 30 and April 7. Available from Factiva (accessed June 2, 2006).

BBC Monitoring Service: Former USSR. 1996. "Temporary Ban on Ethnic Uighur Society in Kyrgyzstan" [Kyrgyz Radio, Bishkek, April 4], April 9. Available from Factiva (accessed May 10, 2006).

———. 1999. "Uighur Community Sets Up Supreme Body, Resolves to Fight for Independence" [Kyrgyz Radio first program, Bishkek, November 3], November 5. Available from Factiva (accessed May 10, 2006).

BBC News Online. 2001. "China Accuses Europe over Uighurs," October 19. Available from http://news.bbc.co.uk/1/hi/world/asia-pacific/1608566.stm (accessed September 22, 2003).

Becker, Jasper. 2001. "China's 'Home-Grown Terror'" [online news]. *South China Morning Post* online, November 16. Available from http://special.scmp.com/waronterrorism/comment/ZZZYAXD8iUC.html (accessed August 1, 2006).

Becquelin, Nicolas. 2000. "Xinjiang in the Nineties." *China Journal* 44:65–90.

———. 2002. "Chinese Hold on Xinjiang: Strengths and Limits." In *La Chine et son occident*, edited by François Godement, 57–80. Paris: Insitut français des relations internationales (IFRI).

———. 2004a. "Criminalizing Ethnicity: Political Repression in Xinjiang." *China Rights Forum*, no. 1:39–46.

———. 2004b. "Staged Development in Xinjiang." *China Quarterly*, no. 178:358–78.

Beissinger, Mark R. 1995. "The Persisting Ambiguity of Empire." *Post-Soviet Affairs* 11, no. 2:149–84.

———. 1998. "Nationalist Violence and the State: Political Authority and Contentious Repertoires in the Former USSR." *Comparative Politics* 30, no. 4:401–22.

Beller-Hann, Ildiko. 1997. "The Peasant Condition in Xinjiang." *Journal of Peasant Studies* 25 no. 1:87–112.

———. 2002. "Temperamental Neighbors: Uighur–Han Relations in Xinjiang, Northwest China." In *Imagined Differences: Hatred and the Construction of Identity*, edited by Günther Schlee, 57–82. Hamburg: Lit.

Benford, Robert D., and David A. Snow. 2000. "Framing Processes and Social Movements: An Overview and Assessment." *Annual Review of Sociology* 26, no. 1:611–39.

Benhabib, Seyla. 2002. "Transformations of Citizenship: The Case of Contemporary Europe." *Government and Opposition* 37, no. 4:439–65.

Bennigsen, Alexandre. 1986. "Soviet Minority Nationalism in Historical Perspective." In *The Last Empire: Nationality and the Soviet Future*, edited by Robert Conquest, 131–50. Stanford, Calif.: Hoover Institution Press.

Benson, Linda. 1990. *The Ili Rebellion: The Moslem Challenge to Chinese Authority in Xinjiang, 1944–49*. Armonk, N.Y.: Sharpe.

———. 1996. "Contested History: Issues in the Historiography of Inner Asia's Uighurs." In *Cultural Contact, History and Ethnicity in Inner Asia*, edited by Michael Gervers and Wayne Schlepp, 87–113. Toronto: Joint Center for Asia Pacific Studies.

Benson, Linda, and Ingvar Svanberg. 1988. "The Kazaks in Xinjiang." In *The Kazaks of China: Essays on an Ethnic Minority*, edited by Linda Benson and Ingvar Svanberg, 1–106. Uppsala: Almquist and Wiksell International.

———, eds. 1998. *China's Last Nomads: The History and Culture of China's Kazaks*. Armonk, N.Y.: Sharpe.

Bermeo, Nancy. 1992. "Surprise, Surprise: Lessons from 1989 and 1991." In *Liberalization and Democratization: Change in the Soviet Union and Eastern Europe*, edited by Nancy Bermeo, 178–200. Baltimore: Johns Hopkins University Press.

Besson, Frédérique-Jeanne. 1998. "Les ouïgours hors du Turkestan oriental: De l'exil à la formation d'une diaspora." *Cahiers d'études sur la Méditeranée orientale et le monde turco-iranien* 25:161–92.

Blank, Stephen. 2004. "Xinjiang and China's Strategy in Central Asia." *Asia Times Online*, April 3. Available from http://www.atimes.com/atimes/China/FD03Ad06.html (accessed June 1, 2004).

Blecher, Marc. 2002. "Hegemony and Workers' Politics in China." *China Quarterly*, no. 170:193–206.

———. 2004. "The Working Class and Governance." In *Governance in China*, edited by Jude Howell, 193–206. Lanham, Md.: Rowman & Littlefield.

Blua, Antoine. 2004. "Human Rights: Kyrgyz Rights Activists Call for End to Deportation of Uighurs to China." Eurasianet.org. Available from http://www.eurasianet.org/departments/rights/articles/pp012504_pr.shtml (accessed October 20, 2004).

Borei, Dorothy V. 1991. "Economic Implications of Empire-Building: The Case of Xinjiang." *Central and Inner Asian Studies* 5:22–37.

Bourdieu, Pierre. 1977. *Outline of a Theory of Practice*. Cambridge: Cambridge University Press.

———. 1991. *Language and Symbolic Power*. Trans. Gino Raymond and Matthew Adamson. Cambridge, Mass.: Harvard University Press.

Bovingdon, Gardner. 1998. "From *Qumulluq* to *Uyghur*: The Role of Education in the Development of a Pan-Uyghur Identity." *Journal of Central Asian Studies* 3, no. 1:19–29.

———. 2001. "The History of the History of Xinjiang." *Twentieth Century China* 26, no. 2:95–139.

———. 2002a. "The Not-So-Silent Majority: Uyghur Resistance to Han Rule in Xinjiang." *Modern China* 28, no. 1:39–78.

———. 2002b. Strangers in Their Own Land: The Politics of Uyghur Identity in Chinese Central Asia. PhD diss., Cornell University.

———. 2005. "Policing the Borders of China's History." Paper presented to annual meeting of the American Historical Association, Seattle, January 7.

Bovingdon, Gardner, and Näbijan Tursun. 2004. "Contested Histories." In *Xinjiang: China's Muslim Frontier*, edited by S. Frederick Starr, 353–74. Armonk, N.Y.: Sharpe.

Bransten, Jeremy. 1997. "Kazakhstan: Exiled Uighurs Step Up Fight Against Beijing" [online news]. RFE/RL, October 14. Available from http://www.rferl.org/features/1997/10/F.RU.971014135113.asp (accessed February 1, 2002).

Brophy, David. 2005. "Rebirth of a Nation: The Modern Revival of Uyghur Ethnicity." Master's thesis, Harvard University.

Brubaker, Rogers. 1993. "East European, Soviet, and Post-Soviet Nationalisms: A Framework for Analysis." *Research on Democracy and Society* 1:353–78.

———. 1996. *Nationalism Reframed: Nationhood and the National Question in the New Europe*. Cambridge: Cambridge University Press.

———. 2002. "Ethnicity Without Groups." *Archives européennes de sociologie* 43, no. 2:163–89.

Buchheit, Lee C. 1978. *Secession: The Legitimacy of Self-Determination*. New Haven, Conn.: Yale University Press.

Bughra, Mehmet Emin (Muhämmad Imin). 1942/1987. *Šärqi Türkistan tarikhi* [*History of Eastern Turkistan*]. Ankara: Ofset Repromat.

———. 1946. *Šärqi Türkistan tarikhi* [*History of Eastern Turkistan*]. Srinagar: Bruka parlis basmakhanesi.

Bulag, Uradyn Erden. 2000. "Ethnic Resistance with Socialist Characteristics." In *Chinese Society: Change, Conflict and Resistance*, edited by Elizabeth J. Perry and Mark Selden, 178–97. London: Routledge.

———. 2002. *The Mongols at China's Edge: History and the Politics of National Unity*. Lanham, Md.: Rowman & Littlefield.

———. 2004. "Inner Mongolia: The Dialectics of Colonization and Ethnicity Building." In *Governing China's Multiethnic Frontiers*, edited by Morris Rossabi, 84–116. Seattle: University of Washington Press.

Bunce, Valerie. 1999. *Subversive Institutions: The Design and the Destruction of Socialism and the State*. Cambridge: Cambridge University Press.

Cai, Yongshun. 2002. "The Resistance of Chinese Laid-off Workers in the Reform Period." *China Quarterly*, no. 170:327–44.

Cai Ke, and Lei Xiaoxun. 2009. "200 to Face Trial for Day of Carnage." *China Daily*, August 24. Available from http://www.chinadaily.com.cn/china/2009xinjiangriot/2009-08/24/content_8605477.htm.

Campion, Gilles. 1997. "Mass Trials, Executions Follow Moslem Riots in China" [newswire]. Agence France-Presse, February 12. Available from Factiva (accessed February 12, 1997).

Cao, Changqing (Cao Changching). 1999a. "Fighting to Free Another Chinese 'Province.'" *Taipei Times*, October 11. Available from http://www.taipeitimes.com/News/insight/archives/1999/10/11/6035 (and subsequent articles through October 17) (accessed July 18, 2003).

———. 1999b. "'The General' Looks to the World for Help." *Taipei Times*, October 11. Available from http://www.taipeitimes.com/News/insight/archives/1999/10/110000006036 (accessed July 18, 2003).

———. 1999c. "Womende mubiao shi Dong Tu de duli"—Fang Xinjiang duli yundong lingdao ren Beiken jiangjun ["Our Objective Is Independence for Eastern Turkistan"—An Interview with General Bekin, Leader of the Xinjiang Independence Movement] [Web page]. Caochangqing.com (originally published in *Ziyou shibao* [Taibei] October 11. Available from http://caochangqing.com/bigs/newsdisp.php?News_ID=274 (accessed June 1, 2005).

Carlson, Allen. 2005. *Unifying China, Integrating with the World: Securing Chinese Sovereignty in the Reform Era*. Stanford, Calif.: Stanford University Press.

Chan, Anita, Richard Madsen, and Jonathan Unger. 1984. *Chen Village: The Recent History of a Peasant Community in Mao's China*. Berkeley: University of California Press.

Chan, Vivien Pik-Kwan. 2002. "Pro-Separatist Artists Under Watch." *South China Morning Post*, January 15, 8. Available from Factiva (accessed January 31, 2009).

Chang, Chih-Yi (Zhang Zhiyi). 1949. "Land Utilization and Settlement Possibilities in Sinkiang." *Geographical Review* 39, no. 1:57–75.

Chang Chih-i (Zhang Zhiyi). 1966. *The Party and the National Question in China*. Edited and translated by George Moseley. Cambridge, Mass.: MIT Press.

Chen Chao, ed. 1990. *Xiandai Xinjiang shi shiji* [*Record of Events in Xinjiang's Contemporary History*]. Ürümci: Xinjiang shehui kexueyuan lishi yanjiusuo (neibu).

Chen Linguo. 1994. *Weidade bulü—Zhonghua minzude xingcheng, fazhan ji qi ningjuli* [*Great Strides: The Formation, Development, and Cohesive Power of the Zhonghua Minzu*]. Hangzhou: Zhejiang renmin chubanshe.

Chen Yuning, ed. 1994. *Zhonghua minzu ningjuli de lishi tansuo* [*A Historical Exploration of the Cohesiveness of the Zhonghua minzu*]. Kunming: Yunnan renmin chubanshe.

Cheung, Po-ling. 1992. "'More Autonomy' for Xinjiang to Resist Separatism." April 1, FBIS-CHI-920063, 21.

Chiang, Kai-shek. 1947. *China's Destiny and Chinese Economic Theory*. Trans. Philip Jaffe. New York: Roy Publishers.

"China Hails Anti-Terror Progress" 2004. [webpage]. Digital Chongwen, February 18. Available from http://www.cwi.gov.cn/include/cmarticle_detail.jsp?cmArticleID=1077073040001 (accessed June 4, 2006).

China Radio International. 2006. *Xinjiang shiju minzu zhi er: Hanzu* [*Minzu Inhabiting Xinjiang over the Long Term (2): Hans*] [online news], June 12. Available from http://www.cnr.cn/xjfw/mlxj/200602/t20060207_504163030.html (accessed June 30, 2006).

"China: Xinjiang Confiscates Publications Which Undermine Unity." 1998. *Xinjiang Ribao 1998/03/13 p. 1 04/04*. FBIS-CHI-96-107.

"China's Growing Problem with Xinjiang." 2000. *Jane's Intelligence Digest*, June 13. Available from http://www.janes.com/security/international_security/news/jid/jid000613_1_n.shtml (accessed February 20, 2006).

Ching Cheong. 1997. "New Analysis—Xinjiang Riot Unlikely to Boost Separatism." *Straits Times*, February 13. Available from Factiva (accessed January 15, 2009).

Choi Chi-yuk, and Vivian Wu. 2009. "Overseas Media Given Freedom to Cover Unrest, but Some Areas Still out of Bounds." *South China Morning Post*, July 8, 2.

"Chongqing to Send 100,000 Farmers to Pick Cotton in Xinjiang." 2006. *China Knowledge 2006*. Available from http://www.chinaknowledge.com/news/news-detail.aspx?id=3868 (accessed August 2, 2006).

Chow, Kai-wing. 1997. "Imagining Boundaries of Blood: Zhang Binglin and the Invention of the Han 'Race' in Modern China." In *The Construction of Racial Identities in China and Japan*, edited by Frank Dikötter, 34–52. Honolulu: University of Hawai'i Press.

Clark, William C. Forthcoming. "Ibrahim's Story."

Clarke, Michael. 2007. "China's 'War on Terror' in Xinjiang: Human Security and the Causes of Violent Uighur Separatism." In *Regional Outlook* 11:1–28. Queensland: Griffith Asia Institute.

Cliff, Thomas Matthew James. 2009. Neo Oasis: The Xinjiang Bingtuan in the Twenty-first Century. *Asian Studies Review* 33 (1):83–106.

Cloud, David S., and Ian Johnson. 2004. "Friend or Foe: In Post-9/11 World, Chinese Dissidents Pose U.S. Dilemma." *Wall Street Journal*, August 3, A1.

Comisso, Ellen. 2006. "Changing Modalities of Empire: A Comparative Study of the Ottoman and Habsburg Decline." In *Empire to Nation: Historical Perspectives on the Making of the Modern World*, edited by Joseph Esherick, Hasan Kayalı, and Eric Van Young, 138–66. Lanham, Md.: Rowman & Littlefield.

Congressional-Executive Commission on China. 2005a. "China's Changing Strategic Concerns: The Impact on Human Rights in Xinjiang." Washington, D.C.: U.S. Government Printing Office.

———. 2005b. "Upgrade in Police Armament in Ürümci Signals Continued Tensions in Xinjiang." CECC Virtual Academy. Available from http://www.cecc.gov/pages/virtualAcad/index.phpd?showsingle=7769 (accessed June 2, 2006).

———. 2009. "Two Young Uyghurs Detained for Distributing Leaflets Calling for Student Demonstration." CECC Virtual Academy, January 12. Available from http://www.cecc.gov/pages/virtualAcad/index.phpd?showsingle=116179 (accessed January 13, 2009).

Connor, Walker. 1984. *The National Question in Marxist–Leninist Theory and Strategy*. Princeton, N.J.: Princeton University Press.

———. 1994. *Ethnonationalism: The Quest for Understanding*. Princeton, N.J.: Princeton University Press.

Cornell, Svante E. 2002. "Autonomy as a Source of Conflict: Caucasian Conflicts in Theoretical Perspective." *World Politics* 54:245–76.

Corntassel, Jeff J., and Tomas Hopkins Primeau. 1995. "Indigenous 'Sovereignty' and International Law: Revised Strategies for Pursuing 'Self-Determination.'" *Human Rights Quarterly* 17, no. 2:343–65.

Crossley, Pamela Kyle. 1999. *A Translucent Mirror: History and Identity in Qing Imperial Ideology*. Berkeley: University of California Press.

Dang Yulin and Zhang Yuxi, eds. 2003. *Dangdai Xinjiang jianshi* [*A Concise History of Contemporary Xinjiang*]. Beijing: Dangdai Zhongguo chubanshe.

Dautcher, Jay Todd. 1999. Folklore and Identity in a Uighur Community in Xinjiang China. PhD diss., University of California at Berkeley.

———. 2000. "Reading Out-of-Print: Popular Culture and Protest on China's Western Frontier." In *China Beyond the Headlines*, edited by Timothy B. Weston and Lionel M. Jensen, 273–94. Lanham, Md.: Rowman & Littlefield.

———. 2004. "Public Health and Social Pathologies in Xinjiang." In *Xinjiang: China's Muslim Borderland*, edited by S. Frederick Starr, 276–95. Armonk, N.Y.: Sharpe.

Davidson, Basil. 1953. *Daybreak in China*. London: Cape.

———. 1957. *Turkestan Alive; New Travels in Chinese Central Asia*. London: Cape.

Deng Liqun. 2006. *Deng Liqun zishu: Shi'er ge chunqiu* (*Deng Liqun in His Own Words: Twelve Seasons*)(*1975–1987*). Hong Kong: Da Feng chubanshe.

Demick, Barbara. 2009. "China Says It Has Evidence Deadly Uighur Uprisings Were Coordinated." *Los Angeles Times*, July 21. Available from http://www.latimes.com/news/nationworld/nation/la-fg-china-riots21-2009jul21,0,4647474.story.

Deutsch, Karl. 1953. *Nationalism and Social Communication: An Inquiry into the Foundations of Nationality*. Cambridge, Mass.: Harvard University Press.

Derbyshire, John. 1999. "Hell, No, Uighur Won't Go." *Weekly Standard*, December 6. Available from Lexis-Nexis (accessed January 15, 2001).

Deutsche Presse Agentur. 2006. "China Warns Oslo of Consequences If Peace Prize Goes to Kadeer" [newswire], September 22. Available from http://www.uyghurcongress.org/En/news.asp?ItemID=1158943854 (accessed September 22, 2006).

Dikötter, Frank. 1992. *The Discourse of Race in Modern China*. Stanford, Calif.: Stanford University Press.

———, ed. 1997. *The Construction of Racial Identities in China and Japan*. Honolulu: University of Hawai'i Press.

Dillon, Michael. 2004. *Xinjiang—China's Muslim Far Northwest*. London: RoutledgeCurzon.

Doktor Rahilä Dawut. 2001. *Uyghur Mazarliri* [*Uyghur Mazars*]. Ürümci: Shinjang khälq näshriyati.

Dolkun Isa (Dolqun Isa). n.d. "Rebuttal of the Chinese Public Security Ministry's 'Terrorist' Accusation" [webpage]. World Uyghur Congress n.d. Available from http://www.uyghurcongress.org/En/AboutWUC.asp?mid=1095738888&mid2=-2118628734&mid3=-1844889938 (accessed June 1, 2006).

Dow Jones International News. 2001. "Laid-off Workers Protest in China's Xinjiang Region," December 26. Available from Factiva (accessed June 1, 2006).

Downs, Erica S. 2004. "The Chinese Energy Security Debate." *China Quarterly* 177, no. 1:21–41.

Dreyer, June Teufel. 1976. *China's Forty Millions: Minority Nationalities and National Integration in the People's Republic of China*. Cambridge, Mass.: Harvard University Press.

———. 1986. "The Xinjiang Uygur Autonomous Region at Thirty: A Report Card." *Asian Survey* 26, no. 7:721–44.

———. 1994. "The PLA and Regionalism in Xinjiang." *Pacific Review* 7, no. 1:41–56.

———. 2000. "The PLA and Kosovo: A Strategy Debate." *Issues and Studies* 36, no. 1:100–119.

Du Wenzhong. 2002. "Zizhi yu gongzhi: Dui xifang gudian minzu zhengzhi lilun de xianzheng fansi" [Autonomy and Collective Rule: A Constitutionalist Reflection on Classic Western *Minzu* Political Theory]. *Minzu yanjiu*, no. 6:1–8.

Duara, Prasenjit. 1995. *Rescuing History from the Nation: Questioning Narratives of Modern China*. Chicago: University of Chicago Press.

Dwyer, Arienne M. 2005. "The Xinjiang Conflict: Uyghur Identity, Language Policy, and Political Discourse." *Policy Studies*, no. 15:1–88.

Dwyer, Michael. 2001. "Beijing Links Crackdown to International Struggle." *Australian Financial Review*, November 20. Available from Factiva (accessed February 1, 2005).

East Turkestan Information Center. 1997a. "Press Conference of the Uyghur Leaders in Almaty" [online news], February 23. Available from http://www.uygur.org/enorg/wunn97/wunn022397.htm (accessed September 1, 2006).

———. 1997b. "Uyghur Leaders Met with the U.S. State Department Officials" [online news], July 15. Available from http://www.uygur.org/enorg/reports97/e0715971.htm (accessed July 2, 2006).

———. 2002. "Situation with Human Rights in East Turkistan After September 11th Events." Munich. Available from http://www.uygur.org/enorg/h_rights/report_9_11_2002.html (accessed September 9, 2006).

Emerson, Rupert. 1962. *From Empire to Nation: The Rise to Self-Assertion of Asian and African Peoples*. Boston: Beacon Press.

Ertughrul Atihan. 2002. "Terrorist Actions of the Communist Chinese Regime in East Turkistan in the Area of Mass Media Channels" [online news]. Eastern Turkestan Information Center, June 18. Available from http://www.uygur.org/enorg/h_rights/etic_report_june_2002.html (accessed July 1, 2003).

Escarra, Jean. 1954. "Daybreak in China, by Basil Davidson" [book review]. *Pacific Affairs* 27, no. 1:71–72.

Esenbel, Selçuk. 2004. "Japan's Global Claim to Asia and the World of Islam: Transnational Nationalism and World Power, 1900–1945." *American Historical Review* 109, no. 4:1140–70.

Esherick, Joseph. 2006. "Going Imperial: Tibeto-Mongolian Buddhism and Nationalisms in China and Inner Asia." In *Empire to Nation: Historical Perspectives on the Making of the Modern World*, edited by Joseph Esherick, Hasan Kayalı, and Eric Van Young, 229–59. Lanham, Md.: Rowman & Littlefield.

Esposito, Bruce J. 1974. "China's West in the 20th Century." *Military Review* 54, no. 1:64–75.

Eurasianet. 2003. "Uighur Issues May Become Factor in China–Kazakhstan Relations." Available from www.eurasianet.org (accessed October 20, 2004).

Fang Yingkai and Li Fusheng. 1997. *Xinjiang bingtuan tunken shubian shi* [*A History of the Xinjiang Production and Construction Corp's Reclaiming Land and Protecting the Borders*]. Ürümci: Xinjiang keji weisheng chubanshe.

Fei Xiaotong, ed. 1989. *Zhonghua minzu de duoyuan yiti geju* [*The Holistic Plural Configuration of the Zhonghua Minzu*]. Beijing: Zhongyang minzu xueyuan chubanshe.

Feng Dazhen. 1992. "Gaodu zhongshi yishi xingtai lingyu fenlie he fan fenlie douzheng—Pingxi 'Weiwu'erren' deng san ben shu de zhengzhi cuowu" [Give the Utmost Attention to the Struggle on the Terrain of Ideology Between Splittism and Anti-Splittism—An Analysis of the

Political Errors in the Three Books Including *Uyghurs*]. In *"Weiwu'er ren" deng san ben shu wenti taolunhui lunwenji* [*Collection of Papers from the Symposium on the Three Books Including Uyghurs*], edited by Feng Dazhen, 1–13. Ürümci: Xinjiang renmin chubanshe.

———. 2003. "Xu er" [Second Preface]. In *Guojia liyi gaoyu yiqie—Xinjiang wending wenti de guancha yu sikao* [*The National Interest Above All Else—Analysis of and Reflections on the Problem of Stability in Xinjiang*], edited by Ma Dazheng, iii–v. Ürümci: Xinjiang renmin chubanshe.

Feuerwerker, Albert. 1968. "China's History in Marxian Dress." In *History in Communist China*, edited by Albert Feuerwerker, 14–44. Cambridge, Mass.: MIT Press.

Finnemore, Martha. 2003. *The Purpose of Intervention: Changing Beliefs About the Use of Force*. Edited by Robert J. Art, Robert Jervis, and Stephen M. Walt. Ithaca, N.Y.: Cornell University Press.

Fitzgerald, John. 1996a. *Awakening China: Politics, Culture, and Class in the Nationalist Revolution*. Stanford, Calif.: Stanford University Press.

———. 1996b. "The Nationless State: The Search for a Nation in Modern Chinese Nationalism." In *Chinese Nationalism*, edited by Jonathan Unger, 56–85. Armonk, N.Y.: Sharpe.

Fletcher, Joseph. 1968. "China and Central Asia, 1368–1884." In *The Chinese World Order: Traditional China's Foreign Relations*, edited by John King Fairbank, 206–24. Cambridge, Mass.: Harvard University Press.

Forbes, Andrew W. D. 1986. *Warlords and Muslims in Chinese Central Asia: A Political History of Republican Sinkiang 1911–1949*. Cambridge: Cambridge University Press.

Foreman, William. 2008. "Attack on Chinese Police Carefully Planned." *Santa Cruz Sentinel*, August 6. Available from http://hosted.ap.org/dynamic/stories/O/OLY_CHINA_SECURITY ?SITE=CACRU&SECTION=HOME&TEMPLATE=DEFAULT (accessed Auust 7, 2008).

Forney, Matthew. 2002a. "China's New Terrorists." *Time*, September 16. Available from http://www. time.com/time/magazine/article/0,9171,501020923-351276,00.html (accessed April 4, 2005).

———. 2002b. "Man of Constant Sorrow: One Uighur Makes Music for the Masses." Time-asia.com, March 25. Available from www.time.com/time/asia/features/xinjiang/culture.html (accessed April 8, 2002).

———. 2002c. "Workers' Wasteland." *Time Asia*, June 17. Available from http://www.time.com/ time/asia/covers/1101020617/cover2.html (accessed July 15, 2006).

Foucault, Michel. 1990. *The History of Sexuality: An Introduction*. Vol. 1. New York: Vintage Books.

French, Howard W. 2006. "Letter from China: Beijing's Growing Urge to Dominate the Media" [online newspaper]. *International Herald Tribune*, September 21. Available from http://www. iht.com/bin/print_ipub.php?file=/articles/2006/09/21/news/letter.php (accessed September 21, 2006).

French, Howard W. 2008. "Protest in Muslim Province in China." *New York Times*, April 2. Available from http://www.nytimes.com/2008/04/02/world/asia/03china.html?_r=1&hp&oref=slogin.

Frum, David. 2006. "Trouble Is Coming to Beijing." *National Post*, June 24, A19. Available from http://web.lexis-nexis.com/universe/document?_m=891adce54dfc8bbf6fffba726a368ee3&_

docnum=1&wchp=dGLbVlz-zSkVA&_md5=1c629f2abd8c1e887c718ca75cfeef85 (accessed July 7, 2006).

Fuller, Graham, and Jonathan Lipman. 2004. "Islam in Xinjiang." In *Xinjiang: China's Muslim Borderland*, edited by S. Frederick Starr, 320–52. Armonk, N.Y.: Sharpe.

Gasster, Michael. 1969. *Chinese Intellectuals and the Revolution of 1911*. Seattle: University of Washington Press.

Gellner, Ernest. 1983. *Nations and Nationalism*. Ithaca, N.Y.: Cornell University Press.

———. 1995. "Nationalism in the Vacuum." In *Thinking Theoretically About Soviet Nationalities: History and Comparison in the Study of the USSR*, edited by Alexander J. Motyl, 243–54. New York: Columbia University Press.

Geng, Shimin. 1984. "On the Fusion of Nationalities in the Tarim Basin." *Central Asian Survey* 3, no. 4:1–14.

George, Paul. 1998. "Commentary no. 73: Islamic Unrest in the Xinjiang Uighur Autonomous Region." Ottawa: Canadian Security Intelligence Service.

"Gezu renmin fennu shengtao difang minzu zhuyi fenzi zuixing" [People of Various *Minzu* Angrily Condemn the Crimes of Local Nationalist Elements]. 1958. *Xinjiang ribao*, May 1.

Ghalip Isma'il. 1996. "Aptonomiyä nizami wä uning alahidiliki" [The Law on Autonomy and Its Characteristics]. *Millätlär ittipaqi* [*Minzu* unity—Uyghur edition], no. 4:28–30.

Gilley, Bruce. 2004. *China's Democratic Future: How It Will Happen and Where It Will Lead*. New York: Columbia University Press.

Gladney, Dru C. 1990. "The Ethnogenesis of the Uighur." *Central Asian Survey* 9, no. 1:1–28.

———. 1991. *Muslim Chinese: Ethnic Nationalism in the People's Republic*. Cambridge, Mass.: Harvard University Press.

———. 1992. "Transnational Islam and Uighur National Identity: Salman Rushdie, Sino-Muslim Missile Deals, and the Trans-Eurasian Railway." *Central Asian Survey* 11, no. 3:1–18.

———. 1996. "Relational Alterity: Constructing Dungan (Hui), Uygur, and Kazakh Identities Across China, Central Asia, and Turkey." *History and Anthropology* 9, no. 4:445–77.

———. 1998. "Internal Colonialism and the Uyghur Nationality: Chinese Nationalism and Its Subaltern Subjects." *Cahiers d'études sur la Méditeranée orientale et le monde turco-iranien* 25:47–63.

———. 2002. "Xinjiang: China's Future West Bank?" *Current History*, September, 267–70.

———. 2004a. *Dislocating China: Muslims, Minorities, and Other Subaltern Subjects*. Chicago: University of Chicago Press.

———. 2004b. "Responses to Chinese Rule: Patterns of Occupation and Opposition." In *Xinjiang: China's Muslim Borderland*, edited by S. Frederick Starr, 375–96. Armonk, N.Y.: Sharpe.

———. 2006. "China's 'Uyghur Problem' and the Shanghai Cooperation Organization." Washington, D.C.: U.S.–China Economic and Security Review Commission.

Gleason, Gregory. 1990. *Federalism and Nationalism: The Struggle for Republican Rights in the USSR*. Boulder, Colo.: Westview Press.

Goffman, Erving. 1974. *Frame Analysis: An Essay on the Organization of Experience*. Cambridge, Mass.: Harvard University Press.

Golden, Peter B. 1992. *An Introduction to the History of the Turkic Peoples: Ethnogenesis and State-Formation in Medieval and Early Modern Eurasia and the Middle East*. Wiesbaden: Otto Harrassowitz.

Goldman, Merle. 2006. "Protesting the Party." *Wall Street Journal*, March 8, 13.

Goldsmith, Benjamin. 2005. "Here There Be Dragons: The Shanghai Cooperation Organization." Center for Defense Information, September 26. Available from http://www.cdi.org/friendly-version/printversion.cfm?documentID=3153&from page=../program/document.cfm (accessed November 26, 2005).

Goldstein, Melvyn C. 1997. *The Snow Lion and the Dragon: China, Tibet, and the Dalai Lama*. Berkeley: University of California Press.

"Gong'anbu gongbu shoupi rending de 'dongtu' kongbu zuzhi ji chengyuan mingdan" [PSB Reveals the First Batch of Confirmed "ET" Terrorist Organizations and Members]. 2003. [online news]. *People's Daily* online, December 15. Available from http://www.people.com.cn/GB/shizheng/1027/2246683.html (accessed March 8, 2004).

Gong Yong. 1997. "Qianlun feifa zongjiao huodong dui Xinjiang shehui zhengzhi wending de weihaixing" [A Brief Discussion of the Nature of the Threat of Illegal Activity to Xinjiang's Social and Political Stability]. Conference paper. Ürümci: Xinjiang University.

Grabot, André. 1996. "The Uighurs—Sacrificed on Central Asia's Chessboard" [newswire]. Agence France-Presse, April 25. Available from Factiva (accessed July 1, 2006).

Greve, Louisa. 2006. "Remarks." Fifth Congress of the Uyghur American Association, May 28, 2006. Available from http://uyghuramerican.org/articles/270/1/Remarks-at-the-5th-Congress-of-the-Uyghur-American-Association-by-Louisa-Greve/Remarks-at-the-5th-Congress-of-the-Uyghur-American-Association-by-Louisa-Greve-NED.html (accessed May 29, 2006).

"A Grim Reminder for the Central Government's Opponents." 2003. *South China Morning Post*, June 13, 13.

Gu Bao. 1983. "Wei Shenme Qingchao Jiang Xiyu Gaicheng Xinjiang" [Why the Qing Changed "Xiyu" to "Xinjiang"] *Xinjiang shehui kexue yanjiu*, no. 143:24–26.

Gunaratna, Rohan, and Kenneth George Pereire. 2006. "An al-Qaeda Associate Group Operating in China?" *China and Eurasia Forum Quarterly* 4, no. 2:55–61.

Guowuyuan xinwen bangongshi. 2002. "'Dong tu' kongbu shili nantuo zuize" [The "ET" Terrorist Forces Cannot Escape Their Crimes], January 21. Available from http://www.peopledaily.com.cn/GB/shizheng/3586/20020121/652705.html (accessed April 2, 2002).

———. 2003. "Xinjiang de lishi yu fazhan" [Xinjiang's History and Development]. Beijing: Guowuyuan.

Guo Zhengli. 1992. *Zhongguo tese de minzu quyu zizhi lilun yu shijian* [*The Theory and Practice of Minzu Regional Autonomy* [*with*] *Chinese Characteristics*]. Ürümci: Xinjiang daxue chubanshe.

Guo Zhenglin and Yu Zhen (Herbert S. Yee). n.d. "Zuqun yishi yu guojia rentong: Xinjiang Wei–Han guanxi wenjuan fenxi" [Ethnic Consciousness and State Identification: An Analysis of a Survey of Xinjiang's Uyghur–Han Relations]. Working paper. Hong Kong: Universities Service Center, Chinese University. Available from http://www.usc.cuhk.edu.hk/wk_wzdetails.asp?id=1935 (accessed September 28, 2005).

Gurr, Ted Robert. 1993. *Minorities at Risk: A Global View of Ethnopolitical Conflicts.* Washington, D.C.: U.S. Institute of Peace Press.

———. 2000. *Peoples Versus States: Minorities at Risk in the New Century.* Washington, D.C.: U.S. Institute of Peace Press.

Hannum, Emily, and Yu Xie. 1998. "Ethnic Stratification in Northwest China: Occupational Differences Between Han Chinese and National Minorities in Xinjiang, 1982–1990." *Demography* 35, no. 3:323–33.

Hannum, Hurst. 1988. "New Developments in Indigenous Rights." *Virginia Journal of International Law* 28, no. 1:649–78.

Hannum, Hurst, and Richard B. Lillich. 1980. "The Concept of Autonomy in International Law." *American Journal of International Law* 74, no. 4:858–89.

Hansen, Mette Halskov. 1999. *Lessons in Being Chinese: Minority Education and Ethnic Identity in Southwest China.* Seattle: University of Washington Press.

Harris, Lillian Craig. 1993. "Xinjiang, Central Asia and the Implications for China's Policy in the Islamic World." *China Quarterly* 133:111–29.

Harris, Rachel. 2001. "Uyghur Pop: 'Amubap Nakhshisi.'" *IIAS Online Newsletter,* no. 26, November. Available from www.iias.nl/iiasn/26/theme/26T3.html (accessed July 15, 2003).

Hastings, Justin V. 2005. "Perceiving a Single Chinese State: Escalation and Violence in Uighur Protests." *Problems of Post-Communism* 52, no. 1:28–38.

Heberer, Thomas. 1989. *China and Its National Minorities: Autonomy or Assimilation?* Armonk, N.Y.: Sharpe.

Hechter, Michael. 1975. *Internal Colonialism: The Celtic Fringe in British National Development, 1536–1966.* Berkeley: University of California Press.

He Fulin, ed. 1996. *Weihu zuguo tongyi [Preserve the Unification of the Motherland].* Ürümci: Xinjiang Renmin Chubanshe.

———. 2002. "Gaodu zhongshi yishi xingtai lingyu de fan fenlie douzheng" [Give the Utmost Attention to the Anti-Splittist Struggle on the Ideological Plane]. *Shiting tiandi* (65). Available from http://www.xjbs.com.cn/sht/gh/65gj/2.htm (accessed August 13, 2005).

He Gang and Shi Weimin. 1994. *Monan qing: Nei Menggu shengchan jianshe bingtuan xiezhen [The Situation South of the Gobi: The True Story of the Inner Mongolia PCC].* Beijing: Falü chubanshe.

He Jihong. 1996. *Xiyu lungao [Articles on the Western Regions].* Ürümci: Xinjiang renmin chubanshe.

Hierman, Brent. 2006. "The Pacification of Xinjiang: Uyghur Protest and the Chinese State, 1988–2002." Manuscript, Indiana University.

Higgins, Andrew. 1992. *Tremors in the Chinese Empire—Uighurs Battle for Independence*, April 19. Available from Factiva (accessed July 1, 2006).

Hobsbawm, E. J. 1990. *Nations and Nationalism Since 1780: Programme, Myth, Reality*. Cambridge: Cambridge University Press.

———. 1992. *Nations and Nationalism Since 1780: Programme, Myth, Reality*. 2nd ed. Cambridge: Cambridge University Press.

Hoh, Erling. 2000. "China—Hear Our Prayer: China's Ethnic Uighur Population Is in the News Again Following Fresh Reports of Rights Violations; yet Their Plight Remains Unknown to Many Outsiders." *Far Eastern Economic Review*, April 13, 24.

———. 2004. "Sultan's Song." *Far Eastern Economic Review*, September 30, 69.

Hong, Yan. 2006. "Image of Internet Police: Jingjing and Chacha Online" [online newspaper]. *China Digital Times*, January 22. Available from http://chinadigitaltimes.net/2006/01/image_of_internet_police_jingjing_and_chacha_online_hon.php (accessed January 22, 2006).

Hoo, Stephanie. 2005. "China Detains Teacher, 37 Students for Studying Qur'an in Muslim Northwest, Activist Says" [newswire]. Associated Press, August 14. Available from Factiva (accessed August 15, 2005).

Hornby, Lucy. 2009. "Protesters Demand China's Xinjiang Leader Resign." Reuter's, September 3. Available from http://www.reuters.com/article/topNews/idUSTRE5821PT20090903 (accessed October 30, 2009).

Hsu, Immanuel C. Y. 1964–1965. "The Great Policy Debate in China, 1874: Maritime Defense Vs. Frontier Defense." *Harvard Journal of Asiatic Studies* 25:212–28.

———. 1965. *The Ili Crisis: A Study of Sino-Russian Diplomacy, 1871–1881*. Oxford: Oxford University Press.

Huang Guangxue. 2001. "Dang de san dai lingdao jiti guanyu minzu gongzuo de zhidao sixiang" [The Guiding Principles Concerning *Minzu* Work Held by the Party's Three Generations of Leadership Groups]. *Zhongguo minzu* [*China Ethnicity*] (7). Available from www.56-china.com.cn/china1-12/7q/2gmz-7m20.htm (accessed May 1, 2004).

Human Rights Watch. 1999. "China: State Control of Religion, Update Number 1." New York: Human Rights Watch.

———. 2005. "Devastating Blows: Religious Repression of Uighurs in Xinjiang" [report]. Available from hrw.org/reports/2005/china0405/china0405.pdf (accessed April 13, 2005).

———. 2006. "China: A Year After New Regulations, Religious Rights Still Restricted." Reuters Alertnet, February 28. Available from http://www.alertnet.org/thenews/newsdesk/HRW/8e2d9ae1f5b37ae6b295e73bf81d3e50.htm (accessed February 28, 2006).

Hurst, William. 2004. "Understanding Contentious Collective Action by Chinese Laid-off Workers: The Importance of Regional Political Economy." *Studies in Comparative International Development* 39, no. 2:94–120.

Hutcheon, Stephen J. 1998. "Pressing Concerns: Hong Kong's Media in an Era of Transition." Cambridge, Mass.: Joan Shorenstein Center on the Press, Politics and Public Policy, Harvard University.

Hutzler, Charles. 1997. "10 Dead in Muslim Riot in West China, Government Says" [newswire]. Associated Press, February 12. Available from Factiva (accessed February 1, 2003).

Imatov, K. 2001. "The Question of the Uyghur Question" (*Slovo kyrgyzstana*, November 1). BBC Monitoring Central Asia, November 3. Available from Factiva (accessed June 21, 2006).

Ingram, Ruth. 2001. "Foreign Media—Xinjiang's Lifeline or Harbinger of Empty Hopes." *Central Asia—Caucasus Analyst*, August 15, 4.

IRINNEWS. 2004. "Central Asia: Uighurs Deported to China Face Persecution." UN Office for the Coordination of Humanitarian Affairs. Available from http://www.irinnews.org/report.asp?ReportID=42060&SelectRegion=Central_Asia&SelectCountry=CENTRAL_ASIA (accessed October 20, 2004).

Jankowiak, William R. 1988. "The Last Hurrah? Political Protest in Inner Mongolia." *Australian Journal of Chinese Affairs*, nos. 19/20:269–88.

Jarring, Gunnar. 1991. *Prints from Kashghar: The Printing-Office of the Swedish Mission in Eastern Turkestan, with an Attempt at a Bibliography*. Stockholm: Swedish Research Institute in Istanbul: Distributor Almqvist and Wiksell.

Ji Dachun, ed. 1993. *Xinjiang lishi cidian* [*Dictionary of Xinjiang History*]. Ürümci: Xinjiang renmin chubanshe.

Ji, Ping. 1990. "Frontier Migration and Ethnic Assimilation: A Case of Xinjiang Uygur Autonomous Region." PhD diss., Brown University.

Ji Ping and Gao Bingzhong. 1994. "Xinjiang Wei–Han minzu jiaorong zhu yinsu de lianghua fenxi" [Quantitative Analysis of Various Factors Affecting Uyghur–Han Relations in Xinjiang]. In *Zhongguo bianjiang diqu kaifa yanjiu* [*Research on Opening Up China's Peripheral Regions*], edited by Pan Naigu and Ma Rong. Hong Kong: Oxford University Press.

Jiang, Wenran. 2006. "Dynamics of China's Social Crisis." *China Brief* 6, no. 2:1–3.

Jiang Zhongzheng (Chiang Kai-shek). 1943/1962. *Zhongguo zhi mingyun* [*China's Destiny*]. Taibei: Zhongyang wenwu gongying she.

"Jiekai Xinjiang 'Dong Tu' fenzi de kongbu miansha" [Pulling Back the Veil from the Terror of Xinjiang's East Turkistan Elements]. 2001. *Sanlian shenghuo zhoukan*, November 2. Available from http://news.sohu.com/05/20/news147092005.shtml (accessed August 1, 2006).

Jin Tianming and Wang Qingren. 1981. "'Minzu' yi ci zai woguo de chuxian ji qi shiyong wenti" [The Problem of the Emergence and Use of the Term "*Minzu*" in Our Country]. In *Minzu yanjiu lunwenji* [Selected Essays on *Minzu* Research], edited by Minzu yanjiusuo, 36–54. Beijing: Zhongyang minzu xueyuan chubanshe.

J K P Š U A R komiteti täšwiqat bölümi. 2000? *Aptonom rayonimizning ide'ologiyä sahäsidiki bölgünçilikkä qarši turuš kürišigä yüksäk ähmiyät beräyli* [*Let Us Give the Highest Attention to the Struggle Against Splittism in the Ideological Realm in Our Autonomous Region*]. Ürümci: n.p.

Johnston, Alastair Iain. 1996. "Learning Versus Adaptation: Explaining Change in Chinese Arms Control Policy in the 1980s and 1990s." *China Journal*, no. 35:27–61.

Kamminga, Menno T. 1992. *Inter-State Accountability for Violations of Human Rights*. Philadelphia: University of Pennsylvania Press.

Kapstein, Matthew. 2004. "A Thorn in the Dragon's Side: Tibetan Buddhist Culture in China." In *Governing China's Multiethnic Frontiers*, edited by Morris Rossabi, 230–69. Seattle: University of Washington Press.

Kashi diqu shizhi ban, ed. 2001. *Kashi nianjian [Kashgar Yearbook]*. Kashgar: Kashgar weiwu'erwen chubanshe.

Kashi diwei xuanchuan bu. 1995. "Fandui minzu fenlie, weihu zuguo tongyi, weihu minzu tuanjie, weihu shehui wending (xuanchuan jiaoyu cailiao)" [Oppose Minzu Separatism, Protect the Unification of the Motherland, Protect Minzu Unity, Protect Social Stability] (propaganda education materials). Kashgar: (internal circulation).

Kaup, Katherine Palmer. 2000. *Creating the Zhuang: Ethnic Politics in China*. Boulder, Colo.: Lynne Rienner.

Kim, Ho-dong. 2004. *Holy War in China: The Muslim Rebellion and State in Chinese Central Asia, 1864–1877*. Stanford, Calif.: Stanford University Press.

Kirby, William C. 2005. "When Did China Become China? Thoughts on the Twentieth Century." In *The Teleology of the Modern Nation-State: Japan and China*, edited by Joshua A. Fogel, 105–14. Philadelphia: University of Pennsylvania Press.

Knaus, John Kenneth. 1999. *Orphans of the Cold War: America and the Tibetan Struggle for Survival*. New York: Public Affairs.

Kolstø, Pål. 2000. *Political Construction Sites: Nation-Building in Russia and the Post-Soviet States*. Trans. Susan Høivik. Boulder, Colo.: Westview Press.

Krasner, Stephen D. 1993. "Sovereignty, Regimes, and Human Rights." In *Regime Theory and International Relations*, edited by Volker Rittenberger and Peter Meyer, 139–67. Oxford: Clarendon Press.

———. 1999. *Sovereignty: Organized Hypocrisy*. Princeton, N.J.: Princeton University Press.

Kristof, Nicholas D. 2006. "Rumblings from China." *New York Times*, July 2, 11.

Kuang Chen and Pan Liang, eds. 2005. *Womende wushi niandai [Our 1950s]*. Beijing: Zhongguo youyi chuban gongsi.

Kuran, Timur. 1992. "Now Out of Never: The Element of Surprise in the East European Revolution of 1989." In *Liberalization and Democratization: Change in the Soviet Union and Eastern Europe*, edited by Nancy Bermeo, 7–48. Baltimore: Johns Hopkins University Press.

Kurlantzick, Joshua. 2003. "The Dragon Still Has Teeth: How the West Winks at Chinese Repression." *World Policy Journal* 20, no. 1:49–58.

Kushko, Yuri. 1997. "Uighur Exiles Claim China 'Revenge' Bus Bombings" [newswire]. Reuters, March 4. Available from Factiva (accessed July 21, 2006).

Lakoff, George. 1987. *Women, Fire, and Dangerous Things : What Categories Reveal About the Mind*. Chicago: University of Chicago Press.

Lakoff, George, and Mark Johnson. 1980. *Metaphors We Live By*. Chicago: University of Chicago Press.

Lakoff, Robin Tolmach. 2001. *The Language War*. Berkeley: University of California Press.

Landau, Jacob M. 1995. *Pan-Turkism: From Irredentism to Cooperation*. Bloomington: Indiana University Press.

Lattimore, Owen. 1950. *Pivot of Asia: Sinkiang and the Inner Asian Frontiers of China and Russia*. Boston: Little, Brown.

———. 1951. *Inner Asian Frontiers of China*. 2nd ed., vol. 21. New York: Capitol Publishing and American Geographical Society.

———. 1962. "The Chinese as a Dominant Race." In *Studies in Frontier History—Collected Papers, 1928–58*, edited by Owen Lattimore, 200–17. Oxford: Oxford University Press.

Lawrence, Susan V. 2000. "Where Beijing Fears Kosovo." *Far Eastern Economic Review*, September 7. Available from Factiva (accessed September 16, 2002).

Le Coq, Albert von. 1986 (1928). *Buried Treasures of Chinese Turkestan*. Oxford: Oxford University Press.

Leibold, James. 2007. *Reconfiguring Chinese Nationalism: How the Qing Frontier and Its Indigenes Became Chinese*. New York: Palgrave Macmillan.

Lenin, Vladimir I. 1914/1975. "The Right of Nations to Self-Determination." In *The Lenin Anthology*, edited by Robert C. Tucker, 153–80. New York: Norton.

Lescot, Patrick. 1988. "600 Uygurs Demonstrate in Xinjiang Capital." *Agence France-Presse*, June 21. FBIS-CHI-88-119.

Li Ailing, Li Hongxun, Ma Yan, and Zhang Guolin. 1992. *Ate'izm tärbiyisi toghrisida qisqiçä oqušluq* [*A Concise Text Concerning Education in Atheism*]. Trans. Tursun Sadiq. Ürümci: Shinjang yashlar osmurler neshriyati.

Li Danhui. 2003. "Xinjiang Sulian qiaomin wenti de lishi kaocha (1945–1965)" [A Historical Investigation of the Problem of Soviet Nationals in Xinjiang, 1945–1965]. *Lishi yanjiu*, no. 3:80–99.

Li Dezhu. 2000. "Xibu da kaifa yu woguo minzu wenti" [Developing the West and Our Country's *Minzu* Problems]. *Qiushi*, no. 11:22–25.

Li Hongjie. 2002. "Lun minzu gainian de zhengzhi shuxing—Cong ouzhou weiyuanhui de xiangguan wenjian kan 'minzu' yu 'zuqun'" [A Discussion of the Political Properties of the Concept of *Minzu*—Viewing "*Minzu*" and "Ethnic Group" Through Relevant Council of Europe Documents]. *Minzu yanjiu*, no. 4:11–20.

Li, Jing. 2005. "Xinjiang Cracks Down on Terrorist Threat." *China Daily Online*, August 26. Available from http://www.chinadaily.com.cn/english/doc/2005–08/26/content_472215.htm (accessed December 1, 2005).

Li Kangping. 1994. *Zhonghua minzu jingshen* [*The Spirit of the Zhonghua Minzu*]. Nanchang: Jiangxi jiaoyu chubanshe.

Li Qi. 2002. "Daji 'Dong Tu' kongbu shili shi guoji fan kongbu douzheng de zucheng bufen" [Striking the 'Eastern Turkistan' Terrorist Forces Is a Component Part of the International Struggle Against Terror]. *Xinjiang shehui kexue*, no. 2:70–75.

———. 2003. *Zhongya Weiwu'er ren* [*Central Asian Uyghurs*]. Edited by Zhongguo shehui kexueyuan Xinjiang fazhan yanjiu zhongxin. Wulumuqi: Xinjiang renmin chubanshe.

Li Shangkai. 1992. "Shilun tufa minzu jiufen de xinli chengyin yu xinli shudao" [A Preliminary Discussion of the Psychological Origins and Resolution of Suddenly Developing *Minzu* Disputes]. In *Xinjiang minzu xinli yanjiu* [*Research on the Psychology of Xinjiang's Minzu*], edited by Li Ze and Li Shangkai, 130–45. Ürümci: XUAR xinwen chubanju (*neibu*).

Li Weihan. 1982. *Tongyi zhanxian wenti yu minzu wenti* [*United Front Problems and Minzu Problems*]. Beijing: Renmin chubanshe.

Li Yuanqing. 1989. "Qianyi Xinjiang renkou de jixie zengzhang" [A Brief Discussion of the Mechanical Increase in Xinjiang's Population]. *Xinjiang shehui kexue*, no. 3:123–24.

———. 1990. "Population Changes in the Uighur Autonomous Region (1949–1984)." *Central Asian Survey* 9, no. 1:49–73.

Lim, Benjamin Kang. 1997. "China Says Smashes Plot to Sabotage Moslem Region" [newswire]. Reuters, August 28. Available from Factiva (accessed October 30, 2002).

Link, Perry. 2002. "China: The Anaconda in the Chandelier." *New York Review of Books* 49, no. 6:67–70.

Link, Perry, Richard Madsen, Chin-chuan Lee, and Yongming Zhou. 2002. "Scholars Under Siege? Academic and Media Freedom in China." Asia Program Special Report no. 102. Woodrow Wilson International Center for Scholars, Washington, D.C. Available from http://www.wilsoncenter.org/topics/pubs/asiarpt_102.pdf (accessed January 12, 2003).

Lipman, Jonathan. 1997. *Familiar Strangers: A History of Muslims in Northwest China*. Seattle: University of Washington Press.

Liu, Alan P. L. 1971. *Communications and National Integration in Communist China*. Berkeley: University of California Press.

Liu Hantai and Du Xingfu. 2003. *Weile zhigao liyi—Zhongguo daji 'Dong Tu' baogao* [*In Service of the Highest Interests—A Report on China's Attacks on "East Turkestan"*]. Ürümci: Xinjiang renmin chubanshe.

Liu, Xiaoyuan. 2004. *Frontier Passages: Ethnopolitics and the Rise of Chinese Communism, 1921–1945*. Washington, D.C., and Stanford, Calif.: Woodrow Wilson Center Press and Stanford University Press.

Liu Yongqian. 1992. "Dui minzu diqu ziyuan kaifa de xinli ceshi" [A Survey of Attitudes Toward Resource Exploitation in *Minzu* Regions]. In *Xinjiang minzu Xinli Yanjiu (Research on the*

Psychology of Xinjiang's Minzu), edited by Li Ze and Li Shangkai, 90–100. Ürümci: XUAR Xinwen chubanju (*neibu*).

Liu Zhixiao. 1985. *Weiwu'erzu lishi—Shang bian* [*The History of the Uyghurs*]. Vol. 1. Beijing: Minzu chubanshe.

————. 1986. "Weiwu'erzu shi Zhonghua minzu bu ke fenge de yi bufen [The Uyghurs Are an Indivisible Part of the Zhonghua Minzu]. *Xinjiang ribao*, July 4.

Liu Zhongkang. 1990. "Bo 'guoqu Malie Zhuyi ya zongjiao, xianzai zongjiao yao yadao Malie Zhuyi' de miulun" [A Refutation of the Preposterous Idea That in the Past Marxism–Leninism Suppressed Religion; Now Religion Will Overwhelm Marxism–Leninism]. *Xinjiang shehui kexue yanjiu* (special issue):50–55.

Llopis-Jepsen, Celia. 2009. "Why Did the NIA Bar Dolkun Isa?" *Taipei Times*, July 22. Available from http://www.taipeitimes.com/News/editorials/archives/2009/07/22/2003449242 (accessed July 25, 2009).

Lloyd, Barbara. 2009. "Angry Chinese Mob Turns on ABC Reporters and Crew." In *The World Newser*. ABC, July 8.

Long Qun and Guo Ning. 2000. "Lun zongjiao dui Xinjiang xinjiao qunzhong zhengzhi xingwei de yingxiang" [A Discussion of the Influence of Religion on the Political Behavior of Xinjiang's Believing Masses]. *Xinjiang shehui jingji*, no. 4:75–78.

Lu Minghui, ed. 1994. *Qingdai beibu bianjiang minzu jingji fazhan shi* [*A History of the Economic Development of the Minzu in China's Northern Borderlands*]. Ha'erbin: Heilongjiang jiaoyu chubanshe.

Lubman, Stanley B. 1999. *Bird in a Cage: Legal Reform in China After Mao*. Stanford, Calif.: Stanford University Press.

Luo Tianliang. 2006. "Timing Rebiya xiedu Nuobei'er heping jiang" [The Nomination of Rebiya Blasphemes the Nobel Peace Prize] [online newspaper]. *Chinanews*, September 19. Available from http://www.xjnews.com.cn/newsshow.asp?id=33703&ntitle=0895f95a63acb269d809e66d d4ea1240 (accessed September 26, 2006).

Luo Yingfu. 1992. *Zongjiao wenti jianlun* [*A Brief Discussion of the Religious Question*]. Wulumuqi: Xinjiang renmin chubanshe.

Lynch, Daniel C. 1999. "Dilemmas of 'Thought Work' in Fin-de-Siecle China." *China Quarterly* 157, no. 1:173–201.

Macartney, C. A. 1934. *National States and National Minorities*. Oxford: Oxford University Press.

Maccartney, Jane. 1996a. "China Gives Tibet Separatists Surrender Ultimatum" [newswire]. Reuters, May 29. Available from Factiva (accessed January 13, 2008).

————. 1996b. "China's Inner Mongolia Warns Against Separatists" [newswire]. Reuters, June 6. Available from Factiva (accessed June 1, 2006).

————. 1996c. "China to Build Steel Great Wall Against Separatism" [newswire]. Reuters, June 4. Available from Factiva (accessed June 1, 2006).

———. 2006. "Beijing Pledges 'a Fight to the Death' with Dalai Lama" [online newspaper]. *Times Online*, August 14. Available from http://www.timesonline.co.uk/article/0,,25689-2312796,00 .html (accessed August 16, 2006).

Mackerras, Colin, ed. 1972. *The Uighur Empire According to the T'ang Dynastic Histories: A Study in Sino-Uighur Relations, 744–840*. Canberra: Australian National University Press.

Mackerras, Colin. 1990. "The Uighurs." In *The Cambridge History of Early Inner Asia*, edited by Denis Sinor, 317–42. Cambridge: Cambridge University Press.

———. 1994. *China's Minorities: Integration and Modernization in the Twentieth Century*. Oxford: Oxford University Press.

———. 2004a. "What Is China? Who Is Chinese? Han–Minority Relations, Legitimacy, and the State." In *State and Society in 21st-Century China*, edited by Peter Hays Gries and Stanley Rosen, 216–34. New York: RoutledgeCurzon.

———. 2004b. "Why Terrorism Bypasses China's Far West." *Asia Times*, April 23. Available from www.atimes.com/atimes/China/FD23Ad03.html (accessed December 4, 2004).

Mackey, Robert. 2009. "Another Media Tour Goes Very, Very Badly for Chinese Authorities." In *The Lede—The New York Times News Blog*, July 7. Available from http://thelede.blogs.nytimes. com/2009/07/07/media-tour-goes-very-very-badly-for-chinese-authorities (accessed October 30, 2009).

Ma Dazheng, ed. 1990. *Zhongguo gudai bianjiang zhengce yanjiu* [*Research on Frontier Policies in Ancient China*]. Beijing: Zhongguo shehui kexue chubanshe.

———. 2003. *Guojia liyi gaoyu yiqie—Xinjiang wending wenti de guancha yu sikao* [*The National Interest Above All Else—Analysis of and Reflections on the Problem of Stability in Xinjiang*]. Edited by Zhong-guo shehui kexueyuan Xinjiang fazhan yanjiu zhongxin. Ürümci: Xinjiang renmin chubanshe.

Ma Rong. 2004. "Lijie minzu guanxi de xin silu—Shaoshu zuqun wentide 'qu zhengzhi hua'" [New Thoughts on How to Understand *Minzu* Relations—"Depoliticizing" the Problem of Ethnic Minorities]. *Beijing daxue xuebao* (*zhexue shehui kexue ban*) 41, no. 6:122–33.

Maddox, Richard. 1997. "Bombs, Bikinis, and the Popes of Rock 'n' Roll: Reflections on Resistance, the Play of Subordinations, and Liberalism in Andalusia and Academia, 1983–1995." In *Culture, Power, Place: Explorations in Critical Anthropology*, edited by Akhil Gupta and James Ferguson, 277–90. Durham, N.C.: Duke University Press.

Madsen, Richard, and Center for Chinese Studies, University of California at Berkeley. 1984. *Morality and Power in a Chinese Village*. Berkeley: University of California Press.

Mähmud Sulayman. 1994. *Seni dedim* [*I Spoke of You*]: Guangdong jinhui yinxiang chubanshe. tape.

Mair, Victor H. 2005. "The North(West)Ern Peoples and the Recurrent Origins of the 'Chinese' State." In *The Teleology of the Modern Nation-State: Japan and China*, edited by Joshua A. Fogel, 46–84. Philadelphia: University of Pennsylvania Press.

Maitra, Ramtanu. 2005. "U.S. on Nepal's Case" [online newspaper]. *Asia Times Online*, July 23. Available from http://www.atimes.com/atimes/South_Asia/GG23Df04.html (accessed July 24, 2005).

Mallory, J. P., and Victor H. Mair. 2000. *The Tarim Mummies: Ancient China and the Mystery of the Earliest Peoples from the West*. New York: Thames & Hudson.

Mao Yongfu and Li Ling. 1996. "Nanjiang san dizhou shehui jingji fazhan de shehuixue sikao" [Sociological Reflections on Socioeconomic Development in Three Regions of Southern Xinjiang]. In *Xinjiang minzu guanxi yanjiu* [*Research on Minzu Relations in Xinjiang*], edited by Yin Zhuguang and Mao Yongfu. Urumchi: Xinjiang renmin chubanshe.

Mao Zedong. 1977 (1956). "Lun shi da guanxi" [On the Ten Major Relationships]. In *Mao Zedong xuanji* [*Selected Works of Mao Zedong*], 267–88. Beijing: Renmin chubanshe.

Marquand, Robert. 2003. "Pressure to Conform in West China." *Christian Science Monitor*, September 29. Available from http://www.csmonitor.com/2003/0929/p06s01-woap.html (accessed September 30, 2003).

Martin, Terry. 2001. *The Affirmative Action Empire: Nations and Nationalism in the Soviet Union, 1923–1939*. Ithaca, N.Y.: Cornell University Press.

McGibbon, Rodd. 2004. "Secessionist Challenges in Aceh and Papua: Is Special Autonomy the Solution?" *Policy Studies*, no. 10:1–96.

McMillen, Donald H. 1979. *Chinese Communist Power and Policy in Xinjiang, 1949–77*. Boulder. Colo.: Westview Press.

———. 1981. "Xinjiang and the Production and Construction Corps: A Han Organization in a Non-Han Region." *Australian Journal of Chinese Affairs*, no. 6:65–96.

———. 1984. "Xinjiang and Wang Enmao: New Directions in Power, Policy, and Integration?" *China Quarterly*, no. 99:569–93.

McNeal, Dewardric L. 2002. "China's Relations with Central Asian States and Problems with Terrorism." Washington, D.C.: Congressional Research Service.

Migdal, Joel S. 1988. *Strong Societies and Weak States: State–Society Relations and State Capabilities in the Third World*. Princeton, N.J.: Princeton University Press.

———. 2001. *State in Society: Studying How States and Societies Transform and Constitute One Another*. Cambridge: Cambridge University Press.

Migdal, Joel S., Atul Kohli, and Vivienne Shue, eds. 1994. *State Power and Social Forces: Domination and Transformation in the Third World*. Cambridge: Cambridge University Press.

Millward, James A. 1996. "New Perspectives on the Qing Frontier." In *Remapping China: Fissures in Historical Terrain*, edited by Gail Hershatter, Emily Honig, Jonathan N. Lipman, and Randall Stross, 113–29. Stanford, Calif.: Stanford University Press.

———. 1998. *Beyond the Pass: Economy, Ethnicity, and Empire in Qing Central Asia, 1759–1864*. Stanford, Calif.: Stanford University Press.

———. 2000. "Historical Perspectives on Contemporary Xinjiang." *Inner Asia* 2, no. 2:121–35.

———. 2004. "Violent Separatism in Xinjiang: A Critical Assessment." *Policy Studies*, no. 6:1–41.

———. 2007. *Eurasian Crossroads: A History of Xinjiang.* New York: Columbia University Press.

Millward, James A., and Peter C. Perdue. 2004. "Political and Cultural History of the Xinjiang Region Through the Late Nineteenth Century." In *Xinjiang: China's Muslim Borderland*, edited by S. Frederick Starr, 27–62. Armonk, N.Y.: Sharpe.

Millward, James A., and Nabijan Tursun. 2004. "Political History and Strategies of Control, 1884–1978." In *Xinjiang: China's Muslim Borderland*, edited by S. Frederick Starr, 63–98. Armonk, N.Y.: Sharpe.

Mirsky, Jonathan. 1998. "China Plays the Dissident Card." *International Herald Tribune*, February 12, 8.

Mishra, Pankaj. 2005. "The Restless Children of the Dalai Lama." *New York Times Magazine*, December 8, 58–63.

Moneyhon, Matthew. 2002. "Controlling Xinjiang: Autonomy on China's New Frontier." *Asia-Pacific Law & Policy Journal* 3, no. 1:120–52.

Mooney, Paul. 2004. "China Faces up to Growing Unrest." *Asia Times Online*, November 16. Available from http://www.atimes.com/atimes/China/FK16Ad01.html (accessed June 11, 2006).

Moore, Donald S. 1998. "Subaltern Struggles and the Politics of Place: Remapping Resistance in Zimbabwe's Eastern Highlands." *Cultural Anthropology* 13, no. 3:344–81.

Moseley, George. 1965. "China's Fresh Approach to the National Minority Question." *China Quarterly*, no. 24:14–27.

Näbijan Tursun. 2008. "The Formation of Modern Uyghur Historiography and Competing Perspectives Toward Uyghur History." *China and Eurasia Forum Quarterly* 6 no.:87–100.

Naby, Eden. 1986. "Uighur Elites in Xinjiang." *Central Asian Survey* 5, no. 3/4:241–54.

———. 1991. "Uighur Literature: The Antecedents." In *Cultural Change and Continuity in Central Asia*, edited by Shirin Akiner, 14–28. New York: Kegan Paul.

Naribilige (Naran Bilik). 1995. "Minzu yu minzu gainian zai bianzheng" [A Further Clarification of *Minzu* and the *Minzu* Concept]. *Minzu yanjiu*, no. 3:9–16.

Nathan, Andrew J. 1986. *Chinese Democracy.* Berkeley: University of California Press.

"947 ming yuan jiang ganbu fen fu Tianshan nan bei" [947 Cadres Sent to Help Xinjiang Traveled to Various Places in Northern and Southern Parts of the Region]. 2005. [*Online News*, originally *Xinjiang Daily*]. Tianshannet, September 1. Available from http://www.tianshannet.com.cn/GB/channel3/17/200509/01/181680.html (accessed October 30, 2005).

Ning Sao. 1995. *Minzu yu guojia: Minzu guanxi yu minzu zhengce de guoji bijiao* [*Minzu and State: An International Comparison of Minzu Relations and Minzu Policies*]. Beijing: Beijing daxue chubanshe.

Norins, Martin R. 1944. *Gateway to Asia: Sinkiang, Frontier of the Chinese Far West.* New York: John Day.

Nurmuhämmät Yasin. 2004. "Yawa käptär" [Wild Pigeon] *Qäšqär ädäbiyati*, no. 5. Available from http://www.rfa.org/english/uyghur/2005/06/27/wild_pigeon/ (accessed June 27, 2005).

O'Brien, Kevin J. 1996. "Rightful Resistance." *World Politics* 49, no. 1:31–55.

———. 2003. "Neither Transgressive nor Contained: Boundary-Spanning Contention in China." *Mobilization: An International Journal* 8, no. 1:51–64.

Oi, Jean C. 1989. *State and Peasant in Contemporary China: The Political Economy of Village Government*. Berkeley: University of California Press.

Olcott, Martha Brill. 1997. "Kazakhstan: Pushing for Eurasia." In *New States, New Politics: Building the Post-Soviet Nations*, edited by Ian Bremmer and Ray Taras, 547–64. Cambridge: Cambridge University Press.

Ong, Russell. 2005. "China's Security Interests in Central Asia." *Central Asian Survey* 24, no. 4:425–39.

"PA." 2005. "China Blocks BBC World Channel" [online news]. *The Scotsman*, March 11. Available from http://news.scotsman.com/print.cfm?id=4241102 (accessed March 14, 2005).

Pan, Philip P. 2002. "In China's West, Ethnic Strife Becomes 'Terrorism.'" *Washington Post*, July 15, A12.

Pan Zhiping, ed. 1999. *Minzu zijue haishi minzu fenlie* [*Minzu Self-Determination or Minzu Splitting*]. Ürümci: Xinjiang renmin chubanshe.

———. 2001. "Women Zhongguo shi nengou jiejue minzu wenti de—Du 'Deng Xiaoping minzu lilun ji qi zai Xinjiang de shijian" [Our China Is Capable of Solving *Minzu* Problems—Reading "Deng Xiaoping's *Minzu* Theory and Its Realization in Xinjiang"]. *Xinjiang shehui kexue*, no. 1:91–92.

Papas, Alexandre. 2005. *Soufisme et politique entre Chine, Tibet et Turkestan: Étude sur les Khwajas Naqshbandis du Turkestan oriental*. Paris: Librairie d'Amérique et d'Orient.

Parish, William L. 1978. *Village and Family in Contemporary China*. Chicago: University of Chicago Press.

Pei, Minxin. 2002. "Self-Administration and Local Autonomy: Reconciling Conflicting Interests in China." In *The Self-Determination of Peoples: Community, Nation, and State in an Interdependent World*, edited by Wolfgang Danspeckgruber, 315–32. Boulder, Colo.: Lynne Rienner.

Perdue, Peter C. 2005a. *China Marches West: The Qing Conquest of Central Eurasia*. Cambridge, Mass.: Harvard University Press.

———. 2005b. "Where Do Incorrect Political Ideas Come From? Writing the History of the Qing Empire and the Chinese Nation." In *The Teleology of the Modern Nation-State: Japan and China*, edited by Joshua A. Fogel, 174–99. Philadelphia: University of Pennsylvania Press.

Perry, Elizabeth J. 2001. "Challenging the Mandate of Heaven: Popular Protest in Modern China." *Critical Asian Studies* 33, no. 2:163–80.

Pipes, Richard. 1968. *The Formation of the Soviet Union: Communism and Nationalism, 1917–1923*. Rev. ed. New York: Atheneum.

Pomfret, John. 2000. "Chinese Workers Are Showing Disenchantment." *Washington Post*, April 23, A23.

"PRC: AFP Reports Further on Clashes in Xinjiang." 1996. *AFP* May 31. FBIS-CHI-96–107.

"PRC: Exiled Leader Claims 20 Dead in Street Fighting in Xinjiang." 1996. *AFP* May 31. FBIS-CHI-96–107.

"PRC: Security Official Says Deaths in Xinjiang 'Pure Lies.'" 1996. *AFP* June 1. FBIS-CHI-96–107.

Pulleyblank, Edwin G. 1956. "Some Remarks on the Toquzoghuz Problem." *Ural-Altaische Jahrbücher* 28, nos. 1–2:35–42.

Pye, Lucian. 1966. *Aspects of Political Development*. Boston: Little, Brown.

"Qazaqstanda Qazaq azayip, Uyghirlar köbeyip zhatir" [In Kazakhstan Qazaqs Are Decreasing, Uyghurs Are Multiplying]. 2000. *Qazaq eli*, April 5.

Qiu Yuanyao, ed. 1994. *Kua shijide Zhongguo renkou: Xinjiang juan* [*China's Population Across the Millennial Divide: Xinjiang Volume*]. Beijing: Zhongguo tongji chubanshe.

Qurban Wäli. 1988. *Bizning tarikhiy yäziqlirimiz* [*Our Historical Scripts*]. Ürümci: Šinjang yašlar-ösmürlär näšriyati.

Rabgey, Tashi, and Tseten Wangchuk Sharlho. 2004. *Sino-Tibetan Dialogue in the Post-Mao Era: Lessons and Prospects*. Vol. 12. Washington, D.C.: East-West Center.

Rahman, Anwar. 2005. *Sincization Beyond the Great Wall: China's Xinjiang Uighur Autonomous Region*. Leicester: Matador.

Raič, D. 2002. *Statehood and the Law of Self-Determination*. New York: Kluwer Law International.

Raman, B. 1999. "Continuing Unrest in Xinjiang." South Asia Analysis Group. Available from http://www.saag.org/papers/paper41.html (accessed February 14, 2003).

———. 2002. "US & Terrorism in Xinjiang: Paper no. 499." South Asia Analysis Group, July 7. Available from http://www.saag.org/papers5/paper499.html (accessed February 14, 2003).

Rashid, Ahmed. 2003. *Jihad: The Rise of Militant Islam in Central Asia*. New York: Penguin.

"'Rebellion' Quelling Detailed." 1990. Xinjiang Television Network (Ürümci), April 22, 1990. FBIS-CHI-90–078.

"Rebiya Kadeer's Funding Sources." 2009. *Global Times*, July 14 [cited July 15, 2009]. Available from http://www.globaltimes.cn/www/english/truexinjiang/urumqi-riot/rebiya-kadeer/2009-07/446397.html.

Renan, Ernst. 1990 (1882). "What Is a Nation?" In *Nation and Narration*, edited by Homi K. Bhabha, 8–22. London: Routledge.

"Rencai gaoji! Xinjiang 20 nian liushi rencai 21 wan" [Human Capital Emergency! Xinjiang's Brain Drain 210 Thousand over 20 Years]. 2002. [newswire]. *China Info*, March 15. Available from http://www.chinainfo.gov.cn/data/200203/1_20020315_30139.html (accessed June 4, 2006).

"Renmin ribao" pinglunyuan. 1975. "Dong dimen renmin de Duliquan bu rong qinfan" [The Right of the People of East Timor to Independence Cannot Be Infringed Upon]. *Xinjiang ribao*, December 10.

Reporters sans Frontières. 2002. "Severe Crackdown in Defence of the State Monopoly on Information" [online news], April 23. Available from http://www.rsf.org/article.php?id_article=1386 (accessed May 28, 2002).

Reuters. 2003. "China Quake Highlights Ethnic Rift in Xinjiang" [newswire], March 25. Available from Factiva (accessed March 25, 2003).

———. 2008. "China Warns Dalai Lama Against Tibetan Autonomy." *International Herald Tribune*. Available from http://www.iht.com/articles/2008/11/10/arts/tibet.php (accessed February 1, 2009).

———. 2009. "Needle Attacks and Rumors Spread in China's Xinjiang." ABS-CBN News Online, September 11. Available from http://www.abs-cbnnews.com/print/70164 (accessed September 14, 2009).

(RFA) Radio Free Asia. 2004. "Police in Xinjiang Detain Protesters," June 18. Available from http://www.rfa.org/english/news/social/2004/06/18/138541/ (accessed June 2, 2006).

———. 2005a. "Chinese Court Jails Uyghur Editor for Publishing Veiled Dissent" [online news], November 10. Available from http://www.rfa.org/english/uyghur/2005/11/10/uyghur_kashgar/ (accessed November 11, 2005).

———. 2005b. "Wild Pigeon: A Uyghur Fable" [online news], June 27. Available from http://www.rfa.org/english/news/arts/2005/06/27/uyghur_literature/ (accessed June 27, 2005).

———. 2006a. "China Bans Officials, State Employees, Children from Mosques," February 6. Available from http://www.rfa.org/english/news/2006/02/06/uyghur_religion/ (accessed February 6, 2006).

———. 2006b. "China Closes Investigative Pages of Top Newspaper," January 24. Available from http://www.rfa.org/english/china/2006/01/24/china_media/ (accessed January 24, 2006).

———. 2006c. "No Word for Wife on Jailed Uyghur Writer's Fate," January 19. Available from http://www.rfa.org/english/news/politics/2006/06/19/uyghur_writer/ (accessed January 20, 2006).

(RFE/RL) Radio Free Europe / Radio Liberty. 2000. *Turkmen Report: July 8, 2000*. Available from http://www.rferl.org/content/article/1347130.html (accessed June 3, 2006).

(RFE/RL) Radio Free Europe / Radio Liberty. 2006. "China, Kyrgyzstan Sign Cooperation Agreements." AFP. Available from http://www.rferl.org/featuresarticle/2006/06/46B8A21F-0352-4FF2-B119-8139397B93D3.html (accessed June 9, 2006).

Richardson, Michael. 1998. "Beijing Watching Indonesia Violence New Attacks Aimed at Ethnic Chinese Viewed as Test for Jakarta." *International Herald Tribune*, August 14, 4.

Roberts, Sean R. 1996. *Waiting for Uighurstan* [documentary film]. Los Angeles: Center for Visual Anthropology, University of Southern California.

———. 1998a. "Negotiating Locality, Islam, and National Culture in a Changing Borderlands: The Revival of the Mäshräp Ritual Among Young Uighur Men in the Ili Valley." *Central Asian Survey* 17, no. 4:673–700.

———. 1998b. "The Uighurs of the Kazakstan Borderlands: Migration and the Nation." *Nationalities Papers* 26, no. 3:511–30.

———. 2004. "A 'Land of Borderlands': Implications of Xinjiang's Trans-Border Interactions." In *Xinjiang: China's Muslim Borderland*, edited by S. Frederick Starr, 216–37. Armonk, N.Y.: Sharpe.

Roeder, Philip G. 1991. "Soviet Federalism and Ethnic Mobilization." *World Politics* 43:196–232.

Rood, Steven. 2005. "Forging Sustainable Peace in Mindanao: The Role of Civil Society." *Policy Studies*, no. 17:1–64.

Rossabi, Morris, ed. 2004. *Governing China's Multiethnic Frontiers*. Seattle: University of Washington Press.

Rotar, Igor. 2005. *Xinjiang: How Long Will Arrested Sufi Muslims Be Held?* Forum 18, September 26. Available from http://www.forum18.org/Archive.php?article_id=659&printer=Y (accessed September 26, 2005).

Roy, Olivier. 2000. *The New Central Asia: The Creation of Nations*. New York: New York University Press.

———. 2002. "Islamic Ferments and State Responses in Central Asia: Is There a Chinese Card?" In *La Chine et son occident*, edited by François Godement, 139–56. Paris: Insitut français des releations internationales (IFRI).

Rudelson, Justin Jon. 1991. "Uighur Historiography and Uighur Ethnic Nationalism." In *Ethnicity, Minorities, and Cultural Encounters*, edited by Ingvar Svanberg, 63–82. Uppsala: Centre for Multiethnic Research, Uppsala University.

———. 1992. "Bones in the Sand: The Struggle to Create Uighur Nationalist Ideologies in Xinjiang, China." PhD diss., Harvard University.

———. 1997. *Oasis Identities: Uyghur Nationalism Along China's Silk Road*. New York: Columbia University Press.

Rudelson, Justin Jon, and William Jankowiak. 2004. "Acculturation and Resistance: Xinjiang Identities in Flux." In *Xinjiang: China's Muslim Borderland*, edited by S. Frederick Starr, 299–316. Armonk, N.Y.: Sharpe.

Ruwitch, John. 2004. "China Convicts 50 to Death in 'Terror Crackdown'" [newswire]. Reuters, September 13. Available from http://www/alertnet.org/thenews/newsdesk/PEK347706.htm (accessed December 9, 2004).

Sabit Abdurakhman. 2002. *Uyghurstan azatliq täškilati wä uning inqilabiy pa'aliyiti (1992–2002 yillarni öz icigä alidu)* [*The Uyghurstan Liberation Organization and Its Revolutionary Activities (Comprising the Years 1992–2002)*. Almaty: n.p.

Said, Edward W. 1993. *Culture and Imperialism*. New York: Knopf.

Salisbury, Harrison. 1970. "Russian Eyes on Sinkiang." *New York Times*, March 3, 10.

Šärqiy Türkistan Jumhuriyiti Sürgündiki Parlamenti wä Hökümiti. 2005. Constitution of the Republic of Eastern Turkistan. Istanbul: Enes Ofset.

Sautman, Barry. 1997. "Myths of Descent, Racial Nationalism and Ethnic Minorities in the People's Republic of China." In *The Construction of Racial Identities in China and Japan*, edited by Frank Dikötter, 75–95. Honolulu: University of Hawai'i Press.

———. 1999. "Ethnic Law and Minority Rights in China." *Law and Policy* 21, no. 3:283–314.

Savadove, Bill. 2005. "Faith Flourishes in an Arid Wasteland; Muslim Sect in Ningxia Accepts Beijing's Authority and Is Allowed to Build a Virtual Religious State." *South China Morning Post*, August 17. Available from Factiva (accessed August 18, 2005).

Säypidin Äzizi. 1995. "Carry Forward the Cause, Create More Glories—Marking the 40th Anniversary of the Establishment of the Xinjiang Uygur Autonomous Region." *Renmin ribao*, September 28, FBIS-CHI-95-221.

Schoenhals, Michael. 1992. *Doing Things with Words in Chinese Politics: Five Studies*. Vol. 41. Berkeley: Institute of East Asian Studies, University of California.

———. 1994. *"Non-People" in the People's Republic of China: A Chronicle of Terminological Ambiguity*. Indiana East Asian Working Papers Series on Language and Politics in Modern China. Bloomington: East Asian Studies Center, Indiana University. Available from http://www.easc.indiana.edu/Pages/Easc/working_papers/framed_4A_PEOPL.htm (accessed July 29 2001).

Schwartz, Ronald D. 1994. *Circle of Protest: Political Ritual in the Tibetan Uprising*. New York: Columbia University Press.

Scott, James C. 1985. *Weapons of the Weak: Everyday Forms of Peasant Resistance*. New Haven, Conn.: Yale University Press.

———. 1986. "Everyday Forms of Peasant Resistance." In *Everyday Forms of Peasant Resistance in South-East Asia*, edited by James C. Scott and Benedict J. Kerkvliet, 5–35. London: Cass.

———. 1990. *Domination and the Arts of Resistance: Hidden Transcripts*. New Haven, Conn.: Yale University Press.

Scott, James C., and Benedict J. Kerkvliet, eds. 1986. *Everyday Forms of Peasant Resistance in South-East Asia*. London: Cass.

Seton-Watson, Hugh. 1977. *Nations and States: An Enquiry into the Origins of Nations and the Politics of Nationalism*. Boulder, Colo.: Westview Press.

Seymour, James D. 2000. "Xinjiang's Production and Construction Corps, and the Sinification of Eastern Turkestan." *Inner Asia* 2, no. 2:171–93.

Shakya, Tsering W. 1999. *The Dragon in the Land of Snows: A History of Modern Tibet Since 1947*. New York: Columbia University Press.

Sheridan, Michael. 2000. "China Hides Its Muslim Separatist War." *Sunday Times*, December 10. Available from Factiva (accessed January 16, 2006).

———. 2008. "Young Tibetans 'Will Resist China with Blood.'" *Times Online*, November 16. Available from http://www.timesonline.co.uk/tol/news/world/asia/article5162348.ece (accessed February 1, 2009).

Shichor, Yitzhak. 2003. "Virtual Transnationalism: Uygur Communities in Europe and the Quest for Eastern Turkestan Independence." In *Muslim Networks and Transnational Communities in and across Europe*, edited by Jorgen S. Nielsen and Stefano Allievi, 281–311. Leiden: Brill.

———. 2004. "The Great Wall of Steel: Military and Strategy in Xinjiang." In *Xinjiang: China's Muslim Borderland*, edited by S. Frederick Starr, 120–60. Armonk, N.Y.: Sharpe.

———. 2005. "Blow Up: Internal and External Challenges of Uyghur Separatism and Islamic Radicalism to Chinese Rule in Xinjiang." *Asian Affairs: An American Review* 32, no. 2:119–35.

———. 2006a. "Company Province: Civil–Military Relations in Xinjiang." In *Chinese Civil–Military Relations: The Transformation of the People's Liberation Army*, edited by Nan Li, 135–50. London: Routledge.

———. 2006b. "Fact and Fiction: A Chinese Documentary on Eastern Turkestan Terrorism." *China and Eurasia Forum Quarterly* 4, no. 2:89–108.

Shue, Vivienne B. 1991. "Powers of State, Paradoxes of Dominion: China 1949–1979." In *Perspectives on Modern China: Four Anniversaries*, edited by Kenneth Lieberthal, Joyce Kallgren, Roderick MacFarquhar, and Frederic Wakeman Jr., 205–25. Armonk, N.Y.: Sharpe.

Shultz, Richard H., and Roy Godson. 1984. *Dezinformatsia: Active Measures in Soviet Strategy*. Washington, D.C.: Pergamon–Brassey's.

Sinor, Denis. 1990. "The Hun Period." In *The Cambridge History of Early Inner Asia*, edited by Denis Sinor, 177–205. Cambridge: Cambridge University Press.

Skrine, C. P., and Pamela Nightingale. 1973. *Macartney at Kashgar: New Light on British, Chinese and Russian Activities in Sinkiang, 1890–1918*. London: Methuen.

Smith, Joanne N. 1999. "Changing Uyghur Identities in Xinjiang in the 1990s." PhD diss., University of Leeds.

———. 2000. "Four Generations of Uyghurs: The Shift Towards Ethno-Political Ideologies among Xinjiang's Youth." *Inner Asia* 2, no. 2:195–224.

———. 2002. "'Making Culture Matter': Symbolic, Spatial and Social Boundaries Between Uyghurs and Han Chinese." *Asian Ethnicity* 3, no. 2:153–74.

———. 2006. "Maintaining Margins: The Politics of Ethnographic Fieldwork in Chinese Central Asia." *China Journal*, no. 56:132–47.

———. 2007. "The Quest for National Unity in Popular Song: Barren Chickens, Stray Dogs, Fake Immortals and Thieves." In *Music, National Identity, and the Politics of Location: Between the Global and the Local*, edited by Ian Biddle and Vanessa Knights, 115–41. Aldershot: Ashgate.

Snow, David A., E. Burke Rochford Jr., Steven K. Worden, and Robert D. Benford. 1986. "Frame Alignment Processes, Micromobilization, and Movement Participation." *American Sociological Review* 51, no. 4:464–81.

Solinger, Dorothy J. 1977. *Regional Government and Political Integration in Southwest China, 1949–1954*. Berkeley: University of California Press.

Sommerville, Quentin. 2005. "China's Grip on Xinjiang Muslims" [online news]. *BBC News*, November 29. Available from http://news.bbc.co.uk/2/hi/asia-pacific/4482048.stm (accessed November 29, 2005).

Song Tianshui. 2005. "Yanfang yanse geming raoluan Xinjiang" [Strictly Guard Against Color Revolutions' Disturbing Xinjiang] [newspaper article]. Chinaelections.org, June 3. Available from http://www.chinaelections.org/NewsInfo.asp?NewsID=6943 (accessed August 21, 2006).

Song Xinwei. 2005. "'Dong Tu' wenti bu duan shengji de yuanyin ji duice" [The Reasons the East Turkistan Problem Continues to Sharpen and Countermeasures]. *Xinjiang shifan daxue xuebao* 26, no. 1:80–83.

Southerland, Daniel. 2005. "China's Changing Strategic Concerns: The Impact on Human Rights in Xinjiang—Statement of Daniel Southerland." Washington, D.C.: Congressional–Executive Commission on China.

Spiegel Interview with Tibet's Communist Party Chief: Dalai Lama "Deceived His Motherland." 2006. *Spiegel Online*, August 16. Available from http://service.spiegel.de/cache/international/spiegel/0,1518,431922,00.html (accessed August 16, 2006).

Stein, Justin J. 2003. "Taking the Deliberative Turn in China: International Law, Minority Rights, and the Case of Xinjiang." *Journal of Public and International Affairs* 14:1–25.

Strauss, Neil. 1999. "In a Far-Flung Corner of China, a Folk Star." *New York Times*, February 7, 30.

Sun Wen (Sun Zhongshan). 1985. *Sanmin zhuyi [The Three People's Principles]*. Edited by Committee on Guomindang Party History. Expanded, with the two texts, "The People's Livelihood" and "Happiness," appended. Taibei: Zhongyang wenwu gongying she.

Sun Yat-sen (Sun Zhongshan). 1919/1994. "The Three Principles of the People." In *Prescriptions for Saving China: Selected Writings of Sun Yat-Sen*, edited by Julie Lee Wei, Ramon H. Myers, and Donald G. Gillin, 222–25. Stanford, Calif.: Hoover Institution Press.

Suny, Ronald Grigor. 1995. "Ambiguous Categories: States, Empires and Nations." *Post-Soviet Affairs* 11, no. 2:185–96.

Svartzman, Jorge. 1997. "Xinjiang Leader Admits Existence of Moslem Party" [newswire]. Agence France-Presse, May 11. Available from Factiva (accessed August 7, 2006).

Svenska Uygur Kommittén. n.d. The Goal of the Swedish Uygur Committe [*sic*] [webpage]. Available from http://www.uygurie.com/English/Goal.htm (accessed August 9, 2006).

Syroezhkin, Konstantin. 2003. "We Don't Want Any Bloodshed" [online magazine]. *Kontinent*, no. 14, July 2. Available from http://www.continent.kz/eng/2003/14/2e.html (accessed July 1, 2006).

Szonyi, Michael. 2000. "Commentary no. 79: Potential for Domestic Instability in the People's Republic of China in the Medium-Term (2001–2006)." Ottawa: Canadian Security Intelligence Service. Available from http://www.csis-scrs.gc.ca/en/publications/commentary/com79.asp (accessed July 25, 2006).

Tanner, Harold M. 1999. *Strike Hard! Anti-Crime Campaigns and Chinese Criminal Justice 1979–1985.* Ithaca, N.Y.: Cornell East Asia Program.

Tanner, Murray Scott. 2005. "Testimony: Chinese Government Responses to Rising Social Unrest." Santa Monica, Calif.: RAND Corporation.

Tarimi, N T. 2004. "China–Uzbek Pact Bad News for Uighurs." *Asia Times Online*, July 30. Available from http://www.atimes.com/atimes/Central_Asia/FG30Ag01.html (accessed September 1, 2004).

Tarrow, Sidney. 1994. *Power in Movement: Social Movements, Collective Action, and Politics.* Cambridge: Cambridge University Press.

Taynen, Jennifer. 2004. "The Rise of Modern Uighur Nationalism." Master's thesis, University of Toronto.

Teichman, Eric. 1937. *Journey to Turkistan.* London: Hodder & Stoughton.

Thwaites, Dilber Kahraman. 2005. "An Uyghur Meshrep Dichotomy." *Central Eurasian Studies Review* 4, no. 2:22–25.

Tian Mengqing. 2000. "Shilun minzu guanxi de tiaojie fangshi ji qi xuanze" [An Exploratory Discussion of Methods for Adjusting *Minzu* Relations and Selecting Among Them]. *Xinjiang shehui jingji,* no. 5:72–74.

"Tighter Security for Chinese Diplomats in Pakistan." 2006. [online news]. India eNews.com, June 26. Available from http://indiaenews.com/print/?article=12707 (accessed June 27, 2006).

Tilly, Charles. 1975. "Reflections on the History of European State-Making." In *The Formation of National States in Western Europe*, edited by Charles Tilly, 3–83. Princeton, N.J.: Princeton University Press.

Toops, Stanley W. 1992. "Recent Uygur Leaders in Xinjiang." *Central Asian Survey* 11, no. 2:77–99.

———. 2004a. "The Demography of Xinjiang." In *Xinjiang: China's Muslim Borderland*, edited by S. Frederick Starr, 241–63. Armonk, N.Y.: Sharpe.

———. 2004b. "The Ecology of Xinjiang: A Focus on Water." In *Xinjiang: China's Muslim Borderland*, edited by S. Frederick Starr, 264–75. Armonk, N.Y.: Sharpe.

Traub, James. 2006. "The World According to China." *New York Times Magazine*, September 3, 24–29. Available from http://www.nytimes.com/2006/09/03/magazine/03ambassador.html (accessed September 4, 2006).

Tsai, Kellee S. 2005. "Capitalists Without a Class: Political Diversity Among Private Entrepreneurs in China." *Comparative Political Studies* 38, no. 9:1130–58.

"Tuanjie qilai hanwei duli—Zhuhe Angela renmin jieshu putaoya zhimin tongzhi de shengli" [Unite to Protect Independence—Congratulations on the Victory of the Angolan People in Ending Portuguese Colonial Rule]. 1975. *Xinjiang ribao*, November 14.

Turani, Anwar Yusuf. 2004. "Jiddi ukhturush Sinteber 12, 2004" [Important Announcement September 12, 2004] [webpage]. East Turkistan National Freedom Center, September 12. Available from http://etnfc.org/page40.html (accessed November 2, 2004).

Turghun Almas. 1986. "Uyghurlarning ana wätini häqqidä" [Concerning the Home Country of the Uyghurs]. *Qäšqär pidagogika inistituti ilmiy zhornili*, no. 1:47–67.

———. 1989. *Uyghurlar* [*The Uyghurs*]. Ürümci: Šinjang yašlar-ösmürlär näšriyati.

Tursun Islam. 2004. *Šärqiy Türkistan jumhuriyitining 60 yili* [*60 Years of the Eastern Turkistan Republic*]. Istanbul: Täklimakan Uyghur näšriyati.

Tyler, Christian. 2003. *Wild West China: The Taming of Xinjiang*. London: John Murray.

Tyler, Patrick E. 1997. "In China's Far West, Tensions with Ethnic Muslims Boil over in Riots and Bombings." *New York Times*, February 28, A8.

Uighur, M. E. 1983. "Sherki Türkistan evazi" [The Voice of Eastern Turkistan]. *Central Asian Survey* 1, no. 2/3:127–30.

"UN Has a Mission to Build New World Order." 2001. *China Daily*, February 15. Available from http://www.chinadaily.net/cndy/history/2001/02/d4-run.215.html (accessed February 19, 2001, link now defunct).

Ünal, Süleyman. 1995. "Dogu Türkistan Öksüz Kaldi" [online newspaper]. *Aksiyon*, December 23. Available from http://www.aksiyon.com.tr/detay.php?id=20144 (accessed September 1, 2005).

"Under the Thumb; China's Far West." 2005. *Economist*, December 1. Available from Factiva (accessed January 15, 2009).

U.S. Department of State. 2003. Patterns of Global Terrorism 2002. Available from http://www .state.gov/s/ct/rls/crt/2002/html/ (accessed December 5, 2004).

———. 2004. China—No Recognition of Any East Turkestan Government in Exile [press briefing], November 22. Available from http://www.state.gov/r/pa/prs/ps/2004/38594.htm (accessed June 3, 2006).

———. 2006. Country Reports on Human Rights Practices: China (Includes Tibet, Hong Kong, and Macau) 2005. Washington, D.C.: U.S. Department of State.

———. 2007. Report on International Religious Freedom: China (Includes Tibet, Hong Kong, and Macau) 2007. Washington, D.C.: U.S. Department of State.

Vidaillet, Tamora. 2001. "China Arrests Nine Muslims in Broad Crackdown" [newswire]. Reuters. Available from Factiva (accessed September 1, 2006).

Walder, Andrew. 1986. *Communist Neo-Traditionalism: Work and Authority in Chinese Industry*. Berkeley: University of California Press.

Walia, Shelley. 2001. *Edward Said and the Writing of History*. Cambridge: Icon Books.

Wang, David. 1998. "Han Migration and Social Changes in Xinjiang." *Issues and Studies* 34, no. 7:33–61.

———. 1999. *Under the Soviet Shadow: The Yining Incident, Ethnic Conflicts and International Rivalry in Xinjiang, 1944–49*. Hong Kong: Chinese University Press.

Wang Lequan. 1999. "Ji mi: Wang Lequan shuji zai Hetian diqu wending gongzuo huiyi shang de jianghua" [Top Secret: Secretary Wang Lequan's Speech at the Stabilization Work Meeting in Hotan District]. n.p.

———. 2003. "Xu yi" [First Preface]. In *Guojia liyi gaoyu yiqie—Xinjiang wending wenti de guancha yu sikao* [*The National Interest Above All Else—Analysis of and Reflections on the Problem of Stability in Xinjiang*], edited by Ma Dazheng. Ürümci: Xinjiang renmin chubanshe.

Wang, Lixiong. 2002. "Reflections on Tibet." *New Left Review*, no. 14:79–111.

Wang Shuanqian, ed. 1999. *Zou xiang 21 shiji de Xinjiang—Zhengzhi juan* [*Xinjiang Heading into the 21st Century—Volume on Politics*]. Ürümci: Xinjiang renmin chubanshe.

Watts, Jonathan. 2009. "Death and Debris on Urumqi's Streets, but in Beijing the Blame Game Begins." *Guardian*, July 6. Available from http://www.guardian.co.uk/world/2009/jul/06/china-urumqi-uighur-united-nations.

Weber, Eugen. 1976. *Peasants into Frenchmen: The Modernization of Rural France, 1870–1914*. Stanford, Calif.: Stanford University Press.

"Weiwu'erzu jianshi" bianxiezu, ed. 1991. *Weiwu'erzu jianshi* [*A Concise History of the Uyghurs*]. Ürümci: Xinjiang renmin chubanshe.

Wen Hui, Wang Peng, and Li Bengang, eds. 1992. *Dangdai xin ciyu da cidian* [*The Big Dictionary of Contemporary Neologisms*]. Dalian: Dalian chubanshe.

Whiting, Allen S. 1955. "Review: Rewriting Modern History in Communist China: A Review Article." *Far Eastern Survey* 24, no. 11:173–74.

———. 1960. "Sinkiang and Sino-Soviet Relations." *China Quarterly*, no. 3:32–41.

Whiting, Allen S., and Sheng Shih-ts'ai [Sheng Shicai]. 1958. *Sinkiang: Pawn or Pivot?* East Lansing: Michigan State University Press.

Whyte, Martin King. 1974. *Small Groups and Political Rituals in China*. Berkeley: University of California Press.

Whyte, Martin King, and William L. Parish. 1984. *Urban Life in Contemporary China*. Chicago: University of Chicago Press.

Williams, Melissa S. 1998. *Voice, Trust, and Memory: Marginalized Groups and the Failings of Liberal Representation*. Princeton, N.J.: Princeton University Press.

Wong, Edward, and Jonathan Ansfield. 2009. "Chinese President Visits Volatile Xinjiang." *New York Times*, August 26. Available from http://www.nytimes.com/2009/08/26/world/asia/26china.html?sq=xinjiang&st=cse&scp=1&pagewanted=print.

Working, Russell. 2001. "Fighting for Independence in the Shadow of a Goliath." *Japan Times Online*, November 6. Available from http://search.japantimes.co.jp/cgi-bin/eo20011106a1.html (accessed November 11, 2001).

World Uyghur Congress. 2006a. "East Turkistan." Available from http://www.uyghurcongress.org/En/AboutET.asp?mid=1107905016 (accessed July 18, 2006).

———. 2006b. "The World Uyghur Congress Successfully Concludes Its Second Assembly," November 28. Available from http://www.uyghurcongress.org/En/PressRelease.asp?ItemID=1164714960&mid=1096144499 (accessed December 1, 2006).

———. 2006c. "WUC Appreciates NED Funding of Its Human Rights Work," July 4. Available from http://www.uyghurcongress.org/En/pressrelease.asp?ItemID=1152260355 (accessed September 1, 2006).

Wright, David C. 1994. "Gong Zizhen and His Essay on the 'Western Regions.'" In *Opuscula Altaica: Essays Presented in Honor of Henry Schwarz*, edited by Edward H. Kaplan and Donald W. Whisenhunt, 655–85. Bellingham: Western Washington University Press.

Wu Qiyu. 1947. "Xinjiang wenti de fenxi ji qi jiejue tujing" [An Analysis of the Problems in Xinjiang and the Means to Their Solution]. *Tianwentai* [*The Observatory*] 1, no. 1:5–13.

Wu Xiongwu. 1994. *Zhonghua minzu jingshen xinlun—Ge minzu jingshen ronghui yu ningju* [*A New Theory of the Spirit of the Zhonghua Minzu—The Fusion and Cohesiveness of the Spirit of the Various Minzu*]. Kunming: Yunnan renmin chubanshe.

Xiaokaiti Yiming. 2002. "Ba guangbo yingshi jiancheng yishi xingtai lingyu fan fenlie douzheng de jianqiang zhendi" [Build Radio, Film, and Television into a Stalwart Front in the Struggle against Splittism on the Ideological Plane]. *Shiting tiandi*, no. 65. Available from www.xjbs .com.cn/sht/gj/65gj/3.htm (accessed August 13, 2005).

Xing Zhaoyuan and Wang Se. 2003. "Rencai dui xibu fazhan zhiguan zhongyao" [Talented People Are Extremely Important to Western Development] [online newspaper]. *Guangming ribao*, December 19. Available from http://www.gmw.cn/01gmrb/2003–12/19/02–46ACE9485C23F25 C48256E00008383C7.htm (accessed December 1, 2005).

Xinhua. 1975. "Balesitan tujidui yingyong daji yiselie qinlüezhe" [Palestinian Guerrillas Bravely Attack Israeli Invaders]. *Xinjiang ribao*, November 15.

———. 1999. "Yongyuan zhongqing zuguo—Bao'erhan houren yan zhong de xin Zhongguo" [Eternally Loyal to the Motherland—New China in the Eyes of Burhan's Descendants] [newswire], September 29. Available from http://211.143.249.205/gerenzhuyie/qinwei/ WWWFILE/guoqing/gqzj/guonei/3091704714.htm (accessed September 1, 2006).

———. 2002. "'Dong Tu'kongbu shili da jiemi: Feifa zuzhi da 50 yu ge"[Major Exposé of East Turkistan Terrorist Forces: There Are More Than 50 Illegal Organizations], February 1. Available from http://news.xinhuanet.com/newscenter/2002–02/01/content_263978.htm (accessed June 1, 2006).

———. 2004. "Chinese Police Call on German Counterparts to Stop Activities of 'Eastern Turkistan'Terrorist Groups" [online news], April 16. Available from Factiva (accessed December 9, 2004).

———. 2005. "China–Kazakhstan Pipeline Starts to Pump Oil." Available from http://www.chinadaily.com.cn/english/doc/2005–12/15/content_503709.htm (accessed February 2, 2009).

———. 2006. "Political Advisory System Can Help China Avoid 'Color Revolution': Advisor" [online newspaper]. *People's Daily Online*, March 10. Available from http://english.peopledaily. com.cn/200603/10/eng20060310 249588.html (accessed August 2, 2006).

———. 2008. "Xinjiang Armed Police Elevated to Greater Role in Fighting Terror." *People's Daily Online*, November 28. Available from http://english.peopledaily.com.cn/90001/90776/90882/6 542813.html (accessed February 1, 2009).

————. 2009. "Thousands of Harmony Makers Sent to Urumqi." *China Daily*, September 7 [cited October 1 2009]. Available from http://www.chinadaily.com.cn/ethnic/2009-09/07/content_8660860.htm.

Xinhuanet. 2002. "9 Yue 12 ri: Fayan ren jiu 'Dong Tu,' donghai chenchuan deng da jizhe wen" [September 12: Spokesperson Answers Reporters' Questions About "East Turkistan," About the Eastern Sea Shipwreck, and Other Matters] [online news], September 13. Available from http://news.xinhuanet.com/newscenter/2002-09/13/content_559871.htm (accessed August 9, 2006).

"Xinjiang 20 nian liushi rencai 21 wan" [Xinjiang's Brain Drain 210 Thousand over 20 Years]. 2001. [newswire]. *Union News Net*. Available from http://www.unn.com.cn/GB/channel445/446/1583/200103/16/45705.html (accessed March 16, 2001).

Xinjiang daxue xuesheng shouce [*Xinjiang University Student Handbook*]. 2005. Ürümci: Xinjiang University.

Xinjiang jiushi ti bianji weiyuanhui, ed. 1993. *Xinjiang jiushi ti* [*Ninety Questions on Xinjiang*]. Ürümci: Xinjiang renmin chubanshe.

"Xinjiang pilu da za qiang shao sha baoli fan zui shijian dang ri fazhan shimo" [Xinjiang Reveals How the Episode of Criminal Beating, Smashing, Looting, Burning, and Killing Unfolded on That Day]. 2009. *Zhongguo xinwen wang*, July 6 [cited July 12, 2009]. Available from http://www.chinanews.com.cn/gn/news/2009/07-06/1762907.shtml.

Xinjiang shehui kexueyuan lishi yanjiusuo [Institute of History at the Xinjiang Academy of Social Sciences], ed. 1987. *Xinjiang difang lishi ziliao xuanji* [*Selected Materials on the Local History of Xinjiang*]. Beijing: Renmin chubanshe.

"Xinjiang shouci pilu minzu fenlie shili zai yishi xingtai lingyu pohuai huodong de liu zhong xingshi" [Xinjiang Reveals for the First Time Minzu Splittists' Six Forms of Sabotaging Activities in the Ideological Sphere]. 2002. [PSB webpage]. Chinano.com, February 1. Available from http://www.chinano.com/police/plnews/gdjs/xinj/item/2002_02/579500.shtml (accessed June 1, 2006).

Xinjiang weiwu'er zizhiqu minzu shiwu weiyuanhui, ed. 1995. *Xinjiang minzu cidian* [*Xinjiang Minzu Dictionary*]. Ürümci: Xinjiang renmin chubanshe.

Xinjiang weiwu'er zizhiqu minzu zongjiao shiwu weiyuanhui, ed. 1999. *Xin shiqi minzu yu zongjiao zhengce fagui xuanbian* [*Selected Policies, Laws, and Regulations on Minzu and Religion in the New Era*]. Ürümci: Xinjiang renmin chubanshe.

Xinjiang weiwu'er zizhiqu renda changwei. 1990. "Xinjiang weiwu'er zizhiqu shishi 'jihui youxing shiwei fa' banfa" [Method of Implementing the "Law on Assembly Marching and Demonstrating" in the XUAR]. Ürümci: Xinjiang weiwu'er zizhiqu renda changwei.

Xinjiang Weiwu'er zizhiqu tongjiju, ed. 1995. *Xinjiang tongji nianjian* [*Xinjiang Statistical Yearbook*] *1995*. Beijing: Zhongguo tongji chubanshe.

————, ed. 1996. *Xinjiang tongji nianjian* [*Xinjiang Statistical Yearbook*] *1996*. Beijing: Zhongguo tongji chubanshe.

———, ed. 2005. *Xinjiang tongji nianjian* [*Xinjiang Statistical Yearbook*] *2005*. Beijing: Zhongguo tongji chubanshe.

Xu Xifa. 1995. *Zhongguo shaoshu minzu jihua shengyu gailun* [*An Introduction to Family Planning for China's Minority Minzu*]. Ürümci: Xinjiang renmin chubanshe.

Xu Yuqi, ed. 1999. *Xinjiang fandui minzu fenlie zhuyi douzheng shihua* [*Narrative History of Xinjiang's Struggle Against Minzu Splittism*]. Ürümci: Xinjiang renmin chubanshe.

"XUAR gaikuang" bianxiezu, ed. 1985. *Xinjiang wiwu'er zhiqu gaikuang* [*An Overview of Conditions in the XUAR*]. Ürümci: Xinjiang renmin chubanshe.

XUAR jiaoyu weiyuanhui gaoxiao lishi jiaocai bianxiezu, ed. 1992. *Xinjiang difang shi—Shiyong ben* [*A Local History of Xinjiang—Trial Edition*]. Ürümci: Xinjiang daxue.

XUAR Local Gazetteer Editorial Committee, ed. 1988. *Xinjiang nianjian* [*Xinjiang Yearbook*] *1988*. Ürümci: Xinjiang renmin chubanshe.

———, ed. 1995. *Xinjiang nianjian* [*Xinjiang Yearbook*] *1995*. Ürümci: Xinjiang renmin chubanshe.

———, ed. 1997. *Xinjiang tongzhi—Junshi zhi* [*Xinjiang General Gazetteer—Military Affairs Volume*]. Vol. 28. Ürümci: Xinjiang renmin chubanshe.

XUAR Party Committee Propaganda Bureau, ed. 1997. *Minzu tuanjie jiaoyu duben* [*A Reader on Education in Minzu Unity*]. Ürümci: Xinjiang qingshaonian chubanshe.

Xue Yu [pseud.]. 2003. "Qianyi Xinjiang de fenlie zhuyi wenti de lishi he jintian zhengfu de duice" [A Simple View of the History of and Current Government's Policies for Handling the Problem of Splittism in Xinjiang] [online article]. *Xuhuan junshi tiankong*. Available from http://www.war-sky.com/cgi-bin/forums.cgi?forum=70&topic=4813 (accessed November 4, 2003).

Yang, Chuang. 2005. "On the Contrast Between the Five Principles of Peaceful Coexistence and the Principle of Humanitarian Intervention." China Institute of International Studies, March 28. Available from http://www.ciis.org.cn/item/2005–03–28/50899.html (accessed September 1, 2006).

Yang Faren. 2000. *Deng Xiaoping minzu lilun ji qi zai xinjiang de shijian* [*Deng Xiaoping's Minzu Theory and Its Practical Application in Xinjiang*]. Ürümci: Xinjiang renmin chubanshe.

Yang Shengmin. 2008. "Pupiande liyi suqiu haishi shaoshu ren de suqiu—Xinjiang wei Han minzu guanxi" [Appealing to the General Interest, or Appealing to a Minority—Survey and Research on Uyghur–Han Relations in Xinjiang]. *Sociology of Ethnicity*, no. 46:9–20.

Yang Zhenhua, ed. 1997. *Shichang jingji yu tunken shubian* [*Market Economics and Reclaiming Land to Garrison the Frontiers*]. Ürümci: Xinjiang renmin chubanshe.

Yao Kuangyi. 2005. "'San gu shili' zhanlue tiaozheng ji dui woguo zhoubian anquan xingshi de yingxiang" [Strategic Adjustments by The "Three Forces" and Their Impact on the Security Environment of Our Country's Neighbors]. Available from http://fanleo.blogchina.com/1148223.html (accessed September 1, 2005).

Yardley, Jim. 2006. "A Spectator's Role for China's Muslims." *New York Times*, February 19, 4. Available from Factiva (accessed July 12, 2006).

———. 2008. "China Meeting for Dalai Lama Envoys." *New York Times*, October 31. Available from http://www.nytimes.com/2008/10/31/world/asia/31tibet.html (accessed October 31, 2008).

Yee, Herbert S. 2003. "Ethnic Relations in Xinjiang: A Survey of Uygur–Han Relations in Ürümci." *Journal of Contemporary China* 12, no. 36:431–52.

———. 2005. "Ethnic Consciousness and Identity: A Research Report on Uygur–Han Relations in Xinjiang." *Asian Ethnicity* 6, no. 1:35–50.

Yin Zhuguang and Mao Yongfu, eds. 1996. *Xinjiang minzu guanxi yanjiu* [*Research on Minzu Relations in Xinjiang*]. Ürümci: Xinjiang renmin chubanshe.

Yongding [pseud.]. 2005. "China's Color-Coded Crackdown." *Foreign Policy Online*, October 18. Available from http://www.foreignpolicy.com/story/files/story3251.php (accessed August 2, 2006).

York, Geoffrey. 2006. "China Mum on Fate of Detained Canadian." *Globe and Mail* (Toronto), July 18. Available from http://www.theglobeandmail.com/servlet/story/LAC.20060718.CHINA18/TPStory/National (accessed July 18, 2006).

Yu, Xingzhong. n.d. "From State Leadership to State Responsibility—Comments on the New PRC Law on Regional Autonomy of Ethnic Minorities." Working paper. Hong Kong: Chinese University, n.d. Available from www.cuhk.edu.hk/gpa/xzyu/work1.htm (accessed 2 May 2004).

Zeng Wenwu. 1986. *Zhongguo jingying xiyu shi* [*A History of China's Administration of the Western Regions*]. Ürümci: Xinjiang weiwu'er zizhiqu difangzhi zongbianshi.

Zerubavel, Eviatar. 2003. *Time Maps: Collective Memory and the Social Shape of the Past*. Chicago: University of Chicago Press.

Zhang Binglin. 1907. "Shehui Tongquan *Shangdui*" [A Discussion of *A History of Politics*] [by Edward Jenks]. *Minbao*, no. 12:1–24.

Zhang Erju, ed. 1988. *Zhongguo minzu quyu zizhi de lilun he shijian* [*The Theory and Practice of Minzu Regional Autonomy in China*]. Beijing: Zhongguo shehui chubanshe.

Zhang Liang [pseud.], comp., and Andrew J. Nathan and Perry Link, eds. 2001. *The Tian'anmen Papers*. New York: Public Affairs.

Zhang Ya. 2005. "Wu–Chang dangwei—Kua xingzheng quyu de lianhe dangwei" [The Ürümci Changji Party Committee—A Trans-Administrative Regional Party Committee]. *China Xiaokang*, no. 11:32–33.

Zhang Yuxi. 1993. "Xinjiang jiefang yilai fandui minzu fenliezhuyi de douzheng ji qi lishi jingyan" [The Struggle and Historical Experience of Opposition to *Minzu* Separatism in Xinjiang Since Liberation]. In *Fan Yisilan zhuyi, fan Tujue zhuyi yanjiu* [*Research on Pan-Islamism and Pan-Turkism*], edited by Yang Faren, 331–63. Ürümci: (neibu).

Zhang Zhirong. 2005. *Zhongguo bianjiang yu minzu wenti: Dangdai Zhongguo de tiaozhan ji qi lishi youlai* [*China's Frontiers and Minzu Problems: Contemporary China's Challenges and Their Historical Origins*]. Beijing: Beijing University Press. Zhang Zhizhong. 1947. "Zhengben qingyuan" [Enact Thoroughgoing Reform]. *Da gong bao*, August 25–30.

Zhao, Gang. 2006. "Reinventing China: Imperial Qing Ideology and the Rise of Modern Chinese National Identity in the Early Twentieth Century" *Modern China* 32, no. 1:3–30.

Zhao, Suisheng. 2004. *A Nation-State by Construction: Dynamics of Modern Chinese Nationalism.* Stanford, Calif.: Stanford University Press.

Zheng Pingjian and Dai Erfu. 2003. "Zhongguo xibu dakaifa zhong de renkou wenti yanjiu: Yi Xinjiang weiwu'er zizhiqu wei li" [Research on Population Problems in China's Open the West Program: The Case of the XUAR]. *Diyu yanjiu yu kaifa* 22, no. 5:17–22.

Zhong Yu. 1958. "Yao gei difang minzu zhuyi yige ying tou tong ji" [We Must Fight Off Local Nationalism]." *Xinjiang ribao*, May 18.

Zhonggong Hetian shiwei bangongshi. 1999. "Guanyu yinfa zizhiqu dangwei changwei, zizhiqu dangwei fu Hetian gongzuozu zuzhang Simayi Tieliwa'erdi he gongzuozu fu zuzhang Zhou Yuan zai Hetian shi wu tao banzi lingdao hui shang de jianghua de tongzhi" [A Notice Concerning the Printing and Distribution of Remarks by Ismayil Tiliwaldi, Head, and Zhou Yuan, Vice Head, of the Working Group from the XUAR Party Committee Standing Committee and Party Committee at the Meeting of Five Leadership Groups in Khotän City]. Khotän: CCP Khotän City Party Committee Office.

Zhonggong Xinjiang weiwu'er zizhiqu weiyuanhui zuzhibu, Zhonggong Xinjiang weiwu'er zizhiqu weiyuanhui dang shi yanjiu shi, and Xinjiang weiwu'er zizhiqu dang'an ju, eds. 1996. *Zhongguo gongchandang Xinjiang weiwu'er zizhiqu zuzhi shi ziliao* [Historical Materials on the CCP Organization in the XUAR] *1937–1987.* Beijing: Zhonggong dangshi chubanshe.

Zhou Enlai. 1980 (1957). "Guanyu woguo minzu zhengce de jige wenti" [A Few Problems with Our Country's *Minzu* Policies]. *Minzu yanjiu* [*Minzu research*], no. 1:1–11.

Zhu Jun. 2004. "'Dong Tu' zuixing bei wang lu" [Memorandum on "Eastern Turkistan" Crimes]. *Jiancha fengyun*, no. 23:16–17.

Zhu Lun. 2002. "Lun minzu gongzhi de lilun jichu yu jiben yuanli" [A Discussion of the Theoretical Basis and Basic Tenets of *Minzu* Collective Rule]. *Minzu yanjiu*, no. 2:1–9.

Zhu Peimin. 2000. *20 shiji Xinjiang shi yanjiu* [*Research on the History of Xinjiang in the 20th Century*]. Ürümci: Xinjiang renmin.

Zhu Peimin, Chen Hong, and Yang Hong. 2004. *Zhongguo gongchandang yu Xinjiang minzu wenti* [*The Chinese Communist Party and Xinjiang's Minzu Problems*]. Ürümci: Xinjiang renmin chubanshe.

"Zizhiqu dangwei kuoda huiyi henhen de fandui difang minzu zhuyi; chedi fensui yi Ziya wei shou de fandang jituan" [Autonymous Regional Party Committee Plenum Resolutely Opposes Local Nationalism; Thoroughly Smash the Anti-Party Cabal Led by Ziya]. 1958. *Xinjiang ribao*, April 30.

"Zizhiqu dangwei kuoda huiyi zuochu jueyi—Kaichu youpai fenzi" [Autonomous Regional Party Committee Plenum Resolves: Expel Rightist Elements]. 1958. *Xinjiang ribao*, April 30.

Zongjiao yanjiusuo Yisilanjiao diaocha zu. 1983. "Xinjiang Kashi, Hetian Yisilanjiao qingkuang diaocha" [An Investigation into the Situation of Islam in Xinjiang's Kashgar and Khotän]. *Xinjiang shehui kexue yanjiu* 126:16–42.

Zordun Sabir. 2000. *Ana yurt* [*Motherland*]. 2nd ed. Vol. 1. Ürümci: Šinjang yašlar ösmürlär näsriyati.

INDEX

9 780231 147514